Enabling Technologies for Wireless E-Business

T0224092

Weidong Kou
Yelena Yesha (Eds.)

Enabling Technologies for Wireless E-Business

With 141 Figures and 15 Tables

 Springer

Editors

Weidong Kou

Chinese State Key Laboratory of ISN
2 South Taibai Road
Xi'an, Shaanxi, 710071
Peoples Republic of China
kou_weidong@yahoo.com.cn

Yelena Yesha

Department of Computer Science and
Electrical Engineering
University of Maryland Baltimore County
1000 Hilltop Circle
Baltimore, Maryland 21250, USA
yeyesha@umbc.edu

ACM Classification: C.2, C.3, H.4, J.1

ISBN 978-3-642-06781-5   e-ISBN 978-3-540-30637-5

Springer is a part of Springer Science+Business Media
springer.com
© Springer-Verlag Berlin Heidelberg 2010
Printed in The Netherlands

Cover design: KünkelLopka, Heidelberg

Foreword

The key message that we have for readers is that wireless is blooming. The following statistics can show readers that this is definitely true:

- According to Strategy Analytics and UK-based Portio Research, at the end of 2005 there were over 2.1 billion mobile subscribers in the world. By the end of 2006 the mobile subscribers will reach to the level of 2.5 billions, and this figure is expected to increase to close to 4 billion by 2012. The worldwide mobile phone penetration is predicted to easily pass the 50% mark by the end of 2009.

- The Ministry of Information Industry of China reported that at the end of 2005, the number of mobile subscribers in the country was close to 400 millions. It is predicted that by the end of 2006, the number of mobile subscribers in China can reach 440 millions. In addition, the number of short messages sent in China in 2005 was over 300 billions, and the associated revenue was close to $4 billion US dollars.

- According to LaNetro Zed based in Madrid of Spain, at the end of 2005, West Europe has over 270 millions of wireless subscribers. Germany is the largest market for mobile phones in Europe, with 74.1 million users, and it has a penetration rate of 90%; Italy is the second largest market in Europe, with over 65.3 million mobile subscribers and a penetration rate of 114%, the highest in the world; the United Kingdom has 64 million subscribers and a mobile phone penetration rate of 106%; the penetration rate in Finland stands at 100% with nearly 5.2 million subscribers.

- In 2005 total number of mobile service subscribers in Russia has grown by 70 percent and reached 125.8 million, according to a recent report in 2006 from AC&M consulting bureau.

- According to Mobile Marketing Association, in the United States the number of wireless subscribers was over 200 millions. The data on the Mobilephonediscuss.com Forums shows that 66% of US households own cell phones.

- In Canada, with the number of subscribers to wireless products and service totaling close to 13.9 million by mid-2004, almost 43% of Canadians now have access to a wireless device. By the end of 2005, it was estimated that this number is probably over 50%.

- Global wireless service revenue is expected to rise 11% to $623.9 billion. The global wireless service industry is expected to generate $800 billion in revenue in 2010, with emerging markets accounting for about 42% of the total.

- Worldwide shipments of mobile phones reached a record 242 million units in Q4 2005, surpassing the previous peak of 200 million units in Q4 2004, according to iSuppli. For all of 2005, 813 million units were shipped, up 14% from 713 million in 2004.

The list of statistics can go on and on. The rapid growth in the number of wireless subscribers along with the emergence of new wireless technologies such as 3G and Wi-Fi, allowing for higher transmission rates will lead to an explosion of new e-business applications and services generally referred to as "wireless e-business".

Wireless e-business allows people to conduct business wirelessly without physical connectivity. A variety of different devices can be used for wireless e-business, including mobile phones, pagers, palm-powered personal computers (PCs), pocket PCs, laptop computers, and other mobile devices or devices connected to the wireless networks.

Because wireless e-business holds the promise to reshape the way businesses conducted, and because it has a huge customer base, the advantages of wireless e-business are endless. The key is that people can break free from spatial and temporal constraints and communicate and transact in business anytime and anywhere. However, there are a number of great challenges, including problems of sustaining connectivity, limited resources such as limited bandwidth and limited frequency spectrum, as well as the issues of security and privacy in a wireless environment. To address these problems and issues, huge efforts have been made to develop a variety of enabling technologies, including new wireless communication technologies, wireless security, wireless application protocols, mobile payment protocols, mobile data management, mobile agents, mobile payment, mobile computing, mobile services, and RFID technologies. Drs. Weidong Kou and Yelena Yesha have edited this book, with assistance from the chapter contributors to cover these technologies.

I believe this is an excellent book for business managers, e-business developers, academic researchers, university students, professors, and professional consultants to acquire comprehensive knowledge on enabling technologies for the blooming wireless e-business. I highly recommend this book!

Robert Mayberry
Vice President, Sensors and Actuators
IBM Software Group

Table of Contents

1 Introduction to Enabling Technologies for Wireless E-Business

W. Kou[*] and Y. Yasha[+]

[*] ISN National Key Laboratory, Xidian University, Xi'an, China
[+] Department of Electrical Engineering and Computer Sciences, University of Maryland, Baltimore County, USA

1.1 Introduction

Wireless e-business allows people to communicate and transact in business via wireless technology, without physical connectivity, such as wires or cabling. Wireless e-business uses many devices, including mobile phones, pagers, palm-powered personal computers (PCs), pocket PCs, laptop computers, and other mobile devices or devices connected to the wireless networks.

Advancements in wireless technologies hold the promise to reshape the way businesses conducted. With wireless technologies, people can break free from spatial and temporal constraints, as they are able to use these technologies to work anywhere and anytime. With wireless e-business, companies can locate inventory items, anytime, anywhere; emergency units are able to respond in real time; and universities are able to manage communications across campuses. The rapid growth in mobile telephony in recent years has provided a strong model for the adoption of undeterred wireless e-business. A number of consulting firms have made various estimations on the growth of the number of mobile phone users worldwide. These estimations are certainly confirmed by the huge increase in the number of mobile phone users in China – the country currently has over 300 million mobile phone users, more than the entire population of the USA. The rapid transition from fixed to mobile telephony will almost certainly be followed by a similar transition from conducting e-business through desktop computers via physical connectivity to wireless e-business through a variety of mobile devices via wireless communication networks in the near future.

To make wireless e-business work effectively, a variety of enabling technologies are needed. First, one must be connected wirelessly. This means that wireless communications networks must be in place. From the first commercial Global System for Mobile Communication (GSM) network launched in 1992 to 3G services launched in Hong Kong, UK, and Italy in recent years, wireless communication networks have penetrated almost every part of the world. The 2G/2.5G and 3G wireless communication systems are the cornerstones of wireless communications. In addition, there are other wireless networks, such as Wi-Fi, Wi-Max, Bluetooth, and infrared. Wireless security is crucial for wireless e-business. Accessing the Internet, digitally signing e-commerce transactions, authentication, and encryption of transaction information, all these wireless e-business activities need security. However, given that wireless e-businesses broadly use mobile devices such as mobile phones, and that these devices have strict processing requirements and storage limitations of wireless environments, ubiquitous wireless security technologies must be ready to satisfy these requirements and overcome these limitations. To enable mobile Internet applications, application environment and various application protocols are needed. In 1997, Ericsson, Motorola, and Nokia formed a forum for creating such protocols. As a result, the wireless application protocol (WAP), a suite of emerging standards, has been defined. The WAP is designed to assist the convergence of two fast-growing network technologies, namely, wireless communications and the Internet. The convergence is based on the rapidly increasing numbers of mobile phone users and the dramatic effect of e-business over the Internet. The combination of these two technologies will have a big impact on current e-business practice, and it will create huge market potential.

To be able to connect mobile people to the information and applications they need — anytime and anywhere, to allow people to have computation capabilities and network resources at hand, and to move the workplace to any place, supporting the broadest spectrum of mobile networks and a wide array of devices on the client side, necessary wireless middleware software and mobile data management are essential. When a mobile user moves with a handheld mobile device and connects to a wireless network, how one can ensure that the connection will not be lost while the user moves out of the range of the wireless network that can reach? Roaming from one wireless network into another is therefore a desired feature for wireless e-business applications.

Mobile content delivery technology deals with delivering the digital contents to mobile devices with limited computing and storage resources. For example, if a digital photo is too large to fit into the memory of a mobile phone, then for the mobile user to see the photo, one must convert the original digital photo into one of a smaller size that can fit into the mobile phone. This converting process is called transcoding.

When a mobile user is located in a place where the businesses are close to him, these businesses may wish to inform the user on either services or products available at a special price, which the user might be interested in. The technology enabling such a capability is called location-aware technology, while related services are called location-aware services.

To transact wireless e-business, mobile payment is essential. Without mobile payment, wireless e-business is not going to be successful as people need to collect the payment when they conduct e-business anytime and anywhere. Mobile payment needs wireless security to ensure secure authentication and data confidentiality. In addition, restriction of mobile devices and wireless communications must be considered while making the payment.

Wireless e-business also needs mobile agent technology. A mobile agent system is a platform that can create, interpret, execute, transfer, and manage agents. The ability to travel, which distinguishes mobile agents from other types of agents, allows them to move to a new host and then to take advantage of being in the same environment to interact with each other locally.

Mobile Web service is an extension of Web service technology. A Web service is a software system designed to support interoperable machine-to-machine inter-action over a network. It is a standard computing unit over the Internet. There are three technologies to make Web service work, namely, Web Services Description Language (WSDL), Simple Object Access Protocol (SOAP), and Universal Description, Discovery, and Integration (UDDI). With WSDL, a legacy system can be wrapped with a standard interface and becomes a Web service. SOAP, on the other hand, provides a standard connection among those Web services so that communications among them can be carried out. UDDI is a registration server, which is available for the convenience of publishing and retrieving Web services. According to the information in UDDI servers, consumers of Web services are able to obtain essential knowledge so as to ensure that the services meet their re-quirements. Mobile Web service extends Web service with considerations of mo-bility, wireless security, restriction of mobile devices, and multimodality.

Radio Frequency Identification (RFID) is a not-quite-new wireless technology that has a wide range of applications from automatically collecting highway tolls, identifying and tracing products and managing supply chain, to controlling access to buildings and offices. A minimum RFID system consists of an RIFD tag, an RFID reader, and a computer host. Each RFID tag holds a microchip surrounded by a printed antenna and protected between laminates, which can be pasted to a product. The chip on the RFID tag holds data in its memory that can identify a manufacturer, a particular product model, and an individual product. An RFID reader is a device to read the tag at a distance. Radio waves from the reader hit the tag with enough power for the tag to retransmit the data back to the reader. The host computer processes the data and passes them to business applications.

Given a number of market demands and needs, including societal shifts toward a more mobile workforce, geographical mobility among corporate individuals, criticality of time and effective decision making within narrow windows of oppor-tunities, increasing need for remote communication, computing and collaboration, increasing availability of wireless connections at affordable rates, new and impor-tant requirements for mobile computing support such as intelligent mobile agents, and mobile knowledge networking, particularly, given a close to one billion mo-bile phone users (if not yet exceeded), which is a huge potential customer base for wireless e-business, we can certainly say that wireless e-business is very promis-ing and will have a very bright future.

1.2 About This Book

As doing e-business wirelessly is becoming a new trend and as there is a huge demand from business executives and managers, technological practitioners, stu-dents, and teachers who wish to know how e-business can be done wirelessly, and what the technologies to support wireless e-business are, this book is a response to this demand by providing readers with comprehensive information on enabling technology for wireless e-business. The target audience of this book includes e-business developers, business managers, academic researchers, university students, professors, and professional consultants. This book can also be used for e-business classes and training courses.

We have invited leading experts in various countries and regions, including USA, Canada, Hong Kong, Taiwan, and China, to contribute to this book. From wireless communication fundamentals to wireless applications, the book covers the major subjects related to enabling technologies for wireless e-business, including wireless security, mobile agents, mobile payment, mobile computing, mobile data management, location-based services, software infrastructure, wireless application protocol, and RFID technologies.

Chapter 2 presents a brief introduction of the fundamentals of wireless communications, including a variety of cellular standards, such as GSM, GPRS, IS-95, cdma2000, and UMTS.

Chapter 3 deals with mobile security issues with the intrinsic restrictions that are inherent in the mobile devices and the wireless environment, and possible practical solutions that can be used to overcome those restrictions, including the wireless equivalent of public key cryptosystem and elliptic curve cryptography, an alternate approach to conventional public key cryptography, which is suitable for applications under resource-constrained conditions.

WAP is a suite of emerging standards to enable mobile Internet applications. The WAP standards have been created as a result of the WAP Forum that was formed in June 1997 by Ericsson, Motorola, and Nokia. The WAP Forum is designed to assist the convergence of two fast-growing network technologies, namely, wireless communications and the Internet. Chapter 4 presents a detailed introduction to WAP, including the application environment and various protocols.

Chapter 5 focuses on a very hot wireless technology, RFID, which has a huge potential in managing products and people, particularly in the areas of supply chain management, manufacturing, asset management, product tracing, and security access control.

An extended form of mobile computing, namely, context-aware mobile computing, is investigated, and the issues in building software infrastructure for supporting this paradigm are discussed in Chap. 6.

Chapter 7 presents an overview of challenges arising in the area of mobile data management and surveys existing solutions, with emphasis on data management in mobile ad hoc networks. Various challenges related to data management in mobile ad hoc networks, information discovery in dynamic networks, and traditional data management issues, such as transactional support or consistency among data objects, are discussed, and possible solutions to these challenges are proposed.

The topic of mobile agents is the focus of Chap. 8. After a brief introduction of the concept of mobile agents, the chapter outlines the advantages and applications of mobile agents, and presents important technologies for implementing mobile agent systems.

Chapter 9 extends the discussions of mobile agents, by presenting how the coordination and information sharing among multiple agents can be done through the tuple space-based coordination model.

Mobile payment is crucial to wireless e-business, simply because without collecting payment instantly regardless of where users are, the wireless e-business cannot survive. Chapter 10 presents a variety of mobile payment technologies.

Chapter 11 deals with mobile content delivery technologies, including messaging services technologies, such as short message service (SMS) and multimedia message service (MMS), and existing transcoding technologies of image, video, audio, and Web pages.

Web service is an effective technique for improving business efficiency by automating the collaboration of heterogeneous information systems. By extending it to the wireless and mobile world, many more people can be connected to the enormous Web of information and services, anywhere and anytime. Chapter 12 presents mobile services, which is the next direction of Web service.

Chapter 13 presents the Location Operating REference (LORE) model, including domains of location operation semantic, privacy and security, management and location-aware agent. To support the rich sets of location-aware wireless applications, based on the LORE model, an infrastructure – Location-Based Services (LBS) middleware—can be built, which has three key components: location server, moving object database, and spatial pub/sub engine.

The book concludes with Chap. 14, in which mobile commerce, horizontal wireless e-business applications, and vertical wireless e-business applications are identified and presented with case studies.

The readers can use the structure of the book effectively. If they have no background knowledge of wireless communications, they can then read chapters of this book sequentially; if they are already familiar with wireless communications, they can skip reading Chap. 2. Of course, the readers, if they wish, can always select a chapter without following a particular order.

Acknowledgments

This work is supported in part by NSFC grant 90304008 from the Nature Science Foundation of China and the Doctoral Program Foundation grant 2004071001 from the Ministry of Education of China.

References

1. W. Kou, Y. Yesha (eds.) (2000) Electronic Commerce Technology trends: Challenges and Opportunities. IBM, Carlsbad.
2. W. Kou (1997) Networking Security and Standards. Kluwer, Boston.
3. W. Kou, Y. Yesha, C. Tan (eds.) (2001) Electronic Commerce Technologies. LNCS 2040. Springer, Berlin Heidelberg New York.
4. M. Sherif (2000) Protocols for Secure Electronic Commerce. CRC, Boca Raton.
5. M. Shaw, R. Blanning, T. Strader, A. Whinston (2000) Handbook on Electronic Commerce. Springer, Berlin Heidelberg New York.

6. K. Finkenzeller (2003): RFID-Handbook, "Fundamentals and Applications in Contact less Smart Cards and Identification," 2nd edition, Wiley, New York.
7. J. Eberspächer, H. Vögel, C. Bettstetter (2001), GSM Switching, Services and Protocols, 2nd edition, Wiley, New York.
8. T. Halonen, J. Romero, J. Melero (2002), GSM, GPRS and EDGE Performance, Wiley, New York.

2 Fundamentals of Wireless Communications

D. Shen and V.O.K. Li

The University of Hong Kong, Pokfulam Road, Hong Kong

2.1 Introduction

Since the introduction of the first generation cellular networks in the 1980s, there has been tremendous growth in wireless communications. In 1992 the first commercial GSM network was launched, which marked the beginning of era of digital cellular networks. Since 2003, Hutchinson has launched 3G services in Hong Kong, UK, and Italy. Today, wireless communication devices have penetrated almost every corner of the world and have become an indispensable part of our daily life. In this chapter, we present a brief overview of 2G/2.5G and 3G wireless communication systems, with particular focus on security-related aspects.

2.2 Global System for Mobile Communication

Global System for Mobile Communication (GSM), is currently the most widely used wireless technology. The number of global GSM customers is estimated to be over 1 billion as of the first quarter of 2004, accounting for over 70% of the global market share.

GSM was proposed in Europe (in fact, the initials were originally derived from Groupe Special Mobile) and was under standardization by the European Telecommunication Standards Institute (ETSI). Currently, the work has largely been transferred to third generation partnership project (3GPP).

2.2.1 Overview

Currently, GSM operates in frequency bands of 400, 800, 900, 1,800, and 1,900 MHz. A GSM channel has a bandwidth of 200 kHz. The modulation scheme is Gaussian minimum shift keying (GMSK), which is a type of continuous 7-phase modulation scheme. Since GMSK has a constant amplitude envelope, it is desirable for simple amplifiers. At the same time, it has a narrow power spectrum with low adjacent channel interference. The duplexing scheme is frequency division duplexing (FDD), with the uplink channel and downlink channels located in different frequency bands. Since the uplink time slot is about three time slots later than the corresponding downlink slot, the mobile station (MS) does not have to send and receive at the same time, thus reducing system design complexity and cost.

In Fig. 2.1, we illustrate the processing of a GSM voice call. At the transmitter, the voice is first digitized and source encoded. Then channel coding (convolutional coding) and interleaving are applied for error correction. To achieve confidentiality over the air interface, encryption is performed. After modulation, the user signal is transmitted over the multipath fading channel. At the receiver, the received signal is first demodulated, and then decrypted. After deinterleaving and channel decoding, source decoding is conducted to restore the speech.

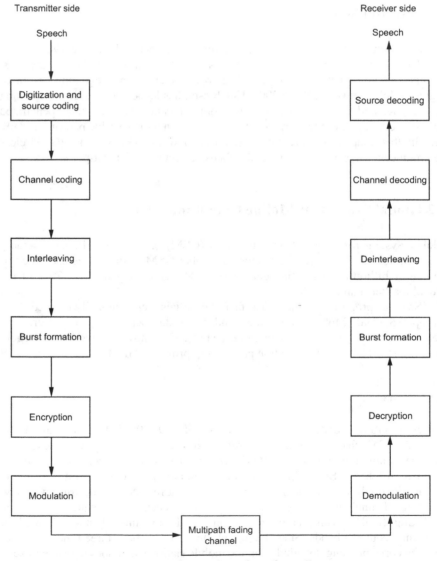

Fig. 2.1. Processing of a voice call

The multiple access scheme of GSM is time division multiple access (TDMA) with optional frequency hopping. A TDMA frame lasts for 4.615 ms, and is divided into 8 time slots, corresponding to a slot time of 576.9 µs. The gross data rate of a frame is 271 kbps or 33.9 kbps for a slot. This data rate is equivalent to 156.25 bit periods in a time slot. There are five types of time slot burst: normal, frequency correction, synchronization, access, and dummy slot burst. In Fig. 2.2, we show the structure of a normal burst. In a normal burst, the first three bits are tail bits. The next 57 bits are data bits, followed by 1 signaling bit, 26 training bits, 1 signaling bit, 57 data bits, 3 tail bits, and finally a guard period of 8.25 bits.

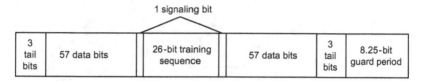

Fig. 2.2. Structure of a normal time slot burst

The TDMA frames are further organized into multiframes. There are two types of multiframes: one type consists of 26 TDMA frames, another with 51 frames. A superframe has 1326 TDMA frames, which is composed of either fifty-one 26-frame multiframes or twenty-six 51-frame multiframes, and lasts for 6.12 s. Then 2,038 superframes are grouped as a hyperframe, corresponding to a period of 3 h 28 min 53.760 s. The organization of frames is plotted in Fig. 2.3.

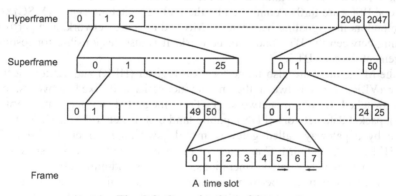

Fig. 2.3. Organization of frames

The cellular structure is adopted in GSM, as shown in Fig. 2.4. In each cell, there is one base transceiver station (BTS), transmitting and receiving radio signals to/from MS. The main tasks for a BTS are:

- Channel coding
- Ciphering and deciphering
- Burst formation, multiplexing, and modulation
- Evaluation and optimization of uplink and downlink transmissions

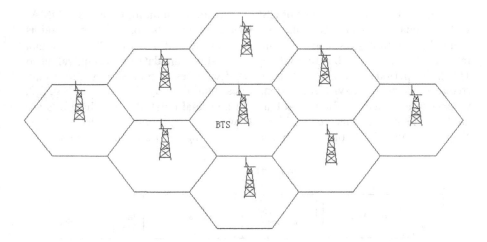

Fig. 2.4. Cellular network structure of GSM

A number of base stations are controlled by one base station controller (BSC). The BTSs and BSC form the base station subsystem. The main responsibility of a BSC is to coordinate the handoff operation. Therefore, a BSC will collect the measurement report of link quality from each mobile to decide whether a handoff is necessary. A BSC also needs the information of available resources in each neighboring BTS. During the handoff process, the BSC will coordinate the call transition from one BTS to another with the involved BTS and MS.

Several BSCs are further controlled by the mobile switching center (MSC). The MSC monitors the signaling between the MS and the core network, and performs switching between the BTS and core network. It is also responsible for resource management for each BTS.

At the MSC, there are also home location register (HLR) and visitor location register (VLR). Calls between the mobile networks and fixed networks, e.g., public switched telephone network (PSTN), integrated service data network (ISDN), packet data network (PDN), public land mobile network (PLMN), etc. are handled by a gateway called gateway mobile switching center (GMSC). The MSC, HLR, VLR, and GMSC are parts of the network and switching subsystem. Network management-related operations, such as administration, security, network configuration and performance management, maintenance, etc. are the responsibility of the operation subsystem. The network control functions are monitored by the operation and maintenance center. The authentication center (AuC) and equipment identity register (EIR) are related to the security aspects. More specifically, the AuC is responsible for authentication and encryption, and the EIR stores equipment identity data. The network architecture is described in Fig. 2.5.

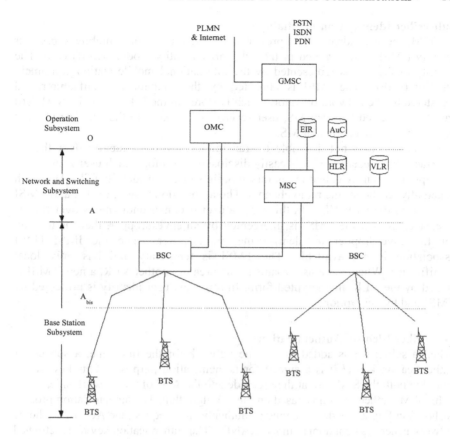

Fig. 2.5. Network architecture of GSM

HLR and VLR are used to support user mobility. When an MS is under an MSC different from its home MSC, the MS will register at the VLR of the MSC. The VLR will also forward the user location information to the HLR. When the MS is called, its HLR is first queried for the current location. Then the HLR will respond with the MS's current location, and the call is routed to the visiting MSC.

2.2.2 Security-Related Aspects

In GSM, the following are related to security:
- Subscriber identity confidentiality
- Subscriber identity authentication
- Signaling information element confidentiality
- Data confidentiality

These are described in the following paragraphs.

Subscriber Identity Confidentiality

In GSM, the user identity is represented by the international mobile subscriber identity (IMSI) and is stored in the subscriber identity module (SIM) card. The identity of the MS is represented by the international mobile station equipment identity (IMEI). The IMEI is allocated by the equipment manufacturer and registered by the network operator, which is stored in the EIR. Since the SIM card can be transferred between MS, user service only relates to the SIM card and is not dependent on a particular MS.

Obviously, it is not desirable to transmit the IMSI frequently over the air interface, since user identity is easily disclosed. Therefore, each user is assigned a temporary identity called temporary mobile subscriber identity (TMSI), which is actually used over the radio channel. The association between IMSI and TMSI is stored in the HLR/VLR. In this way, a user becomes anonymous over the air interface. Even if the TMSI is intercepted by an eavesdropper, there is no way for the eavesdropper to identify the mobile user, since the IMSI–TMSI association is not available. The TMSI is temporary and has only local significance. Whenever a user roams to the area of another VLR, a new TMSI is issued by the VLR, in encrypted form. In this way, user identity is protected by TMSI and by encryption.

Subscriber Identity Authentication

When a subscriber is added to a home network for the first time, a subscriber authentication key (Ki) is assigned for authentication purposes. This key, Ki, is stored in both the SIM card at the user side and the AuC of the network side.

In GSM, authentication is based on the A3 algorithm. The authentication process is shown in Fig. 2.6. After receiving an authentication request, the AuC of the home network generates a random number (RAND). The authentication key Ki is retrieved from the database based on the user identity IMSI. Then a signature response (SRES) is calculated from Ki and RAND from the A3 algorithm. The RAND is also sent to the MS. From the locally stored Ki and the received RAND, the MS calculates its own SRES value and transmits it to the network. At the MSC, the SRES values from the MS and the AuC are compared: if the two agree, the subscriber is authenticated. In this authentication process, RAND is transmitted once from the network to MS, and SRES once from the MS to the network. There is no explicit exchange of user identity information between the MS and the network. The RAND is generated each time on authentication. Thus it is of no use for an attacker to record the transmitted SRES and retransmit some time later, which means the authentication process is secure against the replay attack.

The key Ki can be stored exclusively in the AuC of the home network. When a VLR requests the authentication of a roaming user, a 2-tuple (RAND, SRES) is computed and forwarded by the HLR to the requesting VLR. This approach can provide a high level of security. In this authentication procedure, Ki is only stored in the AuC at the home network and is never transmitted to VLR. This ensures security when a user roams to the network of another operator. An alternative option is to supply Ki to the requesting VLR. Obviously, this approach is less secure.

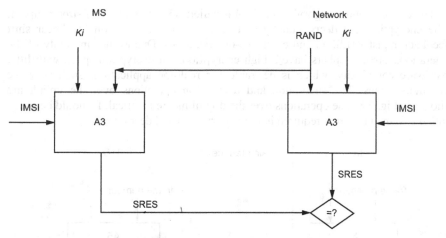

Fig. 2.6. Authentication procedure

Data Encryption

In GSM, user data are protected by encryption. Once a user is authenticated, the cipher key Kc should be generated for encryption and decryption. Kc is also generated from the secret authentication key Ki and the RAND used for authentication, based on the A8 algorithms. The generation of Kc takes place in both AuC and MS. The procedure is illustrated in Fig. 2.7. After Kc is generated, it is used between the MS and the BTS for data protection. At the BTS, the encrypted data from the MS are decrypted. Therefore, data protection in GSM only happens over the air interface, and is not end to end. This is obviously not desirable for certain applications.

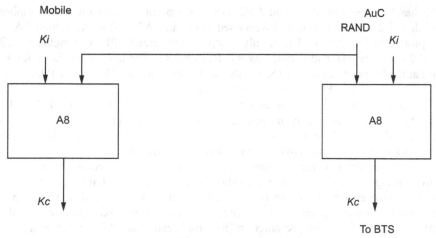

Fig. 2.7. Cipher key generation

The data encryption algorithm in GSM is called A5. A5 is a type of stream cipher. The encryption and decryption by a stream cipher are based on the linear shift feedback register (LSFR) and exclusive-or operations. Due to the simplicity of the operations, stream ciphers have a high encryption and decryption speed with little hardware complexity, which is desirable for realtime applications such as voice communications. The encryption and decryption operations over the uplink are shown in Fig. 2.8. The operations over the downlink are identical. It should be noted that the frame number is required in both encryption and decryption.

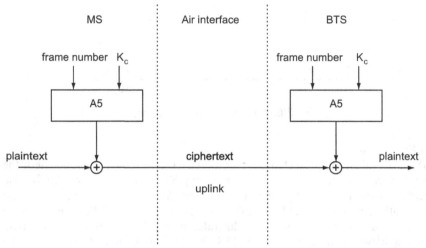

Fig. 2.8. Encryption and decryption over the uplink

2.2.3 Problems with GSM Security

A5 has two versions: A5/1 and A5/2. A5/1 is a proprietary 64-bit stream cipher, while A5/2 can be viewed as a weakened version of A5/1. The schematic of A5/1 is plotted in Fig. 2.9. A5/1 is mainly composed of three LSFRs of lengths 19, 22, and 23 (totally 64), and denoted as R1, R2, and R3. The taps of feedback for R1 are at the bit positions of 13, 16, 17, 18; for R2 they are 20, 21; and for R3at 7, 20, 21, 22. Then the LSFRs are all of maximal length.

In practice, most operators either use A5/2 or no encryption at all. In other words, user data are usually unprotected over the air, which makes it very easy for an eavesdropper. Moreover, users are unaware of the current security level, since network operators do not advertise the adopted security method.

To make things worse, A5 has been discovered to be insecure. Even for the stronger algorithm of A5/1, in a workshop held in New York City in year 2000, it was announced that A5/1 can be cracked [8]. It was claimed that A5/1 can be broken in seconds given sufficient precomputation time and resource. Another attack on A5/1 has been presented in [9], and it can break A5/1 in a few minutes given 2–5 minutes of plaintext conversation. Therefore, the use of encryption in GSM can make things difficult only for an amateur eavesdropper but is unable to protect against well-equipped professionals.

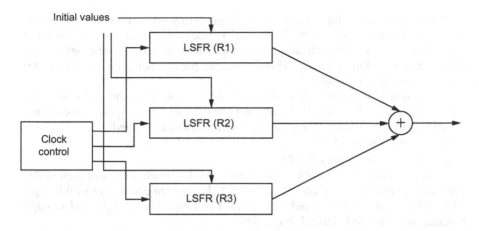

Fig. 2.9. Schematic of A5/1

These are not the only security flaws in GSM. Since the encryption is only between the MS and the BTS, user messages are in the clear in fixed networks. If an attacker can tap into a fixed network, the encryption over the air interface has no significance.

Another security feature in GSM is to hide user identity by using TSMI. However, user anonymity is not always guaranteed. When the user device is to register in a new PLMN, the network will request the true user identity (e.g., IMSI), which is transmitted in the clear.

In all, although GSM is designed with security features, the achieved security still has flaws that prevent the use of security-critical applications such as m-commerce.

2.3 General Packet Radio Service

General packet radio service (GPRS), is part of ETSI's GSM Phase 2+ development. It can be upgraded from GSM without extra infrastructure.

2.3.1 Overview

The original GSM is essentially a circuit-switching technology, and GPRS is to support packet switching within GSM. With circuit switching, a radio channel is dedicated to a user. Even when a user has no traffic to send and the channel is not utilized, it is still "occupied" by the user and cannot be used by other users. Circuit switching is more suitable for voice traffic, since voice usually has a continuous bit stream. However, circuit switching is not appropriate for packet data due to low efficiency and inflexibility. This is because packet data usually have a variable bit rate, which causes an intermittent nature in channel usage.

With packet switching, a channel is occupied only when there are packets to send. When there is no packet, the channel is released and can be used by other users. Therefore, packet switching is more efficient in terms of channel use for packet data with bursty traffic. This is because packet switching enables better resource sharing among users.

GPRS also introduces Internet Protocol (IP) and X.25 to the GSM network, which facilitates the access of data networks, such as corporate local area networks and public Internet. Further, two new services are added:

- Point-to-point (PTP)
- Point-to-multipoint (PMP)

Another feature is that GPRS can support much higher data rates than GSM. The classic GSM circuit switched data (CSD) has a connection rate of 9.6 kbps, while GPRS can reach a speed as high as 171 kbps. This is achieved through bundling several GSM channels for an MS.

2.3.2 Network Architecture

In GPRS, a few new network elements are introduced into the GSM network. The network architecture of GPRS is plotted in Fig. 2.10. The most important ones are the new serving GPRS support node (SGSN) and the gateway GPRS support node (GGSN).

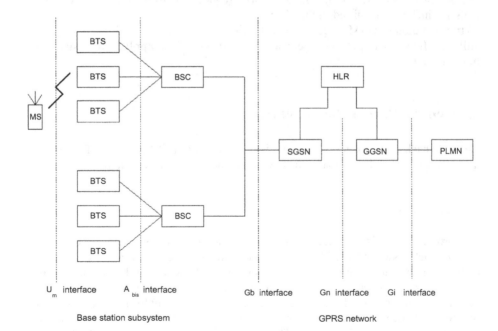

Fig. 2.10. GPRS network architecture

SGSN and GGSN are used to route packet-switched data within the PLMN. The SGSN is the interface to the users, while the GGSN acts as a logical interface between the GPRS system and the external PDN. The SGSN stores the mobility management contexts for the MS and is also responsible for the ciphering of the packet data. Note that for circuit-switched traffic, ciphering is conducted at the BTS. The GGSN stores the routing information for the forwarding of packets. Therefore, GGSN has access to the HLR for user location information. Within the GPRS network, user packets are transmitted through IP tunneling, i.e., packets are encapsulated in the IP packets of the gateways.

The routing of packets between two MSs is illustrated in Fig. 2.11. First the SGSN serving the sender (SGSN-S) receives the transmitted packets from the sender MS. Then SGSN-S forwards the packets to an appropriate GGSN-S. Next, GGSN-S sends the packet to a GGSN at the destination GPRS network (GGSN-D) through the publicPDN. The GGSN-D then routes the packet to the SGSN serving the destination MS (SGSN-D). Finally the destination MS receives the packets from the SGSN-D.

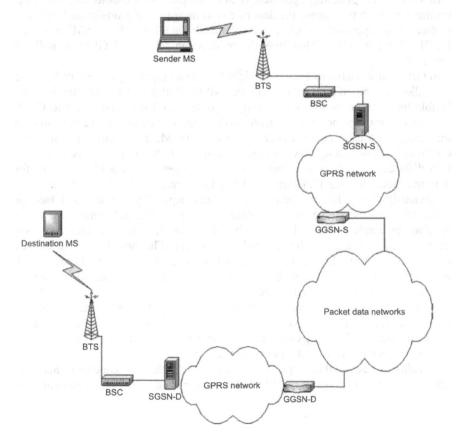

Fig. 2.11. Packet routing in GPRS networks

Since GPRS devices can have voice and packet data traffic, a packet control unit (PCU) is added to distinguish the two types of traffic. The voice traffic is to be transmitted as switched calls by the MSC, and packet data will be handled by the SGSN. Therefore, the PCU is usually placed at the BSC to divert the incoming traffic to either MSC or SGSN. The PCU also has other functionalities such as access control, transmission control, scheduling, buffering, etc.

2.3.3 Air Interface

In GSM, higher data rates can be achieved by bundling several time slots together. This is known in GSM as high-speed circuit-switched data (HSCSD). In HSCSD, a theoretically maximal data rate of 115.2 kbps (8 × 14.4 kbps) is possible. However, since HSCSD is switched by the MSC, the data rate is also confined by the 64-kbps connection rate at the MSC. As a result, HSCSD is practically limited at 57.6 kbps, or by the combination of four time slots.

In GPRS, the bundling approach is also adopted to increase the data rate. Another approach to increase the data rate is to increase the modulation level on a symbol. This approach is taken in enhanced data rates for GSM evolution (EDGE), but not GPRS. Therefore, the modulation scheme of GPRS is still the same as GSM.

In GPRS, it is viable to bundle all eight time slots together, since GPRS traffic is handled by the SGSN rather than the MSC. Further, the data rate is more flexible by introducing four new coding schemes in GPRS, from CS 1 to CS 4. The four coding schemes have variable coding redundancy to achieve different net data rates. Since convolutional codes are used in GSM, the variation in data rates is achieved by puncturing. In GSM, the gross data rate for a time slot is 22.8 kbps. With different degrees of puncturing, CS 1 has a net data rate of 9.05 kbps for each time slot, CS 2 has 13.4 kbps, CS 3 has 15.6 kbps, and CS 4 has 21.4 kbps.

Obviously, CS 1 has the best error resilient capability, while CS 4 has the worst. The CS modes give users the ability to adapt to channel conditions. When the channel condition is bad, CS 1 should be used; when channel condition becomes better, CS 2 can be adopted, and so on. The best CS mode can be selected based on the knowledge of channel quality. This operation is called link adaptation. Link quality can be monitored through the received carrier-to-interference ratio or raw bit error rate.

In fact, CS 4 has no coding protection and can only be used when the channel quality is excellent. Due to checksum, the net rate of CS 4 is 21.4 kbps, lower than the gross data rate 22.8 kbps of a GSM time slot. When all eight time slots are grouped in CS 4 mode, the total rate is 171.2 kbps.

In reality, the actual throughput is more meaningful than the concept of maximal data rate. In fact, the maximal rate of CS 4 is seldom used, and it is also not common to assign all eight time slots to one GPRS node. Most of the time, there could be four time slots bundled over the downlink and one or two time slots over the uplink. The CS mode is usually CS 2 at 13.4 kbps. Therefore, the practical access speed is around 50 kbps over the downlink and 10–20 kbps over the uplink. Obviously, this kind of access speed is only comparable to that of the 56-kbps modem. Higher data rates can be achieved by EDGE through the introduction of higher level modulation. However, EDGE requires hardware modification of the original GSM system, while GPRS can be achieved through software upgrade.

2.3.4 Resource Management

Unlike voice calls and HSCSD connections, there is no need for connection setup in GPRS because of the packet switching mode. Instead, a GPRS node is "attached" rather than "connected." Further, an uplink and a downlink time slots are always allocated in pairs for voice calls, and this is not needed in GPRS.

As a result, the concept of "capacity on demand" is introduced in GPRS. After the initial GPRS attach procedure, there will be no resource dedication unless the user has traffic to send/receive. In GPRS, the radio link control/media access control (MAC) layer is responsible for the management of packet transmission.

For the uplink transmission, a slotted ALOHA random-access based packet reservation mechanism is adopted. When an MS has packets to transmit, it makes a transmission request on the uplink random access channel. The request can be granted by the network and announced over the access grant channel. The response from the network can be either an immediate assignment of network resource, or an allocation of resource for a further resource report from the MS. In the latter case, the MS reports the complete information of resource request. Then the network allocates network resource according to the report from the MS. After the resource allocation, the MS transfers a burst of packets using the allocated resource. The procedure of uplink packet transfer is plotted in Fig. 2.12.

The allocation of downlink resource can be achieved by scheduling algorithms [17]. A simple scheduling algorithm is the round robin algorithm, in which each user is allowed to transmit in turn. Obviously, round robin cannot adapt to user traffic load: when a node has heavy traffic load, it is treated the same way as a node with low traffic load. Round robin can neither provide priority nor service differentiation. There are many more elaborate algorithms that take into account user quality of service (QoS), priority, and even channel condition so that network throughput is maximized [18], [18].

In the MAC protocol, there are three indexing bits for the allocation of an uplink time slot, and five bits for the downlink. As a result, at most eight users can share the same uplink time slot, and 32 on the same downlink time slot. Since the resource is dynamically allocated, a node does not need to be "detached" when there is no traffic to send. This is the so-called "always on" feature of GPRS.

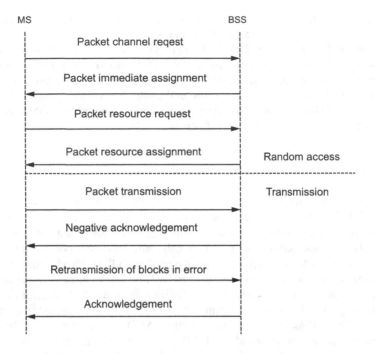

Fig. 2.12. Transmission over uplink of GPRS

2.3.5 Quality of Service

For packet data traffic, the concept of QoS is needed. In voice communications, all voice calls have the same service requirement. For data communication, QoS requirements vary significantly from application to application. For example, email and Web browsing are the best effort services, which do not have stringent delay requirement but are sensitive to loss. On the other hand, applications such as video transmission are sensitive to delay, but are tolerable to a certain degree of loss. Therefore, the QoS requirements are vastly different among all types of applications and should be considered in the GPRS network.

To provide more flexible QoS, GPRS defines different classes of priority, reliability, and delay, which can be used to characterize user QoS profile. There are three possible precedence classes (priority):

- High precedence: the highest level for service fulfillment
- Normal precedence: average level of service commitment
- Low precedence: service commitment is fulfilled after the service of the previous precedence classes has been satisfied

Based on the precedence class, nodes in the GPRS network, such as PCU, SGSN, and GGSN, can decide which packet should be served immediately, and which should be buffered. Therefore, traffic with realtime requirement, such as packet voice and packet video, can be set to be the high precedence class, while email applications can take low precedence. Moreover, it should be noted that the precedence level can also be related to the fee charged by the service provider. Traffic with high precedence can be charged with a premium, while low precedence traffic may enjoy a discount.

When user packets, or service data units (SDU), are buffered and forwarded within the data network, there are possibilities for many erroneous events, including:

- SDU lost: due to transmission error, e.g., over the air interface
- Duplicated SDU: SDU delivered twice, e.g., from incorrect retransmission
- SDU out-of-sequence: received in the wrong order
- SDU corrupt: SDU in error but not detected

There are three types of reliability classes defined in GPRS, as summarized in Table 2.1. The reliability of class 1 would be needed when an application is error sensitive but without sufficient (or no) error correction capability. Class 2 reliability is suitable for applications with good error tolerance or a certain error correction capability. Class 3 reliability copes with traffic that is either insensitive to error or has strong error correction capability.

Table 2.1. Reliability classes in GPRS

reliability class	SDU lost probability	SDU duplicate probability	SDU out-of-sequence probability	SDU corrupt probability
1	10^{-9}	10^{-9}	10^{-9}	10^{-9}
2	10^{-4}	10^{-5}	10^{-5}	10^{-6}
3	10^{-2}	10^{-5}	10^{-5}	10^{-2}

Three delay classes are also defined, as presented in Table 2.2. Therefore, Classes 1–3 can offer guaranteed delay, while Class 4 corresponds to the best effort traffic with no delay guarantee.

Table 2.2. Delay classes in GPRS

delay classes	delay (maximum values)			
	SDU size: 128 octets		SDU size: 1,024 octets	
	mean transfer delay (s)	95 percentile delay (s)	mean transfer delay (s)	95 percentile delay (s)
1 (predictive)	0.5	1.5	2	7
2 (predictive)	5	25	15	75
3 (predictive)	50	250	75	375
4 (best effort)	unspecified			

2.3.5 Security Features

Though the basic security elements in GPRS are similar to those in GSM, there are still certain changes.

To facilitate packet communication, a new user identity is introduced, the packet temporary mobile subscriber identity (P-TMSI). Like TMSI, P-TMSI is also stored in the SIM card. It serves as a temporary user name to the network. P-TMSI is allocated by the SGSN and is updated on a regular basis.

Authentication is required when an MS is to attach or detach from the network. Further, authentication is also needed when packet transfer is to start. The authentication elements are still the triplets: RAND, SRES, and Kc, the same as in GSM. The authentication process is initiated by the SGSN. To authenticate the MS, the SGSN requests AuC to generate the triplet of [RAND, Kc, SRES], and sends the RAND to the MS. The following steps are just like those in GSM. To save signaling overhead between SGSN and AuC, multiple triplets may be generated by the AuC and stored in the SGSN for future use.

A5 is still used as the ciphering algorithm. However, the ciphering is between MS and SGSN. In contrast, ciphering in GSM is between MS and BTS over the air interface. This means user data protection is extended. However, it is still not an end-to-end approach.

2.4 Code Division Multiple Access Systems

Code division multiple access (CDMA), has been selected as the multiple access scheme for a number of 2G and 3G cellular communication systems. In this part, we first provide an overview of the CDMA technology. Then we introduce three cellular systems based on CDMA: IS-95, cdma2000, and Universal Mobile Telecommunications System (UMTS).

2.4.1 Brief Introduction

Basic Operations

CDMA is a type of spread spectrum technology. At the transmitter, the transmitted signal is multiplied with a spreading code. The code rate is usually much higher than the information rate. The ratio between the spreading code rate and the information data rate is defined as the spreading gain or spreading factor. After spreading, signal bandwidth is expanded by a factor of the spreading gain. At the receiver, the same code is applied to restore the information bits. The operation of CDMA is illustrated in Fig. 2.13.

Spreading Codes

In CDMA, different spreading codes are used for user differentiation. The quality of spreading sequences is characterized by the autocorrelation and crosscorrelation properties. Autocorrelation refers to the correlation between a sequence and its phase shifts. Crosscorrelation refers to the correlation between two different spreading sequences. It is desirable that the autocorrelation for nonzero phase shifts and crosscorrelation be as low as possible.

There are two types of spreading codes-one is the orthogonal code and the other is the pseudonoise (PN) code.

When synchronized, orthogonal code has perfect correlation property: the crosscorrelation between different codes is 0. However, this property will be destroyed with imperfect synchronization. Orthogonal codes are commonly used over the downlink. Walsh code is a type of orthogonal code, and is generated from the Hadamard matrices. Variable spreading factor (VSF) orthogonal code is another type of orthogonal code. With VSF, multiple rates are easily supported. In the mean time, the orthogonality property is still preserved over codes with different spreading factors.

The maximal length sequence (m-sequence) is an important type of PN sequence. It is generated from LSFR. It has excellent autocorrelation property: the correlation between different phase shifts is almost 0. Therefore, m-sequences can be used in synchronous networks to differentiate base stations. However, m-sequences may have large crosscorrelation values. The Gold code is derived from m-sequences. It has much better crosscorrelation property. The Kasami sequence is another important type of PN sequence, because it has very low crosscorrelation.

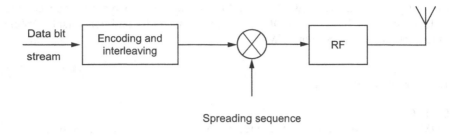

Spreading sequence

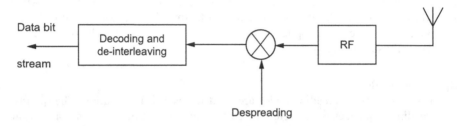

Despreading

Fig. 2.13. CDMA operation

In CDMA systems, the orthogonal codes and PN codes are often used together. The short orthogonal codes are used as channelization codes, while the long PN sequences are called scrambling codes. For example, over the downlink, multiple Walsh codes are used among different users for channelization. At the same time, a common PN sequence is shared among all the users. This PN sequence is unique for each base station and is used to differentiate transmissions from different base stations. This layered use of spreading codes is adopted in the downlink transmission, as presented in Fig. 2.14.

Usually complex spreading is adopted in CDMA, in which the spreading is conducted on the I and Q channels separately. The complex spreading operation is described in Fig. 2.15.

Power Control
Power control is required in CDMA to avoid the "near-far effect." If there is no power control, the strong signals of the nearby users will overwhelm the weak signals from the faraway users. The purpose of power control is to ensure the received power from different users is at a proper level at the BS, so that the signal-to-interference plus noise ratios (SINR) of users are maintained at an acceptable level.

Soft Handoff
In CDMA, the an same frequency band is used in neighboring bands. Therefore, it is possible for a MS to connect to more than one BS at the same time. An

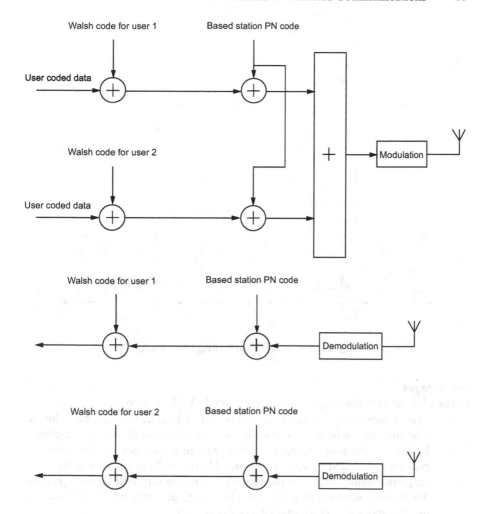

Fig. 2.14. Downlink spreading using Walsh codes and PN code

important benefit of CDMA is its capability to support soft handoff. Soft handoff means an MS can connect to more than one BS during the handoff process. By comparing the signal quality over the links with multiple BSs, the MS can an select the link with the best connection quality. Further, soft handoff allows a MS to have continuous connection with the BS so that the connection is never interrupted. Soft handoff is superior to hard handoff. In hard handoff, the connection between the former BS should be severed before the connection with the new BS is established. This is because in TDMA, the frequency bands are different between two neighboring cells. An MS has to switch frequency during handoff. Therefore, soft handoff is not possible in TDMA.

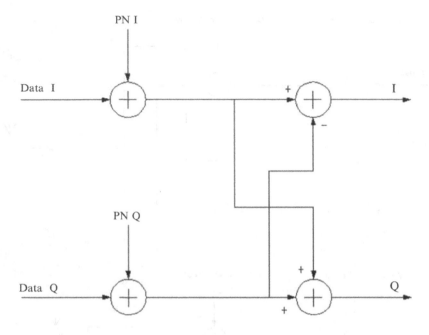

Fig. 2.15. Complex spreading in CDMA

Advantages

CDMA has several advantages over conventional TDMA systems.

- Due to spreading, the influence of cochannel interference can be reduced. The interference rejection capability is proportional to the spreading gain.
- In CDMA, the same frequency can be reused in two neighboring cells. In conventional TDMA systems, two neighboring cells cannot share the same frequency band; otherwise the received signal quality will be corrupted by the strong cochannel interference. Therefore, the frequency reuse factor is usually above 4 in conventional TDMA systems.
- Cell sectorization further increases CDMA capacity. The same frequency is still used in difference sectors. Therefore, system capacity grows with more sectors. In TDMA, different frequency bands have to be used, and the use of sectors is for the reduction of cochannel interference.
- RAKE receiver is adopted to achieve multipath diversity. RAKE can optimally combine multipath signals to explore multipath diversity.
- Soft handoff is possible in CDMA, while TDMA only allows hard handoff.
- Flexible data rates are easily supported by CDMA through the use of spreading codes with variable spreading gains. The higher the spreading gain, the lower the data rate, and vice versa.

- CDMA is more efficient in terms of resource utilization. In CDMA, power can be viewed as a network resource. When a user has no traffic to send, there is no transmission power, thus no resource consumption. In TDMA, if a time slot is assigned to an MS, but the MS has no traffic, the time slot is wasted. For voice traffic, for example, usually voice is active for 40% of the time, and idle in the rest period. Therefore, the voice activity factor is exploited in CDMA for a capacity increase.

2.4.2 IS-95

Overview

IS-95 was standardized by TIA/EIA of the USA. IS-95 is also known as cdmaOne. IS-95 has two substandards: IS-95 A and IS-95 B. IS-95 A is a 2G technology and is mainly designed for voice communication. IS-95 B can provide higher data rates by simultaneously using multiple code channels for each user.

IS-95 has a chip rate of 1.2288 chips per second (cps) and occupies a bandwidth of 1.25 MHz. It operates in the 800-MHz band and 1900-MHz PCS band. The network architecture of IS-95 is essentially similar to that of GSM, i.e., BTS controlled by BSC, and then MSC, etc.

In IS-95, the channelization code over the forward link (downlink) is the Walsh code with a length of 64 bits. Therefore, there are 64 unique Walsh codes, and each Walsh code is called a code channel. On the reverse link (uplink), the Walsh codes are not used to differentiate users, but for 64-ary modulation.

There are two types of PN codes in IS-95: a short sequence that has a period of 2^{15} and a long sequence with a chip period of $2^{42} - 1$. The short code is used for quadrature spreading on both the forward and the reverse links. On the forward link, the short code has a unique phase shift to differentiate transmission from the BS. Global Positioning System (GPS) is thus required for the synchronization among BSs. Over the reverse link, the long code is used to separate reverse link channels. Over the forward link it is used for data scrambling.

In Fig. 2.16, we plot the block diagrams of the forward link. Convolutional code adopted as the forward error correction scheme is IS-95. The long PN code is used for scrambling. Walsh code is used as the spreading code. The short PN code is adopted in quadrature spreading. The modulation scheme over the forward link is QPSK.

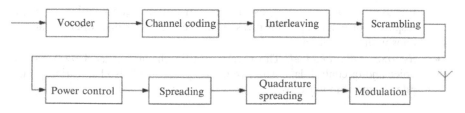

Fig. 2.16. Forward link block diagram for IS-95

The reverse link operations are presented in Fig. 2.17. In orthogonal modulation, one of the 64 Walsh codes is selected to be transmitted in place of six symbols of user data. The modulation scheme over the reverse link is offset-QPSK (O-QPSK). O-QPSK is more efficient than QPSK for the RF of the mobile, since the modulation signal will not pass the origin on the I–Q plane when both I and Q components are 0s.

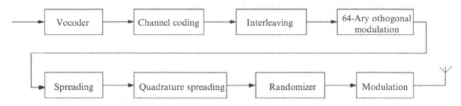

Fig. 2.17. Reverse link block diagram for IS-95

Logical Channels

Over the forward link, IS-95 has 64 logical channels, among which the following channels are devised:

- *Pilot channel*. This channel carries no data information, and bits are set to all zero (all-zero Walsh code). It is transmitted at the highest power and acts as a beacon to MS. Its signal strength is measured at the MS for it to estimate the link quality with the BS. The pilot is also used for system acquisition and power control purposes. Its signal strength is also used to assist handoff decisions.
- *Synchronization channel*. This channel provides MS with critical time synchronization information.
- *Paging channel*. The paging channel contains messages about system parameters, access parameters, call setup, channel assignment information, etc. This channel is used to communicate with an MS when there is no ongoing call with it.
- *Forward traffic channel*. The forward traffic channel is used to carry voice data or control data. All the remaining Walsh codes are available to traffic channels, only subject to the noise limit. The forward traffic channel can have a variable data rate of 1.2, 2.4, 4.8, and up to 9.6 kbps.

The logical channels over the reverse link are:

- *Access channel*. This channel is used when an MS has no call with the BS. It is used to transmit messages such as registration request, call setup, page response, or other signaling messages. The access channel operates at 4.8 kbps with a 20-ms frame.
- *Reverse traffic channel*. The reverse traffic channel is used by MSs for voice and/or control data. The reverse traffic channel also has variable data rates from 1.2 to 9.6 kbps.

Power Control

Power control is required in CDMA systems to solve the near–far problem and to maximize system capacity. In IS-95, power control over the forward and reverse links is different.

There are two types of power control an over the reverse link: open loop and closed loop. In open loop power control, a MS measures the received power and adjusts transmission power accordingly. Open loop power control is used whenever an MS transmits on the access channel. Although open loop power control is simple, it is not accurate. Therefore, closed loop power control should be adopted for enhanced power control accuracy. In closed loop power control, the BS continuously monitors the received signal quality from the MS, based on which the BS decides whether the MS should increase or decrease transmission power. Then the BS finetunes the transmission power at the MS by sending power control commands to the MS. The command instructs the MS to increase or decrease transmission power at a certain step size. The power control rate in IS-95 is 800 Hz, i.e., a power control command is issued every 1.25 ms.

The power control over the forward link is to limit intercell interference and reduce intracell/sector interference. Over the forward link, only closed loop power control is utilized. The MS monitors the frame error rate and reports the measurements to the BS. Based on the measurements, the BS adjusts the transmission power. The power control rate is lower than that over the reverse link. The adjustment can be made every 20 ms.

Handoff

In IS-95, handoff will happen under the following conditions:

- Pilot signal strength drops below a threshold. In this case, handoff can be initiated by both the MS and BS.
- MS transmission power level is exceeded. This happens when the MS transmits at the maximal power while the BS still requests power increase from the MS.
- Excessive load at a BS: some calls may therefore be transferred to other cells.

There are two types of handoff-handoff requested by an MS called mobile-assisted handoff, while that requested by a BS called base station-assisted handoff. As an example, we illustrate the mobile-assisted soft handoff as follows.

The MS measures the pilot channel signal strength from surrounding cells. When a pilot with sufficient signal strength is found, the MS identifies BS as a target BS for handoff. The MS sends a measurement report to the serving BS, which generates a handoff request to the MSC. The MSC then forwards the request to the target BS. The target BS agrees to the request and establishes a connection with the MS. The MS continues to monitor the signal strength from multiple BSs, until the handoff procedure is completed.

Authentication and Encryption

IS-95 uses the following algorithms for security purposes:

- Cellular authentication voice privacy encryption (CAVE) algorithm
- Cellular message encryption algorithm (CMEA).
- ORYX

CAVE is used to generate:

- A-key checksum
- Shared security data (SSD)
- Authentication signatures
- CMEA key and voice privacy mask (VPM)

CMEA is a variable-length block cipher with a 64-bit key and is employed to encrypt the control channel. ORYX is a stream cipher for the encryption of data and is derived from three LSFRs.

In IS-95, mobile identity is also represented by the IMSI. There is also an electronic serial number (ESN) that identifies the MS. In IS-95, authentication is performed under the following scenarios:

- Registration: when an MS does automatic registration
- Unique challenge: when an MS responds to the challenge from BS
- Origination: when an MS originates a call
- Terminations: when an MS is paged and should return a message
- Data burst: when an MS is to send a short data burst, such as short message service (SMS)
- TMSI assignment: when an MS responds to a TMSI assignment

For authentication purposes, each MS is assigned a 64-bit secret key, called A-key. The A-key is assigned when the MS first enters service and is stored in both the MS and its associated HLR/AC (authentication center). Its value is usually constant until the network feels necessary to change it. Authentication is based on the matching of SSD generated by the A-key.

SSD has a length of 128 bits and is stored in both the MS and AC. SSD is divided into two parts: SSD_A and SSD_B, each having 64 bits. SSD_A is used for authentication, while SSD_B for voice privacy and signaling message encryption.

For authentication, authentication signatures are computed and compared at the network side. The calculation of authentication signature is based on the CAVE algorithm, with parameters of a 32-bit RAND, 32-bit ESN, 24-bit AUTH_DATA, and 64-bit SSD_A. The AUTH_DATA depend on the authentication scenarios. The computation of authentication signature is shown in Fig. 2.18.

SSD is regularly updated. The update procedure is similar to that in GSM. The update occurs in both the MS and HLR/AC. The network generates a random number (RANDSSD) and sends it to the MS. Based on RANDSSD, A-key, and ESN, SSD is renewed at MS and HLR/AC. The SSD update procedure is presented in Fig. 2.19.

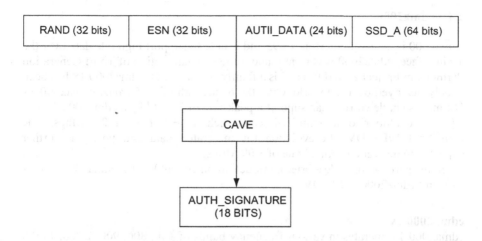

| RAND (32 bits) | ESN (32 bits) | AUTII_DATA (24 bits) | SSD_A (64 bits) |

Fig. 2.18. Computation of authentication signature

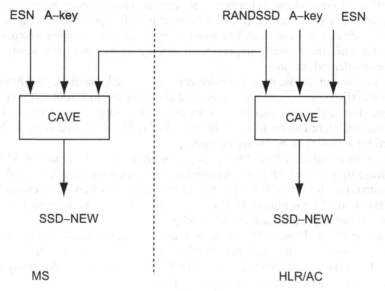

Fig. 2.19. Update of SSD

CDMA can provide a certain degree of privacy with spreading. In IS-95, privacy is further enhanced by encryption algorithms. Voice privacy is provided by the VPM, which is derived from the CAVE algorithm and SSD_B. VPM is generated at the beginning of a call and is used between MS and BS to encrypt user information over the traffic channel. For signaling messages, CMEA is used for encryption. The CMEA key is produced by the CAVE algorithm and SSD_B.

2.4.3 cdma2000

cdma2000 is an evolution from IS-95 and is able to support high rate data over the air interface. cdma2000 is currently under the standardization of Third Generation Partnership Project 2 (3GPP2) and is a family of standards. cdma2000 1x has been widely deployed over the world. Over the bandwidth of 1.25 MHz, cdma2000 1x (1x means single carrier) can support a peak rate of 307.2 kbps. cdma2000 1xEV-DO (1x evolution data optimized) can reach a peak rate of 2.4 Mbps. The cdma2000 1xEV-DV (1x evolution for integrated data and voice) is further expected to deliver a maximal rate of 3.09 Mbps.

In this part, we provide a brief introduction on cdma2000 1x, cdma2000 1xEV-DO, and cdma2000 1xEV-DV.

cdma2000 1x

cdma2000 1x operates in various frequency bands of 450, 800, 900, 1,700, 1,800, 1,900, and 2,100 MHz, and is fully backward compatible with IS-95.

When compared with IS-95, cdma2000 1x has higher voice capacity, supporting 35 voice calls per sector per carrier. In contrast, the voice capacity for IS-95 is 22 voice channels per sector per carrier. This increase in voice capacity is due to a number of factors. Over the forward link, fast power control is employed; a 1/4 code rate is introduced; and transmit diversity can be implemented. Over the reverse link, the capacity improvement mainly comes from the newly adopted coherent demodulation.

For voice and data, there are three commonly used channels. The fundamental channel (FCH) is to carry voice, data, and signaling at rates from 1,200 bps to 14.4 kbps. The high data rates are supported by the supplemental channel (SCH), whose peak rate can be 16 or 32 times of FCH. The dedicated control channel is used for signaling or bursty data access.

For data traffic, cdma2000 1x can support a peak data rate of 153.6 kbps (release 0) and can be further increased to 307.2 kbps (release A). The theoretical maximal rate for cdma2000 1x is 628 kbps, which is achieved by combining two SCHs at 307.2 kbps plus an FCH at a rate of 14.4 kbps. At the peak rate of 153.6 kbps, the average rate is around 50–90 kbps.

At the BS, multiple SCHs can be used over the forward link as long as there are enough Walsh codes and transmission power. At an MS, the number of simultaneous SCHs is limited to two. The SCH can be either individually assigned to an MS, or shared among a number of MSs.

Furthermore, turbo code has been introduced in cdma2000 1x. It has coding rates of 1/2, 1/3, and 1/4, and is derived from two 8-state parallel concatenated codes. Turbo code can deliver better performance than convolution codes with long coding blocks. Therefore, it is only used on the SCH when a frame has more than 360 bits.

Transmit diversity is also adopted in cdma2000 1x, which is called orthogonal transmit diversity. It is an implementation of the orthogonal space time block code. Basically two orthogonal signals are transmitted from two antenna elements at the BS. At the MS, the received signals are optimally combined to achieve the diversity gain.

An important feature in cdma2000 1x is the newly introduced location capability. The gpsOne position technology from Qualcomm has been integrated into device chipset suites. Highly accurate positioning can be achieved through (A-GPS) network assisted-GPS. Conventional GPS requires several minutes to produce location results. With the assistance of the network, A-GPS can provide positioning within seconds. When GPS signal is not available, e.g., for indoor positioning, advanced forward link triangulation and other mixed techniques are adopted to provide location information, at reduced accuracy. The introduction of location features would inevitably promote a wide range of applications such as security, navigation, location-based services, and mobile commerce.

cdma2000 1xEV-DO
The technical specification for 1xEV-DO is IS-856, released by 3GPP2. The chip rate is still 1.2288 Mcps with a bandwidth of 1.25 MHz. The 1xEV-DO is designed to efficiently transfer data. For voice, with the added QoS features, voice over IP can be adopted. With the optimization for data only, the data rate is greatly increased with respect to cdma2000 1x. The peak forward link data rate can be as high as 2.4 Mbps. Average data rate for a user can be as high as 300–800 kbps.

One reason for the enhanced spectrum efficiency is the separation of voice and data. Voice has different characteristics and QoS requirements with data. For example, voice traffic is delay sensitive. A delay over 100 ms is not desirable for voice. To reduce delay, voice traffic common uses short frame size. However, short frame size also leads to added overhead and reduced efficiency. On the other hand, data are bursty in nature and more tolerable of delay. Therefore, long frame size can be adopted to improve efficiency.

Another improvement in efficiency comes from the turbo coding on data frames. Turbo coding is most effective for long frames. For voice, the benefit of turbo coding can hardly be enjoyed.

Besides BPSK and QPSK, higher level modulation schemes 8PSK and 16-QAM are used to achieve data rates above 1 Mbps. The data rates of 1xEV-DO are flexibly adjusted according to the channel condition. The MS constantly monitors the received signal quality from the BS and sends report to the BS on expected channel quality. With favorable channel condition, high transmission rates can be used. When channel quality deteriorates, the data rate is adaptively reduced.

The data rates over the forward and reverse link are asymmetric. This is natural for data services since the data traffic is intrinsically asymmetric, with the forward link dominating the reverse link. The reverse link data rate doubles from 9.6 kbps up to 153.6 kbps.

The power control policy is different between cdma2000 1x and cdma2000 1xEV-DO. For voice traffic in cdma2000 1x, the purpose of power control is to achieve the designated SINR with the least transmission power. In cdma2000 1xEV-DO, the highest power is used to deliver the maximal achievable rate to a user.

Flexible resource management is utilized between BS and MSs to achieve high system throughput. This is viable due to the delay insensitive nature of the data service. The management of resources is the job of the scheduler, which will distribute them in a fair manner to different users. The channel condition should be incorporated into the scheduling process so that throughput and QoS can be properly balanced. For users in deep fades, it is more efficient to divert the time slots to other users with good channel conditions. This is the so-called multiuser diversity in wireless data networks.

1xEV-DO fully supports IP. Therefore, security mechanisms such as virtual private network can be overlaid on top of 1xEV-DO. The 1xEV-DO air interface will be transparent to users, since 1xEV-DO is itself a PDN.

1xEV-DO is used for data sessions only. Dual mode devices will support both cdma2000 1x voice and 1xEV-DO high speed data service. When a call comes to a user with an ongoing data connection, the user is notified. If the user decides to pick up the call, the data service is temporarily suspended during the period of conversation. The device will automatically transfer to the cdma2000 1x air interface. In this way, a user will not miss a call during 1xEV-DO data service, and the transmission between voice and 1xEV-DO data service is seamless and transparent to a user.

cdma2000 1x-EV-DV
The focus of 1xEV-DV is to increase the forward link data rate when supporting both data and voice. High spectral efficiency is achieved with the introduction of a new channel, forward packet data channel (F-PDCH). On F-PDCH, the peak data rate can be as high as 3.09 Mbps.

To improve efficiency, resource sharing is performed among MSs. There are three possible modulation schemes: QPSK, 8PSK, and 16-QAM. Type II hybrid automatic repeat request (H-ARQ) is adopted. In this type of ARQ, incremental redundancy is transmitted with turbo codes.

2.4.4 Universal Mobile Telecommunication System

UMTS is the most widely supported third generation mobile communications system. 3G systems are intended to provide global mobility with a wide range of services, including telephony, paging, messaging, Internet, and broadband data. The International Telecommunication Union started the process of defining the standard for third generation systems, referred to as International Mobile Telecommunications 2000 (IMT-2000). ETSI was responsible for UMTS standardization. In 1998 3GPP was formed to continue the technical specification work.

Services
UMTS offers teleservices (like speech or SMS) and bearer services, which provide the capability for information transfer between access points. It is possible to

negotiate and renegotiate the characteristics of a bearer service at session or connection establishment and during ongoing session or connection. Both connection-oriented and connectionless services are offered for PTP and PMP communication.

The data rates for UMTS are:

- 144 kbps for rural outdoor and satellite
- 384 kbps for urban outdoor
- 2.048 Mbps for indoor or low-range outdoor

Bearer services have different QoS parameters for maximum transfer delay, delay variation, and bit error rate. Four QoS classes are defined in UMTS:

- *Conversational class.* This includes voice and video telephony. The speech codec in UMTS will employ the adaptive multirate technique. It has eight source rates, from 4.75 to 12.2 kbps. Voice activity detector is used with background noise evaluation. In video telephony, UMTS specified H.264M for circuit-switched connections and session initiation protocol for IP multimedia applications.
- *Streaming class.* In this class, multimedia data are transferred as a steady and continuous stream. Some examples are multimedia, video on demand, and webcast. Usually streaming media is less sensitive to delay. Therefore, buffering can be adopted to smooth out delay jitter.
- *Interactive class.* This type of application requires interaction between parties. For example, Web browsing and network gaming belong to the interactive class.
- *Background class.* This is the traditional best effort service, such as email, SMS, and file downloading.

Location services are also provided in UMTS. Similar to cdma2000, the location methods in UMTS include:

1. Cell-id based positioning
2. Positioning based on time difference of arrival
3. Network-assisted GPS (A-GPS)

Architecture

An UMTS network consists of three interacting domains: core network (CN), UMTS terrestrial radio access network (UTRAN), and user equipment (UE). The main function of the core network is to provide switching, routing, and transit for user traffic. Core network also contains the databases and network management functions. Fig. 2.20 shows the UMTS network elements.

The CN architecture for UMTS is based on GPRS. All equipment have to be modified for UMTS operation and services. The CN can be divided into circuit-switched and packet-switched parts. Circuit-switching equipment such as MSC and GSMC remain the same as in GSM. The packet domain is managed by SGSN and GGSN, the same as in GPRS. The external networks also have two types: circuit-switched networks such as PSTN and ISDN, and packet-switched networks such as the Internet.

UTRAN provides the air interface access method for user equipment. In UMTS, the base station is referred to as Node-B, while BSC is called radio network controller (RNC).

The functions of Node-B include:

- Radio transmission and reception
- Modulation/demodulation
- Channel coding
- Microdiversity
- Error handling
- Closed loop power control

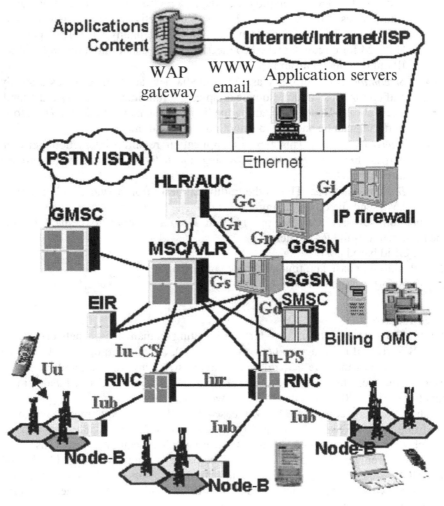

Fig. 2.20. UMTS system architecture

The functions of RNC include:
- Radio resource control
- Admission control
- Channel allocation
- Power control settings
- Handover control
- Macrodiversity
- Ciphering
- Segmentation/reassembly
- Broadcast signaling
- Open-loop power control

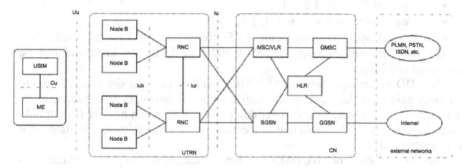

Fig. 2.21. UMST logical elements and interfaces

UE consists of two parts:
- Mobile equipment is the radio terminal used for radio communication.
- UMTS subscriber identity module (USIM) performs the same role as the SIM card. Its functions are mainly related to security aspects, such as authentication.

UMTS has the same types of identity as in GPRS, such as IMSI, TMSI, P-TMSI, IMEI, etc.

UMTS specifies interfaces between logical network elements. The major ones include:
- Uu interface: the interface between UE and UTRAN, which is also the radio interface.
- Cu interface: the interface between USIM card and UE.
- Iu interface: this interface connects UTRAN to the CN.
- Iur interface: the interface between RNCs.
- Iub interface: the interface that connects Node-B with RNC.

Fig. 2.21 illustrates the relationship between the logical network elements and interfaces.

Radio Access

The air interface technology of UTRAN is called wideband CDMA (WCDMA). WCDMA has two basic operation modes: frequency-division duplexing (FDD) and time-division duplexing (TDD).

The major parameters of the FDD standard are summarized as follows:

- Chip rate: 3.84 Mcps
- Bandwidth: 5 MHz
- Channel coding schemes: convolutional coding and turbo coding, which is used for data traffic
- Modulation scheme: QPSK
- Pulse shape: root-raised cosine with a roll of factor of 0.22
- Frame length: 10 ms
- Power control rate: 1,500 Hz
- Power control step size: 0.5, 1, 1.5, 2 dB
- Physical layer spreading factor: 4-256 for uplink, 4-512 for downlink

The maximal data rate for WCDMA FDD mode is 384 kbps and can be increased to 2 Mbps.

The FDD mode requires a pair of 5-MHz bands. In certain situations, there are no such paired bands. Further, the traffic over 3G networks is expected to be asymmetric, which means traffic over downlink will be much heavier than uplink. Therefore, the paired bandwidth allocation is not flexible and suitable for asymmetric traffic.

The TDD mode of WCDMA is better suited for unpaired bands and asymmetric traffic. This is because TDD needs only one frequency band, and the time slots for uplink and downlink can be adaptively adjusted. The major parameters of WCDMA TDD are:

- Chip rate: 1.28 or 3.84 Mcps.
- Bandwidth: 1.6 MHz (at 1.28 Mcps) or 5 MHz (at 3.84 Mcps).
- Channel coding: convolutional and turbo coding.
- Modulation: QPSK.
- Frame length: 10 ms.
- Number of slots/frame: 15.
- Power control rate: 100 or 200 Hz over uplink, 800 Hz over downlink.
- Power control step size: 1, 2, 3 dB.
- Physical layer spreading factor: 1, 2, 4, 8, 16.
- The TDD mode also employs a number of technologies such as joint detection and smart antenna to further improve capacity. It can be expected that good spectral efficiency can be achieved with this TDD mode.

2.4.5 Security Features in cdma2000 and UMTS

UMTS and cdma2000 bear many resemblances in terms of security features. Therefore, we elaborate only on the security schemes in UMTS.

The UMTS security framework is an enhancement and extension of the security features in 2G systems. The major security aspects are still the authentication of UE and encryption between UE and the serving network (SN).

Authentication and Key Agreement
The authentication and key generation procedure in UMTS is called authentication and key agreement (AKA), which is used for authentication and generation of keys for encryption and integrity protection. It should be noted that UMTS allows the UE to authenticate the network. This is called mutual authentication. In contrast, only UE is authenticated in GSM, and a UE can never reject the network. With mutual authentication, it is possible for the UE to reject the network.

The AKA procedure is implemented at the USIM card at UE and AuC of the network. The authentication process at the network side involves home environment (HE) and SN. The HE mainly consists of the HLR and AuC. The SN refers to SGSN for packet-switched data and VLC/MSC for circuit-switched data.

The operation of AKA has two stages. The first stage is to transfer the authentication vector (AV) from the HE to the SN. The AV contains security credentials such as challenge–response authentication data and encryption keys. It should be pointed out that the transfer between HE and SN should be secured. For this purpose, mobile application part (MAP) protocol is used, which provides secure mechanisms for the AV transfer. The second stage is the execution of the one-pass challenge–response procedure at the SN to achieve mutual authentication between the USIM and the network. Similar to GSM, the authentication is also based on a preshared 128-bit secret key, K, which is stored in both USIM and AuC in HE.

In UMTS, a number of algorithms are designed for authentication purpose and are different from those in GSM. The algorithms related to authentication are from f0 to f5*. In Table 2.3, we list the security-related algorithms in UMTS. In practice, the authentication algorithms (from f0 to f5*) are operator specific. This means it is up to the operator to decide the exact algorithms for implementation. 3GPP developed a set of algorithms called MILENAGE as an example set of algorithms.

In the authentication process, the f0 algorithm is used to generate the random number RAND. An authentication token AUTN is also generated by the SGSN/VLR. At the network side, function f1 is invoked to produce message authentication code (MAC-A). Then the challenge message, composed of RAND, AUTN, and MAC-A, is sent to the UE. Within the AUTN, there is also a sequence number (SQN). The function f5 may be optionally used to produce an anonymity key (AK) for the concealment of SQN in the challenge. This is achieved by XORing SQN with AK.

Table 2.3. Security algorithms in UMTS

algorithm	function
f0	random challenge generation function
f1	network authentication function
f1*	resynchronization message authentication function
f2	user challenge–response generation function
f3	cipher key derivation function
f4	integrity derivation function
f5	anonymity key derivation function for normal operation
f5*	anonymity key derivation function for resynchronization
f6	MAP encryption algorithm
f7	MAP integrity algorithm
f8	UMTS encryption algorithm
f9	UMTS integrity algorithm

When UE receives the challenge, UE authenticates the network by comparing the local computed MAC with the received MAC-A. After authentication of the network, an authentication response (RES) is computed by the USIM employing the f2 algorithm. Then RES is sent back to the network for the authentication of UE. In the meantime, a 128-bit cipher key (CK) is calculated by the f3 algorithm, and a 128-bit integrity key (IK) by the f4 algorithm.

Confidentiality and Integrity
In UMTS, confidentiality is achieved through encryption. The CK is 128 bits, which doubles the 64-bit key in GSM. The added bits significantly improve encryption security. Another difference between GSM and UMTS is the scope of encryption. In GSM, ciphering ends at BTS, and information flow between BTS and BSC is in the clear. However, in many practical systems, several links

between BTS and BSC are also through radio. Therefore, encryption takes place between MS and RNC in UMTS.

Encryption ensures the confidentiality of the messages. On the other hand, it is necessary to protect encrypted messages from being maliciously modified. This is achieved by the integrity algorithms. The integrity mechanism is to produce a message authentication code (MAC). In UMTS, integrity protection is only adopted for the signaling messages between MS and RNC.

The encryption and integrity algorithms in UMTS are all based on the Kasumi cipher. Kasumi is a block cipher with eight rounds of operation. It operates on 64-bit data block with a key length of 128 bits.

More specifically, the encryption algorithm is f8. It produces key stream blocks of 64 bits, which is then XORed with the plaintext data. It requires a 128-bit CK that is generated by f3.

The integrity algorithm is f9. It is also based on Kasumi but operates in the cipher-block-chaining mode. It takes the message as the input and operates with the IK produced by f4. The final output from f9 is a 64-bit cipher block. Afterward it is truncated to 32 bits to produce the MAC. The MAC is then transferred together with the encrypted message. At the receiver, the MAC is re-generated and compared with the received MAC. If the two agree, the integrity of the message is affirmed.

2.5 Summary

In this chapter, we presented a brief introduction of the fundamentals of wireless communications. We described the cellular standards of GSM, GPRS, IS-95, cdma2000, and UMTS. We also introduced the security aspects of these standards.

References

1. J. Eberspäher, H.-J. Vögel, C. Be ttstetter, GSM Switching, Services and Protocols, 2nd Edition, Wiley, New York, 2001.
2. T. Halonen, J. Romero, J. Melero, GSM, GPRS and EDGE Performance, Wiley, New York, 2002.
3. D. Goodman, "Second generation wireless information networks," IEEE Trans. Vehicular Technol., vol. 40, no. 2, pp. 366–374, May 1991.
4. M. Rahnema, "Overview of the GSM system and protocol architecture," IEEE Commun. Mag., pp. 92–100, July 1993.
5. A. Mehrotra, L. S. Golding, "Mobility and security management in the GSM system and some proposed future improvements," Proc. IEEE, vol. 86, no. 7, pp. 1480–1497, July 1998.
6. B. Schneier, Applied Cryptography: Protocols, Algorithms, and Source Code in C, 2nd Edition, Wiley, New York, 1996.

7.   N. Ferguson, B. Schneier, Practical Cryptography, Wiley, New York, 2003.
8.   A. Biryukov, A. Shamir, D. Wagner, "Realtime cryptanalysis of A5/1 on a PC," Fast Software Encryption Workshop 2000, New York City, USA, 10–12 April 2000.
9.   P. Ekdahl, T. Johansson, "Another attack on A5/1," IEEE Trans. Inform. Theory, vol. 49, no. 1, pp. 284–289, January 2003.
10.   P. Stuckmann, The GSM Evolution: Mobile Packet Data Service, Wiley, New York, 2003.
11.   G. Sanders, L. Thorens, M. Reisky, O. Rulik, S. Deylitz, GPRS Networks, Wiley, New York, 2003.
12.   M. Mouly, M.-B. Pauttet, "Current evolution of the GSM systems," IEEE Personal Commun., pp. 9–19, October 1995.
13.   G. Brasche, B. Walke, "Concepts, services, and protocols of the new GSM Phase 2+ General Packet Radio Service," IEEE Commun. Mag., pp. 94–104, August 1997.
14.   A. Furuskar, S. Mazur, F. Mller, H. Olofsson, "EDGE: enhanced data rates for GSM and TDMA/136 evolution," IEEE Personal Commun., pp. 56–66, June 1999.
15.   J. Cai, D. Goodman, "General Packet Radio Service in GSM," IEEE Commun. Mag., pp. 122–131, October 1997.
16.   R. Kalden, I. Meirick, M. Meyer, "Wireless Internet access based on GPRS," IEEE Personal Commun., pp. 8–18, April 2000.
17.   H. Zhang, "Service disciplines for guaranteed performance service in packet-switching networks," Proc. IEEE, vol. 83, pp. 1374–1396, October 1995.
18.   Y. Cao, V.O.K. Li, "Scheduling algorithms in broadband wireless networks," Proc. IEEE, vol. 89, no. 1, pp. 76–87, January 2001.
19.   H. Fattah, C. Leung, "An overview of scheduling algorithms in wireless multimedia networks," IEEE Wireless Commun., pp. 76–83, October 2002.
20.   W.C.Y. Lee, "Overview of cellular CDMA," IEEE Trans. Vehicular Technol., vol. 60, no. 2, pp. 291–302, May 1991.
21.   E. Dinan, B. Jabbari, "Spreading codes for direct sequence CDMA and wideband CDMA cellular networks," IEEE Commun. Mag., pp. 48–54, September 1998.
22.   A.J. Viterbi, CDMA: principles of Spread Spectrum Communication, Addison-Wesley, Reading, MA, 1995.
23.   R. Rrasad, CDMA for Wireless Personal Communications, Artech House, USA, 1996.
24.   L. Harte, CDMA IS-95 for Cellular and PCS, McGraw-Hill, New York, 1999.
25.   V. Garg, IS-95CDMA and cdma2000: Cellular/PCS Systems Implementation, Prentice-Hall, Englewood Cliffs, NJ, 2000.
26.   V. Vanghi, A. Damnjanovic, B. Vojcic, The cdma2000 System for Mobile Communications, Prentice-Hall, Englewood Cliffs, NJ, 2004.
27.   T. Ojanpera, R. Prasad, "An overview of third-generation wireless personal communication," IEEE Personal Commun., pp. 59–65, December 1998.

28. T. Ojanpera, R. Prasad, "An overview of air interface multiple access for IMT-2000/UMTS," IEEE Commun. Mag., pp. 82–95, September 1998.
29. D. Knisely, S. Kumar, S. Laha, S. Nanda, "Evolution of wireless data services: IS-95 to cdma2000," IEEE Commun. Mag., pp. 140–149, October 1998.
30. B. Sarikaya, "Packet mode in wireless networks: overview of transition to third generation," IEEE Commun. Mag., pp. 164–172, September 2000.
31. J.-H. Park, "Wireless Internet access for mobile subscribers based on the GPRS/UMTS network," IEEE Commun. Mag., pp. 38–49, April 2002.
32. R. Parry, "cdma2000 1xEV-DO: a 3G wireless Internet access system," IEEE Potential, pp. 10–13, October/November 2002.
33. A. Soong, S.-J. Oh, A. Damnjanovic, Y.C. Yoon, "Forward high speed wireless packet data service in IS-2000 – 1xEV-DV," IEEE Commun. Mag., pp. 171–177, August 2003.
34. A. Samukic, "UMTS Universal Mobile Telecommunication Service: development of standards for the third generation," IEEE Trans. Vehicular Technol., vol. 47, no. 4, pp. 1099–1104, November 1998.
35. E. Dahlman, B. Gudmundson, M. Nilsson, J. Skold, "UMTS/IMT-2000 based on wideband CDMA," IEEE Commun. Mag., pp.70–80, September 1998.
36. J. Huber, D. Weiler, H. Brand, "UMTS, the mobile multimedia vision for IMT-2000: a focus on standardization," IEEE Commun. Mag., pp. 129–136, September 2000.
37. H. Holma, A. Toskala, WCDMA for UMTS: Radio Access for Third Generation Mobile Communications, 2nd Edition, Wiley, New York, 2002.
38. K. Boman, G. Horn, P. Howard, V. Niemi, "UMTS security," Electron. Commun. J., pp. 191–204, October 2002.
39. G. Koien, "An introduction to access security in UMTS," IEEE Wireless Commun., pp. 8–18, February 2004.
40. G. Rose, G. Koien, "Access security in cdma2000, including a comparison with UMTS access security," IEEE Wireless Commun., pp. 19–25, February 2004.

3 Wireless Security

W.-B. Lee

Feng Chia University, 100 Wen Hua Road, Taiwan

3.1 Introduction

Following the rapid development of the wireless communication services and the vast advancement of the mobile commerce community at large, security issues that are of crucial importance to the wired environment are resurfacing and creating a similar degree of impact. At heart, these security requirements for the wireless are essentially equivalent to the wired counterpart, which necessitates meeting the three fundamental demands below.

- Confidentiality: The assurance that the data is not revealed to unauthorized parties.
- Authentication: The assurance that the identities which the communicating entities proclaim are indeed their true identity.
- Integrity: The assurance that data received are exactly as sent by the genuine sender (i.e., contain no modification, insertion, deletion, or replay).

Furthermore, as our lives are gradually becoming more and more dependant on information and with wireless communication increasingly gaining dominance as the means for electronic and mobile commerce, one other additional security attribute that must be taken into account.

Non-repudiation: Provides protection against denial by one of the entities involved in a communication of having participated in all or part of the communication.

Although these topics are already intensely discussed, and many practical methods and mature approaches have taken shape, there are still significant differences that forbid us to fit these wired solutions onto the wireless systems due to a few intrinsic limitations. These limitations can be organized into two major categories, those relating to the mobile devices and those concerning wireless network environments.

3.1.1 Mobile Device

Due to power and size limitations, mobile device processors are usually consequently restricted, and incapable of performing complicated computations. On the other hand, memory capacity is equally limited, although extension memory card can be added, there are still of little assistance, and hardly help improve the

overall performance. These combined restrictions attach the following influences on security.

- Because the processor on mobile devices is on average computationally in-
ferior to ordinary desktop computers, they usually do not accommodate
adequate performance when dealing with computationally intensive public
key encryption/decryption operations (e.g. RSA [3.1]).
- The memory storage on mobile devices is respectively smaller, thus placing restrictions on both the size of key length and digital certificate.

3.1.2 Wireless Network Environment

With respect to wired network, the wireless medium supports narrower bandwidth.
Even as the 2.5G and 3G standards states to offer a transmission rate of up to
384kbps for the mobile transmission and 2Mbps for stationary communication,
these figures are, for the most part, overly optimistic. Under realistic circumstances, various factors such as signal strength, environmental disturbances and
communication density can alter the actual experience. Also, due to the open-
ness of wireless channel, the coverage area of the wireless signal must also be
carefully calculated to avoid possible eavesdropping or other active attacks. All
in all, the influences, which limited bandwidth and radio wave have on security,
are as follows:

- Because bandwidth is limited, the transmission load is naturally restricted.
When the digital certificate or encrypted message becomes overly lengthy,
transmission cost will rise, and users will experience extra waiting time. It
is therefore important to minimize the payload transmitted.
- Due to the intrinsic property of wireless network, eavesdropping on the
transmission content can easily be carried out without being causing detection, thus it is necessary to set up appropriate safety measures to lower the
risk of privacy violation.

While porting security mechanisms seen in the wired network, for example en-
cryption/decryption, digital signature etc., to achieve security requirements such as
confidentiality, authentication and integrity on the wireless environment, we must
lower the computation cost in order to comply to the mobile devices' computation
capability, reduce the key lengths and the immense quantity of digital signature information to allow their storage within mobile devices, manage the bandwidth
consumption to accommodate the relatively slow transmission rate, and also select
radio wave coverage area to reduce the chance of information leakage.

This chapter focuses on the discussion of wireless related security issues. The
use of public key cryptosystem is competently adapted to such tasks; nevertheless,
in order for it to work correctly, a complete certification infrastructure must be in
place to guarantee the validity of individual's public key. Thus we explain how
such an infrastructure can be setup in the wireless environment. Section 3.2 will

present a method that wireless environment is used to ensure the legitimacy of public key. As promising as public key cryptosystems may appear, they still have the serious shortcoming of consuming an excess amount of time and even with symmetric key cryptosystem jointly employed to enhance the calculation speed, the huge computation load, consequent of the public key operation, is still beyond those that mobiles devices are capable of handling. As a result, in Section 3.3 we introduce elliptic curve cryptosystem – a faster and much more efficient member (in terms of key length) of the public key cryptosystem that nicely suited for implementation in the wireless environments. Furthermore, due to the characteristic of mobility, putting a centralized server in charge of storing and maintaining each entity's authentication information and handling most of the computation work is necessary to ease the task of achieving mobile security. This topic will be pursued on Section 3.4. And finally, summary is given in Section 3.5.

3.2 Mobile Certificate

Generally, in the field of cryptography, the primary means of achieving information communication security are through encryption. The method of encryption can be largely classified into symmetric and asymmetric cryptosystems, also referred to respectively as secret key and public key cryptosystems. In symmetric cryptosystem (e.g., DES [3.2], AES [3.3]), each communicating party shares a secret key to secure the communication, observable from Fig. 3.1.

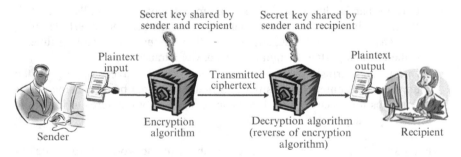

Fig. 3.1. Symmetric key cryptosystem framework

As the basic functional units of the symmetric cryptosystems are comprised of substitution and transposition, they can be exceedingly fast and extremely suited for implementation on hardware. Due to the above reason, symmetric cryptosystems are well adapted for use on the wireless environment; however, for reasons that will be explained, symmetric cryptosystems are not entirely adequate for solving all the security problems.

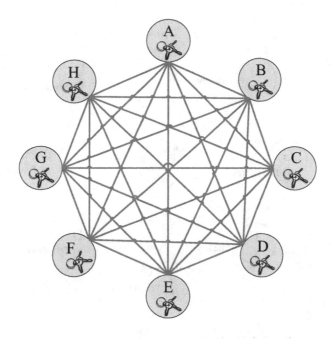

Fig. 3.2. Key management problem ($n(n-1)/2$ keys)

- Key management problem: In E-commerce, the ratio of transacting partners is proportional to the number of keys that must be managed, and this growth becomes impractical for the mobile devices when transaction demands increases. As can be seen in Fig. 3.2, it's easy to understand that, for n participants, $n(n-1)/2$ keys need to be kept secret.
- Inability to support non-repudiation mechanism: With symmetric cryptosystem, the two communication participants will have the same secret key, thus making it impossible to distinguish the originator of the cipher, causing non-repudiation practically infeasible.

From the previous discussion we can reason that symmetric cryptosystem alone is not enough for the securing of wireless systems, and must take into account another method – public key cryptosystem – to provide non-repudiation, for example. In public key cryptosystem, every user owns a pair of keys; one for encryption and another for decryption. The key used for decryption, also known as the private key, is usually kept secret and includes applications such as signing a digital signature. The encryption key, also referred to as the public key, can be used for encryption as well as the verification of the owner of digital signatures (shown in Fig. 3.3). Due to the public key is assumed to be known to everyone, communicating members that

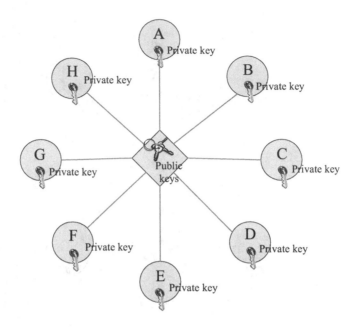

Fig. 3.3. Public key management (*n* public keys)

employ asymmetric cryptosystems need only maintain their own pair of keys and can successfully accomplish the requirement of non-repudiation through the use of digital signature. However, public key cryptosystem based its principles on mathematical hard problems, such as factoring very large numbers and solving discrete logarithm, as opposed to the simpler operations of substitution and transposition found in symmetric cryptosystems, and hence require greater burden. If directly applied onto the mobile devices, it will most likely be too much of a burden.

In remedy of this situation, current applications usually entail the use of a symmetric key cryptosystem to encrypt the message and an asymmetric key cryptosystem to encrypt the key used for the symmetric cryptosystem. This method of mixing symmetric and asymmetric cryptosystem is both secure and efficient. However, before any public key cryptosystem can be safely applied, one must first make certain of its authenticity, furthermore, the identity of the public key's owner must be correctly associated. For these purposes, a trusted authority is required to create, for each public key, a corresponding certificate to ensure its authenticity and connection with the rightful owner. This entire framework is the so called public key infrastructure (PKI).

The core of PKI is X.509 [3.4], where the digital certificate is used to assure the identity of the subject and signed by a trusted third party, the so called certification authority (CA). Hence, verifying the correctness of the certificate is a fundamental building block for public key applications.

However, verification of the X.509's certificate must couple with the ability of greater processing power and a lot of memory spaces. Unfortunately, it is not suitable for the modern mobile devices, because wireless network is a resource constrained environment. Hence, the length of certificate should be shortened for transmission over wireless network. Besides, the restrictions in the resource of wireless mobile devices greatly limit the deployment of the X.509' Certificate Verification Framework [3.5]. For example, RSA algorithm defined in X.509 must use 512-bit key. However, RSA 512-bit key generation takes approximately 4 minutes on mobile phone's processor. Singing with the key takes about 7 seconds. The issues are much worse with the 1024-bit RSA where the key generation takes 30 minutes. Such limitations lead to the challenge of tuning existing wired technologies or developing new one to make them suitable to these mobile devices in the wireless world. Therefore, the PKI has also been modified to the form of WPKI [3.6].

WAP forum established the WPKI framework not as a new PKI standard but as an extension of the traditional PKI to the wireless environment. It utilizes two approaches to satisfy the mobile device's requirement: 1) It makes use of elliptic curve cryptography, and 2) It reduces certain fields within the X.509 certificate to cut down on the total length. The specifics will be illustrated more clearly in Section 3.2.1. Aside from those differences, WPKI is also a certificate-based infrastructure.

At present, many international organizations are studying the WPKI technology. In particular, USA, Japan and various European countries have independently demonstrated the maturity of their own information security techniques and industry. For example, WAP PKI proposed by WAP Forum, i-mode security infrastructure presented by Japanese firm NTT DoCoMo and the PALM security structure developed by the American company are all examples of complete working models that are supporting practical applications within the wireless domain today.

3.2.1 Certificate Formats

In an effort to lower the amount of public key certificate storage, WPKI certificate format specification adopted two measures; first is to continue the use of X.509 standard with a few reductions on the excess fields; secondly, elliptic curve cryptography is used to replace the traditional public key cryptosystems on the task of encryption and digital signatures. The primary benefit of this change is that extra storage can be conserved since the size of the certificate is reduced and also the transmission cost additionally minimized. The result of the above efforts is that both the storage size and the computation cost have decreased tremendously for the WPKI solution.   Fig. 3.4 will illustrate the differences of certificate formats between X.509 and WPKI. WPKI has an additional merit, which lies in its conformance with the traditional PKI certificate format, this compatibility advantage, can best be seen when integration of the wireless network and wired is called for.

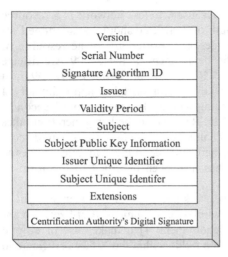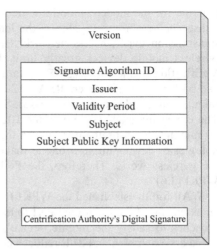

Fig. 3.4. Certificate formats of X.509 and WPKI

3.2.2 Certificate URLs

Generally, there are two ways to transfer certificate to mobile device: one involves storing the certificate within the mobile device prior to delivery such as in the form of the SIM card; the other entails transmitting the certificate through wireless network to the mobile device.

Due to the problems of limited storage capacity and the mobility characteristic, storing the certificate and querying for the certificate doesn't seem like a practical solution.

Accordingly, wireless network removes the storage certificates on mobile devices, and instead maintain a copy of certificate URL which points to the location where the real certificate is stored. When verifiers need to confirm a particular client's identity, they can follow the certificate URL address to arrive at the location on which the client's certificate is stored, to accomplish the verification work. This method of transferring the payload from the resources-constrained mobile devices to the relatively resource-affluent verifiers can effectively mitigate the computation and bandwidth obstacle.

3.2.3 Certificate Revocation

Although X.509 defines many schemes for revocation of public key certificates while the user identity and the corresponding public key are no longer regarded as legal one, these X.509 Certificate Revocation List (CRL) [3.7] schemes are not suitable for mobile client because a large CRL must be sent to the mobile client.

The restriction of storage and bandwidth environment cause mobile client difficult to support the X.509 CRL. Besides, the mobile client also must consume power and bandwidth to contact an on-line certificate status responder, such as OCSP protocol [3.8], to query the current status of mobile client's certificate.

One way to resolve this problem is to adopt the short-lived gateway certificates that issued continuously for each small period of time, and the revocation of the short-lived certificate is done by simple dis-continual issuing of the certificate. In such a way, the risk of impersonation is minimized by the short expiration date. However, this method would raise the effort of CA and WAP gateway. The reason is that WAP gateway must usually generate a key pair and the corresponding certificate, and the CA must validate the requested certificate and issue a WTLS certificate frequently.

In order to protect the wireless communication for transaction security, WPKI's huge potential will undoubtedly be further explored. Its technology will continue to enhance and will eventually become the center of wireless security research.

3.3 Elliptic Curve Cryptography for Mobile Computing

Elliptic Curve Cryptography is a branch of public-key cryptography proposed by Victor Miller and Neal Koblitz [3.9] in the mid 1980s. It is an alternative method to the older RSA system and offers the relative advantages of higher performance in terms of speed and space usage. This makes it especially suited for implementation on devices with limited computation capability, storage area, battery power, and communication bandwidth.

An elliptic curve is the set of solutions (x, y) which satisfy an elliptic curve equation of the form $y^2=x^3+ax+b$. If $4a^3+27b^2 \neq 0$, then the elliptic curve $y^2=x^3+ax+b$ can be used to form a group. An elliptic curve group over real numbers consists of the points on the corresponding elliptic curve, together with an extra point O called the point at infinity.

Each choice of the numbers (a, b) yields a different elliptic curve. For example, the elliptic curve with equation $y^2 = x^3 - 4x + 0.67$ is shown below in Fig. 3.5.

Elliptic Curves over Z_p

Calculations over the real numbers are slow and inaccurate due to round-off error. Cryptographic applications require fast and precise arithmetic; thus elliptic curve groups over the *finite* fields of F_p are used in practice.

An elliptic curve with the underlying field of F_p can be formed by choosing the variables (a, b) within the field of F_p. The elliptic curve includes all points (x, y) which satisfy the elliptic curve equation modulo p, where x and y are numbers in F_p.

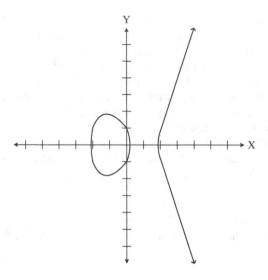

Fig. 3.5. The graph of $y^2 = x^3 - 4x + 0.67$

For example: $y^2 \bmod p = x^3 + ax + b \bmod p$ has an underlying field of F_p if a and b are in F_p.

If $x^3 + ax + b$ contains no repeating factors (or, equivalently, if $4a^3 + 27b \bmod p$ is not 0), then the elliptic curve can be used to form a group. An elliptic curve group over F_p consists of the points on the corresponding elliptic curve, together with a special point O called the point at infinity. There are finitely many points on such an elliptic curve.

As a very small example, consider an elliptic curve over the field F_{23}. With $a = 1$ and $b = 0$, the elliptic curve equation is $y^2 \pmod{23} = x^3 + x \pmod{23}$.

The 23 points which satisfy this equation are: (0,0) (1,5) (1,18) (9,5) (9,18) (11,10) (11,13) (13,5) (13, 18) (15, 3) (15, 20) (16, 8) (16, 15) (17, 10) (17, 13) (18, 10) (18, 13) (19, 1) (19, 22) (20, 4) (20, 19) (21, 6) (21, 17), we can easily verify these points to be correct, for example, the point (9, 5) satisfies this equation since:

$$x^3 + x \equiv 9^3 + 9 \equiv 729 + 9 \equiv 2 \bmod 23 \equiv 25 \equiv 5^2 \equiv y^2 \bmod 23$$

These points are graphed as below in Fig. 3.6:

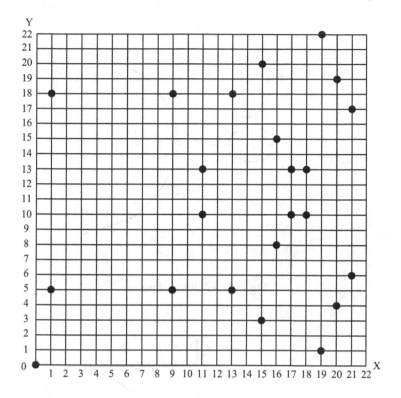

Fig. 3.6. Points of equation $y^2 - x^3 + x$ over F_{23}

Elliptic Curve over F_p Addition

Elliptic curve groups are additive groups; that is, their basic function is addition. The addition of two points in an elliptic curve is defined geometrically as follows:

Suppose that P and Q are two distinct points on an elliptic curve, and the P is not $-Q$. To add points P and Q, a line is drawn through these two points. This line will intersect the elliptic curve in exactly one more point, called $-R$. The point $-R$ is reflected in the x-axis to the point R. The law for addition in an elliptic curve group is $P + Q = R$ and illustrated in Fig. 3.7.

When $Q = -P$, then $P + Q = O$. In this case that $x_1 = x_2$ but $y_1 \neq y_2$, the line through P and Q is a vertical line, which therefore intersects E at O. Reflecting O across the x-axis yields the same point O. Therefore, in this case $P + Q = O$. This condition is illustrated in Fig. 3.8.

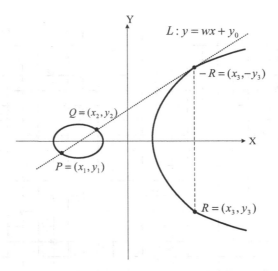

Fig. 3.7. Addition of points

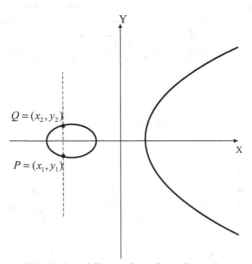

Fig. 3.8. Adding point when $Q = -P$

When $Q = P$, to double this point, draw the tangent line and find the other points of intersection S. Then $P + Q = P + P = 2P = S$. This condition is illustrated in Fig. 3.9. Intuitively, for a point $P = (x, y)$ and a positive integer n, we can define $n \cdot p = P + P + \ldots + P$ (n times); that is, multiplication is defined as repeated addition.

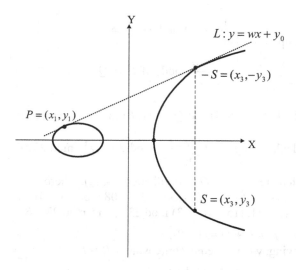

Fig. 3.9. Doubling of points

Algebraic Description of Addition

Reviewing from Fig. 3.7, to calculate $P + Q$, where $P \neq Q$, $P = (x_1, y_1)$ and $Q = (x_2, y_2)$, we must first derive $L: y = w \cdot x + y_0$ that passes through P and Q, where

$w = \dfrac{y_2 - y_1}{x_2 - x_1}$ is the slope and $y_0 = y_1 - w \cdot x_1$.

Next, finding the intersection points $-R = (x_3, y_3)$ of the line L and elliptic curve, where $x_3 = w^2 - x_1 - x_2$, $y_3 = -(w \cdot x_3 + y_0)$.

Finally, obtaining $R = (x_3, y_3) = P + Q$.

When $P = Q = (x_1, y_1)$, only the calculation of slope $w = \dfrac{dy}{dx} = \dfrac{3x^2 + a}{2y_1}$ of L is different. The rest is the same as when $P \neq Q$.

In summary, if $P = (x_P, y_P)$ and $Q = (x_Q, y_Q)$ with $P \neq -Q$, then $R = P + Q = (x_R, y_R)$ is determined by the following rules:

$x_R = (w^2 - x_P - x_Q) \bmod p$, and

$y_R = (w(x_P - x_R) - y_P) \bmod p$,

$$\text{where the slope } w = \begin{cases} (\dfrac{y_Q - y_P}{x_Q - x_P}) \bmod p \text{ if } P \neq Q \\ (\dfrac{3x_P^2 + a}{2y_P}) \bmod p \text{ if } P = Q \end{cases}.$$

For example, if $P = (15, 3)$ and $Q = (21, 6)$ in $y^2 = x^3 + x$ over F_{23}, to find $R = P + Q$, then

Step 1) Calculate slope $w = (\dfrac{6-3}{21-15}) \bmod 23 = (\dfrac{3}{6}) \bmod 23 = (\dfrac{1}{2}) \bmod 23 = 12$.

Step 2) Calculate $R = P + Q$'s coordinates (x_R, y_R), where
$x_R = (12^2 - 15 - 21) \bmod 23 = 108 \bmod 23 = 16$, and
$y_R = (12(15 - 16) - 3) \bmod 23 = -15 \bmod 23 = 8$.

Thus derive $R = P + Q = (16, 8)$.
In the following, we will demonstrate what if $R = P + P$.

Step 1) Compute $w = (\dfrac{3 \cdot (15)^2 + 1}{2 \cdot 3}) \bmod 23 = (\dfrac{9}{6}) \bmod 23 = (\dfrac{3}{2}) \bmod 23 = 13$

Step 2) Find R's coordinates (x_R, y_R), where
$x_R = (132 - 15 - 15) \bmod 23 = 139 \bmod 23 = 1$, and
d
d
$y_R = (13(15 - 1) - 3) \bmod 23 = 179 \bmod 23 = 18$.

So deduce $R = 2P = (1, 18)$.

Compared to Fig. 3.6, we can discover the resulting points $(16, 8)$ and $(1, 18)$ still remain on the elliptic curve, because all the points $y^2 = x^3 + x$ over F_{23} forms a group, therefore, addition of any points within this group, will land eventually in the group.

3.3.1 Analog to DLP

At the foundation of public key cryptosystems is a mathematical function that is computationally infeasible to solve. Here, the difficulty of solving the Elliptic Curve Discrete Logarithm Problem (ECDLP) is the core of the Elliptic Curve Cryptosystem, and described as follows.

Given an elliptic curve E defined over a finite field F_q, a point $P \in E[F_q]$ of order n, and a point Q, determine a number l such that $Q = lP$.

ECDLP looks fairly similar to the Discrete Logarithm Problem (DLP) discussed over the $GF(P)$, and there is indeed a way to map ECDLP to DLP, and

Diffie-Hellman Key Exchange is illustrated to explain how a DLP based protocol can be transformed to one that is based on ECDLP.

First we explain what discrete logarithm problem is: Given elements r and g of the multiplicative group Z_P^* and a prime p, find a number k such that $r = g^k \bmod p$.

As seen from above definition, we discover the two have a similar structure. The Discrete Logarithm Problem is to find k over Z_P^* such that $r = g^k \bmod p$ and ECDLP find an integer l with $Q = lP$. Both must be within an Abelian group, and only differs in the domain of the Abelian group (Z_P^* and $E[F_q]$). Therefore, the original multiplication operation over Z_P^*, $g^a \cdot g^b \bmod p$ correspond to Elliptic Curve's addition operation $aP + bP$, and the exponential operation over Z_P^*, g^a $\bmod p$ would correspond to Elliptic Curve's multiplication operations aP. Otherwise, the two Abelian groups have their own multiplicative inverse and orders. Table 3.1 is an example of a Mapping Table. It is not difficult to imagine that the DLP based cryptosystems such as the Diffie-Hellman Key Exchange, DSA etc. can directly be converted to the ECDLP based system, and enjoy the benefits brought by ECC. In the following, we will use the Diffie-Hellman Key Exchange as an example to explain this process.

Diffie-Hellman Key Exchange (DKE)

In 1976, Diffie and Hellman [3.10] proposed a key exchange method to allow two users to safely negotiate on a key without any prior shared key arrangements for future communication encryption. The security of the algorithm based its difficulty on the discrete logarithm problem.

Table 3.1. DLP and ECDLP mapping table

Discrete Logarithm over Z_P^*	Elliptic Curve Discrete Logarithm Problem over $E[F_q]$
$y = g^x \bmod P$	$Q = lP$
$g^a \cdot g^b = g^{b+a} \bmod p$	$aP + bP = (a+b)P$
$g^{ab} = (g^a)^b \bmod p$	$abP = b(aP)$
$a^{-1} \bmod q$	$a^{-1} \bmod n$
$g^q = 1 \bmod p$	$nP = O$
$g^{ab} = g^{ba} \bmod p$	$abP = baP$
$1 \le a, b \le q$	$1 \le a, b \le n$

First, a large prime number q (greater than 1024-bit) and q's primitive root α are chosen. The method user A and user B employ to exchange a key is shown in Fig. 3.10, explanations is as follows:

Step 1)   User A chooses a secret random number $X_A < q$, and calculates $Y_A = \alpha^{X_A} \bmod q$ to deliver to B.

Step 2) B also chooses a secret random number $X_B < q$, and pass the value $Y_B = \alpha^{X_B} \bmod q$ to A.

Step 3) A applies its secret X_A and the received Y_B to derive key $K = Y_B^{X_A} \bmod q$. Likewise, B too derives $K' = Y_B^{X_B} \bmod q$, where $K' = K$.

A and B will both hold a copy of the same key, because

$$K = Y_B^{X_A} = (\alpha^{X_B})^{X_A} = (\alpha^{X_A})^{X_B} = Y_A^{X_B} = K' \bmod q.$$

Select Private $X_A < q$

Compute public $Y_A = \alpha^{X_A} \bmod q$

Select Private $X_B < q$

Compute public $Y_B = \alpha^{X_B} \bmod q$

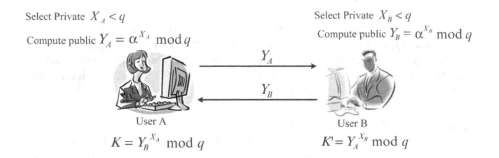

Y_A

Y_B

User A

User B

$K = Y_B^{X_A} \bmod q$

$K' = Y_A^{X_B} \bmod q$

Fig. 3.10. Diffie-Hellman key exchange

According to the previous mapping relations, the elliptic curve based key exchange mechanism can be accomplished as follows.

Elliptic Curve Diffie-Hellman Key Exchange (ECDKE)

First pick a prime number $p \approx 2^{160}$ and two parameters a and b to define an equation $y^2 = x^3 + ax + b \bmod p$, such that it becomes an elliptic curve group $E[F_q]$. Next choose from $E[F_q]$ a generating point $G = (x_1, y_1)$, under the condition that the minimal value of n must be a very large prime number and satisfy $nG = O$.

The key exchange protocol is stated as follows and illustrated in Fig. 3.11:

Step 1) A chooses an integer X_A less than n to be its private key. It then generates a public key $Y_A = X_A \times G$.

Step 2) B chooses a private key X_B, and calculates Y_B likewise.

Step 3) A and B exchange public keys Y_A and Y_B. At this time both A and B will individually be able to compute their mutual key $K = X_A \times Y_B$, and $K' = X_B \times Y_A$, where $K' = K$.

A and B will be computing the same key since,

$$K = X_A \times Y_B = X_A \times (X_B \times G) = X_B \times (X_A \times G) = X_B \times Y_A = K'$$

Select Private $X_A < n$

Compute public $Y_A = X_A \times G$

Select Private $X_B < n$

Compute public $Y_B = X_B \times G$

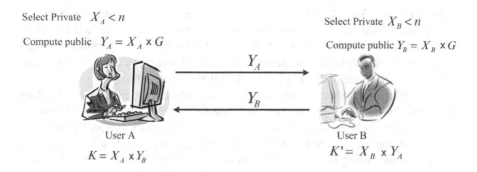

$$Y_A$$

$$Y_B$$

User A

$$K = X_A \times Y_B$$

User B

$$K' = X_B \times Y_A$$

Fig. 3.11. Elliptic Curve Diffie-Hellman key exchange

3.3.2 ECC properties and benefits

In the preceding illustration of Diffie-Hellman Key Exchange approaches, the one based on discrete logarithm must choose a modulus q to be an integer greater than 1024-bit, whereas the one based on ECDLP will be adequate with a modulus p of size greater than 160-bit. The result of this huge reduction in key length signifies computation cost decrease for mobile device processors, as well as key storage capacity and transmission load drop, consequently, ECC is a better choice for implementation on the bandwidth limited wireless network environments.

The reason why ECC is able to achieve such high level of security with such a short key length is because of the difficulty of solving ECDLP.

To understand the superiority, two well known mathematical hard problems, factoring and solving discrete logarithm, the security foundation of RSA and Diffie-Hellman Key exchange protocol respectively, are examined firstly.

To factor an integer n into its prime factors, and the computation complexity of the most efficient algorithm is approximately

$$\exp((1.923 + o(1))(\log n)^{\frac{1}{3}} (\log \log n)^{\frac{2}{3}}). \qquad (1)$$

To solve the DLP over Z_P^*, the current best algorithm is Dan Gordon's general number field sieve method [3.11], which has a computation complexity of

$$\exp((1.923 + o(1))(\log n)^{\frac{1}{3}} (\log \log n)^{\frac{2}{3}}). \qquad (2)$$

For ECC in a finite field F_q, q is a prime or prime exponent with the order n, a large prime or divisible by a large prime, then the most efficient method for calculating the discrete logarithm in E is Shanks and Pollard's full exponential algorithm. The computation time is approximately $\sqrt{q}$ elliptic curve additive operations. Compared with Equation (1) and (2), the ECDLP is more difficult.

Practically, for instance, 40,000 elliptic curve addition operations can be done in one second for an elliptic curve over finite field $F_{2^{160}}$ with a computer executing at 1 MIPS (million instructions per second). Then to solve an ECDLP will take approximately 10^{12} MY (MIPS year). On the other hand, scholar Odlyzko [3.12] estimates using Dodson and Lenstra's number field sieve method, to factor a 1024-bit integer, it will take approximately $3 \cdot 10^{11}$ MY. Thus an ECC over the 160-bit field $F_{2^{160}}$ will exhibit similar strength as RSA's 1024-bit. Due to the fact that factoring and solving DLP are computationally hard problems of equivalent degree, it's not hard to observe from Equation (1) and (2), 160-bit ECC and 1024-bit DLP also exhibit similar strength.

ECC is also suitable under finite field F_{2^m}, because it involves direct bit manipulation, therefore, is especially convenient on hardware devices. Take finite field $F_{2^{155}}$ operations for example, a total of 12,000 gates is all that's need to fit on a integration chip who's size is only 5% of smart card's processors.

Due to these advantages, ECC is especially suited for implementation on computationally limited and hardware sized constrained systems (e.g., smart card, PCMCIA card and mobile devices).

3.3.3 Current Status and Related Research

The developments of ECC to this point have received a great deal attention. Since 1994 when IEEE first drafted the ECC standards P1363 [3.13] till year 2000, when it became final, continuously, several organizations began work on devising standards for ECC. Using ECDSA as an example, ISO (International Standards Organization) established in 1998 the ISO 14888-3 standard [3.14], and in 1999 ANSI created the ANSI X9.62 [3.15] and X9.63 [3.16] standard, IEEE and FIPS independently in 2000 issued the P1363 and FIPS 186-2 standards [3.17]. These standards are already widely adopted by various wireless associated standards for security mechanisms. For instance, WAP's WTLS protocol [3.18] used IEEE P1363, X9.62 and X9.63 standards.

Still, in the field of theoretical research, both ECC's security and efficiency are continuously improved by expert around.

To improve the efficiency, many enhancements on the elliptic curve's ECDLP calculations have been proposed and the Scalar Multiplication's Addition Chain method is presented as an example.

To compute $d \cdot P$, where d is an integer, and P a point on ECC. Intuitively, it will take $d-1$ times of addition operation to complete the computation.

However, with Scalar Multiplication Addition Chain method, d is firstly expressed in binary format

$d = 2^{n-1} + d_{n-2} \cdot 2^{n-1} + \ldots + d_1 \cdot 2 + d_0$, where

$d_i \in \{0\}$ or $\{1\}$, for $i = 0, 1, 2, \ldots, n-2$.

And, $d \cdot P = 2^{n-1} P + \displaystyle\sum_{0 \le i \le n-2, d_i = 1} 2^i P$.

Therefore, only $n-1$ elliptic curve double adding are needed with Addition Chain method.

$$
\left.
\begin{aligned}
2P &= (P + P) \\
2^2 P &= (2P + 2P) \\
2^3 P &= (2^2 P + 2^2 P) \\
&\vdots \\
2^{n-1} P &= (2^{n-2} P + 2^{n-2} P)
\end{aligned}
\right\} n - 1 \text{ elliptic curve double adding}
$$

Consequently, the time complexity is reduced from $O(d)$ to $O(\log d)$.

Take $100 \cdot P$ for example, instead 99 rounds of addition operation as
$$100P = \underbrace{P + P + \ldots + P}_{99 \text{ additions}},$$

with Addition Chain method, we have
$$100 \cdot P = (1100100)_2 \cdot P = (2^6 + 2^5 + 2^2)P = 64P + 32P + 4P$$

In the following, only 6 elliptic curve double adding are need for 64P.

$$
\left.
\begin{aligned}
2P &= (P + P) \\
2^2 P &= (2P + 2P) \\
2^3 P &= (2^2 P + 2^2 P) \\
2^4 P &= (2^3 P + 2^3 P) \\
2^5 P &= (2^4 P + 2^4 P) \\
2^6 P &= (2^5 P + 2^5 P)
\end{aligned}
\right\} 6 \text{ elliptic curve double adding}
$$

In fact, the value of 32P and 4Pare both obtained in the process, thus, two more elliptic curve addition (64P + 32P + 4P) are enough to complete the job. The interested readers may refer to [3.19] for more advanced details on multiplication enhancement methods.

On issues of security, many new characters of Elliptic Curve Discrete Logarithm Problem are being discovered.

Menezes, Okamoto, and Vanstone (MOV) [3.20], in 1993, showed the ECDLP in $E[F_q]$ can be efficiently reduced to one in $F_{q^m}^{\times}$ for a very special class of curves called super-singular curves. Since DLP in finite fields can be attacked by the index-calculus methods, they can be solved faster than ECDLP, as long as the field F_{q^m} is not mush larger than F_q.

Besides, the so-called anomalous curves were discovered independently by Semaev [3.21], Smart [3.22], and Satoh and Araki [3.23]. The DLP for these curves can be solved quickly. Other attacks such as Side Channel Attack, Baby-Step Giant-Step [3.24], and etc. are continuously discovered.

Fortunately, until now, no subexponential-time algorithm for ECDLP is found. Whether or not there exists a subexponential-time algorithm for ECDLP is still an important open problem, and one of great relevance to the security of ECC.

Other then the research effort put forth by the academic society, the commercial industry is also showing great interest in ECC. For instance, the Certicom introduced the ECC Challenge [3.25] in November 1997. The challenge is to compute the ECC private keys from the given list of ECC public keys and associated system parameters. This is the type of problem facing an adversary who wishes to completely defeat an elliptic curve cryptosystem. Since 1997, the 79-bit, 89-bit, 97-bit and 109-bit challenges have been solved. The latest challenge to be met is the ECC-163 challenge with the field size of 131-bit; Certicom declared that the 131-bit challenges will require significantly more resources to solve. In fact, it would be approximately one hundred million times harder to solve ECC-163 than ECC-109.

Although the study of ECC is still in progress, that no subexponential-time algorithm has been discovered for the ECDLP makes people feel largely confident with the security of ECC.

3.4 Server Assisted Mobile Security Infrastructure

Owing to the characteristics of mobility, user authentication procedure is crucial in the visited network for detecting unauthorized accesses and for accounting purposes. Mobile users invariably will need to enter a foreign network and under such circumstances, mutual authentication is bound to be a vital concern. When a resourceful and trusted authentication server is involved to assist mobile users and the service provider, this task can be simplified. Thus in this section we consider WPAN, WLAN, and WWAN and explain the roles server play within server-assisted security architecture to simplify user authentication operations.

3.4.1 WPAN Security Infrastructure

In WPAN, Bluetooth is presently most popular technology. Bluetooth networks exhibit a master-slave relationship between its networked devices. We will introduce Bluetooth from three perspectives; these include server assisted security architecture, Bluetooth authentication, and Bluetooth vulnerabilities.

The Security Architecture
WPAN architectures use decentralized networking, in which the information is maintained at the end device rather than in a centralized database. Like an ad hoc networking topology, WPAN is designed for dynamically connecting mobile devices such as PDAs, laptops, and cell phones. Thus, there is no fixed infrastructure in WPAN.

The basic Bluetooth topology is comprised of several piconets, in which up to eight Bluetooth devices may be networked together in a master-slave relationship. In each piconet, one of the devices would be chosen as a master, which is capable of directly connecting with up to seven slaves, and the others are slaves. Note that, a slave in a piconet can act as the master for other piconets, which then create a chain of piconets as illustrated in Fig. 3.12.·

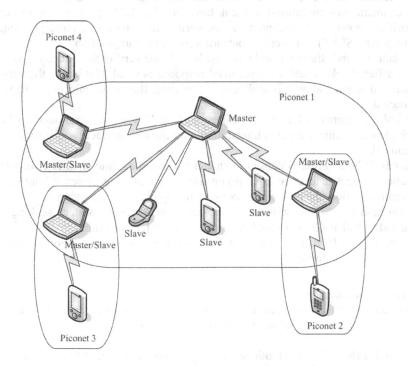

Fig. 3.12. Typical Bluetooth network

Although there is no specific server in the Bluetooth architecture scenario, but in actuality, the chosen master within a piconet is really treated as a virtual server. In general, once the master is chosen, a slave device can connect to other devices through the help of the master device. Thus, the master can act as a virtual server for the slaves within the same piconet by taking the responsibility of providing user authentication and key management within its piconet.

The criterion for selecting a master or verifier from among the group of connectable devices is to pick out the device that is best equipped in terms of battery power and computation capabilities, so that the server has the better resources to do a job well.

Bluetooth Authentication

The Bluetooth authentication is achieved through challenge-response mechanism. Two devices, a master and a slave, interacting in an authentication procedure are referred to as the verifier and the claimant, respectively. The challenge-response protocol validates devices by verifying the knowledge of a Bluetooth link key.

The Bluetooth authentication is stated as follows and illustrated in Fig. 3.13.

The claimant delivers its 48-bit address (BD_ADDR) as request to the verifier; the verifier sends the claimant a 128-bit random challenge (AU_RAND).

The claimant uses the request, the link key, and the challenge as inputs of the E1 algorithm known by the claimant and the verifier to compute the corresponding 32-bit response (SRES). The verifier performs the same computation.

The claimant sends the computed response back to the verifier for authentication.

The verifier checks whether the received response is valid. If it holds, the verifier assures that the claimant is authentic. Otherwise, the communication will be disconnected.

The link key generated from the corresponding PIN code is assumed to be never disclosed outside and never transmitted over the air-interface, so the security is guaranteed.

Under WPAN, a master is chosen to cluster the members into smaller coverage area, called piconet, it is easy to facilitate the communication. Even a long distance communication, the path can be constructed by chaining the piconet.

It's not hard to imagine, without the existence of a server (master), seeking a specific individual itself is a problem because the effective communication distance is limited to 10 meters, not to mention making a communication channel after the individual is found.

Bluetooth Vulnerabilities

An overview of some known problems with native Bluetooth security is summarized in [3.26]. The vulnerabilities are briefly depicted as follows.

1.   Weak PINs: The Bluetooth security relies on PINs varied between 1 and 16 bytes for establishing trusted relationships between devices. Users have a tendency to choose short PINs typical being 4-digit, the PIN used for the generation of link and encryption keys can be easily guessed.

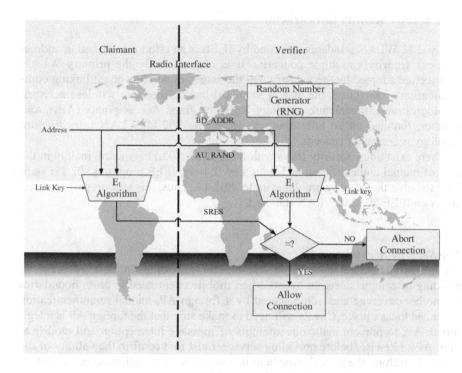

Fig. 3.13. Bluetooth authentication operations [3.26]

2. Scalability problem: Establishing PINs in large Bluetooth networks with numbers of users is difficult, which frequently yields security vulnerabilities.

3. Reusable link key: The link key is static and shared. In this situation, a malicious user can compromise the security between two other users if he has communicated with either the two.

4. One-way-only authentication: Only one-way authentication that the verifier validates the claimant's identity exists. The one-way-only challenge-response authentication is easily subject to man-in-middle attacks.

5. No end-to-end security: Only individual links are authenticated and encrypted. This implies that data is decrypted at intermediate points.

6. Limited security service: The Bluetooth networks provide neither audit nor non-repudiation. These two services are indispensable for the establishment of m-commerce.

3.4.2 WLAN Security Infrastructure

The 802.11 WLAN standards proposed by IEEE is an effort established to address wireless security's multiple concerns. It is also currently the primary WLAN architecture adopted by the industry. On the issues of wireless client linking communication architecture, the 802.11 standard has defined two wireless network topologies: an infrastructure topology based on fixed Access points (APs), and another, founded on ad hoc topology. Here, the 802.11 WLAN infrastructure topology is our major concern.

There exist a few security flaws within the IEEE 802.11 standard, mainly in the area of mutual authentication and static key. Lately, IEEE proposed 802.11i standard to solve the security problems under 802.11. Thus, this section will focus its target on IEEE 802.11i WLAN standard.

The Security Architecture

WLAN infrastructure topology is suitable for providing wireless coverage of building or campus areas. In events when mobile client need to cross boundaries to another coverage area administered by a foreign AP, mutual re-authentication will need to take place. Clients will need to make sure that the foreign AP is a legitimate AP, to prevent malicious attempts of message interception and modification. APs, likewise, before providing service, must first confirm the validity of the client. Therefore, the critical issue here is how mutual authentication can be established under this relatively disbelieving condition.

In the WLAN infrastructure shown as Fig. 3.14, beside from the client and the AP, there is still an authentication server that holds the ability to authenticate APs, and to prove to the client, AP's legitimacy. In this way, with help from the authentication server, the client can easily authenticate the AP. To verify whether the client is authorized to the network resources by an AP, the users must register at the network provider with contracted/subscribed users' information. After registration, the authentication server can verify the legitimacy of clients according to the contracted/subscribed users' information. Therefore, intuitively, mutual authentication between the AP and the client involves the authentication server taking the responsibility of proving the legitimacy of the AP to the client and vise versa.

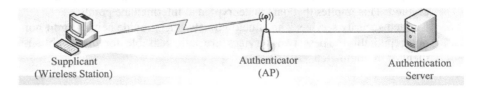

Supplicant   Authenticator   Authentication
(Wireless Station)   (AP)   Server

Fig. 3.14. IEEE 802.11-serial WLAN infrastructure

IEEE 802.11i WLAN Authentication

In order to fix the security problems of the IEEE 802.11 WLAN, IEEE 802.11i authentication provides three main security features: mutual authentication, integrity check, and fresh key generation. This section will use mutual authentication as an example to explore the workings of IEEE 802.11i WLAN security mechanisms. If readers are interested in the integrity and the fresh key features of IEEE 802.11i authentication, they can obtain further details from [3.27].

To guarantee the mutual authentication, IEEE 802.11i standard makes use of 802.1x standard and the Extensible Authentication communication protocol (EAP) to enforce compulsory mutual authentication. The 802.1x standard can dynamically distribute encryption keys to construct authentication architecture. This architecture is comprised of three different elements: a client (supplicant), an AP (Authenticator), and an authentication server (Remote Authentication Dial-In User Service; RADIUS server). EAP is an extension of PPP (Point-to-Point Protocol) and is primarily used in applications of mutual authentication between the clients [3.28]. Due to different security demands and considerations, several authentication methods, including password, token, certificate, Smart Card or Kerberos are integrated into EAP to increase the flexibility. This approach is originally adopted in 802.1x and now inherited by the new coming 802.11i.

For instance, password is adopted by Cisco Lightweight Extensible Authentication communication protocol (Cisco LEAP) [3.29], server certificate is adopted by Protected EAP (PEAP) [3.30], and client and/or server certificates are optionally adopted in EAP-Transport Layer Security (EAP-TLS) [3.31].

For clearer explanation, we use the Cisco LEAP as an example to further explain server-assisted security infrastructure. The Cisco LEAP mutual authentication process is illustrated as Fig. 3.15.

Initially, the client and the authentication server share a secret user password. When the client wants to access the resource through the AP, the AP requires that the client transmits his own username to the authentication server. For assisting the AP in authenticating the client, the authentication server delivers a challenge to the client and waits for an appropriate response from the client. The client replies the response to the authentication server by using the Cisco LEAP algorithm, mixes challenge and user password together. For the replied response, the authentication server derives another expected response by using the user password with the Cisco LEAP algorithm, and then checks if the derived value and the received one from the client match. If it holds, the authentication server transmits evidence to the AP for declaring that the client is authentic.

For the purpose that the client wants to authenticate the AP, the process is similar to the above mentioned scenario. Finally, the client can realize that the AP is legal while receiving the evidence for the AP authentication from the authentication server. Therefore, the mutual authentication can be achieved through the assistance of the authentication server.

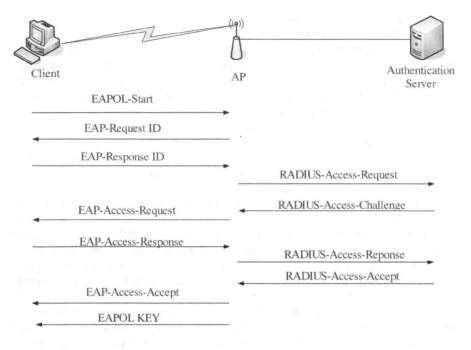

Fig. 3.15. Cisco LEAP mutual authentication process

Because the supporting from the authentication server behind an AP, the mobile client can roam into a foreign area without registration in advance and gain the service from the foreign network. It is, of course, also a cost-effective approach to negotiate the session key between the client and the AP in WLAN environment while the mutual authentication is done.

Vulnerabilities

The native mode of 802.11 has been proven to contain security concerns. The major security threats are summarized in [3.26]. These security concerns have already been corrected in the latest IEEE standard 802.11i [3.27]. Because 802.11i is still a relatively new standard, its security is yet to be tested. So far, only He and Mitchell [3.32, 3.33] have revealed that 4-way handshake between the AP and the client in the 802.11i authentication exist Denial-of-Service (DoS) attack. In addition, care must be exercises when choosing the different authentication mechanisms, as insecure modules could accordingly endanger the entire system's security. An example can be seen from Cisco LEAP that uses a static password to complete the authentication process which is vulnerable to dictionary attacks [3.34]. System administrator should evaluate the options for the authentication mechanisms based on the tradeoff between usage convenience, ease of management and security requirements.

3.4.3 WWAN Security Infrastructure

This section talks about the most used GSM communication system and the current most popular 3G systems. There are many standards for the 3G systems, but we pick Universal Mobile Telecommunications System (UMTS) for its compatibility with GSM, to better demonstrate how the server assisted security mechanism operates.

The Security Architecture

WWAN covers a very broad service area in a hierarchical structure consisting of many Visited Location Registers (VLRs). With such vast amount of VLRs, their computation and storage ability are naturally limited by cost, causing it infeasible to store all the subscriber data, and a more powerful centralized server is called for, which is HLR/AuC (Home Location Register/ Authentication Center).

Fig. 3.16 shows the GSM communication infrastructure and, in general, the AuC would be attached to a HLR in a secure environment.

The Authentication Center (AuC) securely stores the secret keys of all subscribers for later user authentication purposes. Other personal information not involved with authentication is stored on the HLR. Besides, it is assume that there is a secure channel between HLR/AuC and the visited network for delivering sensitive information, such as user authentication information for assisting visited network providers in authenticating the user.

The VLR, which is the visited network providers, authenticates the user based on the information obtained from HLR/AuC. It is no doubt that HLR/AuC is the key to successfully authenticate both the MS and the VLR. The authenticating capability of the HLR/AuC comes from the key shared with MS. Based on the knowledge of this key, the corresponding authenticator can be derived to convince to the VLR that the MS is the alleged one. This way, the user is approved to access the resources within visited network without obstacle.

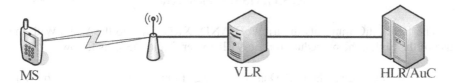

MS   VLR   HLR/AuC

Fig. 3.16. GSM communication infrastructure

GSM Authentication

Fig. 3.17 illustrates the GSM authentication process. The challenge/response security mechanism is used for authentication in the GSM. Because the HLR/AuC shares a secret key Ki with the MS, the HLR/AuC can retrieve the MS's secret key Ki and generate a random number RAND to help the VLR verify the MS locally when the MS is checking in the visited network.

Below shows the associated procedure.

1. Apply the secret key Ki and the random RAND to the A3 algorithm to compute XRES = A3(Ki, RAND), where the A3 is an algorithm known between the HLR/AuC and the MS.
2. Apply the secret key Ki and the random RAND to the A8 algorithm to compute K_C = A8(Ki, RAND), where the A8 is also an algorithm known between the HLR/AuC and the MS.

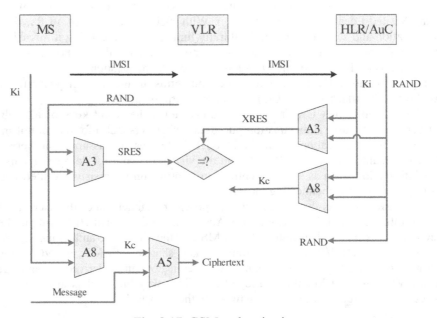

Fig. 3.17. GSM authentication

The HLR/AuC transmits the triplet (RAND, XRES, K_C) to the VLR. With the use of the triplet, the procedure for the VLR to verify the MS is as follows.

1. The VLR sends the RAND as a challenge to intend the MS to send back an appropriate response.
2. Upon receiving the RAND, the MS computes SRES and K_C as the same as HLR/AuC's process, and then sends the result back to the VLR.

After receiving the SRES returned from the MS, the VLR will verify whether the responded SRES matches the expected XRES. Because the secret key is only known by the HLR/AuC and the MS, the VLR can be convinced that the MS is authentic only if the secret key is well-protected and SRES=XRES. Furthermore, to secure the communication between the MS and VLR, a session key K_C can also be derived and verified in the authentication process. After that, the transmitted message can be encrypted and decrypted by A5 with the session key K_C. Because of the secrecy of the session key, the confidentiality between MS and VLR can be guaranteed.

Vulnerabilities
The problems with native GSM security are summarized as follows [3.35, 3.36, 3.37].

1. SIM/ME interface: SIM/ME interface of MS lacks proper protection and can be potentially exploited to cause messages to be leaked out. However, the system's security is yet guarded by the SIM algorithm.
2. Attacks on the algorithm A3/8: In April 1998, Wagner and Goldberg successfully cracked COMP-128 which made use of A3/8. With around 160,000 chosen plaintext attack attempts launched, Ki could be compromised.

Attacks on the algorithm A5/1: A5/1 has also been found to contain a weakness. Biryukov and Shamir [3.38] devised the method of "time-memory trade-off", which exploits connections between algorithm state and key stream sequence to derive Kc.

UMTS Authentication
Third generation (3G) mobile phones are characterised by higher rates of data transmission and a richer range of services and Universal Mobile Telecommunications System (UMTS) is one of the new 3G systems. An important characteristic of UMTS is that the new radio access network is connected to an evolution of the GSM core network.

The principles of UMTS security are, therefore, build on the security of GSM by adopting the security features from GSM that have proved to be needed and that are robust, and correcting the problems with GSM by addressing security weaknesses [3.35, 3.38].

The new security features for UMTS, not addressed in GSM, are listed as follows.

1. Provide mutual authentication and integrity protection of critical signalling procedures to give greater protection against false base station attacks.
2. Establish a cipher key and integrity key and assure user that cipher/integrity keys' freshness.
3. Encryption terminates at the radio network controller.
4. Adopt open design algorithms f1 to f9 with longer key length (128-bit) instead of mystery A3, A5, and A8 algorithms.

UMTS adopts the same architecture as GSM; embracing its benefits and replacing the existing security problems. Like GSM, UMTS also employs a server assisted security model. Therefore, HLR/AuC is responsible for overseeing individual's security requirements: mutual authentication, integrity, and anonymity. The way to accomplish this goal is through guarding of a master key shared with independent MS. For a specific security service the pre-shared master key is used in accompanying with a dedicated algorithm, to generate a corresponding service key. Because only MS and HLR/AuC holds the master key, only they will be able to generate the service keys, and since HLR/AuC will subsequently bestow the possession of the service keys to the VLR, VLR and MS will be able to locally authenticate each other to initiate the services.

All the communication networks discussed in this section used various levels of server assistance with the common goal of achieving the different security mechanisms.

3.5 Summary

In this chapter, we outlined various practical solutions that can be used to overcome those intrinsic restrictions that are inherent in the mobile devices and the wireless environment to realize the many security requirements. We discussed the wireless equivalent of public key cryptosystem; the use of WPKI certificate to resolve verification of public key's ownership. Furthermore, we introduced elliptic curve cryptography, an alternate approach to conventional public key cryptography, which is suitable for applications under resource-constrained conditions.

Despite so, several practical issues concerning ECC still remain to be resolved. For instance, finding an efficiently way to determine an appropriate base point G and a suitable elliptic curve is still undergoing more research. And ever since Koblitz demonstrated, in the 2001 EuroCrypto, the effectiveness of the Weil Paring property on the Super Singular Elliptic Curve for handling authentication problems, a dilemma between choosing the more secure Non-Singular Elliptic Curve or the relatively less secure but offering the Paring property Super Singular Elliptic Curve, has emerged.

Finally, due to the mobility characteristics, mobile devices will invariably face authentication difficulties when entering a foreign visited network. With the help of the server, much of the authentication complication can be relieved.

Additionally, if we want to enjoy the advantages of a broader coverage area and better mobility transmission performance from both WWAN and WLAN, the interoperability among these two heterogeneous networks must be solved. Within the sever-assisted model, the role of a server is the answer to this problem. Of course, the vulnerabilities inherited from the underlying environments must be also carefully evaluated to facilitate the possible solution.

For the time being, the topic of mobile security while not obstructing the practical demand of efficiency will remain as an area of active research for many years to come.

References

1. R. Rivest, A. Shamir and L. Adleman (1978) A method for obtaining digital signatures and public key cryptosystems, Communications of the ACM, 21, pp. 120-126.
2. W. Barker (1991) Introduction to the Analysis of the Data Encryption Standard (DES). Laguna Hills, CA: Aegean Park Press.
3. J. Daemen and V. Rijmen (2001) Rijndael: The Advanced Encryption Standard. Dr. Dobbš Journal.
4. Public-Key Infrastructure (X.509) PKIX, http://www.ietf.org/html.charters/pkix-charter.html
5. Internet X.509 Public Key Infrastructure Certificate and CRL Profile, R. Housley, et al., January 1999.
6. WPKI, Wireless Public Key Infrastructure Definition, WAP Forum, 24 April 2001.
7. Internet X.509 Public Key Infrastructure Certificate and CRL Profile, R. Housley, et al., January 1999.
8. Internet X.509 Public Key Infrastructure – On-line Certificate Status Protocol - OCSP, IETF RFC 2560, M. Myers, R. Ankney, A. Malpani, S. Galperin, and C. Adams, June 1999.
9. N. Koblitz (1987) Elliptic Curve Cryptosystem, Mathematics of Computation, 48, 203-209.
10. W. Diffie and M. E. Hellmn (1976) New Directions in Cryptography, IEEE Transactions on Information Theory. V. IT-22, n.6, pp. 644-654.
11. B. Dodson and A. Lenstra (1995) NFS with four large primes: an explosive experiment, Advances in Cryptology-CRYPTO95.
12. A.M. Odlyzko (1995) The future of integer factorization, CryptoBytes, l(2).
13. IEEE P1363, Standard Specifications for Public Key Cryptography, ballot draft, 1999. Drafts available at http://grouper.ieee.org/groups/1363/index.html.
14. ISO/IEC 14888-3, Information Technology - Security Techniques - Digital Signatures with Appendix - Part 3: Certificate Based-Mechanism, 1998.
15. ANSI X9.62, Public Key Cryptography for the Financial Services Industry: The Elliptic Curve Digital Signature Algorithm (ECDSA), 1999.
16. ANSI X9.63, Public Key Cryptography for the Financial Services Industry: Elliptic Curve Key Agreement and Key Transport Protocols, working draft, August 1999.
17. National Institute of Standards and Technology, Digital Signature Standard, FIPS Publication 186-2, February 2000. Available at http://cstc.nist.gov/fips.
18. WAP Wireless Transport Layer Security Specification, WAP Forum, 5 November 1999.
19. P.L. Montgomery (1985) Modular Multiplication without trial division, Mathematics of Computation, 44, pp. 519-521.

20.   Menezes, T. Okamoto and S. Vanstone (1993) Reducing elliptic curve logarithms to logarithms in a finite field, IEEE Transactions on Information Theory, 39, pp. 1639-1646.
21.   Semaev (1998) Evaluation of discrete logarithms in a group of p-torsion points of an elliptic curve in characteristic p, Mathematics of Computation, 67, pp. 353-356.
22.   N. Smart (1999) The discrete logarithm problem on elliptic curves of trace one, Journal of Cryptology, 12, pp. 193-196.
23.   T. Satoh and K. Araki (1998) Fermat quotients and the polynomial time discrete log algorithm for anomalous elliptic curves, Commentarii Mathematici Universitatis Sancti Pauli, 47, pp. 81-92.
24.   D. Shanks (1971) Class number, a theory of factorization and genera. In 1969 Number Theory Institute (Proc. Sympos. Pure Math., Vol. XX, State Univ. New York, Stony Brook, Ny. 1969), pp. 415-440. Amer. Math. Soc., Providence, RI.
25.   Certicom ECC Challenge, November 1997, http://www.certicom.com.
26.   Tom Karygiannis and Les Owens (2002) Wireless Network Security: 802.11, Bluetooth and Handheld Devices, NIST Special Publication 800-48.
27.   IEEE P802.11i/D10.0 (2004) Medium Access Control (MAC) Security Enhancements, Amendment 6 to IEEE Standard for Information technology – Telecommunications and information exchange between systems – Local and metropolitan area networks – Specific requirements – Part 11: Wireless Medium Access Control (MAC) and Physical Layer (PHY) Specifications.
28.   L. Blunk and J. Vollbrecht (1998) PPP Extensible Authentication Protocol (EAP), IETF RFC 2284.
29.   Wireless LAN Security White Paper, Cisco Systems, http://www.cisco.com/warp/public/cc/pd/witc/ao1200ap/prodlit/wswpf_wp.pdf.
30.   H. Andersson, S. Josefsson, G. Örn, D. Simon, and A. Palekar (2002) Protected EAP Protocol (PEAP), IETF.
31.   B. Aboba and D. Simon (1999) PPP EAP TLS Authentication Protocol, IETF RFC 2716.
32.   C. He and J.C. Mitchell (2004) Analysis of the 802.11i 4-Way Handshake, Proceedings of the 2004 ACM workshop on Wireless security, pp. 43-50.
33.   C. He and J.C. Mitchell, Security Analysis and Improvements for IEEE 802.11i,
      http://www.isoc.org/isoc/conferences/ndss/05/proceedings/papers/NDSS05-1107.pdf, 2005.
34.   Dictionary Attack on Cisco LEAP Vulnerability, Reversion 2.1, Cisco Systems, http://www.cisco.com/warp/public/707/cisco-sn-20030802-leap.pdf.
35.   P.S. Pagliusi (2002) A Contemporary Foreword on GSM Security, Proceedings of the International Conference on Infrastructure Security, LNCS No. 2437, pp. 129-144, Springer-Verlag.

36. K. Boman, G. Horn, P. Howard and V. Niemi (2002) UMTS Security, Electronics & Communication Engineering Journal, 14(5), pp. 191-204.
37. G.M. Koien (2004) An Introduction to Access Security in UMTS, IEEE Wireless Communication, 11(1), pp. 8-18.
38. Biryukov, A. Shamir, and D. Wagner (2002) Real Time Cryptanalysis of A5/1 on a PC, in FSE 2000, LNCS No. 1978, Sp.

4 Wireless Application Protocol

W. Kou

ISN National Key Laboratory, Xidian University, P.R. China

4.1 Introduction

The wireless application protocol (WAP) is a suite of emerging standards to enable mobile Internet applications. The WAP standards have been created as a result of the WAP Forum that was formed in June 1997 by Ericsson, Motorola, and Nokia. The WAP Forum is designed to assist the convergence of two fast-growing network technologies, namely, wireless communications and the Internet. The convergence is based on rapidly increasing numbers of mobile phone users and the dramatic effect of e-business over the Internet. The combination of these two technologies will have a big impact on current e-business practice, and it will create huge market potential.

In this chapter, a detailed introduction to WAP is presented, including the application environment and various protocols. The security aspect in the present Internet environment is dealt with in Sect. 4.3.

4.2 Wireless Application Protocol

4.2.1 Overview

The WAP standards consist of a variety of architecture components, including an application environment, scripting and markup languages, network protocols, and security features. These components and features together define how wireless data handsets communicate over the wireless network, and how content and services are delivered. With the WAP standards, a wireless data handset can establish a connection to a WAP-compliant wireless infrastructure, request and receive the content and services, and present them to the end user. This WAP-compliant wireless infrastructure may include the handset, the server side infrastructure, such as the proxy server (WAP gateway), the Web server, the application server, and the network operator (telecommunication company). The WAP architecture is shown in Fig. 4.1.

The WAP architecture can also be presented through the WAP protocol stack shown in Fig. 4.2. The WAP protocol stack covers the complete picture from

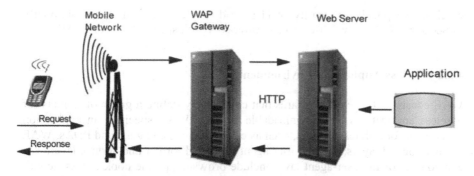

Fig. 4.1. The WAP architecture

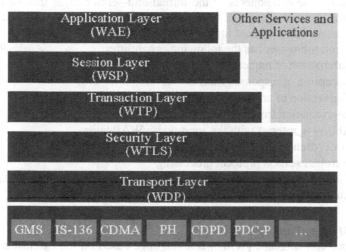

Fig. 4.2. The WAP protocol stack

bearers to applications. The bearers are the various wireless networks that WAP currently supports. The transport layer is an interface common to the underlying wireless network, and it provides a constant service to the upper layers in the WAP stack, such that the bearer services are transparent to the upper layers. In other words, with the transport layer, the specific network characteristics can be masked. The security layer provides security for the transport layer, based on the industry standard protocol and the transport layer security (TLS) protocol. The transaction layer provides a lightweight transaction-oriented protocol for mobile thin clients. The session layer provides the application layer with the capability to select connection-oriented or connectionless services. The application layer deals with a general-purpose environment for applications.

The WAP protocols in Fig. 4.2 include wireless application environment (WAE), wireless session protocol (WSP), wireless transaction protocol (WTP), wireless transport layer security (WTLS), and wireless datagram protocol (WDP). In Sects. 4.2.2–4.2.6, we discuss these protocols with special focus on WAE.

4.2.2 Wireless Application Environment

WAE consists of a set of standards that collectively define a group of formats for wireless applications and downloadable content. WAE specifies an application framework for wireless devices, such as cellular phones, pagers, and PDAs. WAE has two logical layers, namely, user-agent layer and format-and-service layer. The components of the user-agent layer include browsers, phone books, message editors, and other items on the user device side, such as wireless telephony application (WTA) agent. The components of the format-and-service layer include common elements and formats accessible to the user agents, such as WML, WMLScript, and WAP binary XML content format (WBXML).

A WAP microbrowser has the following capabilities:

- Submission of requests to the server
- Reception of responses from the server
- Conversion of and parse the data
- Interpretation from WML and WMLScript files
- Ability to interact with the appropriate WAP layer
- Local cache and variable management
- Wireless session protocol processing
- Effective management of local hardware resources, such as RAM, ROM, small screen, and input and output

Wireless Markup Language

Wireless markup language (WML) is a language based on the extensible markup language (XML). WML is optimized for small screens and limited memory capacity, and for content intended for lightweight, wireless devices such as mobile phones and personal digital assistants (PDAs).

A WML document is called deck. A page of a WML document is called card. A deck consists of one or more cards. Each deck is identified by an individual URL address, similar to an HTML page. A WML deck requires a browser that will format the deck for the benefit of the user. The browser determines the final shape of the deck. Sometimes, people use the analogy of HTML to explain WML. In the analogy, a WML deck corresponds to an HTML page. However, there are differences between a WML deck and an HTML page. While each HTML file is a single viewable page, a WML deck may contain multiple cards, each of which is a separate viewable entity. WML files are stored as static text files on a server. During the transmission from the server to the browser, the WML files are encoded in binary format by the wireless connection gateway and then sent to the browser. This is also different from HTML, where there is no need for such an encoding process.

WML contains commands for navigation in decks. Each WML command has two core attributes, namely, id and class. The id is the attribute for an individual name to the elements inside a deck, while the class is the attribute that links the element to one or several groups. A WML deck, at its most basic level, is constructed from a set of elements. Elements are identified by tags, which are enclosed in angular brackets. Each element must include a start tag (<el_tag>) and an end tag (</el_tag>). The content is included between the start and end tags. An empty element that has no content can be abbreviated by a single tag (<el_tag/>).

Because WML is based on the XML language, a WML document must follow the XML rule to contain the XML-specified document type definition (DTD) at the beginning of the WML code, which is referred to as deck header or document prolog, as follows:

<?xml version="1.0"?>
<!DOCTYPE wml PUBLIC "-//WAPFORUM//DTD WML 1.1//EN"
http://www.wapforum.org/DTD/wml_1.1.xml>

A deck is defined by the <wml> and </wml> tags that are required in every WML document. Within a deck, each card is defined by the <card> and </card> tags. Both <wml>···</wml> and <card>···</card> are formatting commands. The <wml>···</wml> commands summarize the deck. The <card>···</card> commands summarize the text, images, input fields, and any other objects of a card in the deck.

Cards are the basic units of WML, defining an interaction between a mobile device and the user. Each card may contain three different groups of elements: content elements (such as text, tables, and images), tasks and events (such as <onevent>, <timer>, and <do>), and data entry (such as <input> and <select>).

WMLScript

WMLScript is a simple scripting language based on ECMAScript (ECMA-262 standard) with modifications to better support low-bandwidth communication and thin clients. WMLScript is part of the WAP application layer.

WMLScript complements the WML by adding simple formatting capabilities to make the user interfaces more readable, for example, the capabilities of checking the validity of user input and generating messages and dialog locally to reduce the need for expensive round-trip to show alerts. These capabilities are not supported by WML as the content of WML is static. WMLScript provides programmable functionality that can be used over narrowband communication links in clients with limited capabilities. With WMLScript, more advanced user interface functions can be supported and intelligence can be added to the client. WMLScript also provides access to the device and its peripheral functionality, and reduces the amount of bandwidth that is needed for sending data back and forth between the server and the client.

WMLScript is similar to JavaScript. For example, WMLScript includes a number of operators such as assignment and arithmetic operators, which are similar to those in JavaScript. However, there are major differences between WMLScript and JavaScript. First, WML contains references to the URL address of a

WMLScript function, whereas JavaScript functions are normally embedded in the HTML code. Second, WMLScript must be compiled into binary WMLScript code prior to its execution in a WAP device, while there is no such requirement for JavaScript.

Although WMLScript is based on ECMAScript as mentioned earlier, there are differences between WMLScript and ECMAScript. First, like JavaScript, ECMAScript is not encoded in a binary form while WMLScript has to be. Second, to form WMLScript, many advanced features of the ECMAScript language have been dropped to make WMLScript smaller and easier to compile into binary WMLScript code.

WMLScript syntactically resembles C language. It has basic types, variables, expressions, and statements. Unlike C, WMLScript cannot be used to write stand-alone applications. There is no built-in support for reading and writing files. Because it is an interpreted language, scripts or functions can run only in the presence of an interpreter, which is supplied as part of the WAP user agent. WMLScript is a weakly typed and object-based language, in which variables must be declared before they can be used in expression. In WMLScript, there is no main program or routine. Functions are created to perform specific tasks and they are invoked through a WML call. When a WMLScript function is invoked, the WAP gateway accesses the source code, compiles it into binary WMLScript code, and then sends the execution function to the WAP user agent. WMLScript code is written in normal text files with the file extension "wmls."

Each WMLScript file contains at least one function. Each function is composed of statements that perform the appropriate processing. The structure of a WMLScript function is as follows:

```
extern function function_xyz (parameter list)
{// start of the statements
        statement_1;
        statement_2;
        statement_n;
}// end of the statements
```

With this structure and the file extension "xmls," a simple WMLScript example to set a day of the week, which is included in the file named "setday.xmls," is listed as follows:

```
extern function SetDay(givenDay)
{
        if (givenDay > 0 && givenDay <=7) {
                var newDay=givenDay;
        }
        else {
                newDay=1;
        }
        return newDay;
}
```

To invoke a WMLScript function, a reference to the WMLScript function must be included in a WML document. The call will be routed from the WAP browser through the WAP gateway to the server. The server then sends the binary WMLScript code to the WAP browser. The WAP browser has an interpreter, which is able to execute WMLScript programs in their binary format. Using our example, the reference to the WMLScript can be as simple as follows:

```
<do type="ACCEPT" label="Set Day">
<!--Calling the WMLScript function: -->
    <go href="setday.xmls#SetDay($(givenDay))"/>
</do>
```

Wireless Telephony Application Interface and Wireless Telephony Applications
One of the major mobile services is voice. How can we set up a call or receive an incoming call using a WAP-enabled mobile device? This is the problem that wireless telephony application interface (WTAI) addresses. WTAI is designed to allow wireless network operators access the telephony features of WAP device. Through either a WML deck/card or WMLScript, using the WTAI function libraries, a mobile phone call can be set up and an incoming call can be received. In addition, text messages can be sent or received, and phonebook entries can be manipulated on the WAP device.

Wireless telephony application (WTA) is a collection of telephony-specific extensions for call and feature control mechanisms that make advanced mobile network services available to the mobile users. It provides a bridge between wireless telephony and data. The WTA applications can use the privileged WTAI.

From the architecture point of view, a WTA server communicates with the WAP gateway to deliver and manage telephony services; on the client side, there is a WTA framework, which has three components as follows:

1. *User agent.* This agent supports the WTAI libraries, renders WML, and executes WMLScripts.
2. *Repository.* It provides persistent client-side storage for wireless telephony applications.
3. *Event handling.* This deals with incoming-call and call-connected events to be delivered to a wireless telephony application for processing, which may also invoke WMLScript library interfaces to initiate and control telephony operations.

Wireless telephony supports in WAP make WAP suitable for creating mobile applications through voice services. The compact form, encryption, and error handling capabilities of WAP enable critical wireless payment transactions.

WBXML
WAP binary XML content format (WBXML) is defined in the binary XML content format specification in the WAP standard set. This format is a compact binary representation of the XML. The main purpose is to reduce the transmission size of XML documents on narrowband communication channels.

A binary XML document is composed of a sequence of elements and each element may have zero or more attributes. The element structure of XML is preserved while the format encodes the parsed physical form of an XML document.

This allows user agents to skip elements and data that are not understood. In terms of encoding, a tokenized structure is used to encode an XML document. The network byte order is big-endian, that is, the most significant byte is transmitted first. Within a byte, bit-order is also big-endian, namely, the most significant bit first.

4.2.3 Wireless Session Protocol

WSP is a protocol family in the WAP architecture, which provides the WAP application layer with a consistent interface for session services. WSP establishes a session between the client and the WAP gateway to provide content transfer: the client makes a request, and then the server answers with a reply through the WAP gateway. WSP supports the efficient operation of a WAP microbrowser running on the client device with limited capacity and communicating over a low-bandwidth wireless network. The WSP browsing applications are based on the HTTP 1.1 standard, and incorporated with additional features that are not included in the HTTP protocol, for example, the connection to the server will not be lost when a mobile user is moving, resulting in a change from one base station to another. The other additional features that WSP supports include:

- *Binary encoding.* Given the low bandwidth of the wireless network, the efficient binary encoding of the content to be transferred is necessary for mobile Internet applications.
- *Data push functionality.* Data push functionality is not supported in the HTTP protocol. A push is what is performed when a WSP server transfers the data to a mobile client without a preceding request from the client. WSP supports three push mechanisms for data transfer, namely, a confirmed data push within an existing session context, a non-confirmed data push within an existing session context, and a nonconfirmed data push without an existing session context.
- *Capability negotiation*: Mobile clients and servers can negotiate various parameters for the session establishments, for example, maximum outstanding requests and protocol options.
- *Session suspend/resume.* It allows a mobile user to switch off and on the mobile device and to continue operation at the exact point where the device was switched off.

WSP offers two different services, namely, the connection-oriented service and the connectionless service. The connection-oriented service has the full capabilities of WSP. It operates on top of the wireless transaction protocol (WTP), supports session establishment, method invocation, push messages, suspend, resume and session termination. The connectionless service is suitable for those situations where high reliability is not required, or the overhead of session establishment and release can be avoided. It supports only basic request-reply and push, and does not rely on WTP.

4.2.4 Wireless Transaction Protocol

The wireless transaction protocol operates on top of a secure or insecure datagram service. WTP introduces the notion of a transaction that is defined as a request with its response. This transaction model is well suited for Web content requests and responses. It does not handle stream-based applications (such as telnet) well.

WTP is responsible for delivering the improved reliability over datagram service between the mobile device and the server by transmitting acknowledge messages to confirm the receipt of data and by retransmitting data that have not been acknowledged within a suitable timeout period. WTP supports an abort function through a primitive error handling. If an error occurs, such as the connection being broken down, the transaction is aborted.

WTP is message oriented and it provides three different types of transaction services, namely, unreliable one-way, reliable one-way, and reliable two-way. The transaction type is set by the initiator and is contained in the service request message sent to the responder. The unreliable one-way transactions are stateless and cannot be aborted. The responder does not acknowledge the message from the initiator. The reliable one-way transactions provide a reliable datagram service that enables the applications to provide reliable push service. The reliable two-way transactions provide the reliable request/response transaction services.

4.2.5 Wireless Transport Layer Security

The wireless transport layer security (WTLS) protocol is a security protocol based on the *transport layer security protocol* (TLS) [10] (see Sect. 4.5). TLS is a derivative of the *secure sockets layer* (SSL), a widely used security protocol for Internet applications and payment over the Internet. WTLS has been optimized for the wireless communication environment. It operates above the transport protocol layer.

WTLS is flexible due to its modular design. Depending on the required security level, we can decide whether WTLS is to be used or not. WTLS provides data integrity, data confidentiality, authentication, and denial-of-service protection. Data integrity is to ensure that data sent between a mobile station and a wireless application server are unchanged and uncorrupted. Data confidentiality is to ensure that data transmitted between the mobile station and the wireless application server are private to the sender and the receiver, and one not going to be understood by any hackers. Authentication is to check the identity of the mobile station and the wireless application server. Denial-of-service protection is to prevent the upper protocol layers from the denial-of-service attacks by detecting and rejecting data that are replayed or not successfully verified.

4.2.6 Wireless Datagram Protocol

The wireless datagram protocol (WDP) in the WAP architecture specifies how different existing bearer services should be used to provide a consistent service to the upper layers. WDP is used to hide the differences among the underlying bearer networks. WDP layer operates above the bearer services and provides a consistent interface to the WTLS layer.

Different bearers have different characteristics. The bearer services include short message, circuit-switched data, and packet data services. Since WAP is designed to operate over the bearer services, and since the bearers offer different types of quality of service with respect to throughput, error rate, and delays, the WDP is designed to adapt the transport layer to specific features of the underlying bearers. The adaptation results in a family of protocols in the WDP layer, dealing with each supported bearer network protocol. When a message is transmitted through WAP stack, depending on the underlying bearer network, a different WDP protocol may be used. For example, for an IP bearer, the user datagram protocol (UDP) must be adopted as the WDP protocol, and for a short message service (SMS) bearer, the use of the source and destination port numbers becomes mandatory.

4.2.7 Gateway

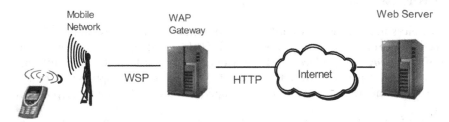

Fig. 4.3. WAP gateway

A WAP gateway (shown in Fig. 4.3) is a proxy server that sits between the mobile network and the Internet. The purpose of this proxy server is to translate between HTTP and WSP. The reason for the translation is that the Web server connected to the Internet understands only the HTTP protocol, while the WAP-enabled mobile client understands only the WSP. The WAP gateway also converts an HTML file into a WML document that is designed for small-screen devices. In addition, the WAP gateway compiles the WML page into binary WML, which is more suitable for the mobile client. The WAP gateway is transparent to both the mobile client and the Web server.

Fig. 4.4 shows the WAP model using the WAP gateway. How the WAP gateway processes a typical request for a document can be illustrated as follows:

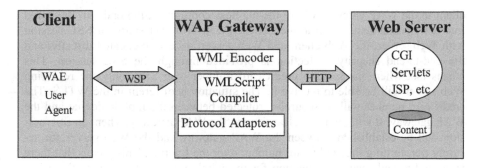

Fig. 4.4. WAP model

1. The mobile user makes a request for a specific document using the WAP phone.
2. The WAE user agent on the WAP phone encodes the request and sends it to the WAP gateway.
3. The WAP gateway decodes and parses the encoded request.
4. The WAP gateway sends an HTTP request for the document.
5. The Web server answers with a response to the WAP gateway.
6. The WAP gateway parses and encodes the response.
7. If the content type is WML, then the gateway compiles it into binary WML.
8. The WAP gateway sends the encoded response to the WAP phone.
9. The WAE user agent on the WAP phone interprets and presents the document to the mobile user.

4.3 Wireless Application Security

Wireless application security is becoming increasingly important as transaction-based mobile commerce applications (such as mobile payment, banking, and buying stock via cellular phones or other handheld devices) take off.

The basic security needs for mobile commerce are similar to those for electronic commerce over the wired Internet, such as authentication, confidentiality, nonrepudiation, and data integrity. However, implementing them in the wireless world is more difficult than in the wired world. This is simply because of the limitations that wireless have, including limited bandwidth, high latency, and unstable connections. In addition, the limited battery and processing power that the wireless devices have also make the sophisticated security algorithms difficult to run on these devices.

As discussed in Sect. 4.2, WAP specifies an SSL-like security protocol, namely, wireless transport layer security (WTLS). However, there are some drawbacks in WTLS. First, WTLS provides only security protection from the mobile client to the WAP gateway where the wireless communication ends. In the wired Internet environment, when a Web client (Web browser) starts an SSL session with Web server, the Web client and Web server are communicated directly, and the end-to-end security protection is provided through the SSL session. This means that when one sends a credit card number over SSL, only the receiving Web server will be able to receive it. The situation is different in the WTLS. The credit card number will be securely protected between the mobile device and the WAP gateway. It will be in the clear form at the WAP gateway. Then, an SSL session will be established between the WAP gateway and the Web server for securely transmitting the credit card number over the Internet. This means that there is no end-to-end security protection for the wireless transactions since there is a potential security hole in the WAP gateway. Second, the CCITT X509 certificate is too large for the mobile phones, and the limitations of the processing power and battery for the wireless devices make it difficult to perform the sophisticated computation of the public-key encryption. In summary, WAP security has two issues: (1) there is no end-to-end security protection and (2) there is a lack of certificates for mobile devices.

Research is being done on these two security issues. As a result, simplified certificates have been defined for mobile devices. The research on how to use currently available mobile devices to perform the computation of public-key encryption is ongoing. For example, elliptic curve cryptography (ECC) requires far fewer resources and it looks very promising for wide deployment to CPU-starved wireless devices.

4.4 Summary

The convergence of wireless technologies and the e-business over the Internet has led to emerging and fast growth of wireless e-business, including mobile commerce. As a result, wireless e-business has attracted increasing attention of academic researchers and business leaders. Being able to conduct e-business anywhere and anytime is becoming a reality. However, because of the limitations that wireless has, conducting e-business in the wireless world is more difficult than in the wired world. Understanding the wireless application protocol that the wireless e-business relies on is important for developing and deploying wireless e-business. In this chapter, our discussion was focused on wireless application protocol and related wireless security.

4.5 Appendix

4.5.1 Overview of the Transport Layer Security

The transport layer security (TLS) [10] is a protocol that provides privacy and data integrity between two communicating applications. The TLS is application protocol independent, that is, higher-level protocols can layer on top of the TLS protocol transparently. The TLS protocol is composed of two layers:

1. *TLS record protocol.* This protocol provides connection security and is used for encapsulation of various higher-level protocols, such as the TLS handshake protocol discussed here. It has the following two basic properties

    o   *The connection is private.* Data encryption is used for ensuring the communication privacy and is based on symmetric cryptographic algorithms, such as DES or RC4. The keys for symmetric encryption are generated uniquely for each connection and are based on a secret negotiated by another protocol (e.g., the TLS handshake protocol). The record protocol can also be used without encryption.

    o   *The connection is reliable.* A message integrity check based on a keyed MAC is used for protecting message transport. Secure hash functions, such as SHA and MD5, are used for MAC computations. In such cases, another protocol uses the record protocol and negotiates security parameters, and the record protocol can operate without a MAC.

2. *TLS handshake protocol.* This protocol allows the server and client to authenticate each other, and negotiate an encryption algorithm and cryptographic keys. It has the following three basic properties

    o   The authentication between the server and client can be based on a public-key cryptographic algorithm, such as RSA or DSS. Although the authentication can be mutual, the mutual authentication is optional. Generally speaking, one-way authentication is required.

    o   It is secure for the negotiation of a shared secret between the server and client.

    o   The negotiation is reliable.

Because the TSL is a derivative of SSL, the actual handshake exchanges are similar to that of SSL. Description of the main SSL exchanges can be found later in this book.

Acknowledgments

This work is supported in part by NSFC grant 90304008 from the Nature Science Foundation of China and the Doctoral Program Foundation grant 2004071001 from the Ministry of Education of China.

References

1.   WAP. http://www.ini.cmu.edu/netbil.
2.   Wireless Application Protocol Forum Ltd (1999) Official Wireless Application Protocol. Wiley, New York.

3.   S. Mann, S. Sbihli (2000) The Wireless Application Protocol. Wiley, New York.

4.   S. Singhal, et al. (2001) The Wireless Application Protocol. Addison-Wesley, New York.

5.   J. Schiller (2000) Mobile Communications. Addison-Wesley, New York.

6.   U. Hansmann, et al. (2001) Pervasive Computing Handbook. Springer, Berlin Heidelberg New York.

7.   C. Sharma (2001) Wireless Internet Enterprise Applications. Wiley, New York.

8.   Y.B. Lin, I. Chlamtac (2001) Wireless and Mobile Network Architectures. Wiley, New York.

9.   Dornan (2001) The Essential Guide to Wireless Communications Applications. Prentice-Hall, New York.

10. T. Dierks, C. Allen (1999) The TLS Protocol Version 1.0. http://www.ietf.org/rfc/rfc2246.txt.

5 RFID Technologies and Applications

D. Kou[+], K. Zhao[*], Y. Tao[*], and W. Kou[*]

[+] University of Waterloo, Ontario, Canada
[*] ISN National Key Laboratory, Xidian University, P.R. China

5.1 Introduction

Commercialism plays a critical role in contemporary society. To stay ahead of competitors, businesses must find a better, more cost-effective method of production quickly and efficiently through research and development, or make investment toward technological improvement. At the same time, companies must successfully adopt these improvements quickly in order to respond to the demands of the market.

Corporations must differentiate which technologies are beneficial to them, and which are unnecessary in order to flourish in competitive markets. Any technology that speeds up decision making and increases productivity, while reducing production costs is considered beneficial. Fundamentally important production stages include supply chain management, warehouse control, product tracking, and security to name a few.

Since the birth of modern wireless technological era, there is no other technology that has drawn more attention to itself than RFID in terms of product management.

RFID is now rapidly becoming prominent in the contemporary business world. It has attracted extensive attention from the business community and has many applications such as access control, security management, purchasing, manufacturer, supply chain management, and distribution logistics.

Given the benefit of communicating without relying on line-of-sight access, RFID offers a genuine solution to handling product management, whether from the supply chain perspective or from the inventory perspective. RFID provides an effective way to communicate and transfer data without the need of physical contact. RFID tags on products are not easily damaged, as they can sustain high amounts of pressure, as well as survive in varying temperatures. This, along with many additional benefits (discussed in later sections) that RFID brings to corporations, makes it a very real and viable business solution.

5.1.1 What is RFID?

Radio Frequency IDentification (RFID) is a standard term to describe technologies that utilize radiowaves to capture and identify data. RFID uses wireless technology to convey data between microchip-embedded transponders and readers. The transponders or tags, consisting of a microchip and an antenna, are attached to objects that need identifying. The reader, using one or more antennae, reads the data held on the microchip. By emitting radiowaves to the tag and receiving signals back, the reader is able to communicate with the transponder.

5.1.2 History

RFID systems have been around for decades and have been used in many different applications. But it was not until recently that RFID has started to receive enormous amount of attention from business corporations and commercial retailers.

One of the earliest uses of RFID was during WWII, when the long-ranged transponder system was explored. Identification, Friend or Foe (IFF) was one of the first practical uses of RFID, where military forces attempted to identify whether aircrafts were friendly or hostile.

The earliest commercial impact RFID had was during the late 1960s, when the electronic article surveillance (EAS) equipment was designed to counter theft and shoplifting. Although the EAS equipment consisted of only one-bit tags, it was an effective method to counter theft. Because only one-bit tags were used, the system could only detect whether an item was present, or absent. However, the system proved cost efficient, as the tags were relatively cheap and provided an effective way to prevent theft.

One of the first passive, read–write RFID tags was invented in the early 1970s. The transponder now included a way to store data, using a memory chip. It also responded to signals transmitted to write data into the memory, as well as data read from the memory. Furthermore, it transmitted a return signal out of the memory to the reader. The transponder also had a way to internally generate power to operate. This new invention was groundbreaking, as it opened the door for many new possibilities. With the ability to alter data in the tag, RFID tags became much more useful in the practical world.

Following this invention in the 1970s, many tracking applications began to appear. RFID played a significant role in animal tracking, which is still used in modern society. Special tags are applied beneath the skin of animals, be it domestic, stock, or wild. The earliest form of animal tracking was used to analyze the migration route of different species of birds. The tag is usually in the form of a little glass pill, where information about the animal pertaining to its age, physical attributes, and health conditions can be stored and updated. The pill is placed under the skin of the animal and can in no way harm the carrier.

With the increasing uses of RFID in the 1980s, RFID systems were beginning to break out in a significant way, emerging from the hidden shell of the past with a bang into the 1990s and the twenty-first century, where commercialism plays such an influential role.

5.1.3 Modern World Applications

One of the key uses of RFID introduced in the 1990s was implementing automated tollgates. Electronic tollgates began to appear in North America and across Europe, aided by a video surveillance system. Cars are equipped with a RFID tag that automatically sends the data once it passes through the tollbooth. The RFID readers on the tollbooths send a signal to activate the tags on the cars, and tag automatically transmits the data to the reader. Cars could now pass through tollgates without having to stop at tollbooths, which increased traffic flow drastically.

While RFID is not the leading technology associated with product identification, its potential benefits are evident. While other forms of product identification, such as barcodes, require line-of-sight readers, the advantage of using RFID to identify products relies heavily on the wireless transferring of data. No direct contact needs to be made between the tag and the scanner for the information to be accessed. This is much more efficient and time conserving as compared to barcodes. Instead of having to scan each product individually, the RFID reader automatically retrieves the necessary data from the tags. Furthermore, barcodes on similar products are identical, thus there is no way of differentiating between one from another, and this can easily be used to duplicate and create counterfeit products.

Because RFID uses wireless technology, it can play a monumental part in terms of the supply chain. Suppliers of major retailers can use RFID technology for the sole basis of inventory/warehouse management. Instead of having to scan the product separately, a mobile reader can be used to scan the tags to retrieve the product data. During the shipping phase, the products can then be tracked from the time they leave the warehouse to the time they arrive at the retailer. Once they reach the retailer, the new information will be stored on the tags.

Since RFID tags can be relatively small in size, they can also have a large effect on the manufacturing/production chain. By using RFID tags, each step of the production chain can be traced and recorded. Once a phase is finished, the tag can be updated and the new information stored. This ensures product quality, in addition to facilitating the production process. Any error made during production can be traced back using the RFID tags.

Fraud and counterfeit prevention is another aspect of RFID technology. In many countries, fraudulent products are made to resemble products of brand name companies. With the use of RFID, products can be uniquely branded during production. By embedding or attaching an RFID tag to the product, it is impossible for counterfeiters to forge the product without destroying it. For example, during the production phase an RFID tag is sealed to the lid of a vintage wine bottle. Once the bottle is opened, the RFID tag is destroyed, so it cannot be read again. If someone attempts to forge the brand name from the used wine bottle to resell, the RFID tag will no longer be readable, thereby making it impossible for the counterfeiter to show that the wine was authentic. The consumer would immediately know whether the product was real or not.

Table 5.1 shows a simplistic comparison between barcodes and RFID tags.

Table 5.1. Comparison between barcodes and RFID tags

	barcodes	RFID
readability (%)	80–85	95–99
line-of-sight	necessary	unnecessary
resistance to environment	low	high
resistance to heat	low	high
rate of failure	high	low
production cost	low	high
unique product identification	poor	good
easy integration into other systems	no	yes
Security issues	low	high

The popularization of wireless and mobile communication equipments brings along customers' need of location service. Customers need to confirm the goods' 3D coordinate and track their movement. The exist location service system mainly includes GPS system based on satellite location, the location system based on infrared or ultrasonic, and the location system based on mobile network. The RFID location and tracking system takes advantage of the tags' unique identification feature to the goods, and measures the goods' location according to the signal intensity of radio frequency between the reader and the object. It is mainly used in in-door locations that are difficult to be hacked by the GPS system. The typical RFID location and tracking system includes the Cricket system developed by the MIT Oxygen project, the LANDMARC system of the Michigan State University, and the RADAR system of Microsoft. By aiming at the RFID tag's inexpensive cost and introducing RFID tags as reference points, the location accuracy can be improved and the system cost can be reduced at the same time.

5.2 Components

5.2.1 Basic Components

RFID systems consist of two basic components: the reader (or scanner) and the tag (or transponder). The reader can contain one or more antennae to communicate with the tag. The tag, placed on the object to be identified, usually includes a microchip and an antenna.

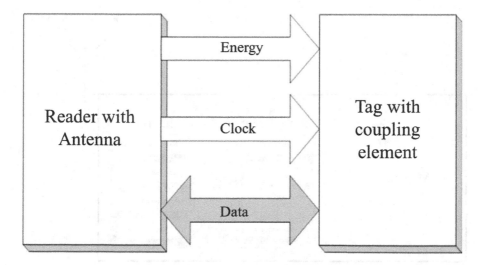

Fig. 5.1. Basic components of an RFID system

The communication between the reader and the tag uses a defined radio frequency and protocol. The reader transfers data to the tag, along with a clock signal from the reader to the tag to effectively label when the product was last checked. Some readers also provide energy to the transponder to activate and initiate the data transfer.

The tag itself carries the data used for object identification. Once the reader activates the tag, it can begin to read or write data onto the tag. A tag can be activated differently depending on the type of transponder used.

5.2.2 The Tag

There are three main types of RFID tags: active, passive, and semipassive. Each type of tag is used for different application purposes, as their range and frequency limit them to certain viable functions.

Active RFID tags have a power source such as a battery attached to the tag, in addition to larger memory and longer ranges than passive or semipassive tags. Active tags are able to broadcast data continuously on a set interval (from every few seconds to a few hours). Since active tags are used when identifying products that are deemed valuable and expensive, such as cars, the active tag must be able to communicate to the reader at long ranges and store much more information than passive tags. The typical read range of an active tag is usually somewhere between 20 and 100 m, and the batteries on the active tags last up to several years. The costs of active tags can range between $10 and $50 depending on memory size, the power of the battery, and the material used to design the tag.

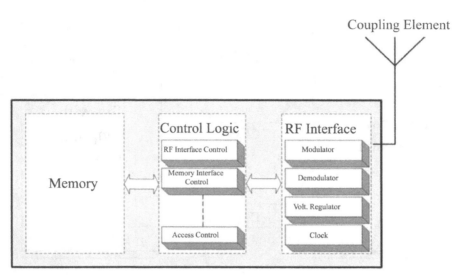

Fig. 5.2. Passive tag structures

Unlike active tags, passive RFID tags do not have a power source, but instead generate power through induction. They rely on electromagnetic fields to generate power. The antennae on both the tag and reader usually have a small coil, and when placed near one another, form an electromagnetic field. The tag draws its energy from the field and uses this to feed the microchip on the tag. Because the coils on both the reader and tag must be close to one another in order to form a magnetic field, the range of passive tags is much smaller than that of an active tag. The typical range of a passive tag to the reader ranges from a few inches to 10 m. However, because passive tags do not have a power source, it can be quite small, and therefore less expensive to produce. Passive tags can be as tiny as 0.4 mm × 0.4 mm and as thin as a sheet of paper. The current cost of a passive tag ranges between 20 and 50 cents, making it an ideal type of tag to be used in manufacturing and the supply chain.

Semipassive tags have their own battery, which is used to run the microchip. However, they may only respond to incoming transmissions and they communicate by using the power provided on the reader.

Table 5.2. Characteristics of the three tag types

	passive	active	semipassive
power source	passive	battery	battery
transmitter	passive	active	passive
max. range (M)	10	100	100

5.2.3 Tags and Their microchips

Tags are usually passive unless activated by the reader. When the reader is near the tag, and the tag is in the "interrogation zone," the microchip on the tag is activated. Simple tags are read only, where the reader can only access the data but cannot update or manipulate the data. Read–write tags are more expensive, but the reader can access the stored data within the tag as well as have the capability to change or update the data. Some more advanced tags include both a read-only chip and a read-write chip. The memory contained in the chip is programmed during production stages, and it would depend largely on the function of the tag and whether a large amount of memory is necessary for its designated task. The size of the tags would depend largely on which power supply, if any, was used, as well as the size of the antenna.

Table 5.3. Attributes of different microchip types

	attributes of microchip types
read-only chip	read-only chips contain a unique license plate number that cannot be altered. The reader is only able to retrieve information from the tag without altering its contents. Read-only tags are cheaper to produce than WORM or read/write tags because they require the least amount of memory
write-once read many (WORM) chip	WORM chips allow a user to encode the tag during its first usage, but after that the code is locked and inaccessible. The data can still be read off the tag, but the data can no longer be altered. Production costs for WORM tags are greater than read-only chips as they require slightly more memory
read/write chip	read/write chips allow continuous updates on the tag to include new information. This is exceptionally critical during the supply chain, where products should be updated every time they are shipped off, and when they arrive at the retailer. Read/write tags require the most memory and thus are the most expensive amongst the three types of chips

5.2.4 Tag Conclusion

Although passive tags are the cheapest tags to produce at the moment, they are still not feasible in terms of production costs for many suppliers and retailers. The market expectation is to produce tags for less than $0.05 so as to enable widespread use of RFID. Economically, the supply and demand for RFID tags are too low for prices to drastically reduce anytime soon. Furthermore, many companies are not willing to invest enough money into RFID technology, because many of its applications are fairly new and are yet to be embraced by the general public. While RFID technology is evidently increasing, companies are not willing to risk ordering large supplies of RFID tags at this level and cost.

While the cost efficiency of using passive tags over active tags is undeniable, factors such as accuracy and reliability have made the use of active tags more common today. However, as research and development an passive tags begins to intensify, the commercial implications of passive RFID tags will undoubtedly drive costs down as there will be a high demand for them.

The following is a list of the most common RFID tags currently used:
- Label: the tag is of a flat, thin, flexible form
- Ticket: a flat, thin, flexible tag on paper
- Card: a flat, thin tag embedded in tough plastic for long life
- Glass bead: a small tag in a cylindrical glass bead, used for applications such as animal tagging (e.g., under the skin)
- Integrated: the tag is integrated into the object it tags rather than applied as a separate label, such as molded into the object
- Wristband: a tag inserted into a plastic wrist strap
- Button: a small tag encapsulated in a rigid housing

5.2.4 The Reader

The RFID reader has three main functions: energizing, demodulating, and decoding. The reader, using a tuned antenna-capacitor circuit, emits a low-frequency radiowave field. This is used to power up the tag. The information sent by the tag must be demodulated (like an AM radio). The encoded information is decoded by the reader's on-board microcontroller.

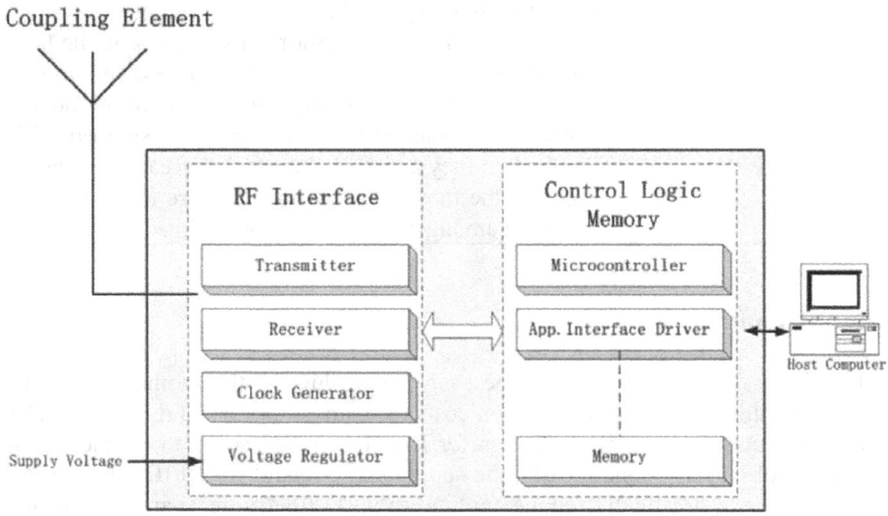

Fig. 5.3. RFID reader's structure

Depending on the application and technology used, some interrogators not only read, but also remotely write to, the tags. Several types of reader exist. A number of companies manufacture them, and more are being developed for supply-chain RFID applications. Reader types include handheld, mobile mounted (forklift or cart), fixed read-only, and a combination of reader/encoder. In a typical distribution center, a set of readers would be configured to read any set of tags passing between them. Such a configuration is called a portal. Portals may be located in receiving dock doors, packaging lines, and shipping dock doors. Mobile mounted and handheld readers can be used to check tags that are not picked up through the portal, or to locate product in the DC or on trucks. An RFID reader's structure is shown in Fig. 5.3.

In both the reader and the tag, the antenna can be sized and shaped in different forms. Because of the small size of the tag, it can be formed to fit almost any situation. Since there is no contact required, the RFID system allows great freedom of movement. Placement of the tag and reader is no longer critical.

5.2.5 Anticollision

Because many tags may be available in the presence of a reader, the reader must be able to receive and manage many replies at once, potentially hundreds per second. Collision avoidance algorithms are used to allow tags to be sorted and individually selected. A reader can instruct some tags to wake up and others to go to sleep to suppress chatter. Once a tag is selected, the reader is able to perform a number of operations, such as reading the identification number and writing information to the tag in some cases. The reader then proceeds through the list to gather information from all the tags. This is like the relation between the teacher and students. When the teacher asks questions, if more than one student raises a hand, only one can be chosen by the teacher. Fig. 5.4 shows the communication between a reader and three tags, and that the reader will communicate with only one tag at a time.

5.2.6 Operating Frequency

There are several operating frequency bands that can be used for the RFID systems according to the radio licensing regulations:
- Low frequency: between 125 and 134 kHz
- High frequency: 13.56 MHz
- UHF: 868 to 956 MHz
- Microwave: 2.45 GHz

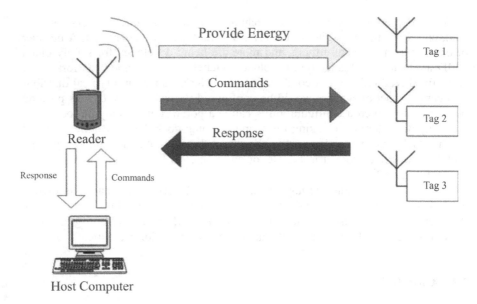

Fig. 5.4. A reader communicating with three tags

UHF tags cannot be used globally as there are no global regulations for their usage. Factors that affect the choice of a suitable frequency for the applications include absorption in water, reflection on surfaces, energy demand, size of electronic parts, and speed of data transmission [1, 4].

Below 135 kHz (LF):
- Short range –contact near to one meter
- Low data rates due to a lower bandwidth
- Penetrate nonmetallic materials (e.g., water)
- Do not penetrate/transmit around metals
- Used in access control, livestock, and wireless commerce

13.56 MHz (HF):
- ISM band
- Higher data rates and range
- Penetrate nonmetallic materials (e.g., water)
- Do not penetrate/transmit around metals
- Used in supply chain, wireless commerce, ticketing, and product authentication

860–930 MHz (UHF):
- High data rate/long range
- Effective around metals
- Do not penetrate water
- Differences in frequency (Europe, USA, Japan)
- Used in supply chain, and toll tags

2.45 GHz (UHF):

- ISM band (same as Bluetooth, WLAN)
- High data rate, long range
- Effective around metals
- Do not penetrate water
- Used in logistics, and toll tags

5.3 Middleware Technology

5.3.1 Features

RFID middleware technology handles RFID requirements by leveraging standard application development, data management, and process integration. RFID middleware includes basic features like reader integration and coordination, product ID data track-and-trace tools, and baseline filtering capabilities. The core capabilities are listed as follows:

- Reader and device management
- Data management
- Application integration
- Partner integration
- Process management and application development
- Packaged RFID content
- Architecture scalability and administration

The capability of reader and device management allows users to configure, monitor, deploy, and issue commands directly to readers through a common interface, such as a command to turn off the reader. Like managing many other devices, a plug-and-play-like feature is desirable to dynamically sense the presence of the reader and link to it. In many applications such as those for container shipping business, in addition to RFID tags, there are other sensors such as temperature sensors. It is also important that RFID middleware have a capability of integration with other sensors, wireless and Internet technologies.

Data management is the ability of RFID middleware to be able to intelligently filter and route it to the appropriate destinations once product ID data are captured from readers. There are potentially hundreds of tags that may be present to a reader. The data management capability must allow the reader to filter out duplicate reads, and aggregate and manage product ID data in either a federated or central data source. It may also include more complex algorithms like content-based routing.

The application integration capability provides the messaging, routing, and connectivity features required to reliably integrate RFID data into existing SCM, ERP, WMS, CRM, or other applications and systems. It is the capability that the enterprise service bus (ESB) offers in the services-oriented architecture (SOA). It minimizes the disruption by using an ESB to handle integration logic and improves flexibility through the adoption of service-oriented interfaces. A service-oriented architecture is essentially a collection of services. A service is a function that is well defined, self-contained, and does not depend on the context or state of other services. These services communicate with each other. The application integration capability of RFID middleware also provides a library of application programming interfaces (APIs) and adapters to integrate with third-party applications developed using proprietary technologies or standard technologies such as J2EE, XML, and SOAP.

Partner integration is the RFID middleware capability that allows sharing RFID data with partners to improve collaborative processes, such as demand forecasting and vendor-managed inventory. It provides B2B integration features, for example, partner profile management, support for B2B transport protocols, and integration with the EPCglobal Network. Partner integration is one of the most promising benefits of RFID.

The capability of process management and application development allows RFID middleware platforms to orchestrate RFID-related end-to-end processes that touch multiple applications such as inventory replenishment. The key features of process management and composite application development include workflow, role management, process automation, and UI development tools.

Packaged RFID content is an important part of RFID middleware platforms. It includes packaged routing logic and product data schemas. It also includes integration with typical RFID-related applications and processes such as shipping, receiving, and asset tracking.

Architecture scalability and administration is very important. First, regarding the scalability, since RFID adoption produces a lot of data, RFID middleware must be able to process the increased volume of data by dynamically balancing processing loads across multiple servers and automatically rerouting data upon server failure.

5.3.2 An Example: IBM's RFID Middleware

There are a number of vendors in the marketplace that offer RFID middleware solutions, such as IBM, HP, Oracle, and Sun Microsystems, to name a few. In this section, we use IBM's RFID middleware as an example to explain the RFID architecture and the RFID middleware solutions.

IBM's RFID middleware technologies [10] are built on existing WebSphere and DB2 technology. IBM's RFID middleware technologies include assured message delivery function, scalable and robust data management and reconciliation technologies, industry-leading enterprise application integration, and prebuilt process automation templates and tools for clients implementing RFID in their business applications. IBM's RFID architecture is shown in Fig. 5.5.

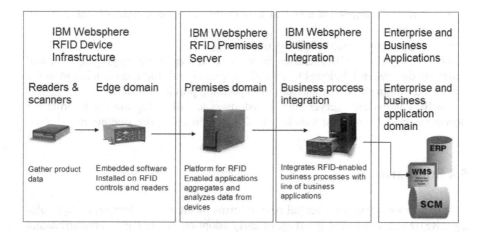

Fig. 5.5. IBM's RFID architecture

An IBM RFID implementation is made up of three elements: devices, Web-Sphere RFID Premises Server, and a WebSphere integration server. Devices include RFID readers, scanners, printers, light stacks, motion sensors, programmable logic controllers, and so on. These devices are embedded with IBM's Web-Sphere RFID Device Infrastructure, which is an RFID-enabled middleware product that IBM provides to select partners to place on their devices. The WebSphere RFID Device Infrastructure is targeted for deployment in distribution centers, warehouse environments, manufacturing plants, and energy generation and distribution centers. It provides important capabilities at the very edge of the network as it:

- Acts as an integration point for a variety of RFID readers and other infrastructure devices
- Filters and aggregates RFID data to eliminate duplicate or false data reads from one or more readers, and identifies RFID events at the edge of the network
- Helps reduce network traffic and enhances the scalability of the RFID solution architecture
- Provides a messaging and event buffer to help assure delivery of RFID events to the RFID Premises Server
- Integrates remote firmware and software distribution management

IBM WebSphere RFID Premises Server is a software that aggregates, monitors, interprets, and escalates RFID events to detect critical business operational events. The WebSphere RFID Premises Server provides the following functions:

- Interpret the RFID information
- Filter, aggregate, monitor, and escalate RFID events to help detect critical business operational events or track the location of physical objects
- Store and cache of local data, including complete database functionality

- Create business context that can enable automatic operational decision making
- Help assure reliable delivery of messages

The WebSphere RFID Premises Server can, for example, aggregate case and pallet tag data when it belongs to a single shipment and find the association to the Advanced Shipment Notice and the corresponding purchase order.

An IBM integration server allows customers to fully integrate the information flowing in from the edge of their business with their enterprise operations.

5.4 Standards

Standardization plays an essential role in terms of the mass adoption of technologies. RFID today is still in the stage of early adoption, while RFID standardization is still in development, especially in retail and supply chain.

Currently, several organizations are active in the standardization of RFID technology. Leading institutions include the International Organization for Standardization (ISO), which is the worldwide union of national standardization institutions; EPCglobal, which is the joint venture of European Article Numbering and Uniform Code Council (EAN,[1] UCC[2]); and Ubiquitous ID Center, a Japanese industry RFID consortium. Some of the other institutions that work on RFID standards include the American National Standards Institute (ANSI) and the Automotive Industry Action Group (AIAG). The Chinese government has also declared developing its own standard for product information.

Although there is a variety of RFID standard activities around the globe, RFID standards can be roughly classified into two groups, namely, application standards and technology standards. The standard structure is shown in Fig. 5.6.

In the following sections, we present three selected RFID standardization efforts, including ISO, EPCGlobal, and the Ubiquitous ID Center from Japan.

5.4.1 ISO

The International Organization for Standardization (ISO) is a union of national standard institutions from 145 countries working toward international standardization. The ISO has been active in the standardization of RFID internationally. ISO has had three committees that deal with RFID technology:

---

[1] EAN was formed in 1977. EAN is a UPC[1]-compatible system that sets standards. Currently, EAN has 99 members, representing 101 companies.

[2] UCC is a nonprofit organization that supervises and manages the Uniform Product Code (UPC), the barcode standard in North America. UCC has more than 250,000 member companies.

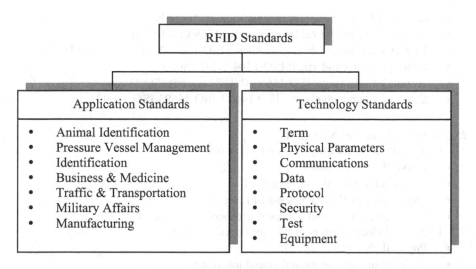

Fig. 5.6. RFID standard structure

- TC104 (for freight containers)
- TC204 (for road informatics)
- TC122 (for packaging)

The ISO has proposed ISO 18000 for standardizing the air interface protocol, the specifications for allowing readers to communicate with tags. According to [9], ISO 18000 does not specify criteria related to data content or the physical implementation of the tags and readers.

ISO/IEC 18000 – RFID for Item Management

The ISO/IEC 18000 standard has been developed by ISO/IEC SC31 WG4, Radio Frequency Identification for Item Management. The aim is to provide parameter definitions for communications protocols within a common framework for internationally useable frequencies for RFID. The standard tries to determine the use of the same protocols for all frequencies such that the problems of migrating from one to another are diminished. It is also to minimize software and implementation costs, and to enable system management and control and information exchange. The ISO 18000 series of standards comprise:

- Part 1: definition of parameters to be standardized.
- Part 2: parameters for air interface communications below 135 kHz
- Part 3: parameters for air interface communications at 13.56 MHz
- Part 4: parameters for air interface communications at 2.45 GHz
- Part 6: parameters for air interface communications at 860–930 MHz
- Part 7: parameters for active air interface communications at 433 MHz

Besides ISO 18000, several other standards are listed here:
- Supply chain and parcel tracking: ISO 15693/ISO 18000
- Libraries and inventory management: ISO 15693/ISO 14443/ISO 18000
- Smart passports and visas: ISO 14443/ISO 18000
- Airport baggage tags: ISO 15693 (UHF version)/ISO 18000
- Smart cards and envelopes: ISO 14443/ISO 45693/ISO 18000

ISO Identified Tag Contactless IC
1. ISO 10536 compact coupling tag (0–1 mm)
    - Physical characteristics
    - Size and location of coupling field
    - Electronic signals and process of reset
    - Response for reset and transport protocol
2. ISO 14443 close quarters proximity tag (0–10 cm)
    - Physical characteristics
    - Radiofrequency energy and signal interface
    - Initialization and anticollision
    - Transport protocol
3. ISO 15693 close quarters vicinity tag (0–100 cm)
    - Physical characteristics
    - Contactless interface and initialization
    - Protocol
    - Application/publication enroll

5.4.2 EPCglobal

EPCglobal is a Belgium-based nonprofit joint venture between EAN and UCC. The mission of EPCglobal is to establish and maintain the Electronic Product Code (EPC) Network as the global standard to commercialize the use of RFID technology from the tags to data integration for immediate, automatic identification of any item in the supply chain in the world.

Within EPCglobal, the Hardware Action Group (HAG) develops specifications for key hardware components of the EPC Network, including tags and readers. The EPC system defines several classes of products:
- Class 0: read only passive tags, preprogrammed by the manufacturer
- Class 1: "write-once read-many" passive tags that can be programmed by the manufacturer or by the user
- Class 2: read/write passive tags, with memory or encryption functionality
- Class 3: semipassive read/write tags, plus a battery-assisted power source to provide increased range and other functionalities on chip – memory, sensors, etc.

- Class 4: active tags that can be reprogrammed many times, class 3 capabilities, plus active communication, and the ability to communicate with other active tags
- Class 5: Readers that can power class 1, 2, and 3 tags, as well as communication with class 4 and with each other

Electronic Product Code (EPC)

Like many other product codes used in commerce, EPC identifies the manufacturer and product type. However, EPC has an added set of digits for identifying each individual item. These digits collectively provide a unique identification for an item. An EPC number contains the following items and its structure is shown in Fig. 5.7:

- Header for identifying the length, type, structure, version, and generation of EPC
- Manager number for identifying the company
- Object class for identifying the class of objects to which an individual item belongs

Additional fields can be added to the structure of EPC for encoding and decoding information from different product codes. In this case, EPC is just an information reference to the stored information about the individual item.

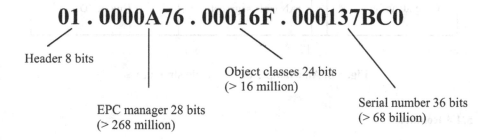

01 . 0000A76 . 00016F . 000137BC0

Header 8 bits

Object classes 24 bits
(> 16 million)

EPC manager 28 bits
(> 268 million)

Serial number 36 bits
(> 68 billion)

Fig. 5.7. The structure of EPC (96 bits)

5.4.3 Ubiquitous ID Center

The Ubiquitous ID Center was formed to establish and popularize the core technology for automatically identifying physical objects and locations and to work toward the ultimate objective of realizing a ubiquitous computing environment.

In the ubiquitous ID architecture, real-world objects are embedded with ubiquitous ID tags (unique ubiquitous identification code or ucode tags). These ucode tags store ID codes (ubiquitous IDs) to distinguish their objects, along with some additional identifying information. The information that cannot be stored in ucode tags is maintained in the database across the network.

The ucode is the most fundamental element in the ubiquitous ID architecture that the Ubiquitous ID Center has developed. Currently, there are many different code systems applied to objects in the distribution sector and other fields. For example, JAN (Japanese Article Number) codes, EAN (European Article Number) codes, and UPC (Universal Product Code) codes are used in barcodes, while ISBN (International Standard Bibliographic Number) codes are used for books and other publications. These codes are assigned to the types of products, and they are not used to distinguish individual product item. In contrast, the ucode is used to identify individual items. As a code, the ucode is 128 bits long and can be extended as needed in 128-bit units to 256, 384, or 512 bits.

The greatest advantage of ucode is that it can be used as a metacode system that can encompass various existing identification codes. With a length of 128 bits, it can accommodate many of these different numbers and identifications: from JAN, UPC, and EAN barcodes to ISBN and ISSN publication IDs, and from IP addresses assigned by hosts for Internet connections to a telephone number. We use the JAN code as an example to explain how ucode works. The standard JAN code is a 13-digit decimal. Expressing each digit of the decimal with 4 bits, we can express the entire JAN code with 52 bits. The corresponding 128-bit ucode is shown in Fig. 5.8.

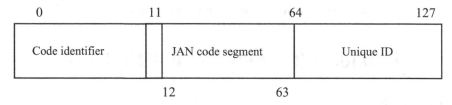

Fig. 5.8. An example of the ucode structure

5.4.4 Remarks

Currently, there is no common RFID global standard. As a result, many companies hesitate to adopt RFID because of potential compatibility issues. Some people worry that a universally accepted standard will never evolve. Let us take frequency as an example. It is clear that low frequency (9–135 KHz) and high-frequency (13.56 MHz) RFID tags can be used globally without a license. However, ultrahigh frequency (300–1200 MHz) cannot be used globally as there is no single global standard. In North America, UHF can be used unlicensed for 902–928 MHz, but this range of UHF is not accepted in France as it interferes with its military bandwidths. In Europe UHF is under consideration for 862–870 MHz. For Australia and New Zealand, 915–927 MHz is the range of UHF for unlicensed use. For China, South Korea, and Japan, there is no regulation for the use of UHF yet. However, initial proposals have been made: for China, the proposed UHF is 915 MHz; for South Korea, the UHF range between 910 and 914 MHz is proposed; for Japan, the UHF range between 950 and 956 MHz is under consideration. The frequency 2.45 GHz is the frequency of microwave. The detailed allowable radiofrequency spectra around the world are shown in Fig. 5.9.

These concerns are reasonable if RFID is used for solutions across continents, or at least across companies. However, if RFID is used for close loop applications, for example, within a company in the same location, then these concerns are no longer valid. There are many close loop applications in which RFID is applicable, such as security access control in a company location, asset management, warehouse management, and manufacture management.

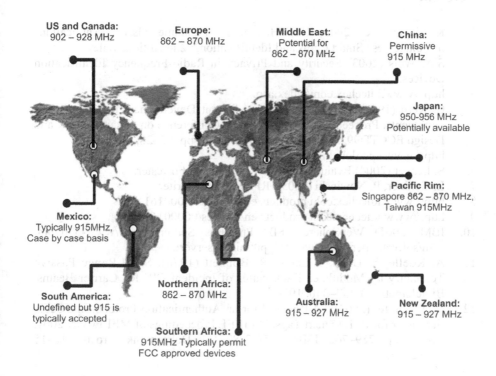

Fig. 5.9. Allowable radiofrequency spectra around the world

5.5 Summary

This chapter introduced RFID technology and its applications. The fundamentals of RFID technologies, tags and readers, middleware, and standards were covered. RFID applications were also discussed.

There is no doubt that RFID has a huge business potential, including many applications such as access control, security management, purchasing, manufacturer, supply chain management, and distribution logistics, even though there are still unsolved issues such as there is no single global RFID standard and there are still not enough industries/companies that have adopted this technology. Given the great business potential and the advances of RFID technology, wide deployment of RFID is just a matter of time, perhaps within a couple of years or so.

References

1.   K. Finkenzeller (2003) RFID-Handbook, "Fundamentals and Applications in Contact less Smart Cards and Identification," 2nd edition, Wiley.
2.   S.A. Weis (2003) Security and Privacy in Radio-Frequency Identification Devices.
3.   http://www.idtechex.com/index.asp.
4.   C. Kern (1999) RFID-Technology – Recent Development and Future Requirements. Proceedings of the European Conference on Circuit Theory and Design ECCTD99, 30.08.–02.09.1999, Vol. 1, pp. 25–28, Stresa, Italy.
5.   http://www.epcglobalinc.org.
6.   S. Leaver (2004) Evaluating RFID Middleware, Forrester.
7.   L. Geldner, P. Nowiński (2003), RFID Reader/Writer
8.   http://www.idtechex.com/products/en/articles/00000161.asp.
9.   http://www.idtechex.com/products/en/articles/00000169.asp.
10.   IBM (2005) WebSphere RFID Premises Server, http://www-306.ibm.com/software/pervasive/ws_rfid_premises_server/.
11.   A. Koelle, S. Depp, J. Landt, R. Bobbett (1976), Short-Range Passive Telemetry by Modulated Backscatter of Incident CW RF Carrier Beams. Biotelemetry, 3:337–340, 1976.
12.   M. Feldhofer (2004), "A Proposal for an Authentication Protocol in a Security Layer for RFID Smart Tags," In IEEE Proceedings of MELECON 2004, Vol. 2, pp. 759–762, ISBN 0-7803-8271-4, Dubronvnik, Croatia, 12–15 May 2004.

6 Software Infrastructure for Context-Aware Mobile Computing

C.L. Wang, X.L. Zhang, N. Belaramani, P.L. Siu, Y. Chow, and F.C.M. Lau

Department of Computer Science, The University of Hong Kong, Pokfulam Road, Hong Kong

6.1 Introduction

6.1.1 New Environment

Computing has been an ever-changing paradigm since the beginning of its creation. In the past decade, small, wireless devices, such as personal digital assistants, cell phones, and handheld PCs, etc. have become extremely popular. These light-weight devices, together with the ubiquitous wireless connections, have successfully supplemented desktop computing, allowing us to move about with computation capabilities and network resources at hand. Recent advances in embedded technologies are another thrust, aiming ambitiously to "computerize" everything. We shall see more and more smart widgets like watches, toys, or shoes, and intelligent appliances, such as microwave ovens and refrigerators, all empowered by embedded processors. We shall live and work in resource-rich environments, where devices of different functionalities and capabilities would readily offer their services to us, and these same devices, static or mobile, would be interconnected via wired or wireless connections, achieving a true ubiquity of computation and information services.

The scope of computation will be dramatically extended. It could happen anytime, anywhere, for any length of time, span any number and types of devices, and offer exciting services to support our everyday activities. We would be free to move around, having our computational tasks follow us and execute continuously, and taking advantages of the environments' resources. This implies an extended form of mobile computing, i.e., context-aware mobile computing, in which the user's mobility is decoupled from the device's mobility, and the main goal of the supporting computational systems is to satisfy the requirements of the mobile user and provide appropriate services fitting their situations.

6.1.2 New Features

Context-aware mobile computing sets itself apart from conventional computing paradigms with the following new features:

- *Environmental heterogeneity.* Heterogeneity is a definite trait of future computing environments. The range of computing devices widens continuously, and they dramatically differ in computing capabilities, including storage, processing power, screen size, networking, to name a few. Such devices would seamlessly interact and coordinate among themselves to fulfill a user's requirement. Heterogeneity in this context is a double-edged sword: on the one hand, specialties of various devices allow for different user preferences; on the other hand, there is the challenge to bridge the differences of those devices. Meanwhile, as users move across spatial locations, they come upon different configurations of these physical spaces, including the devices equipped and the software installed.

- *Dynamism.* Dynamism comes from both the environment and the user. From the environment, variation in resource conditions, including memory consumption, battery life, network bandwidth, etc., induces changes that must be carefully attended to. User mobility introduces explicit changes of the execution location. On the other hand, human thoughts and behaviors tend easily to be in a state of flux. Some users might serendipitously change their goal or course of actions in reacting to a changed situation. To deal with changes is in fact a frequent and constant task for the computational systems.

- *Support for mobile people.* In traditional mobile computing genres, device mobility and code mobility have been extensively explored. The former considers mobile users moving with their devices across physical locations and geographical regions, without dropping the connection. The latter addresses dynamically relocating the execution and changing the bindings of code fragments to devices in which the execution would continue [8]. In context-aware mobile computing, however, the focus is on the people who are mobile. A user may or may not carry a device; rather, the environments along the way are responsible for receiving and executing the user's tasks. This differs from the code relocation in that (1) a task may span a set of local devices in each environment and (2) the task may not be resumed using the same code segments, due to changes in the environment. These issues were seldom addressed in previous mobile computing research.

- *Context awareness.* Context awareness refers to the ability of a computational system to understand the situation at hand and adjust its behavior accordingly. As emphasized by Dey [7], context is any information that can be used to characterize the situation of an entity. An entity is a person, place, or object that is considered relevant to the interaction between a user and an application, including the user and the application themselves. It typically includes location; identity; activity and state of people, groups, and objects. Context awareness has become increasingly a reality because of the availability of inexpensive and powerful sensors for monitoring the environment. When computation moves beyond the desktop and into our environments, mechanisms must exist to reveal the relevant conditions, whether physical or computational. By understanding a mobile user's situation, computer systems could derive knowledge, such as the user's intent, and then act proactively on behalf of the user. Context awareness therefore guides the adaptation of the computation, in a way similar to how we adjust our behavior under different situations, to maximize the user's benefits.

These new features pose great challenges that have not been completely met by existing solutions. Better or new software infrastructure supports need to be investigated for realizing context-aware mobile computing.

6.2 Context-Aware Mobile Computing Infrastructure

6.2.1 New Requirements

Admittedly, some issues related to context-aware mobile computing have already emerged in conventional distributed computing and mobile computing areas. The solutions however are inadequate. Software infrastructures for context-aware mobile computing should be designed anew, taking explicitly into consideration the following requirements.

Mobility support. Mobility support has its root in mobile computing and distributed computing, which deal with device mobility and computation mobility, respectively. In the future, support for mobility at a higher level will also be needed, targeting at user-level tasks and their continuity. In a heterogeneous environment, the execution of a task suspended at one location could hardly be restored as is at another location. Therefore, existing solutions for task mobility, such as process or thread migration, might not be entirely applicable. Rather, the system should strive for a reasonable configuration of environmental resources to fulfill a user's task, and at the same time maintain the execution continuity to achieve user's satisfaction.

Dynamic adaptation. Dynamic adaptation is the modification of an application during its execution. The heterogeneity and dynamism of future environments make it an apparent and important requirement. As indicated in [24], the need for adaptation arises when a significant mismatch exists between a resource's supply and demand. Mobility is a typical cause, since the source and destination environments may very likely differ in hardware/software configurations. Dynamic adaptation is thus required to map the previous task onto the new environment. Also, context-aware mobile applications need to adapt, according to situations that may require different behaviors. It is usually burdensome, if not impossible, for applications to handle the whole chore of adaptation; therefore, system support for dynamic adaptation is necessary. Various adaptation techniques have been previously addressed – from lower-level techniques of dynamically changing routing information to changing the quality of data, altering the composition of an application, etc.

[19]; however, they are not readily amenable to meeting the requirements in context-aware mobile computing.

Context-awareness support. Many would agree that it is difficult to build real context-aware mobile applications. The challenges reside in both the provision and the usage of context. The efficient gathering of context data from various sensors, the proper synthesis of information, and the in-time delivery to context consumers are complex tasks involved in providing context. On the other hand, the appropriate application model and use pattern of context are still under investigation. Most existing approaches to context-aware application development are ad hoc in nature, making the development hard to evolve and to reuse the technologies and context information. System support is thus required for the supply of context, and the deployment and execution of context-aware mobile applications.

User orientation. User orientation is the ultimate goal of computation. Traditionally, computers interact with users at a low level of abstraction – that of applications and individual devices. A user explicitly invokes an application that is preinstalled on a device to use the functionality it provides. In future, however, the notion of application will become obsolete; users should be able to interact with computing systems at a much higher level. This lets the user focus on the tasks to accomplish and delegate the low-level activities to systems support.

6.2.2 Representative Projects

There are many ongoing research projects, addressing different aspects of context-aware mobile computing. This section reviews three representative ones: the Aura project of CMU [1], the Gaia project of UIUC [9], and the one.world project of UW [17]. The emphasis will be on their respective approaches to tackling the new requirements as listed earlier.

Aura at CMU

The Aura project at CMU identifies *user attention* as the most precious resource. It features the concept of "task-driven computing," wherein systems are used to support high-level activities of users, i.e., tasks. A *task* embodies a user's computing intention, which typically involves several applications and information resources. The *task model* captures this knowledge and other task-related information, including user preferences about the alternative ways to carry out a task and the QoS tradeoffs. The infrastructure exploits the task model to automatically configure and reconfigure the environment on behalf of a user, thus releasing him/her from the low-level management activities.

A task is represented as a set of *abstract services*. The type of each abstract service stands for *a unit of abstract functionality*, e.g., the ability to display a document. Computing devices and available software services that implement such functionality are wrapped as *service suppliers*. Upon task instantiation, the infrastructure binds each abstract service to a concrete service supplier. This indirection process ensures the same task to be realized in different ways, according to the environment's resource conditions.

Aura promotes *task-based adaptation* [20], indicating that the ultimate goal of adaptation is to maximize an environment's utility for a user's task. Therefore, user intent and preferences should be used to guide the system's decision on how to best configure the environment. This knowledge is typically missing in current adaptive systems. Aura achieves the dynamic adaptation through two approaches, changing the binding of abstract service to another supplier and changing the fidelity level of a supplier. (Related projects in Aura, such as Coda and Odyssey, also address system-level adaptation like cyber foraging and off-loading [1].) Such adaptations take place when resource availability changes, the task QoS requirements change a task migration request is issued, etc. Aura relies on an econometric-based notion to quantify the system utility and defines the *cost of configuration* to judge whether an adaptation is worthwhile.

Aura advocates task mobility, i.e., a user-level task can be suspended at one place and resumed later at another. Upon migration, a task management module coordinates with the service suppliers for capturing the user-perceivable state of the current task, which typically includes the set of services supporting the task, the user-level settings associated with each of those services, the materials being worked on, interaction parameters (window size, cursor position, etc.), and the user's preferences for QoS tradeoffs. The current suppliers are then deactivated. At the new environment, reconfiguration is conducted to reinstantiate the task, and the newly selected suppliers are resumed with the user-level state.

A contextual information service (CIS) [14] provides applications with a virtual database view of physical entities and available resources in the local environment. It explicitly provides support for on-demand computation of context information and meta-attributes, such as accuracy, confidence, sample time, sample interval duration, etc. The CIS defines four classes of interested entities: people, devices, physical spaces, and networks. It also considers several simple relations among these classes. However, the support for semantic inference and the exploitation of contextual facts are limited.

GAIA at UIUC

The GAIA project at UIUC aims at support for developing that and deploying applications over active spaces. Gaia proposes a middleware adopts the concepts of a conventional operating system and abstracts the space as a single reactive and programmable entity. It manages and coordinates the resources, provides support for application deployment, and offers a set of basic services that are used by all applications. It also comprises an application framework, offering a set of building blocks for mobility, adaptation, and dynamic binding services.

Gaia models its application based on an extended model-view-controller framework. Each application is composed of several input (view), output (presentation), and logic (model) components. Each component can individually exploit a different device for execution. At runtime, an application is partitioned across a set of devices for input/output, processing, and interacting with the user.

Applications in Gaia are built with no assumptions of the spaces. Instead, each application is described in a space-independent description file (AGD) that lists the application components and their requirements. Gaia customizes the application by finding and configuring the target space according to the specified requirements in the AGD and generates an application customized description (ACD), which records the concrete configuration information, such as what specific components to use, how many instances to create, where to instantiate the components, etc.

Gaia investigates *structural adaptation* of an application. During the execution of an application, each of its components can be individually replaced, multiplied in number, and relocated. Such an application can thus display different forms during its lifetime, termed as *application polymorphism*. To guarantee the consistency, Gaia introduces the *semantic similarity* between application components, based on predefined ontological hierarchies. The replacement of a component is only allowed if the substitute allows the user to perform the same task, thereby preserving the semantics of an application.

Gaia supports intra-space and inter-space application mobility. Intra-space mobility moves the interactive components of an application (input/output) to different devices inside the same active space. For interspace mobility, Gaia captures the structure and current state (application-level state) of the migrating application in the ACD file, and configures the targeted space according to the ACD requirements and the space's capabilities. Typically, the *structural adaptation* is also needed, as the source and destination spaces might differ in hardware/software equipment. Finally, the user's perceivable application-level state is resumed and the application is reinstantiated.

Gaia's context support includes a common, reusable context model, an infrastructure that gathers context information from different sensors and delivers context information to applications, and a mechanism that allows applications to specify different behaviors in different contexts. Contexts in Gaia are modeled as first-order predicates, with operations like conjunction, disjunction, negation, and quantification. Higher-level contexts can be deducted from basic sensed contexts using rule-based approaches. The structures of different context predicates are specified in ontology, which is used to check the validity of context predicates and to facilitate writing different context-aware rules.

one.world

one.world identifies the challenges in building applications that constantly adapt to dynamic environments. It proposes dedicated systems' support to ease the programmers' task, which features the separation of data and functionality, the exposure of changes to applications, and the ad hoc composition of applications and devices.

one.world abandons the commonly adopted object abstraction for data and functionality. It represents data using tuples, which essentially are records with named and typed fields, and implements functionality in forms of components. This separation of data and functionality allows them to evolve independently and facilitates data sharing. A special abstraction, called *environment*, groups the data tuples and functional components to form applications. It hosts and isolates applications, serving as the combined role of file system directories and nested processes.

Asynchronous events underlie the system's communication mechanism, i.e., all components' interactions. They also expose changes to the applications. Upon execution, application components function as event handlers to directly deal with changes, such as the user's switching of devices and variation in the execution conditions, etc.

one.world relies on virtual machines to provide a common execution platform, thus allowing applications to be run on a wide range of devices. To address the environmental dynamism, *discovery service* is explicitly provided for the programmers. Applications therefore will actively locate and connect to services on other devices, instead of always assuming the availability of resources. one.world also promotes migration as the application's default behavior and offers the primitives to ease the programming. *Checkpointing* captures the execution state of an environment tree (i.e., all nested environments) and saves it as a tuple. *Migration* provides the ability to move or copy an environment and its contents, including all stored tuples, application components, and nested environments.

The adaptation in one.world is mainly achieved by migrating the application among devices. It is issued when a user's location changes, when the resource scarcity happens, or when a server replication is needed, etc. one.world deals with migration in a rather straightforward way: First, the virtual machine provides a uniform execution environment across different devices and hardware architectures; second, an application's execution state is checkpointed and stored in its associated environment; third, the environment containing the application's code, state, and persistent data is copied or moved to another device; finally, the discovery service ensures an application to restore access to the appropriate resources in the new execution environment.

6.3 A Case Study – The Sparkle Project

The Sparkle project at HKU [13] proposes a component-based software infrastructure for supporting context-aware mobile computing, which features a flexible and intuitive *functionality adaptation* technique. In the literature, various adaptation techniques have been previously addressed – from lower-level techniques of dynamically changing routing information to changing the fidelity of data. However, functionality adaptation, i.e., dynamically changing how an application carries out its functionality, is not very well explored. Techniques do exist, however, with limited flexibility and adaptive capability. For example, many reconfigurable component systems support updating software components at runtime. This often involves bringing the system to a state in which changes can occur, by capturing the system state, changing the component, restoring the state, and informing the system that the new component can be used. Such mechanisms are often used for upgrading long-running applications or operating systems, which cannot be switched off, and not so much for adapting to changes in resource availability or environmental context.

Sparkle regards functionality adaptation a key to meet the requirements of context-aware mobile computing. In its vision, computation essentially is used to realize certain functionality; the same functionality can potentially be realized by many different implementations; through dynamically selecting the most appropriate one, based on the runtime situation, including user factors and resource conditions, computation can flexibly adapt to the scenario at hand. The Sparkle project implements this idea via a new application model and underlying system support.

6.3.1 Facet-Based Application Model

Traditional applications typically have intertangled code and are deployed as a bundled whole. Such applications are not suitable for context-aware mobile computing environments for the following reasons:

- *Fixed functionality and hard to adapt.* The functionality an application provides is often bounded. Extension or upgrade is only possible with add-on patches. With limited user customization support, an application forces all users to put up with the same "look-and-use." Altering part of such an application often has effects that ripple through the entire software, which are difficult to contain and might even render the application inoperable. Run-time modification is virtually intractable. Therefore, the tightly coupled structure of traditional application is not appropriate for future environments, which demand highly adaptive software.

- *Uneconomical usage of device.* A user typically uses only a subset of an application's functionality. Possibly due to economic considerations, traditional applications tend to bundle as much functionality as possible in a single package. Tucking the whole into a small device is neither necessary nor economical, considering the limited storage. Ideally, software should be supplied according to the situation and what is really needed by the user.

To tackle these problems, Sparkle proposes to model an application as a set of components, instead of a monolithic chunk. During execution, the components are dynamically downloaded from the network and linked to the runtime environment to form an application on the fly. After use, these components can be unloaded and thrown away. Note that "network" here can be taken just a placeholder; it could be any mechanism supplying components upon demand.

Components in Sparkle are called *facets*. Each facet implements a single well-defined *functionality*. Essentially, a functionality can be viewed as a contract defining what should be done. The contract includes input and output specifications, pre- and post-conditions, and some side effects. Each functionality typically has different facets as implementations that vary in capability and requirements. A facet consists of two parts (1) *Shadow*, which provides meta-information about the facet, including the facet ID, the funcID of the functionality it achieves, input and output specification, its resource requirements, the functionality it requires to finish its task, etc. The shadow is represented in human- and machine-readable XML format. (2) *Code segment*, which is the body of the executable code that implements the functionality. The code segment can consist of several Java classes.

However, there is only one class that contains the publicly callable method corresponding to the functionality contract.

Facet is designed to be *disposable*. It has no persistent state; therefore each invocation is independent of the previous ones. This allows it to be discarded from the runtime immediately after use. The feature is especially desirable for freeing up resources and memory on small devices. A facet may depend on other functionalities to realize its own operations. Such functionalities are called its *facet dependencies*. Note that facet dependencies are decided by a particular facet's implementation. Therefore, even facets for the same functionality could have different facet dependencies.

Each application in Sparkle is associated with a special abstraction, called *container*, which stores an updatable user interface and a list of *facet specifications*. The user interface is a machine-dependent representation that bridges the user and the facets. Users invoke the container to bring up the user interface and request facets with the corresponding specifications. The container is also the place where the state information and application data are stored.

6.3.2 The Sparkle System Architecture

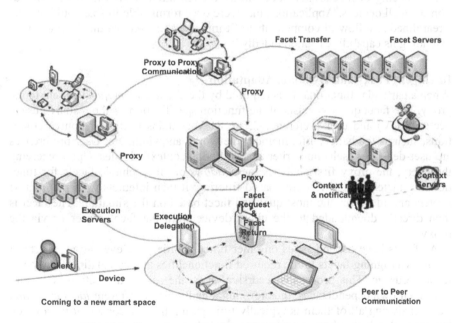

Fig. 6.1. Overview of the Sparkle system architecture

An overview of the Sparkle system is shown in Fig. 6.1. In Sparkle, facets are hosted on *facet servers*. A *client system* on each device takes charge of retrieving and executing the facets. It requests for facets from *proxy servers* or peer clients. Proxy servers analyze the requirements specified in the query and the current context, then select and return a suitable facet to the client. There are *execution servers* around to provide a "computational grid" for devices to delegate execution of facets to. A client may also retrieve data from a peer, or it may ask a peer to execute a facet for it. *Context servers* gather, store, and process contextual data extracted from the low-level data sources and supply high-level contexts to the systems and applications.

Client System and Streamlined Execution

The client system provides an execution environment for facets. It is written in pure Java and is small enough to be installed on various client devices, thus enabling the portability of facets. The main responsibility of a client system is to handle the routine of dynamic facet composition, hiding the details from the programmers. It accepts facet specifications from the client and negotiates with proxies and peers for suitable facets. It then loads and links them up with the runtime, and then discards them after usage. A local facet cache is included both to improve the performance of facet retrieval and to enable peer-to-peer sharing of facets. The client system also sees to the dynamic discovery of proxies and peers, keeps track of resource availability, and deals with mobility. The dynamic loading, executing, and unloading of facets have successfully broken through the limited configuration of small devices. Applications that were once formidable in size could thus be streamlined as a flow of components to fit into a resource-constrained device, thus extending its capabilities "unboundedly."

Intelligent Proxy and Dynamic Adaptation

When a particular functionality is required by the client, a *facet query* is sent to the proxy. The facet query consists of the function specifications – the resource usage vector (RUV) and user preferences. The RUV contains runtime resource conditions, such as the battery life, memory, network bandwidth, etc. User preferences are user-dependent selection criteria, specified in contextual rules. Upon receiving the query, the proxy first analyzes the *shadows* of all reachable facets for functionality matching and resource-based filtering; it then interacts with the context servers and identifies the most qualified facet based on the situation. The facet is then directly downloaded to the client device from the facet server or via the proxy.

As facets have dependencies on other functionalities, the evaluation of a facet involves assigning facets to the required functionalities and calculating the overall resource usage. This process is recursive, since the assigned facets may in turn have their own dependencies, thus forming a multitude of different *facet execution tree*. Analyzing all of them is typically time-prohibiting. A conservative solution is proposed, which adopts a reasonable prediction on the resource usage for executing a functionality without aiming at an accurate facet execution tree.

Sparkle introduces the possibility of dynamic functionality adaptation via the postponed binding of the abstract functionality to the concrete implementation. This concept is shared by peer projects such as Aura and Gaia. The difference is that the execution in Sparkle does not require the complete instantiation of all abstract functionalities; rather, the selection is made step by step, i.e., the facet is brought in one at a time. As different facets have different dependencies, the subsequent steps are not statically fixed, but left to run-time decision. This introduces more flexibility and dynamic adaptability to computation.

Sparkle also proposes to enhance the facet-matching algorithm with ontological support [15]. In reality, the same functionality may mean different things for different users or in different situations. An ontology-based description of functionality as well as user knowledge could fill in the gap between user cognition and the concepts of computational systems.

Mobility Subsystem and Flexible Migration
Sparkle conceives a more flexible mechanism to support mobility in future environments. It regards "lightweight" and "adaptive" as two new requirements that challenge existing solutions. The *lightweight mobile code system* (LMCS) and the *context-aware state management system* are thus proposed.

LMCS handles strong mobility of mobile code and caters to various modes of mobility (e.g., code on demand, remote evaluation). Different from conventional migration techniques, its design targets a lightweight solution for small devices. LMCS discretizes the transmission of code and execution state, and relies on a state-on-demand (SOD) scheme for executing the mobile code. Upon a migration request, LMCS inspects all active facets under the current execution tree and captures the execution state via a Java byte-code instrument technique. It then moves the container, the state, and the identifiers of the active facets to the other device. At the receiving end, the container is extracted; the facets are refetched from the proxies; and the execution is resumed with the corresponding states.

LMCS differs from most conventional solutions in two aspects. First, the migration does not transfer the code; rather, at the destination device, the facets are again retrieved from the proxy. Second, the SOD scheme chops the execution state into segments and ships only a portion of the required stack frames for each migration hop. Both contribute to the saving of bandwidth consumption from unnecessary transfers. Further, SOD suits especially well when a user's movement induces a tight sequence of migration hops. The computation thus is naturally distributed along the trail in a resource-economic way. Figure 6.2 shows the difference between traditional migration solution and that of LMCS.

The *context-aware state management system* (CASM) enables manipulation of data state during the migration. It is motivated by the observation that migrating an application (or a task) between heterogeneous devices or spaces should typically involve application adaptation as well, such as substituting a component or altering the structure of the application. In this sense, the application state captured before migration could hardly be used after the adaptation. Aura and Gaia share this vision; however they choose to avoid this issue by raising the level of state. Both projects assume that exchangeable parts would stick to the same state specification; therefore, the captured high-level state can still be used *as is* to resume an application.

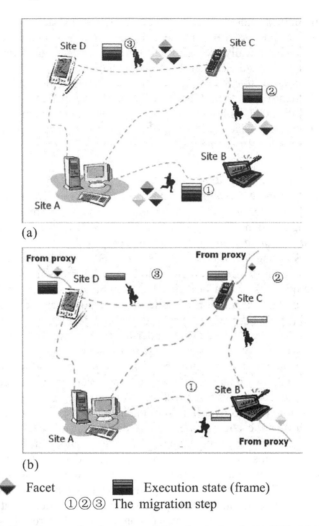

Fig. 6.2. Migration mechanism in traditional solution in LMCS. (**a**) The typical migration mechanism in traditional solution. The code and execution state are shipped together from device to device. (**b**) The mi-gration mechanism in LMCS. Each time only a portion of the execution state in. The associated facet is brought in on demand at the destination device. The memory and bandwidth usage is thus reduced

In contrast, Sparkle explicitly takes care of the need for transforming the state by aiming at a more flexible binding of migration and adaptation. By observation, Sparkle categorizes the state into three groups, namely fixed, mutable and dispos-able. *Fixed state* is essential to computation and typically not affected by contex-tual changes. Such state will be transferred intact. *Disposable state* is what becomes irrelevant after migration (adaptation), for example, certain variables probably no longer exist after substituting the code. Such a state will typically be filtered off at the source device to reduce the communication cost. *Mutable state* is typically context sensitive and would better be adapted to new requirements, for example, the volume of a music player should be raised at a noisy place. Adjusting such a state will be arbitrated by predefined context-aware rules. In the current implementation, Sparkle focuses on data state, i.e., the internal variable values at a point of execution. Fig. 3 demonstrates a typical scenario and rationale of the CASM.

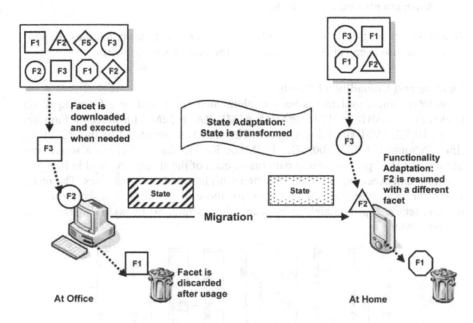

Fig. 6.3. Scenario of mobile function and state adaptation

Context-Aware Middleware Support
Sparkle lays a middleware (CAM) for context-aware support, which automatically collects data from environmental sources and derives high-level context information. It has a dual purpose. First, it runs on context servers and supplies the necessary context information to the proxies for smarter facet selection. Second, it eases developing context-aware applications with simple, unified application programming interfaces. It allows developers to specify context-aware rules and monitors the interested events on behalf of the applications. The middleware adopts an ontology-based context model, in order to facilitate the validating, reusing, and managing of context information. An inference engine, based on Jena ontology server, is exploited to reason over two kinds of rules, including the transitive rules of the ontology and the user-defined application-specific rules.

Context consumers, such as the applications and the proxies, incorporate a client of CAM to communicate the requirements and receive the event notification. They could also explicitly query specific properties of interested entities. For current implementation, the CAM has established several ontologies for campus life and a set of context-aware applications have been developed. (See Sect. 6.3.3 for experimental details).

6.3.3 Experiments and Evaluations

Sparkle has been used in several applications to demonstrate its features. Experiments have also been conducted to evaluate the system's performance.

Loading and Unloading of Facets

A prototype client system has been implemented and tested on a Compaq iPAQ Pocket PC (206MHz Intel StrongARM, 64MB RAM+32MB Flash ROM, Familiar Linux v0.5.2, JVM Blackdown-1.3.1). The iPAQ is connected to the PC proxy (Intel Pentium II MMX 300MHz, 128MHz, RedHat Linux 7.1) via a serial connection of 115 kbps. The timing patterns of each of the stages involved in bringing in a facet and executing it are investigated with facets of different sizes. The result shows the most time-consuming stages are those of getting facets from the network (latency, approximately 2.3s; transmission rate, 80 kbps) and loading the received bytes.

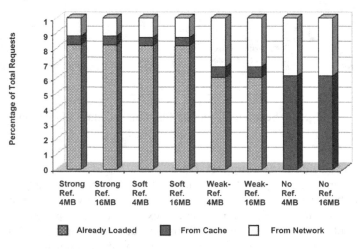

Fig. 6.4. Different types of references and sizes of heap on the IPAG

Another experiment tests the performance with relation to different types of Java references to dereference facet instances, i.e., to discard the facet. When an application requests a facet, the performance will be gained if the facet is still loaded, i.e., has not been discarded after the previous usage. This experiment runs a benchmark application with 21 facets and 724 facet calls. The ratio of the number of facet calls, which had facets still loaded in the runtime, is compared to those that could be retrieved locally as well as to those that had to be retrieved from the network. The reduced percentage of calls forwarded to the network implies a better performance. The heap size is set to 4 and 16 MB, so as to also investigate the effect of memory availability on performance.

The result shown in Fig. 6.4 suggests that soft references are probably best suited for the client system. Strong references disallow the discard of facets, which goes against the "throwable" philosophy. The benefit of weak references when compared to "no references" is not as significant in the presence of a cache.

An image processing application, *SparkleViewer*, has been built to demonstrate the feasibility of facet-based programming. The application consists of 15 facets, each providing a different functionality, out of which ten were root facets. The structure of the application is depicted in Fig. 6.5. The root facets essentially provide the functionality to open, blur, find edges, and flip images. The other facets provide functionalities such as matrix convolvers and converters. Fig. 6.6 shows the screen shots of this application.

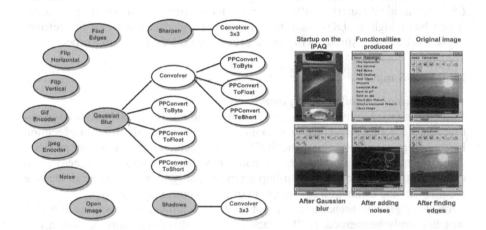

Fig. 6.5. Facets of the Sparkleviewer application

Fig. 6.6. Screen photo of the Sparkleviewer application

Functionality Adaptation

Through dynamically selecting facets for a client request, the intelligent proxy takes main responsibility for achieving functionality adaptation. In the literature, there seems to exist no mechanism for directly evaluating the quality of functionality adaptation; therefore, a metric is defined, called adaptation quality index (AQI):

$$AQ1 = \text{resource\_index} \times \text{weight (resource)}$$
$$+ \text{capability\_index} \times \text{weight (capability)}$$
$$+ \text{preferences\_index} \times \text{weight (preferences)}$$

The *resource index* is a fraction of the resource usage for executing a functionality and the client's available resources; the *capability index* is a fraction of a facet's capability and the largest possible capability for the functionality; and the *preferences index* is a fraction of a facet's score and the total scores of the user preferences. The experiment assumed the three factors to have equal weights. The test runs on a PC with Intel Pentium 4 2.26GHz PC to examine the quality as well as the performance of functionality adaptation.

A chess game called Othello has been developed for testing, which consists of 19 different functionalities. Five facets of different capabilities are designed for each functionality, giving a total of 95 facets available for the application. In the experiment, different requesting ranges and user preferences are used. The proxy system yields different selection results according to the execution context. The average AQI in selecting a facet is around 65% of the ideal functionality. If variations in user preferences are ignored, it can be as high as 0.85. Also, the processing and decision times for returning a facet are measured, being on average, 300 ms and 260 ms respectively.

Migration Support

- *Lightweight Mobile Code System*
LMCS was tested on two standard PCs (Intel Pentium III 650MHz 128MB memory, Linux 2.4.18). Three recursive applications, which exhibit different execution behaviors, are used to evaluate the SOD scheme, including the Fibonacci program (Fib), the quicksort program (QSort), and the N-Queen program (NQueen). Two experiments, single-hop and multi-hop migration, have been conducted to analyze the memory and bandwidth consumption of the scheme, respectively.

In the single-hop scenario, a state of 17 frames formed by executing Fib (35) was uniformly segmented, so that each of the resulting segments contained two stack frames. The experiment result shows that only 529 bytes of memory on average are needed to migrate the execution, which is much lower than that needed in a typical execution without SOD; hence SOD is advantageous in supporting migration in a memory-limited environment.

The testing result under the multihop scenario (Table 6.1) also supports the conclusion that adopting SOD could reduce the memory and bandwidth consumption. More detailed discussion can be found in [6].

Table 6.1. Bandwidth and memory usage for three applications based on the multihop scenario

Testing application	Fib (35)	QSort (5,000)	NQueen-1 (10)	NQueen-2 (10)
Number of hops	12	12	40	40
Total bandwidth used in MB (normal)	0.327	1.7	33.6	33.9
Total bandwidth used in MB (with SOD)	0.315	0.574	32.18	16.36
Total % bandwidth saved by SOD	3.64	66.5	4.22	51.8
Avg. normal code size in KB	27	143	768	848
Avg. initial memory usage with SOD in KB	5.97	15.77	686	259

- *Context-Aware State Management*

A universal browser (UB) application has been developed to demonstrate the usage of context-aware state management. Unlike traditional Web browsers, the UB targets "browsing whatever you want." The special graphical user interface allows users to dynamically retrieve the functionalities they want, such as playing games, editing photos, etc. Figure 6.7 shows a UB running on a PC. When a user migrates the UB, the data state is categorized into three types and processed according to the context. For example, the screen resolution as a mutable type is degraded from 1,400 × 1,050 to 320 × 480.

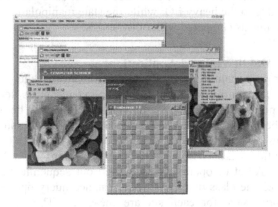

Fig. 6.7. The screen photo of the UB application with three functions: a Web browser, an image editor and a Bomberman game

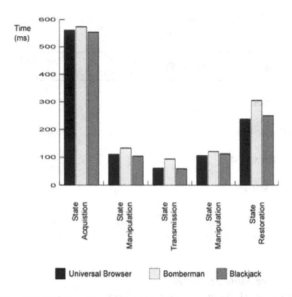

Fig. 6.8. Timing for each migration stage manipulation

Experiments have been done to evaluate the performance with state manipulation. The time needed for each migration stage has been measured for three applications, including the UB, the Bomberman, and the Blackjack games. They each are migrated from one desktop PC (Intel Pentium 4 2.26GHz, Windows 2000) to a notebook PC (Intel Pentium III 1133 MHz, Windows XP). The result is shown in Fig. 6.8. It can be observed that the state acquisition state consumes most time, which is mainly due to the heavy I/O; while the state manipulation phase does not occupy so much time as compared with other stages.

Context-Aware Middleware and Applications

Scalability is an important concern for context-aware middleware support. As changes happen frequently, the number of context instances keeps increasing. Albeit this, the performance of the server operations should be guaranteed. An experiment has been conducted to evaluate the responsiveness and memory usage of the context-aware middleware (CAM), based on a normal PC as the context server (Intel Pentium4 2.26GHz, 512MB memory, Linux 3.0). The server runs Jena version 2.2. A set of operations is carried out sequentially, including two adds, one remove, one class query, and one instance query operations. The total time and memory usage for each set are measured. The number of context instances is increased from 0 to 1,800. The processing time is averaged to 3.4 s, with variations within 0.2 s. The total memory usage gradually increases from 16 to 20 MB. The results show that the system does not degrade much with the number of instances increasing.

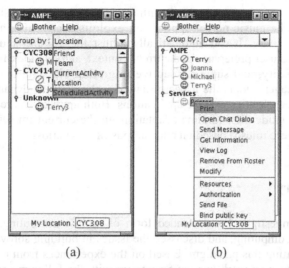

Fig. 6.9. Screen photo of the content- aware instant messenger application. (a) The options for dynamic grouping of the buddy. (b) A resource buddy printer and the available operations on it

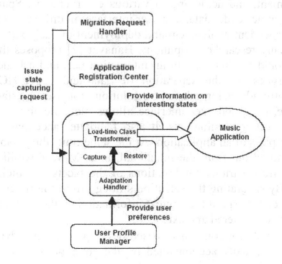

Fig 6.10. The migration manager and working mechanism

Two context-aware applications, including an instant messenger and a music player, have been developed to demonstrate the usage of CAM. The instant messenger application advocates the concept of *"everything is your buddy,"* and features situation-aware buddy grouping, context-aware service discovery, etc. Figure 6.9a shows the dynamic grouping options based on the buddies' situations.

Figure 6.9b shows a "printer buddy," with available interactions listed at the right mouse click. The music player application exploits user profile and context to finetune its behavior. It can automatically adjust the volume and sound effect according to the user preference and current context, actively look for a music file with better quality, and support adaptive migration via state manipulation. A migration manager adopts the aspect-oriented technology to dynamically weave the migration capabilities into the applications. Both applications rely on context-aware rules to guide their runtime adaptation. In the current implementation, the definition of these rules is based on real campus life scenarios.

6.4 Summary

This chapter investigated an extended form of mobile computing, i.e., context-aware mobile computing, and discussed the issues in building software infrastructure for supporting this paradigm. Based on the experiences from both the related projects and our own work, we have come up with the following suggestions for future research.

- We advocate reinventing an application model for context-aware mobile computing. The application model needs to meet the need for change, evolvement, and deploying in various environments. Sparkle intentionally separates code, data, and user interface, in order to prepare the space for independent evolvement and deployment of each part. This is in line with many researchers' opinions. Banavar [2] proposes that an application should be divided into an interaction part and a logic part; Grimm [12] argues for the separation of data and code. HCI research is constantly advancing adaptation solutions for user interface. Separation of code, data, and user interface allows more flexible combinations to cater to different situations. It also facilitates accessing, adapting, and reusing parts of an application. At the same time, the personality features are factored out from the functional units. More flexibility can thus be gained from various combinations of the facets and their implementations. By separating the selection strategy from the functional units, the system could exploit the context information on the spot, and the strategy can easily be altered and extended.
- We also vote for component-based development. The advance of a technology is usually accompanied by the continuous refinement of small widgets. User orientation is another reason, as people care more about peculiarities nowadays. Software developers (or end users) could thus concentrate on deriving fancy small components that are special, fashionable, or perfect in doing a single task. Software in the future could be sold and purchased component by component.
- We identify mobility support as an essential task. Due to environmental heterogeneity, a computational task could hardly be restored as it is after migration. To maintain user-perceivable continuity is thus a new

requirement. We believe in context-aware mobile computing systems, a flexible mobility support is most appropriate. Since it is difficult to predict the runtime requirements, the system must be able to analyze the situation and decide on the strategy for migration. For example, if the source and destination devices are similar in configuration, process migration may be the most reasonable solution; in other cases, as long as the receiving environment can support the user task, some high-level state mapping is sufficient. Tradeoffs between accuracy, response, performance, and user satisfaction must be considered in having the judgment. In Sparkle, we also propose the state manipulation mechanism, which could directly incorporate intelligence into the migration action. Future work will continue to formalize this problem and to yield more useful results.

- More effort is needed for designing and developing real context-aware applications for real-life scenarios. This would enhance understanding of context-aware features and help to devise the appropriate system supports and application models. The research community has identified the challenges in realizing context awareness, but many issues remain open in practically every aspect of this area. Recent works, including context-aware toolkits, context fabric, and various context modeling technologies, are heading in the right direction. However, the five questions of "what, who, where, when, and how of context-awareness" [18] still remain unanswered. This would continue to be an exciting area for research.

Acknowledgments

This research is supported in part by two CERG grants (HKU 7146/04E and 7519/03E) from the Hong Kong Government.

References

1. The Aura project. http://www-2.cs.cmu.edu/~aura/.
2. G. Banavar et al., "Challenges: an application model for pervasive computing", In Proceedings of MOBICOM 2000: The Sixth Annual International Conference on Mobile Computing and Networking, Boston, MA, USA, 6–11 August 2000, pp. 266–274.
3. N. Belaramani, C.L. Wang, and F.C.M. Lau, "Dynamic component composition for functionality adaptation in pervasive environments", The Ninth International Workshop on Future Trends of Distributed Computing Systems (FTDCS2003), San Juan, Puerto Rico, 28–30 May 2003.
4. N. Belaramani, Y. Chow, V.W.M. Kwan, C.L. Wang, and F.C.M. Lau, "A Component-based Software Architecture for Pervasive Computing", Chap. 10, pp. 201–222, "Intelligent Virtual World: Technologies and Applications

in Distributed Virtual Environments", Chap. 10, pp. 191–212, World Scientific, Singapore, July 2004.

5.   G. Chen, D. Kotz, "A survey of context-aware mobile computing research", Technical report, TR2000-381, Dartmouth College, Hanover, NH, 2000

6.   Y. Chow, W.Z. Zhu, C.L. Wang, and F.C.M. Lau, "The state-on-demand execution for adaptive component-based mobile agent systems", The Tenth International Conference on Parallel and Distributed Systems (ICPADS 2004), Newport Beach, California, 7–9 July 2004, pp. 46–53.

7.   A.K. Dey, "Providing architectural support for building context-aware Applications", PhD thesis, Georgia Institute of Technology, 2000.

8.   Fuggetta and G. Vigna, "Understanding code mobility", IEEE Transactions on Software Engineering, 24(5), May 1998.

9.   The Gaia project. http://choices.cs.uiuc.edu/gaia/.

10.   D. Garlan, D. Siewiorek, A. Smailagic, and P. Steenkiste, "Project Aura: toward distraction-free pervasive computing", IEEE Pervasive Computing, April–June 2002.

11.   R. Grimm, J. Davis et al., "Systems directions for pervasive computing", Proceedings of the Eight Workshop on Hot Topics in Operating Systems (HotOS-VIII), Elmau, Germany, May 2001, pp. 147–151.

12.   R. Grimm, J. Davis et al., "System support for pervasive applications", ACM Transactions on Computer Systems, 22(4):421–486, November 2004.

13.   HKU Sparkle Project. http://www.csis.hku.hk/~clwang/projects/sparkle.html.

14.   G. Judd and P. Steenkiste, "Providing contextual information to pervasive computing applications", IEEE International Conference on Pervasive Computing (PERCOM), Dallas, 23–25 March 2003.

15.   L.C.Y. Kong, C.L. Wang, and F.C.M. Lau, "Ontology mapping in pervasive computing environment", International Conference on Embedded and Ubiquitous Computing (EUC-04), Aizu, Japan, 26–28 August 2004, pp. 1014–1023.

16.   V.W.M. Kwan, F.C.M. Lau, and C.L. Wang, "Functionality adaptation: a context-aware service code adaptation for pervasive computing environments", The 2003 IEEE/WIC International Conference on Web Intelligence, Halifax, Canada, 13–17 October 2003, pp. 358–364.

17.   The one.world project. http://www.cs.nyu.edu/rgrimm/one.world/.

18.   D.R. Morse, A.K. Dey, and S. Armstrong, "The what, who, where, when and how of context-awareness", Workshop Abstract in the Proceedings of the 2000 Conference on Human Factors in Computing Systems (CHI 2000), The Hague, The Netherlands, 1–6 April 2000, p. 371.

19.   P.K. McKinley, S.M. Sadjadi, E.P. Kasten, and B.H.C. Cheng," Composing adaptive software", IEEE Computer, 37(7):56–64, July 2004.

20.   V. Poladian, J. Sousa et al., "Task-based adaptation for ubiquitous computing", IEEE Transactions on Systems, Man, and Cybernetics, Part C: Applications and Reviews, Special Issue on Engineering Autonomic Systems, To appear.

21.   Ranganathan, S. Chetan, and R. Campbell, "Mobile polymorphic applications in ubiquitous computing environments", Mobiquitous 2004: First

International Conference on Mobile and Ubiquitous Systems: Networking and Services, Boston, August 2004.

22. M. Román, C.K. Hess et al., "Gaia: a middleware infrastructure to enable active spaces", In IEEE Pervasive Computing, October–December 2002, pp. 74–83.

23. M. Roman, H. Ho, and R.Campbell, "Application mobility in active spaces", In First International Conference on Mobile and Ubiquitous Multimedia, Oulu, Finland, 11–13 December 2002.

24. M. Satyanarayanan, "From the Editor in Chief: the many faces of adaptation", IEEE Pervasive Computing, 3(3):4–5, July–September 2004.

25. W.N. Schilit, "A system architecture for context-aware mobile computing", PhD thesis, Columbia University, 1995.

26. P.P.L. Siu, C.L. Wang, and F.C.M. Lau, "Context-aware state management for ubiquitous applications", International Conference on Embedded and Ubiquitous Computing (EUC-04), Aizu, Japan, 26–28 August 2004. pp. 776–785.

27. J. Sousa and D. Garlan, "Aura: an architectural framework for user mobility in ubiquitous computing environments".

28. Z. Wang, D. Garlan, "Task-driven computing", Technical report, CMU-CS-00-154, May 2000.

7 Data Management for Mobile Ad Hoc Networks

F. Perich[+], A. Joshi[+], and R. Chirkova[*]

[+]University of Maryland, Baltimore County, USA

[*]North Carolina State University, USA

7.1 Introduction

The overall goal of data management and processing in mobile ad hoc networks is to allow individual devices to compute what information each device needs, when the device needs it, and how it can obtain the information. This chapter identifies the fundamental challenges and outlines ongoing and needed future work to achieve this goal.

Until recently, research on mobile data management was dominated by the client–proxy–server model requiring an infrastructure support. In this model, mobile devices connect to the Internet and serve as client end points. They initiate actions and receive information from servers, which reside on the network and provide the infrastructure support to the clients. This earlier research focused primarily on the development of protocols and techniques that deal with disconnection management, low bandwidth, and device resource constraints. This allows applications built for the wired world, e.g., World Wide Web and databases, to run in wireless domains using proxy-based approaches [8, 46]. In systems based on the cellular network infrastructure or wireless local area network infrastructure, the traditional client–proxy–server interaction is perhaps an appropriate model where the client database can be extremely lightweight [10], has a (partial) replica of the main database on the wired side [43, 75], or where selected data are continuously broadcast into the environment and cached by the clients [1, 35].

With the widespread use of short-range ad hoc networking technologies, such as Bluetooth [9], an alternative data management model becomes necessary. These networking technologies allow spontaneous connectivity among mobile devices, including handhelds, wearables, computers in vehicles, computers embedded in the physical infrastructure, and (nano)sensors. Mobile devices can suddenly become both sources and consumers of information. There is no longer a clear distinction between clients and servers, instead devices are now peers. To further complicate the matter, there is also no longer a guarantee of infrastructure support. Consequently, for obtaining data, devices cannot simply depend on the help of some fixed, centralized server [61]. Instead, the devices must be able to cooperate with others in their vicinity to pursue individual and collective tasks. This will lead devices to become more autonomous, dynamic, and adaptive with respect to their environments.

This chapter describes the origins of this novel mobile peer-to-peer computing model and relates it to traditional mobile models.

More importantly, this chapter introduces problems that arise in traditional mobile data management systems as well as additional problems specifically related to mobile ad hoc networks. The three fundamental sources of these problems represent the underlying wireless ad hoc networking technologies, the traditional issues relating to data management in any mobile computing paradigm, and the problems related to context awareness.

This chapter also surveys proposed solutions to each problem category. Despite the fact that wireless ad hoc networking technologies and peer-to-peer based data management paradigms attempt to solve similar problems, the chapter illustrates that there is a very limited effort on crosslayer interaction, which is essential for mobile ad hoc networks. This gap between the research on networking, data management, and context awareness in pervasive computing environments is the fundamental problem of allowing a device to compute *what* information the device needs, *when* the device needs it, and *how* it can obtain the information.

To overcome this problem, this chapter then presents the MoGATU model [58–63] – a novel peer-to-peer data management model for mobile ad hoc networks. The key focus of MoGATU is to narrow the gap to its minimum by enabling mobile devices to proactively learn their current context and adjust their computing functionality according to their users' needs and preferences. MoGATU abstracts all devices using communication interfaces, information managers, information consumers, and information providers. The information manager is the fundamental component of the model. It is responsible for majority of the data management and communication functionality. It is composed of multiple components, which are responsible for (1) data and service discovery, (2) query processing, (3) join query processing, (4) caching, (5) transactions, (6) reputation, and (7) data-based routing among peer devices.

7.2 Origins of Mobile Peer-to-Peer Computing Model

Mobile computing applications can be classified into three categories – client–server, client–proxy–server, and peer-to-peer – depending on the interaction model.

In the client–server model, a large number of mobile devices connect to a small number of servers residing on the wired network, organized in a cluster. This model is a direct evolution of the distributed object-oriented systems like CORBA and DCOM [72]. Here, mobile devices terminal-like client end points, initiating actions and receiving information from servers on the network. The servers then represent powerful machines with high bandwidth wired network connectivity and the capability to connect to wireless devices. Primary data and services reside on, and are managed by, the servers. Servers are also responsible for handling lower level networking details, such as disconnection and retransmission.

The advantages of this model are simplicity of the client design and straight-forward cooperation among cluster servers. The main drawback, however, is the prohibitively large overhead on servers to handle each mobile client separately, in terms of transcoding and connection handling, which severely decreases system scalability.

In the client–proxy–server model, a proxy is introduced between the client and the server, typically on the edge of the wired network. The logical end-to-end connection between a server and a client is split into two physical connections – server-to-proxy and proxy-to-client. This model increases overall system scalability since servers interact only with a fixed number of proxies, which in turn are responsible for handling transcoding and wireless connections to the clients.

There have been substantial research and industry efforts [8, 13, 47, 88] in developing client–proxy–server architectures. Additionally, intelligent proxies [68] may act as a computational platform for processing queries on behalf of resource-limited mobile clients.

Transcoding, i.e., conversion of data and image formats to suit target systems, is an important problem introduced by client–server and client–proxy–server architectures. Unlike mobile devices, servers and proxies are powerful machines that can handle data formats of any type and image formats of high resolution. Therefore, data on the wired network must be transcoded to suit different mobile devices. It is important for a server or a proxy to recognize the characteristics of a client device. Standard techniques for transcoding, such as those included in the WAP stack, include XSLT [56] and Fourier transformation. The W3C CC/PP standard [51] enables clients to specify their characteristics when connecting to HTTP servers using profiles.

The widespread use of short-range ad hoc networking technologies created an additional model based on peer interaction. In this peer-to-peer model, all devices, mobile and static, are treated as peers. Suddenly, mobile devices act as both servers and clients. Ad hoc networking technologies, such as Bluetooth, allow mobile devices to utilize peer resources in their vicinity in addition to accessing servers on the wired network. Server mobility is, however, an important issue in this model. The set of services available to a client dynamically changes with respect to location and time. Consequently, this requires mobile devices to implement protocols for data and service discovery [16, 69], and collaboration and composition [19, 55]. Although the disadvantage of this model is the burden on the mobile devices in terms of energy consumption and network traffic handling, the key advantage is that each device may have access to more up-to-date location dependent information and interact with peers without the need of an infrastructure support. Particularly, the second advantage plays an important role in enabling and revolutionizing mobile ad hoc networks.

7.3 Challenges

The aim of mobile ad hoc networks is to extend the vision of mobile computing paradigm and enable people to accomplish their tasks *anywhere* and *anytime*, by using all computing resources, i.e., data and services, currently available in their vicinity. This goal, however, raises many challenges in multiple research areas.

There are three key sources of these issues and challenges (1) one set of challenges emanates from the networking component, and includes problems relating to device discovery, message routing, and physical limitation of the underlying networking technology, (2) a second set of challenges is due to a device's difficulty to be context aware by discovering and maintaining location of other devices and information in a network, since the topology is dynamic, (3) the third key source of challenges is then the actual data management layer with issues such as transactional support or consistency among data objects.

Figure 7.1 illustrates the various layers that are essential for designing and developing a data management framework for mobile ad hoc networks. Correspondingly, this section describes each layer individually by identifying key challenges and offering a survey of existing approaches.

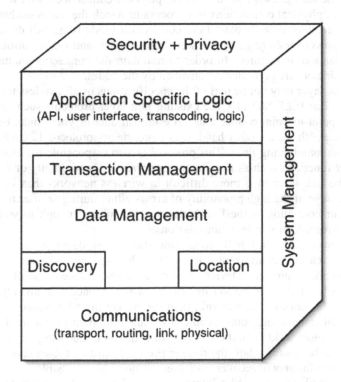

Fig. 7.1. Layered data management framework for mobile ad hoc networks

7.3.1 Communications Layer

The communications layer represents wireless ad hoc networking technologies that enable mobile devices to communicate with other devices in their vicinity. It is responsible for establishing and maintaining logical end-to-end connections between two devices, for data transmission and for data reception. This layer encompasses the first four layers of the standard seven-layer open standards interconnection stack – physical, medium access control (MAC), network, and transport layers.

The primary task of the physical and MAC layers is to provide node discovery, and establish and maintain physical connections between two or more wireless entities. Each ad hoc networking technology implements these functions differently. For example, in Bluetooth, node discovery is accomplished through the use of the *inquiry* command by the baseband (MAC) layer. In IEEE 802.11b, the MAC layer employs the RTS–CTS (i.e., request-to-send and clear-to-send) mechanism in order to enable nodes to discover each other, when they are operating in an *ad hoc* mode. When IEEE 802.11b nodes operate in an *infrastructure* mode, a base station periodically broadcasts beacons, which other nodes use to discover the base station and to establish physical connections with it. The establishment of physical connections is a process in which the nodes exchange operational parameters such as baud rate, connection mode (e.g., full duplex or half duplex), power mode (e.g., low power, high power), and timing information for synchronization, if required. In order to maintain the connection, some or all of these parameters are periodically refreshed by the nodes.

The link layer may not be part of the specifications of all wireless technologies. Some, such as IEEE 802.11b, use existing link layer protocols such as HDLC or PPP (for point-to-point connections) to establish data or voice links between the nodes. Bluetooth, on the other hand, uses a proprietary protocol, L2CAP, for establishing and maintaining links. This protocol is also responsible for other common link layer functions such as framing, error correction, and quality of service. The task of the link layer in is more difficult in wireless networks than in wired networks because of the high probability of errors either during or after transmission. Thus, error correction at the link layer must be robust enough to withstand the high bit-error rate of wireless transmissions.

The network layer in mobile computing stacks must deal with device mobility, which may cause existing routes to break or become invalid with no change in other network parameters. Device mobility may also be the cause of packet loss. For example, if the destination device, to which a packet is already en route, moves out of range of the network, then the packet must be dropped. Thus, both route establishment and route maintenance are important problems that the network layer must tackle. As the mobility of a network increases, so do route failures and packet losses. Thus, the routing protocol must be robust enough to either prevent route failures or recover from them as quickly as possible.

Mobile applications, unlike Internet applications, tend to generate or require small amounts of data (of the order of hundreds or at most thousands of bytes). Thus, protocols at the transport layer should be aware of the short message sizes, packet delays due to device mobility, and noncongestion packet losses. TCP is ill-suited for wireless networks. Numerous variations of TCP and transport protocols designed exclusively for wireless networks ensure that both ends of a connection agree that packet loss has occurred before the source retransmits the packet. Additionally, some of these protocols choose to defer packet transmission if they detect that current network conditions are unsuitable.

Routing in Ad Hoc Networks
Routing is perhaps the most important component of mobile ad hoc networks. Routing allows devices to communicate with others outside their immediate wireless radio range. In the past few years, there has been significant effort in developing routing algorithms. Three representative algorithms are introduced in this section. Destination-sequential distance vector routing algorithm (DSDV) [65] is a representative of a table-driven approach. Dynamic Source Routing Algorithm (DSR) [45] represents an alternative source-initiated approach, and Ad hoc on-demand distance vector routing algorithm (AODV) [66] is a hybrid of the two approaches.

DSDV [65] is a table-driven algorithm based on the Bellman–Ford routing mechanism [24]. Every node in the network maintains a routing table containing a list of all possible destinations and the number of hops to reach them. Additionally, every entry in the table is assigned a sequence number as obtained from the destination node. Every node periodically transmits routing table updates to maintain consistency in the network topology. Duplicate routes with the same sequence number are rejected and only the shortest route is accepted. The algorithm therefore responds to topology changes by detecting them and propagating the information to all nodes in the network. Finally, the algorithm attempts to conserve the available bandwidth by propagating only partial routing information whenever possible.

DSR [45] is a source-initiated on demand routing protocol – an alternative to table-driven routing algorithms. DSR creates a route only upon an explicit source initiated request. When a device requires a route to a destination, it initiates a route discovery process within the network. Upon discovering a proper route, a route maintenance procedure is executed to maintain the route until every path from the source is no longer available. DSR consists of a route learning and maintenance policy accompanied by a route discovery process. When a mobile device needs to send a message, it first verifies the destination by matching it with known routes. Alternatively, the device initiates a route discovery and waits for a *route reply* message that is generated by the destination device. The reply is routed back from destination throughout the same path as it was received on. Lastly, route maintenance is accomplished through the use of *route error* and *acknowledgment* messages.

AODV [66] is an on-demand table-driven algorithm. AODV is an improvement upon DSDV because not every node is required to maintain a complete list of routes for all other nodes in the network. Instead, each node in the network maintains route information for only those paths in which it is actively involved. Similar to DSR, this algorithm consists of two parts: *path discovery* and *path maintenance*.

Each node maintains a sequence number and broadcast ID. During the path discovery, a source node broadcasts a route request with a unique ID for the desired destination. When an intermediate node knows a path to the destination, it replies with that information by reversing the path, otherwise it broadcasts the request further. This algorithm therefore requires the use of symmetric links because path replies and other messages are sent back along the reverse path of the path discovery messages. To reflect topology changes, the algorithm considers two possibilities. When a source node moves, it reinitiates the *path discovery* procedure. When an intermediate or destination node moves, its upstream neighbor detects the change and propagates *link failure* message to the source node along the reverse path. The source node may then choose to again reinitiate the *path discovery* procedure for the given destination.

7.3.2 Discovery Layer

The discovery layer helps a mobile device with discovering data, services, and computation resources. These may reside in the vicinity of the mobile device or on the Internet. Due to resource constraints and mobility, mobile devices may not have complete information about all currently available sources. The discovery layer assumes that the underlying network layer can establish a logical end-to-end connection with other entities in the network. The discovery layer then provides upper layers with the knowledge and context of available sources.

There has been considerable research and industry effort in service discovery in the context of wired and wireless networks. Two important aspects of service discovery are the *discovery architecture* and the *service matching mechanism*. Discovery architectures are primarily either based on *lookup registry* or *peer-to-peer* oriented.

Lookup registry-based discovery protocols register information about the source to some centralized or distributed registry. Devices query this registry in order to obtain knowledge about the source, including its location and invocation parameters. This type of architecture can be further subdivided into two categories: centralized registry-based, and federated or distributed registry-based architectures. A centralized registry-based architecture contains one monolithic centralized registry, whereas a federated registry-based architecture consists of multiple registries distributed across the network. Protocols such as Jini [3], Salutation and Salutation-lite, Universal Plug and Play (UPnP) [69], UDDI and Service Location Protocol (SLP) [79] are examples of a lookup registry-based architecture.

On the other hand, peer-to-peer discovery protocols query each node in the network to discover available services on that node. Broadcasting of requests and advertisements to peers is a simple, albeit inefficient, service discovery technique in peer-to-peer environments. Reference [16] describes a distributed peer-to-peer service discovery protocol (SDP) using caching, which significantly reduces the need to broadcast requests and advertisements. Bluetooth SDP is another example of a peer-to-peer. In SDP, services are represented using 128-bit unique identifiers.

SDP does not provide any information on how to invoke the service. It only provides information on the availability of the service on a specific device.

SDPs discussed in this section use simple interface, attribute, or unique identifier-based matching techniques to locate appropriate sources. Jini uses interface matching, SDP uses identifier matching, while SLP and Ninja secure service discovery systems (SDSs) discover services using attribute-based matching. The drawbacks of these techniques include lack of rich representation of services, inability to specify constraints on service descriptions, lack of inexact matching of service attributes, and lack of ontology support [17]. Semantic matching is an alternative technique that addresses these issues. Both DReggie [17] and Bluetooth semantic service discovery protocol [6] use a semantically rich language, called DARPA agent markup language (DAML), to describe and match both services and data. Semantic descriptions of services and data allow greater flexibility in obtaining a match between the query and the available information. Matching can now be inexact. This means that parameters such as functional characteristics, and hardware and device characteristics of the service provider may be used in addition to service or data attributes to determine whether a match can occur.

SLP [37] is a language-independent protocol for automatic resource discovery on IP networks utilizing an agent-oriented infrastructure. The basis of the SLP discovery mechanism lies on predefined service attributes, which can be applied to universally describe both software and hardware services. The architecture consists of three types of agents: User Agent, Service Agent, and Discovery Agent. The User Agents is responsible for discovering available Directory Agents, and acquiring service handles on behalf of end-user applications that request services. The Service Agent is responsible for advertising the service handles to Directory Agents. Directory Agent is responsible for collecting service handles and maintaining the directory of advertised services. SLP uses multicasting for service registration and discovery, and unicasting for service discovery responses from Directory/Service Agents.

The Ninja Secure SDS [25] is a research level service discovery engine developed at University of California, Berkeley. The architecture consists of clients, services, and SDS servers. The SDS server architecture is a scalable, fault-tolerant, secure, and highly available service discovery repository. SDS servers are hierarchically arranged for scalability and availability purposes across both local and wide area networks. Service descriptions and messages used to send query and answers between devices are encoded using extensible markup language (XML). Additionally, the SDS uses encryption to ensure interaction privacy and uses capability-based access control to limit the clients in discovering only permissible services. Ninja services and clients then use well-known global SDS multicast channels to communicate with the service discovery servers.

UPnP [78] extends the original Microsoft Plug and Play peripheral model to support service discovery provided by network devices from numerous vendors. UPnP works and defines standards primarily at the lower-layer network protocol suites, so that the devices can natively, i.e., language and platform independently, implement these standards. UPnP uses the Simple Service Discovery Protocol (SSDP) for discovery of services over IP networks, which can operate with or without a lookup service in the network. In addition, the SSDP operates on the top of the existing open standard protocols utilizing HTTP over both unicast (HTTPU) and multicast UDP (HTTPMU). When a new service wants to join the network, it transmits an announcement to indicate its presence. If a lookup service is present, it can record this advertisement to be subsequently used to satisfy clients' service discovery requests. Additionally, each service on the network may also observe these advertisements. When a client wants to discover a service, it can either contact the service directly through the URL that is stored within the service advertisement, or it can send out a multicast query message, which can be answered either by the directory service or directly by the service.

Jini [74] is a distributed service-oriented architecture developed by Sun Microsystems. A collection of Jini services form a Jini federation. Jini services coordinate with each other within the federation. The overall goal of Jini is to turn the network into an easily administered tool on which human and computational clients can find services in a flexible and robust fashion. One of the key components of Jini is the Jini lookup service (JLS), which maintains the dynamic information about the available services in the Jini federation. Every service must discover one or more JLS before it can enter a federation. When a Jini service wants to join a Jini federation, it first discovers one or many JLSs from the local or remote networks. The service then uploads its service proxy (i.e., a set of Java classes) to the JLS. This proxy can be used by the service clients to contact the original service and invoke methods on the service. Service clients interact only with the Java-based service proxies. This allows various types of services, both hardware and software services, to be accessed in a uniform fashion. For instance, a service client can invoke print requests to a PostScript printing service even if it has no knowledge about the PostScript language.

DReggie [18] extends the matching mechanisms in Jini and other SDSs by providing a semantic-based matching. The key idea in DReggie is to enable SDSs to perform matching based on semantic information associated with the services as an alternative to strictly syntactic (i.e., string matching) techniques. The semantic information of services consists of their extensive descriptions including, but not limited to, capabilities, functionality, portability, and system requirements. Semantic service matching introduces the possibilities of fuzziness and inexactness of the response to a service discovery request. In the DReggie system, a service discovery request contains the description of an "ideal" service – one whose capabilities match exactly with the requirements. Thus, matching now involves comparison of requirements specified with the capabilities of existing services; however, depending on the requirements, a match may occur even if one or more capabilities does not match exactly.

The Bluetooth Enhanced Service Discovery Protocol (ESDP) [5], similar to DReggie, extends an existing discovery protocol, which in this case uses UUID-based matching, specified in Bluetooth architecture. ESDP presents a more sophisticated matching mechanism using semantic information to decide the success or failure of a query. The initial version employed the RDF/RDF-S [12, 53] data model, while the current version utilizes the DARPA Agent Markup Language + Ontology Inference Layer [26] to describe, register, and discover services at peer devices.

7.3.3 Location Management Layer

The responsibility of the location management layer is to provide location information to a mobile device. Location information changes dynamically with mobility of the device and is one of the key components of context awareness. A location can be used by upper layers to filter location-sensitive information and obtain location-specific answers to queries, e.g., weather of a certain area and traffic condition on a road. The current location of a device relative to other devices in its vicinity can be determined using the discovery layer or the underlying communications layer. Common technologies use methods such as triangulation and signal strength measurements for location determination. GPS [40] is a well-known example of the use of triangulation based on data received from four different satellites. Cell phones use cell tower information to triangulate their position. On the other hand, systems such as RADAR [7], which are used for indoor location tracking, work as follows. Using a set of fixed IEEE 802.11b base stations, the entire area is mapped. The map contains (x,y) coordinates and the corresponding signal strength of each base station at that coordinate. This map is loaded onto the mobile device. Now, as the user moves about the area, the signal strength from each base station is measured. The pattern of signal strengths from the stored map that most closely matches the pattern of measured signal strengths is chosen. The location of the user is that corresponding to the (x,y) coordinates associated with the stored pattern. Outdoor location management technologies have achieved technical maturity and have been deployed in vehicular and other industrial navigational systems. Location management, indoor and outdoor, remains a strong research field with the rising popularity of technologies such as IEEE 802.11b and Bluetooth.

The notion of location can be dealt with at multiple scales. Most "location determination" techniques actually deal with position determination, with respect to some global (lat/long) or local (distances from the "corner" of a room) grid. Many applications are not interested in the absolute position as much as they are in higher order location concepts (inside or outside a facility, inside or outside some jurisdictional boundary, distance from some known place, at a mountain top, in a rain forest region, etc.). Absolute position determinations can be combined with GIS type data to infer locations at other levels of granularity.

Expanding the notion of location further leads us to consider the notion of context. Context is any information that can be used to characterize the situation of a person or a computing entity [28]. So for instance, context covers things such as location, device type, connection speed, and direction of movement. Context even arguably involves a user's mental states (beliefs, desires, intentions), etc. This information can be used by the layers described next for data and service management. However, the privacy issues involved are quite complex. It is not clear who should be allowed to gather such information, under what circumstances should it be revealed, and to whom. So for instance a user may not want her GPS chip to reveal her current location except to emergency response personnel. A more general formulation of such issues can be found in [20], which defines semantically rich policies and a decision logic-based reasoner for specifying and reasoning about a user's privacy preferences as related to context information.

7.3.4 Data Management Layer

The actual data management layer deals with access, storage, monitoring, and data manipulation. Data may reside locally and also on remote devices. Similar to data management in traditional Internet computing, this layer is essential in enabling a device to interact and exchange data with other devices located in its vicinity and elsewhere on the network. The core difference is that this layer must also deal with mobile computing devices. Such devices have limited battery power and other resources in comparison to their desktop counterparts. The devices also communicate over wireless logical links that have limited bandwidth and are prone to frequent failures. Consequently, the data management layer often attempts to extend data management solutions for Internet computing by primarily addressing mobility and disconnection of a mobile computing device. Distributed database systems and distributed file systems in mobile computing environments address the challenges introduced by sharing data that can reside on both devices in a fixed infrastructure and mobile devices. The systems attempt to provide solutions for two challenges raised by the communication characteristics, mobility, and portability of the environments. The first question relates to the location of the database – on the mobile device or the wired network. The latter is typically assumed. So, a mobile device may require access to data that reside on the wired network, but may not be able to obtain due to network disconnection or low bandwidth. Often, the solution is to replicate or cache data on the mobile device to ensure access. This brings up the issue of updates. For a transaction to succeed, a mobile device must be able to commit its updates at the appropriate data manager residing on the wired network. Additionally, when data are modified at the primary side, all mobile devices should receive corresponding updates for their replicas. Mobile data management solutions thus attempt to extend the traditional distributed database systems by addressing challenges that arise due to the following conditions:

- Wireless networks have limited bandwidth and are prone to frequent failures
- Channels in wireless networks may be asymmetric
- Mobile devices have limited battery power
- Mobile devices have limited resources

Mobile ad hoc networks only exacerbate the issues. This can be illustrated by classifying the mobile ad hoc network model along four orthogonal axes that represent autonomy, distribution, heterogeneity, and mobility of mobile databases [29]. *Autonomy* refers to control distribution. It indicates the degree to which each mobile device can operate independently from the servers in the fixed infrastructure. It is a function of numerous factors defining the restrictions on execution of transactions as well as consistency requirements. *Dimension* classifies the data distribution model among all mobile and fixed devices in the system. At one extreme, all data can reside only on one device (usually the server), while at the other extreme all data can reside on all devices within one system (i.e., full replication). *Heterogeneity* defines the hardware as well as software (primarily protocol) heterogeneity supported by a system. Lastly, *mobility* defines the degree of mobility that a particular system provides.

Mobile ad hoc networks are highly autonomous since there is no centralized control of the individual client databases. They are heterogeneous as entities can only *speak* to each other in some neutral format. The mobile ad hoc networks are clearly distributed as parts of data may reside on different devices and there is replication as entities cache data and their respective metadata. Mobility is of course given – in mobile ad hoc networks, devices can change their locations and no fixed set of entities is *always* accessible to a given device. The last point is perhaps most important. It is also the main reason why a direct use of solutions developed for mobile information access is inappropriate. In mobile distributed systems, disconnections of mobile devices from the network are viewed only as temporary events. Additionally, these systems often assume that all data *managers* are located at fixed positions in the wired network and that their locations are known by every client a priori [14, 52, 54]. Finally, an additional limitation is the naming schema for defining data and for locating both data and devices in the traditional system. Here, each client must know the precise server location as well as its corresponding database schema to utilize the data properly.

Much like the arguments in [29], the status of data management in wireless networks versus wired networks can be compared to that of distributed data management versus centralized data management in the late 1960s. The issues are often the same, but the solutions are different. Therefore, first the traditional challenges of any distributed data management are described, which are then followed by additional challenges specific to mobile ad hoc networks. This overview is based on [29, 33, 42, 57, 87].

Query Processing and Optimization

Query processing is highly affected by the addition of mobility to distributed data management systems in mobile environments. The mobility of a device can affect both the type of queries as well as the optimization techniques that can be applied.

Traditional query processing approaches advocated *location transparency*, where a query should return the same outcome irrespective of the client's location. These techniques thus considered only the aspects of data transfer and processing to optimize a given query. On the other hand, in the mobile computing environment, the query processing approaches promote *location awareness* [52]. For example, a mobile device can ask for the location of the closest Greek restaurant, and the server should understand that the starting search point refers to the current position of the device.

Caching

With the possibility of disconnection of mobile devices from the wired infrastructure, the mobile devices require data be cached on their locally available storage. Data caching allows mobile devices to operate even in disconnected mode. At the same time, this may require a weaker notion of consistency as the mobile device may operate on stale data without the knowledge that the primary copy located in the wired infrastructure was altered. Hence, different consistency constraints as well as intelligent caching methods are required to allow a disconnected mode of operation.

Replication
Another issue arises when one mobile device holds a complete replica of a database. The traditional replica control protocols are often based on implicit assumptions, which are no longer valid in the mobile environment. They assume that the communication among devices is symmetric. They also assume that all replicas are always reachable. This is not the case in the mobile environment. This may limit the ability to synchronize the replica located on the mobile device. It may also limit the ability of accepting data modification even in the wired infrastructure, as one of the replica owners may be unavailable to vote.

Name Resolution
Name resolution also plays an important role in data management in mobile environments. As devices may move from one location to another or become disconnected, it is necessary to provide a global naming strategy to be able to locate a mobile station, which may hold the required data. This can be solved by broadcasting a request for the device such as a device discovery in Bluetooth networks. This however introduces reachability limitations as well as a high communication overhead. Alternatively, name resolution can be done by creating a "home" base station for each mobile device, which keeps track of the particular mobile device's location, and can act as proxy to transmit messages to the mobile device if reachable over the network. This solution was studied extensively in [64].

Transaction Management
The bandwidth limitations and possible long spanned disconnections of mobile devices require a new model for transactions as well as transaction-processing techniques. This functionality is further described in Sect. 3.5. Additionally, mobile ad hoc networks impose the following issues that are primarily related to the randomness of every device's neighborhood at any instance of time. The neighborhood, also referred to as vicinity, consists of all reachable devices that a particular (mobile) device can communicate with and all available data that are accessible at that time.

Spatiotemporal Variation of Data and Data Source Availability
As devices move, their vicinity changes dynamically affecting data and data source availability. Additionally, current wireless networking technologies cannot support stable connections under high mobility.

Lack of a Global Catalog and Schema
As the neighborhood changes dynamically, a mobile device has no prior knowledge of the current set of available data. There is no global catalog that it may contact and ask for a location of a given data item.

No Guarantee of Reconnection

When a device moves away from a current neighborhood, it may affect any ongoing interaction among other devices of that neighborhood. As there is no guarantee that the mobile devices will ever again be able to communicate among themselves, this may cause an inconsistent global state.

No Guarantee of Collaboration

The issues of privacy and trust are very important for mobile ad hoc networks where random devices interact in random transactions [77]. A device may have reliable information but refuses to make it available to others. A device may be willing to share information; however that information is unreliable. Lastly, when a device makes information available to other devices, questions regarding protection of future changes and sharing of that data arise.

One consequence of these challenges is that query answering is highly serendipitous. The answer obtained will depend on information sources accessible in the current vicinity. Consequently, each device in mobile ad hoc networks must gather information proactively and much of the interaction among devices should happen in the background, without an explicit human intervention [33, 60]. This requires that devices adapt themselves to the needs and preferences of their users and the current context.

Approaches for Disconnected Operation

This section presents related work on data management challenges from the disconnected operation perspective. This work is primarily based on client–server model, where clients are mobile devices with intermittent connectivity operating under various processing and energy-related constraints. The primary concept is to leverage the traditional client–server model from the wired infrastructure networks to operate also in wireless environments. The authors of the work described later usually relax one of the properties of the wired solutions to allow a seamless (yet limited) operation in the new environment. Commonly, a proxy point is added between the client and server or a weaker notion of transactions is introduced allowing mobile clients to operate in a disconnected mode.

Within a mobile database environment, cached data on mobile clients can take the form of materialized views. In order to efficiently maintain such materialized views while taking into consideration disconnected operations, [54] presents a mechanism within the fixed network they refer to as *view holder* that maintains versions of views required by a particular mobile host (MH). A view defines a function from a subset of base tables to a derived table, where (base) tables are the common data structures within a relational database system. A view is materialized by physically by storing the derived table in the form of tuples. In distributed environments with client–server configuration, such as mobile databases, materialized views can be stored at the client side to support local query processing. Materialized views operate in a fashion similar to data caches. Available data can be quickly processed through the materialized views without the requirement of accessing a remote database server. Due to communication costs and frequent disconnections of wireless networks information stored within the mobile computer becomes crucial to maintaining productivity. If the data needed to complete a task are present on the mobile computer, remote access may be eliminated and processing may continue even though disconnection has occurred. The authors argue that most of the transactions in a database environment are read only, and thus the main focus of this chapter was on optimizing read-only transactions on mobile computers. The authors do not consider write transactions, and only suggest that in the occurrence of a write transaction, the transaction should be performed directly with the data sources and not through the materialized views stored on the mobile client. Their proposed layered system architecture for read-only transactions thus consists of four layers: data servers, data warehouses, MHs, and view holders. The data server layer is responsible for periodically constructing a maintenance transaction to update the data warehouse. A data warehouse, using a versioning maintenance algorithm, is created where the views are static and the number of consecutive versions of each view also remains static. Hence, the amount of space made available for versions of a particular attribute is known and fixed. A view holder is a mechanism for providing dynamic and customizable view maintenance so that the cache or view consistency achieved between the data stored on the MH and the data sources match the availability or cost of the network and the capabilities of the MH. A view holder will maintain a version of a view requested by an MH for as long as the MH needs it. So, the view holder can be seen as a buffer, holding versions of a specialized view for a particular MH. Space allocated for the updated attributes of a view must be done dynamically since it is not known beforehand how many versions will be maintained. The assumption is the views requested by an MH are very likely to be a small and specialized amount of the information from within the data servers and/or data warehouses. To avoid these huge storage requirements, versions of the requested data are dynamically maintained by the view holder. It is possible some of the data sources, including data warehouses, may not support explicit versions of data. In such a case, the view holder will query the source to extract the data at a given moment. A timestamp for this implicit *version* could be the last time the tuple, attribute, or table was modified and found by querying the catalog of the data source.

Reference [52] presents optimization techniques of query processing in mobile database systems of queries that include location information. Query processing in mobile database systems is a special challenge due to the resource limitations and constantly changing location of the MH. The authors concentrate on the optimization of queries that include location information and suggest the use of a location management component. The location management component is responsible for updating the information about the actual location of the MH and resides on the wired network either at the location of home station for a particular MH or at some other centralized and fixed location on the wired network. All ad hoc queries that use location information about the MH have to access the location component. Depending on the localization strategy used, the ad hoc queries are associated with a different cost. Therefore, the authors develop and present a cost model for query optimization incorporating mobility specific factors like energy and connectivity. Additionally, the authors argue that a query processing in mobile database systems is significantly different from that in stationary systems and must be performed using different techniques. The query processing subsystem of a DBMS is organized into several phases: translation, optimization, and execution. The authors concentrate primarily on query optimization. In the phase of query optimization, potential query execution plans are generated and evaluated using a cost function. The cheapest plan is chosen for execution. In stationary systems, disk and main memory accesses are the foremost optimization criteria. In a mobile environment, additional constraints like the energy consumption of a query have to be taken into account. Mobile database systems must be able to choose an execution site for the different phases depending on their current environment and should be able to revise that decision as flexible as possible. The authors then examine different localization strategies for mobile users. To validate their optimization strategies, the authors have developed a simulation model of mobile query processing and performed various experiments. They show that no single localization strategy performs acceptably under all conditions and identify the critical factors for adapting a query processing subsystem to the employed location management strategy.

Reference [14] considers an infrastructure-based mobile network model consisting of MHs and mobile support stations utilizing an IP-type communication and addressing. According to their description, an MH is an intelligent device, which can move freely while maintaining its connection to the network. The mobile support station is connected to the network via a wired medium and provides a wireless interface that allows the MH to interact with the static network. Each mobile support station is responsible for a geographical cellular region and is required to maintain the addresses of the MHs, which are located within its region. Similar to [52], the authors consider location-dependent queries under disconnected operation mode. To overcome the issue of mobility, the authors introduce the concept of a mailbox for each MH. The mailbox is the recipient of all the query messages and results from the network and must be always accessible by its respective MH owner. Mailboxes thus provide a central repository for all of the MH's query responses and logs. This is similar to the concept of voice mailboxes in standard telecommunication cellular and wired networks. Additionally, the mailbox can be used during the process of a mobile transaction recovery, as all messages destined for a particular MH are always sent to it. Therefore, any DBMS is able to resolve and recover from any transactional conflicts by simply interacting with the MH's mailboxes and does not require the MHs to be always accessible over the wireless network. Lastly, it helps reducing the load on the system as the messages may be sent only within the wired network between the query processor and the mailbox for the particular MH. The authors then consider issues related to the cellular region-based infrastructure, namely, mobile support router hand-off and zone-crossing. Mobile support router hand-off occurs when a mobile computer moves within a given cellular zone, while zone-crossing occurs when a mobile computer moves between two cellular zones. The authors address these problems using a mobile protocol adapted from the Columbia host protocol proposal [44].

Reference [66] presents a replication schema appropriate for environments where connectivity is partial, weak, and variant such as in mobile computing. She considers a distributed database with data located both at mobile and stationary hosts to allow autonomous operation during disconnections. Transactions are distributed and can be initiated at both mobile and stationary hosts. As an alternative for requiring a mutual consistency of all copies of data items, their proposed approach allows bounded inconsistencies. Pitoura groups together all data located at strongly connected hosts to form a cluster. While all data inside a cluster are consistent, various degrees of inconsistency are defined for replicas at different clusters. To maximize local processing and to reduce network access, her proposed mechanism enhances the interface offered by the database systems with operations using weaker consistency guarantees, which allow access to data that exhibit bounded inconsistency. Pitoura introduces two new types of operation, weak reads and weak writes. These operations allow users to operate on data with bounded inconsistency. The traditional read and write operations are referred to as strict read and strict write, respectively. Additionally, Pitoura defines two strict and weak transactions. The strict transaction again represents the traditional notion of transaction in distributed database systems, while weak transaction is defined as transaction consisting of strict operations and at least one weak operation. The weak transaction, however, requires two types of commit: local and global. The local commit point is expressed by an explicit commit protocol, and updates made by locally committed weak transactions are visible only by weak transactions in the same cluster. These updates become permanent and visible by strict transactions only after reconciliation when local transactions become globally committed. Pitoura then continues by presenting an implementation, wherein schema distinguishes copies into quasi and core. Core copies are copies whose values are up-to-date and permanent, while quasi copies are copies whose values may be obsolete and are only conditionally committed. Lastly, Pitoura introduces protocols for enforcing the schema and evaluates the performance of the weak consistency schema for various networking conditions.

Reference [27] presents the system architecture of the Bayou System, which is a platform of replicated, highly available, variable-consistency, mobile databases on which one can build collaborative applications. The emphasis is on supporting application-specific conflict detection and resolution, and on providing application-controlled inconsistency. The system is intended to run in a mobile computing environment that includes portable machines with less-than-ideal network connectivity, and the goal of the system is to support data sharing among mobile users. The authors predominantly consider the issue of disconnected operations, which they call an experience of extended and sometimes involuntary disconnection from many or all of the other devices with which a particular mobile device wishes to share data. The system architecture is based on client–server model, where servers store data, and clients read and write data managed by servers. A server is any machine that holds a complete copy of one or more databases, which loosely denotes a collection of data items instead of the traditional database notion. Clients are able to access data residing on any server to which they can communicate, and any machine holding a copy of a database must also act as a server accessible by others. Therefore, in their architecture, servers do not have to reside on a wired network, and instead any mobile device can also operate as a server. For example, when several users become disconnected from the rest of the system, they can continue to actively collaborate among themselves if at least one user is able to utilize its mobile device as the group's server. To allow any two devices that are able to communicate with each other to propagate updates between themselves, the system employs a peer-to-peer reconciliation. Therefore, even machines that never directly communicate can exchange updates via inter-mediaries. Reconciliation can be structured as an incremental process, so that even servers with very intermittent or asymmetrical connections can eventually bring their databases into a mutually consistent state. To resolve update conflicts, the system detects and resolves them in an application-specific manner. A write operation, thus, includes not only the data being written or updated but also a dependency set. The dependency set is a collection of queries and their expected results. A conflict is detected if the queries are executed at a server and do not return the expected outcome. The write operation also specifies how to automati-cally resolve conflicts using a procedure called *mergeproc*. This procedure is invoked when a write conflict is detected. Hence, Bayou's write operation consists of a proposed update, a dependency set, and a *mergeproc*. Both the dependency set and *mergeproc* are dictated by an application's semantics and may vary for each write operation issued by the application. The verification of the dependency check, the execution of the *mergeproc*, and the application of the update set are done atomically with respect to other database accesses on the server.

Reference [80] presents a mobile transaction-processing system Pro-Motion. The underlying transaction-processing model of Pro-Motion is the concept of nested-split transactions. Nested-split transactions are an example of open nesting, which relaxes the top-level atomicity restriction of closed nested transactions where an open nested transaction allows its partial results to be observed outside the transaction. Consequently, one of the main issues for describing the local transaction processing on the MH is visibility and allowing new transactions to see uncommitted changes (weak data), which may result in undesired dependencies and cascading aborts. At the same time, when an update is made on a disconnected MH, subsequent transactions using the same data would be unable to proceed until a connection occurs and the mobile transactions could commit. Pro-Motion con-siders the entire mobile subsystem as one extremely large, long-lived transaction, which executes at the server with a subtransaction executing at each MH. Each of these MH subtransactions, in turn, is a root of another nested-split transaction. The results of local transactions on MH are automatically made visible for subsequent local access. In this way, local visibility and local commitment can reduce the blocking of transactions during disconnection and minimize the probability of cas-cading aborts. It is built on generalized client–server architecture with a mobile agent called compact agent, a stationary server front-end called compact manager, and an intermediate array of mobility managers to help manage the flow of up-dates and data between the other components of the system. Its fundamental build-ing block is the compact, which functions as the basic unit of replication for caching, prefetching, and hoarding. A compact is defined as a satisfied request to cache data, with its obligations, restrictions and state information. It represents an agreement between the database server and the MH where the database server delegates control of some data to the MH to be used for local transaction processing. The database server need not to be aware of the operations executed by individual transactions on the MH, but, rather, sees periodic updates to a compact for each of the data items manipulated by the mobile transactions. Compacts are defined as objects encapsulating the cached data, methods for the access of the cached data, current state information, consistency rules, obligations, and the interface methods. The management of compacts is performed by the compact manager on the database server and the compact agent on each MH cooperatively. Compacts are obtained from the database by requesting when a data demand is created by the MH. If data are available to satisfy the request, the database server creates a compact with the help of compact manager. The compact is then recorded to the compact store and transmitted to the MH to provide the data and methods to satisfy the needs of transactions executing on the MH. It is possible to transmit the missing or outdated components of a compact, which avoids the expensive transmission of already available compact methods on the MH. Once the compact is received by the MH, it is recorded in the compact registry, which is used by the compact agent to track the location and status of all local compacts. Each compact has a common interface, which is used by the compact agent to manage the compacts in the compact registry list and to perform updates submitted by transactions run by applications executing on the MH. Compact agent also performs disconnected processing when the MH is disconnected from the network and the compact manager is processing transactions locally. The compact manager maintains an event log, which is used for managing transaction processing, recovery, and resynchronization on the MH. Local commitment is permitted to make the results visible to other transaction on the MH, accepting the possibility of an eventual failure to commit at the server. Transactions, which do not have a local option, will not commit locally until the updates have committed at the server. As more than one compact may be used in a single transaction, the commitment of a transaction is performed using a two-phase commit protocol where all participants reside on the MH. On the other hand, resynchronization occurs when the MH reconnects to the network and the compact agent reconciles the updates committed during the disconnection with the fixed database.

Reference [30] defines a mobile transaction model, called kangaroo transaction (KT), which addresses the movement behavior of transactions in a mobile computing environment. This transaction model incorporates the property that transactions in a mobile environment hop from one base station to another as the mobile device moves. The model captures this movement behavior and the data behavior reflecting the access to data located in databases throughout the static network. The authors assume an architecture where each base station hosts a data access agent (DAA), which is used for accessing data in the database. When DAA receives a transaction request from a mobile user, the DAA forwards it to a specific base station or a fixed host that contains the required data. DAA acts as a mobile transaction manager (MTM) and data access coordinator for the site. It is built on top of an existing global database system, which assumes that the local DBMS performs the required transaction-processing functions including recovery and concurrency. DAA is, however, unaware of the mobile nature of some nodes or of the implementation details of each requested transaction. A hopping property is added to model the mobility of the transactions. Each subtransaction represents the unit of execution at one base station and is called a joey transaction (JT). The authors define a Pouch to be the sequence of global and local transactions, which are executed under a given KT. Each KT has a unique identification number consisting of the base station number and unique sequence number within the base station. When a mobile unit moves from one cell to another, the control of the KT changes to a new DAA at another base station. The DAA at the new base station creates a new JT as result of the hand-off process. JTs have sequenced identification numbers consisting of both the KT identification number and an increasing number. The mobility of the transaction model is captured by the use of split transactions. The old JT is committed independent of the new JT. If a failure of any JT occurs, which in turn may result in undoing the entire KT, a compensation for any previously completed JTs must be assured. Therefore, a KT could be in a split mode or in a compensating mode. A split transaction divides an ongoing transaction into serialized subtransactions. Earlier created subtransaction may be committed and the remaining ones can continue in its execution. However, the decision on as to abort or commit a currently executing subtransaction is left to the main DBMS. Previous JTs may not be compensated so that neither splitting mode nor compensating mode guarantees serializability of KTs. Although compensating mode assures atomicity, isolation may be violated because locks are obtained and released at the local transaction level. With the compensating mode, joey subtransactions are serializable. The MTM keeps a transaction status table on the base station DAA to maintain the status of those transactions. It also keeps a local log into which the MTM writes the records needed for recovery purposes. Most records in the log are related to KT status and some compensating information.

Approaches for Data Dissemination and Replication
This section presents related work on data dissemination and replication within wireless networks. The work on data dissemination assumes that servers have a relatively high bandwidth broadcast capacity while clients cannot transmit or can do so only over a lower bandwidth link. The data dissemination models are concerned with read-only transactions, where mobile clients usually issue a query to locate particular information or a service based on the current location of the device. Another model for data dissemination can be applied when a group of clients shares the same servers and they can, in general, also benefit from accepting responses addressed to other clients in their group.

Reference [1] presents a broadcast-based mechanism for disseminating information in a wireless environment. To improve performance for nonuniformly accessed data, and to efficiently utilize the available bandwidth, the central idea is that servers repeatedly broadcast data to multiple clients at various frequencies. The authors superimpose multiple disks of different sizes and speeds to create an arbitrarily fine-grained memory hierarchy, and study client cache management policies to maximize performance. The authors argue that in a wireless mobile network, servers may have a relatively high bandwidth broadcast capacity while clients cannot transmit or can do so only over a lower bandwidth link. Such systems have been proposed for many application domains, including hospital information systems, traffic information systems, and wireless classrooms. Traditional client–server information systems employ a pull-based algorithm, where clients initiate data transfers by sending requests to a server. The broadcast disks on the other hand exploit the advantage in bandwidth by broadcasting data to multiple clients at the same, and thus employ a push-based approach. In this approach, a server continuously and repeatedly broadcasts data to the clients, which effectively causes a creation of a disk from which clients can retrieve data as it goes by. The authors then model and study performance of various cache techniques at the client side and broadcast patterns at the server side within their architecture. The inherent limitations of this approach, however, restrict the clients to employ read-only transactions. In addition, it requires the client to wait for incoming data until it appears on the broadcast disk, even though the client may momentarily have a near-perfect wireless connectivity to a particular server.

Reference [75] presents an intelligent hoarding approach for caching files on the client side for mobile networks. The authors consider the case of a voluntary, client-initiated disconnection as opposed to involuntary disconnection that was under the scrutiny of many approaches described earlier. Therefore, the authors attempt to present a solution for intelligently caching important data at the client side, in their case files, once the client has informed the system about its planned disconnection. This is known as the hoarding problem, wherein hoarding tries to eliminate cache misses entirely during the period of client disconnection. The authors first describe other approaches consisting of doing nothing, utilizing explicitly user-provided information, logging user's past activity, and by utilizing some semantic information. Their approach is based on the concept of prefetching, and can be referred to as transparent analytical spying. The algorithm relies on the notion of working sets. It automatically detects these working sets for a user's applications and data. It then provides generalized delimiters for periods of activity, which is used to separate time periods for which a different collection of files is required.

Infostations [35] is a system concept proposed to support *many time, many where* wireless data services, including voice mail. It allows mobile terminals to communicate to Infostations with variable data transmission rate to obtain the optimized throughput. The main idea is to use efficient caching techniques to hoard as data as possible when connected to services within an island of high bandwidth coverage, and use the cached information when unable to contact the services directly. This idea is very similar to the previously described work by [75].

Reference [38] discusses an optimistically replicated file system designed for use in mobile computers. The file system, called Rumor, uses a peer model that allows opportunistic update propagation among any sites replicating files. This work describes the design and implementation of the Rumor file system, and the feasibility of using peer optimistic replication to support mobile computing. The authors discuss the various replication design alternatives and justify their choice of a peer-to-peer based optimistic replication. Replication systems can usefully be classified along several dimensions based on update type, device classification, and propagation methods. Conservative update replication systems prevent all concurrent updates, causing mobile users who store replicas of data items to have their updates frequently rejected, particularly when connectivity is poor or nonexistent. Optimistic replication on the other hand allows any device storing a replica to perform a local update, rather than requiring the machine to acquire locks or votes from other replicas. Optimistic replication minimizes the bandwidth and connectivity requirements for performing updates. At the same time, optimistic replication systems allow conflicting updates to occur. The devices can be classified either into client and servers to as peers. In the client–server replication, all updates must be first propagated to a server device that further propagates them to all clients. Peer-to-peer systems, on the other hand, allow any replica to propagate updates to any other replica. Although the client–server approach simplifies the system design and maintenance, the peer-to-peer system can propagate updates faster by making the use of any available connectivity. Lastly, the last dimension differentiates between an immediate propagation versus a periodic reconciliation. In the first case, an update must be propagated to all replicas as soon as it is (locally) committed, while in the latter case a batch method can be employed to conserve the constrained resources, such as bandwidth and battery. The authors, therefore, decided to design Rumor as an optimistic, peer-to-peer, reconciliation-based replicated file system. Rumor operates on file sets known as volumes. A volume is a continuous portion of the file system tree, larger than a directory but smaller than a file system. Reconciliation then operates at the volume granularity, which increases the possibility of conflicting updates and large memory and data requirement for storage and synchronization. At the same time, this approach does not introduce a high maintenance overhead. Additionally, the Rumor system employs a selective replication method and a per-file reconciliation mechanism to lower the unnecessary cost.

Reference [41] has investigated an epidemic update protocol that guarantees consistency and serializability in spite of a write-anywhere capability and conduct simulation experiments to evaluate this protocol. The authors argue that the traditional replica management approaches suffer from significant performance penalties. This is due to the requirement of a synchronous execution of each individual read-and-write operation before a transaction can commit. An alternative approach is a local execution of operations without synchronization with other sites. In their approach, changes are propagated throughout the network using an epidemic approach, where updates are piggy-backed on messages. This ensures that eventually all updates are propagated throughout the entire system. The authors advocate that the epidemic approach works well for single item updates or updates that commute; however, when used for multioperation transactions, these techniques do not ensure serializability. To resolve these issues, the authors have developed a hybrid approach where a transaction executes locally and uses epidemic communication to propagate all its updates to all replicas before actually committing. Transaction is only committed, once a site is ensured that updates have been incorporated at all copies throughout the system. They present experimental results supporting this approach as an alternative to eager update protocols for a distributed database environment where serializability is needed. The epidemic protocol relieves some of the limitations of the traditional approach by eliminating global deadlocks and by reducing delays caused by blocking. Additionally, the authors claim that the epidemic communication technique is more flexible than the reliable, synchronous communication required by the traditional approach, and justify this by presenting results of their performance evaluations. These results indicate that for moderate levels of replication, epidemic replication is an acceptable solution while significantly reducing the transmission cost.

7.3.5 Transaction Management Layer

This sublayer deals with the managing transactions initiated by devices in mobile ad hoc networks. For a transaction to succeed, a device must be able to commit its updates at the appropriate data manager that can be located in the wired network or on some of the device's peers in the current vicinity. Additionally, when data are modified at the primary side, all mobile devices should receive corresponding updates for their replicas.

Reference [57] defines transaction as a basic unit of consistent and reliable computing, consisting of a sequence of database operations executed as an atomic action. This definition encompasses the four important properties of a transaction: atomicity, consistency, isolation, and durability (i.e., ACID properties). *Atomicity* refers to the fact that a transaction is treated as a unit of operation. *Consistency* refers to a transaction being a correct transformation function from mapping one consistent state of a database onto another consistent state. *Isolation* requires that the data changes triggered by a transaction are hidden from others until the transaction commits. Lastly, *duration* of a transaction implies that an outcome of committed transaction is permanent and cannot be subsequently removed. Another important feature of a transaction is that it always terminates, by either committing the changes or by aborting all its updates.

The transaction problems in mobile environments arise due to the traditional concurrency control technique. The control technique often relies on locking, where a client wishing to modify data on the server database must first acquire a valid lock. For example, in the two-phase commit protocol (2PC) [32, 57] each participant and coordinator enter a state, where they are waiting on a message from one another. The only other escape from the idle state is only triggered by an expired timer. Since mobile devices may become involuntarily disconnected, this technique raises serious problems. If a lock is established on a mobile device, which becomes disconnected, the lock may be active for a long time, thus blocking the termination of a transaction. On the other hand, when a lock is established on a wired device by a mobile device, which since becomes disconnected, the data availability is reduced. These problems have spurred numerous solutions [14, 27, 30, 54, 67]. These approaches are usually based on modeling a novel breed of mobile transactions by proposing different transaction-processing techniques, such as [30], and/or by relaxing the ACID properties as for example in [80].

Having relaxed the ACID properties, one can no longer guarantee that all replicas are synchronized. Consequently, the data management layer must address this issue. Traditional replica control protocols, based on voting or lock principles [31], assume that all replica holders are always reachable. This is often invalid in mobile environments and may limit the ability to synchronize the replica located on mobile devices. Approaches addressing this issue include data division into volume groups and the use of versions for pessimistic [27] or optimistic updates [38, 50]. Pessimistic approaches require epidemic or voting protocols that first modify the primary copy before other replicas can be updated and their holders can operate on them. On the other hand, optimistic replication allows devices to operate on their replicas immediately, which may result in a conflict that will require a reconciliation mechanism [41]. Alternatively, the conflict must be avoided by calculating a voting quorum [48] for distributed data objects. Each replica can obtain a quorum by gathering weighted votes from other replicas in the system and by providing its vote to others. Once a replica obtains a voting quorum, it is assured that a majority of the replicas agree with the changes. Consequently, the replica can commit its proposed updates.

7.3.6 Security and Privacy Plane

The issues related to security and privacy are very important in mobile ad hoc networks. The three main reasons for this are the lack of any notion of security on the transmission medium, the lack of guaranteed integrity of data stored on mobile devices in the environment, and the real possibility of theft of a user's mobile device.

Despite the increased need for security and privacy in mobile environments, the inherent constraints on mobile devices have prevented large-scale research and development of secure protocols. Lightweight versions of Internet security protocols are likely to fail because they ignore or minimize certain crucial aspects of the latter, in order to save computation and/or memory. The travails of the wired equivalent privacy (WEP) protocol designed for the IEEE 802.11b are well known [81]. The IEEE 802.11b working group has now released WEP2 for the entire class of 802.1x protocols. Bluetooth also provides a link layer security protocol that consists of a *pairing* procedure, which accepts a user-supplied passkey to generate an initialization key. The initialization key is used to calculate a link key, which is finally used in a challenge–response sequence, after being exchanged. The current Bluetooth security protocol uses procedures that have low computation complexity, so they are susceptible to attacks. To secure data at the routing layer in client–server and client–proxy–server architectures, IPSec [49] is used in conjunction with Mobile IP. Research in securing routing protocols for networks using peer-to-peer architectures has resulted in interesting protocols such as Ariadne [86] and security-aware Ad hoc routing [85]. The wireless transport layer security (WTLS) protocol is the only known protocol for securing transport layer data in mobile networks. This protocol is part of the WAP stack. WTLS is a close relative of the secure sockets layer protocol that is de jure in securing data in the Internet. Transaction and application layer security implementations are also based on SSL.

7.3.7 System Management Plane

The system management plane provides interfaces so that any layer of the stack in Fig. 7.1 can access system level information. System level information includes data such as current memory level, battery power, and the various device characteristics. For example, the routing layer might need to determine whether the current link layer in use is IEEE 802.11b or Bluetooth to decide packet sizes. Transaction managers will use memory information to decide whether to respond to incoming transaction requests or to prevent the user from sending out any more transaction requests. The application logic will acquire device characteristics from the system management plane to inform the other end (server, proxy, or peer) of the device's screen resolution, size, and other related information. The service discovery layer might use system level information to decide whether to use semantic matching or simple matching in discovering services.

7.4 Peer-to-Peer Data Management Model

This section presents the MoGATU model introduced by [58–63], which attempts to answer mobile data management challenges raised by traditional mobile computing environments and those challenges specific to mobile ad hoc networks. The goal of the model is to allow mobile devices present in the environment to utilize efficiently their current resource-rich vicinity while pursuing their individual and collective tasks. The model makes three propositions:

1. *Postulate 1: All devices in mobile ad hoc networks are peers.* The widespread adoption of short-range ad hoc networking technologies allows mobile devices to interact with other devices in their current vicinity without the need of a back-end wired infrastructure. As a result, a mobile device can be both an information consumer, i.e., a client in the traditional mobile model, or an information provider, i.e., a server in the traditional mobile model. Consequently, there are no explicit clients and servers in this paradigm anymore. Instead, they become peers that can both consume and provide different services and data.
2. *Postulate 2: All devices in mobile ad hoc networks are semiautonomous, self-describing, highly interactive, and adaptive.* The characteristics of mobile ad hoc networks imply that a device's vicinity is highly volatile. Since all devices in the vicinity may be mobile, there is no guarantee about the duration of a connection among any pair of mobile devices. Consequently, mobile devices must be autonomous in order to operate correctly while their vicinity changes constantly. Additionally, as mobile devices move and as new data may arrive at any moment, there is no guarantee about the type of information available at any given time and space. Mobile devices must be adaptive to this nature of the environment in that they must be able to change their functionality and needs based on what

is currently available to them. Mobile devices must also be self-describing. They must be able to articulate their needs, which together with adaptivity will allow them to better utilize their vicinity. Finally, mobile devices must be highly interactive by offering data and services to their peers and by querying the information available on those peers.

3. *Postulate 3: All devices in mobile ad hoc networks require crosslayer inter- action between their data management and communication layers.* It is insufficient for mobile devices to employ mobile data management solu- tions that do not consider the underlying network characteristics. At the same time, it is simply not enough to attempt to solve the underlying net- working problems, including device discovery and routing of traffic between devices, independently from the data management aspect. Such solutions would waste the limited bandwidth and other resources. They would also fail due to the inability to allow mobile devices to completely satisfy their individual and collective tasks. As argued in Sect. 7.3, it is imperative that all mobile devices employ a model that considers both the networking and the data management aspects of the environments.

Figure 7.2 illustrates the corresponding representation of mobile devices from the MoGATU model's perspective. Applying definitions from [84], the model can be classified as *chained architecture* with a *random* replication and local *incre- mental policy*.

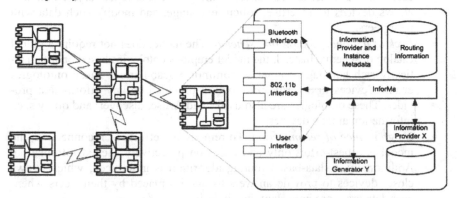

Fig. 7.2. Device abstraction in the MoGATU model

The model is a chained architecture because each data source, or consumer, registers with a local information manager only. Remote information managers present on other devices in the system are unaffected. When a query is placed, first the local information manager attempts to answer it. If it is unable to answer the query, only then the information manager, forwards the query to some remote Manager to which it is currently connected, i.e., to which it is *chained*.

The model employs a random replication policy because any mobile device can obtain and cache a specific data objects. There is no prior knowledge that can de- termine the location of all copies of a specific data object with respect to time and space.

The model also employs a local incremental update policy because there is no guarantee how long two devices may be able to communicate with each other. In order to overcome short session durations and network bandwidth limitations, information managers do not attempt to *load* all information their peers have available. Instead, an information manager only learns incrementally the capabilities of its peers as it queries them or through receiving remote advertisements.

Specifically, the MoGATU model addresses the data management challenges from Sect. 3.4 as follows:

- *Autonomy.* As described earlier, all devices are treated as independent entities acting autonomously from others.
- *Mobility.* The model does not place any restriction on the mobility patterns of devices.
- *Heterogeneity.* Mobile ad hoc networks are highly heterogeneous in terms of devices, data resources, and networking technologies. The model addresses this issue by having each device implement an information manager. Each stored information and service that is able to generate additional information is further abstracted by information providers. Lastly, networking technologies are abstracted in terms of communication interfaces that allow devices to interact regardless of the underlying networks.
- *Distribution.* Mobile devices may have multiple information providers, each holding a distributed subset of the global data repository. The model allows devices to advertise, solicit, exchange, and modify such data with their peers.
- *Lack of a global catalog and schema.* The model does not require a global catalog or schema. Instead, the model employs ontologies based on a semantically rich language – a set of common vocabularies. These ontologies enable devices to describe information provided by any information provider. These ontologies are also used to advertise, discover, and query such information among devices.
- *No guarantee of reconnection.* To remedy the effects of reconnection, the model is a best-effort only and relies on proactively cached information. Additionally, a data-based routing algorithm is introduced, which allows closer devices to provide answers to queries placed by their peers whenever data are more important than its origin.
- *Spatiotemporal variation of data and data source availability.* The model encourages every device to gather information proactively without human interaction. A user profile is used for representing the necessary information in order to allow devices to act independently. The profile is also annotated in a semantically rich language and is used by devices for adapting their caching and querying behavior.

The model abstracts each peer device in terms of information providers, information consumers, and information managers. Additionally, the model defines abstract communication interfaces for supporting multiple networking technologies. This is illustrated in Fig. 7.2.

Information providers, described in later, represent the available data sources. Every information provider holds a partial distributed set, a *fragment*, of heterogeneous data available in the whole mobile ad hoc network. The data model, described in Sect. 7.4.1, is a set of ontologies with data instances expressed in a semantic language. Each information provider stores its data in the data's base form according to the ontology definition. Data involving one ontology are already expressed in base form and stored in the format in which they were obtained. For data involving multiple ontologies, a provider decomposes the data into their base forms and maintains a view linking to the base forms. Using this approach a view is represented as a list of pointers to the respective base fragments. It may be impossible to maintain global consistency among all information providers because the mobile ad hoc network frequently remains partitioned. As a result, mobile nodes attempt to be vicinity-consistent only.

Information consumers, described later, represent entities that query and update data available in the environment. Information consumers can represent not only human users but also proactive agents that actively prefetch context-sensitive information from other devices in the environment.

Lastly, an instance of an information manager, described later, must exist on every mobile device. Information managers are responsible for network communication and for most of the data management functions. Each information manager is responsible for maintaining information about peers in its vicinity. This information includes the types of devices and information they provide. An information manager also maintains a data cache for storing information gathered from other mobile devices and for caching information generated by its local providers.

Not illustrated in Fig. 7.2 is the fact that each information manager also includes a user's profile reflecting some of the user's beliefs, desires, and intentions (BDI). The BDI model has been explored in multiagent interactions [11]. For profiles, it significantly extends [21], which explicitly enumerates data and its utility. In contrast, by using the BDI concept, profiles adapt to the environment by varying both data and their utility over time and present situations. Therefore, a profile enables proactive device behavior because mobile devices can adapt their operation and functionality dynamically based on the current context and user's needs without waiting explicitly for a user's input. The information manager uses the profile for adapting its caching strategies and for initiating collaboration with peers in order to obtain desired information.

7.4.1 Data Representation Model

Every mobile device holds a subset of globally available *heterogeneous* data. Since the mobile ad hoc networks are, by definition, open systems there are no restrictions or rules specifying the type and format of available data. In order to support heterogeneous devices but at the same time allow these devices to interact, it is important that these devices *speak* using a common language.

The efforts of the semantic Web community attempt to address similar issues by defining a semantically rich language – the Web ontology language (OWL)

[82]. This semantically rich language allows the specification of numerous types of data in terms of classes and their properties, and also defines relationship among the classes and the properties. It is advantageous to employ their proposed solution. In fact, as advocated in [60], the use of ontologies in these environments is vital.

By adhering to an already existing language, the syntax and rules do not have to be reinvented by defining new formal language. Second, by utilizing a language used by the semantic Web community, mobile devices will be able to use the resources available in their current vicinity as well as the vast resources available on the Internet. Therefore, the model assumes that information instances, profiles, and other data objects are represented using the OWL.

By using ontologies, the model, however, imposes a requirement that each device is able to parse OWL-annotated information. This is not to say that all devices will, or must, understand all ontologies. Rather, the model anticipates a scenario where each device has some knowledge over a set of ontologies. For new or unknown ontologies already present in the environment, a device can at least detect some metadata information by applying default OWL rules. This will allow a device to match queries with information providers' advertisements without any knowledge about the particular data. For example, this may allow a device that understands ontology A to use data annotated in an unknown ontology B, if B is a subClassOf A. For example, a device may not be able to deduce that Joy Luck is a Chinese restaurant, but it will at least know that Joy Luck is a restaurant.

Since each device is required to only parse OWL-annotated information, the introduction of ontologies in the system does not require much more processing resources than already available.

7.4.3 Application Layer

The application layer defines the specific logic employed by mobile devices. The logic specifies the interface for allowing users to operate over the devices. It also defines logic for devices to initiate actions and interact with other mobile devices. This logic can be abstracted in two types. One type represents information consumers, i.e., applications that search for information, while the other type of logic represents information producers. Information producers are those applications that can store or produce information requested by other applications, which can reside on the same or remote devices.

The model can be represented using the layered approach illustrated in in Fig. 6.1. Communication interfaces are responsible for the functionality of the communications layer. Information providers and information consumers are specific instances defining the application logic at the application layer. Lastly, the information manager combines the tasks of data and transaction management layers and their discovery and location sublayers. Figure 7.3 illustrates this possible reordering of the various components of the MoGATU model.

7.4.2 MoGATU Architecture Model

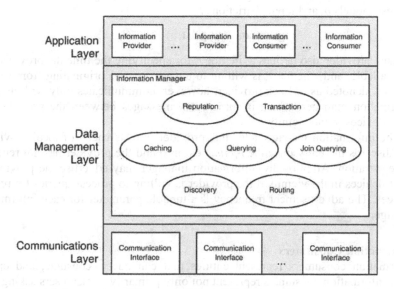

Fig. 7.3. Layered architecture of the MoGATU architecture model

Information Providers

Every device may hold one or more information providers. An information provider manages and provides an interface to a distributed subset of the global data repository. The data can be stored on the device or generated on-demand. The managed subset may be inconsistent with other *copies* located on other devices, as there is no guarantee that the devices can interact, and the subset may even be empty. In MoGATU, any entity is an information provider whenever it is able to accept some query and generate a proper response. For example, an information provider can represent a clock, a calendar, or any other application on a mobile handheld device. Given the variety of information providers, the response of each provider is based on the query, available stored data, and provider-specific mechanisms, including reference rules, for generating new data.

Each information provider describes its capabilities in terms of ontologies defined in a semantically rich language. The MoGATU model employs OWL. Moreover, the design is based on the OWL-S standard [76], which attempts to comprehensively describe services for the World Wide Web. Using this approach, each provider can describe itself by defining the service model it implements, the process model that provides the information, and the input, i.e., query, restrictions, and requirements. Moreover, the language supports efficient discovery and matching approaches required for locating information providers, cached answers, or for answering queries [18].

Upon start-up, each information provider registers itself with the local information manager by sending a registration message including the service model s, process models p, and input restrictions I:

$$\text{registration} = (s, p, I, t, a) \qquad (1)$$

Each provider also defines a lifetime t, for specifying the time the provider will be available, and whether it is willing to answer queries originating from remote devices, denoted as a. Each provider, however, communicates only with its local information manager, which in turn routes messages between the provider and other devices in the vicinity.

The information manager adds this provider into its cache of local providers, and discards the entry once the *lifetime* expired and the provider has not renewed its registration. Additionally, information manager may advertise the provider to other devices in the vicinity if the provider is willing to process queries for remote devices. The advertisement frequency is a tunable parameter for each information manager.

Information Consumers

Information consumers represent entities that can query, consume, and update data. Information consumers represent not only primarily human users asking their mobile devices for context-sensitive information but also autonomous software agents. Like information providers, consumers register with local information managers by sending a registration message. The presence of information consumers is, however, not advertised to remote devices.

When a consumer needs to obtain a specific data, the consumer constructs an *explicit query*. It sends the query to its local information manager. The manager routes the query to appropriate local information providers or other matching providers located on remote peer devices for processing, and awaits a response.

Like data they operate over, queries are also defined using an OWL-based ontology. Specifically, the queries are written using OWL-S. A query is specified by a tuple consisting of a set of used ontologies (O), selection list (σ), filtering statement (θ), cardinality (Σ), and temporal (τ) constraints:

$$\text{query} = (O, \sigma, \theta, \Sigma, \tau) \quad (2)$$

Each query defines the set of ontologies used for constructing the filtering clause and for final projection of the matching data instances. The set can include a specific ontology multiple times if the filtering clause consists of a join over multiple data streams represented in that ontology. The size of the ontology list, therefore, specifies the *degree* of the query. The degree represents the number of joins that must be performed for obtaining an answer. The filtering clause represents a combination of Boolean conjunctive and disjunctive predicates. A device uses its cached data and context information, including current geographical position and time of the day, as inputs to these predicates. This allows a mobile device to place a *dynamic* query asking for the closest local gas station. It also allows a device to pose a *static* query, for example, asking for a Chinese restaurant located on the W 72nd Street. Along with string and numeric comparisons the filtering clause supports basic calculations, such as addition and multiplication. Additionally, the filtering clause supports more advanced predicates based on the ontology specification, such as a distance computation between two geographical objects. The cardinality constraints of the query specify the minimum and maximum size of a required answer. Lastly, the temporal constraint specifies the relative deadline when the query should be completed. This is used by the device to query periodically its peers when time permits and the device has not yet cached a sufficient answer, given an implicit query.

7.4.4 Data Management Layer

This section describes the most important layer for data management in mobile ad hoc networks. It details the information manager, which is responsible for proactive profile-driven discovering, processing, combining, and storing of data available in the environment. The information manager is also responsible for evaluating the integrity of peer devices and the accuracy of peer provided information, to provide the best results to its local information consumers.

Information Manager
An information manager is responsible for majority of data management functions and partially for underlying network communications. From the data management perspective, information manager must be able to discover available sources, construct dynamic indexes and catalogs, support queries, and provide caching mechanisms for addressing the dynamic nature of the environments. From the networking perspective, information manager must also be able to discover and interact with remove devices, and route messages between them.

Each information manager maintains information about providers and consumers present on the same device as the information manager. This information includes the *lifetime* of each provider, their service models, process models, and their query restrictions. Each information manager also maintains information about peers in its vicinity. This information includes the identity of devices – a unique identification number similar to an Internet protocol address, and types of information they can provide, i.e., provider advertisements. Lastly, information manager maintains a data cache for storing information obtained from other mobile devices as well as the information provided by its local providers, i.e., answers to previous queries. Additionally, each information manager may include a user profile reflecting the user's preferences and needs. The information manager uses the profile to adapt its caching strategy and to initiate collaboration with peers in order to obtain missing required information.

Complexity Levels
Since devices can range from sensors to laptops the framework does not require all devices to implement the same set of functionalities. Instead, the framework

differentiates among five types of information managers based on their complexity levels.

In the simplest case (type 0), the information manager maintains at most one local provider. It does not cache any remote information and it does not possess any reasoning or parsing mechanisms. This information manager only periodically *broadcasts* data sent to it by the provider. This type of information manager is well suited for extremely resource-limited devices, such as a store beacon whose only task is to advertise the presence of its store.

On the other hand, devices wishing to interact in more intelligent manner and those that possess more resources must implement an information manager that is able to maintain information about multiple local and *remote* providers. These types of information manager must also be able to parse messages, route message to other peer devices, and proactively query peers. Based on the varying collaboration level four additional types of information managers are possible:

1. Information manager does not cache any remote advertisements or answers to queries.
2. Information manager caches remote advertisements only for the lifetime specified in the message or until replaced by another entry.
3. Information manager caches both advertisements and answers.
4. Information manager caches all advertisements and answers, and makes them available to other peers. This type of an information manager can effectively serve as a temporary partial catalog for all peers in the current vicinity.

In order to present all functionalities of the information managers, the following description assumes the most advanced type of an information manager, i.e., type 4. The remaining part of this section presents the most important components of the information manager, including:

- Data and service discovery component
- Query processing component
- Join query processing component
- Caching component
- Transaction component
- Reputation component

Data and Service Discovery Component

An important aspect of the framework is to discover local and remote information providers. The discovery allows each information manager to construct a temporary catalog representing current data and data sources in the vicinity. The MoGATU framework supports both push- and pull-based approaches, i.e., each information manager can advertise its capabilities from solicit capabilities of other peers. The frequencies of advertisements and soliciting queries are tunable parameters. In order to restrict the number of messages in the environments, solicitation and advertisements are limited to *one-hop* neighbors only.

Query Processing Component
While advertising and soliciting for Information providers is an important functionality, the key objective of an information manager is to provide querying capabilities. The querying is initiated by an information consumer, which sends the information manager a query annotated in OWL, as defined in Sect. 7.2.

The query includes a set of used ontologies (O), selection list (σ), filtering statement (θ), cardinality (Σ), and temporal (τ) constrains. The set of ontologies also represents the service model that can be used to answer the query. A query can represent a selection over a certain data set or it can involve a join over multiple data streams. The later scenario is addressed in "Join Query Processing Component".

An information manager matches the query against entries in its cache. Each entry in the cache represents an unexpired answer to a previous query (otherwise it would be removed), or an advertisement for some local or remote provider. The information manager parses the query and each entry according to OWL rules and relationships specified in the involved ontologies. The information manager compares service models s, i.e., the set of required ontologies, and validates the query against inputs restrictions i, i.e., the filtering and selection statements of the specific query. For cached answers, the information manager matches input values of the query, against those in the cached answer. The approach is equivalent to using traditional forward chaining methods, used by DATALOG/Prolog-based query processing techniques [34, 36]. The information manager first tries to find and return a cached answer. Otherwise, the information manager tries to find a local or a remote provider, in that order.

Join Query Processing Component
Often, an information consumer can ask a query that requires a device to join *horizontally* data streams from multiple devices holding the same type of data. The device may also have to join *vertically* data streams from different devices as they become available. The term *data stream* is used to represent any source that is able to provide data given a specific query and also to represent the "streaming"-data sources defined by the sensor network community.

To allow devices to answer queries involving multiple sources, a collaboration protocol is defined based on the principles of contract nets [4, 73]. The collaborative query processing protocol enables a mobile device to query its vicinity and locate peer data sources matching a given query. The protocol allows the information manager to obtain data matching any query, irrespective of whether the query is a *selection* or a *join*. It extends the traditional concept of nested loop joins and the simple selection query algorithm from above.

The collaborative query processing protocol allows two or more information managers to cooperate by executing any combination of select–project–join queries. The protocol accomplishes the task by subdividing queries. Each subquery can be assigned to a different device. The assignment is determined according to the available resources of devices present in the vicinity. For example, the collaborative query processing protocol allows a tourist to use her handheld device to ask for the closest, cheapest Laundromat that is open given her current location, time of the day, and a price range. The protocol also allows the tourist to ask for the closest Laundromat adjacent to a Chinese restaurant – a query requiring a join over two data *streams*.

Caching Component

Another key component of an information manager is caching. Each information manager stores query answers together with advertisements and registrations of local and remote providers in a cache. To provide answers to, at least the expected, user explicit queries, i.e., to overcome the spatiotemporal variation of data and data source availability, an information manager must utilize the cache in the most effective manner. MoGATU supports the traditional LRU and MRU replacement algorithms; however, as shown in [60], these two approaches are highly ineffective. This is because an information manager must utilize the knowledge included in a user's profile to improve cache *effectiveness*.

For caching, the information manager should use the profile in two ways (1) to allocate space for specific data type and (2) to assign utility value to each entry. In the first case, the information manager uses the profile to determine types of standing queries. The information manager uses these types to reserve portions of the cache for the related data types, e.g., traffic. MoGATU applies the first heuristic for defining two hybrid LRU+P and MRU+P algorithms and both heuristics for defining a semantic cache algorithm S+P [60].

Transaction Component

Maintaining data consistency between devices in distributed mobile environments has always been, and continues to be, a challenge. To operate correctly, devices involved in a transaction must ensure that their data repositories remain in a consistent state. While stationary nodes often embody powerful computers located in a fixed, wired infrastructure, this is not an option for mobile devices in wireless ad hoc networks. Since most traditional transactions rely on infrastructure help, the use of such transactions is limited in these environments.

To address the problem, MoGATU also defines a novel transaction model – the neighborhood-consistent transaction model (NC-Transaction) [61]. The focus of NC-Transaction is on maintaining consistency of transactions. This has generally been termed as the most important ACID property of transactions for mobile environments [30]; however, it is not critical for read-only transactions [59].

NC-Transaction provides a higher rate of successful transactions in comparison to models designed for traditional mobile computing environments. NC-Transaction maintains neighborhood consistency among devices in the vicinity. It does not ensure global consistency, a task often impossible since there is no guarantee that two devices will ever reconnect in mobile ad hoc networks.

NC-Transaction accomplishes neighborhood consistency and high successful termination rate by employing active witnesses and an epidemic voting protocol. NC-Transaction defines witnesses as devices in vicinity that can *hear* both transacting devices and agree to monitor the status of a transaction. Each witness can cast a vote to commit or abort a transaction. A transacting device must collect a quorum of the votes, defined as a percentage of all witness votes, to decide on the final termination action for a transaction. By using a voting scheme and redundancy of witnesses, NC-Transaction ensures that transacting devices terminate in a consistent state. Additionally, information stored by each witness can be used to resolve conflicts between devices involved in a transaction.

Trust Component for Evaluating Data and Source Integrity
In the preceding discussion it was assumed that all Information Providers and information managers are reliable. These components explicitly assume that answers provided are correct and do not verify the veracity of the information or their providers. This assumption is suitable for most mobile client–server environments; however, it is not suitable for peer-to-peer environments as they lack the intrinsic stability of *anchored* sources. In mobile peer-to-peer environments, some sources may provide faulty information due to malice or ignorance, which can lead to incorrect conclusions. Consequently, devices need a mechanism to evaluate the integrity of their peers and the accuracy of peer provided information.

To address this problem, MoGATU introduces an additional feature of an information manager. This feature depends on distributed trust and beliefs to evaluate data and device integrity [63]. In this belief-driven model, each device maintains and shares beliefs regarding the degree of trust it has for its peers. This trust is determined by previous experience and reputation made by other devices in the environment. Additionally, each device associates a value indicating its belief in the accuracy of the information the device holds. Each device, when querying its peers, uses the trust it has placed in the peers, in conjunction with the peers' accuracy belief of their information, to determine the reliability of the responses to its query.

7.4.5 Communications Layer

The lowest level of MoGATU deals with the networking aspect of the mobile ad hoc networks. The communication layer is responsible for discovering devices and for reliable exchange of data among devices. This layer is implemented using communication interfaces, which abstract different ad hoc networking technologies, such as Bluetooth or AdHoc IEEE 802.11 standards.

Communication Interface
To support multiple types of networking interfaces and to abstract these types from an information manager, each device implements at least one communication interface. A communication interface provides a common set of interfaces for discovering neighboring devices and for communicating with them.

Every communication nterface registers its capabilities with its local information manager. Upon start-up, the communication interface sends a registration message including the network type n and process model p encoded in OWL:

$$registration = (n, p). \quad (3)$$

The network type is a specific service instance of the OWL-S ontology, while the process model allows the information manager to interact with communication interfaces in the same manner as with information providers. While a communication interface is responsible for sending and receiving date over the transmission medium, the information manager is still *network aware*. This is because it can infer the network constraints and requirements from the information contained in the registered capabilities. The advantage of using an abstract representation for the underlying networks is twofold:

First, the addition of a new networking technology does not require changes to the information manager component. An information manager is not burdened by different packet formats and message sizes for different networking technologies. Moreover, the abstraction allows an information manager to route data across multiple network technologies at once. An information manager can accept data over one network technology and route it through an interface of another network technology. For example, this allows an information manager to talk to its peer using Bluetooth while the peer forwards the data to another peer using its AdHoc IEEE 802.11 interface. One such scenario is illustrated in Fig. 7.4.

This is because each information manager only maintains information about what communication interface it needs to use in order to interact with a specific peer. Additionally, since the underlying network is hidden, information managers use only the identity of the peer information manager as a destination of data instead of the network-specific address, which could otherwise be incompatible with other network standards. This is similar to the concept of Internet protocol addresses allowing devices connected to the Internet to communicate over heterogeneous network technologies like Ethernet and ATM.

An information manager can thus abstract its current vicinity as a graph, where nodes represent other devices in the environment and edges represent a connection between two peers over any technology. The information manager can then apply any link state or dynamic vector routing algorithm for computing path to a desired destination, e.g., AODV, DSDV, or DSR.

In *data-intensive* environments, an answer can often be provided by more than one device, e.g., cached by information managers, or available by local providers. The querying source may not be interested in whom it interacts with as long as it receives a correct answer. To improve the performance of the system, an information manager can intercept routed queries at the communication level.

MoGATU defines a hybrid mechanism combining discovery and routing for queries or data discovery among peer information managers in multihop networks. The algorithm uses a source-initiated approach similar to AODV and DSR. The algorithm works on a best-effort basis as it attempts to rebuild disconnected routes; however, it does not guarantee message delivery. Moreover, each information manager can intercept all messages it receives or routes to provide *shortcuts* for cached routes. Here, each information manager maintains a route entry for one-hop peers. The information manager also maintains a route entry for peers more than one hop away if those peers are used in on-going interactions or the information manager is caching advertisements for those peers.

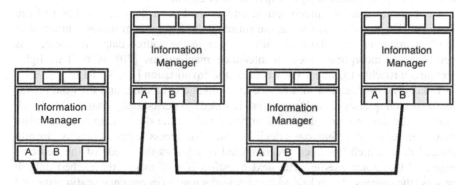

Fig. 7.4. Sample routing across multiple networking technologies

7.5 Future Work

This section outlines the future work that is required for achieving the overall goal of data management and processing in mobile ad hoc networks to allow individual devices to compute *what* information each device needs, *when* the device needs it, and *how* it can obtain the information. In particular, because of restrictions on query-answering power in mobile ad hoc networks, one important direction of work will be on intelligently applying precomputed information.

For processing user queries, many devices use cached information, which can also be referred to as materialized views. In many current approaches, the cached data mainly represent stored answers to queries that a device issued in the past. Much is to be gained if one changes the current approaches to caching data on devices, by doing *purpose-driven* data caching and view materialization. Since previously cached information is kept around in order to enable processing of current queries, the first step is to determine which precomputed information would benefit precisely the expected current queries. In many scenarios, expected queries can be extracted from the current context, from past queries on the given device, or from user profiles stored on the device.

Once the system has collected a workload of expected queries, purpose-driven data caching can be done *in advance*, to enable maximally efficient processing of queries. For instance, rather than caching full answers to some past queries, it makes sense to precompute and store on a device partial answers to multiple expected queries. A variety of approaches are possible, from purely ad hoc to fully formal approaches [2, 22]. As mobile ad hoc networks use relatively simplified ways of query processing, approaches based on multiquery optimization, such as [71], may be, however, able to guarantee better solution optimality than in standard standalone or distributed database scenarios. Additionally, to further improve the quality of stored data, precomputed for a given set of expected queries, it may be possible to use constraints that come from user profiles. Finally, it is also worth exploring restrictions on the size of cached data that need to be stored on a device to enable efficient processing of expected queries, such as [23].

Once useful data are precomputed and cached on a device, one has to keep them consistent and up to date as the source data may be continuously updated in the network over time. To deal with changes in the source data over time, it is necessary to incorporate view-maintenance mechanisms [70] as well as light-weight approaches to concurrency control and invalidation [15, 39, 83].

Finally, as the location of a device may change over time, and thus the prevalent expected queries also change, there is a need to periodically change the *definitions* of the derived data that need to be stored on the devices, to accommodate new expected queries. Suppose a device already has access to "good-quality" locally cached data, which has been precomputed to address the needs of the device's expected important queries. The next question is *how* to use the cached data to process the queries. As mobile ad hoc networks tend to experience spatio-temporal data variation and have no guarantee of reconnection or collaboration in query processing, in many cases the best we can hope for is to get *approximate* answers to the queries. Among others, the reasons are that not all sources can be taken into account when answering a query and that stored data are not necessarily up to date. A promising direction here is to explore purpose-driven approximate query answering, where a device chooses just some of the more useful sources for the purposes of the task related to the query. We can call this direction *purpose-driven* data integration, where, in particular, part of query processing is to use the advertised purposes of other data sources to collect only the information that is the most relevant for the query. In approximate query answering, we need to do formal analysis of the quality of answers to the queries using the currently available data. Another aspect of collaborative query answering is trust and security; one interesting direction here is to use, in query processing, trusted devices in the current context to verify the quality of information from potentially unreliable primary sources of the data [63].

7.6 Summary

This chapter presented an overview of challenges arising in the area of mobile data management and surveyed existing solutions, with emphasis on data management in mobile ad hoc networks. The chapter described origins of the mobile peer-to-peer computing model and related it to the traditional mobile data management models. The chapter then concentrated on the specific data management challenges due to three sources. One set of challenges is due to the nature of ad hoc networking, including problems such as device discovery, message routing, and restricted bandwidth. Next set of challenges relates to an information discovery in dynamic networks. The last set of challenges represents traditional data management issues, such as transactional support or consistency among data objects.

While describing the problems, the chapter surveyed proposed solutions to each problem category.

An important theme of this chapter is the fact that despite wireless ad hoc networking technologies and peer-to-peer based data management paradigms attempting to solve similar problems, there is a very limited effort on crosslayer interaction, which is essential for mobile ad hoc networks. The gap between the research on networking, data management, and context-awareness in pervasive computing environments is the fundamental problem of allowing a device to compute *what* information the device needs, *when* the device needs it, and *how* it can obtain the information. As an effort to address this issue, this chapter presented the MoGATU model [58–63] – a novel peer-to-peer data management model for mobile ad hoc networks. The chapter outlined the underlying conceptual model and basic assumptions of MoGATU, which treats all devices in the environment as semiautonomous peers guided in their interactions by profiles and local context. The chapter also presented the MoGATU abstraction of each device in terms of information providers, information consumers, and information managers, and details their respective concepts and functionality.

Finally, this chapter offered future work, which is required in order to bring the data management and processing in mobile ad hoc networks close to their goal to allow individual devices to compute *what* information each device needs, *when* the device needs it, and *how* it can obtain the information.

References

1. S. Acharya, R. Alonso, M. Franklin, and S. Zdonik. Broadcast disks: data management for asymmetric communication environments. In Proceedings of ACM SIGMOD, pp. 199–210, 1995.
2. F. Afrati and R. Chirkova. Selecting and using views to compute aggregate queries. In Proceedings of ICDT, 2005.
3. K. Arnold, B. Osullivan, R.W. Scheifler, J. Waldo, A. Wollrath, B. O'Sullivan, and R. Scheifler. The Jini Specification (The Jini Technology). Addison-Wesley, Reading, MA, June 1999.
4. S. Avancha, P. D'Souza, F. Perich, A. Joshi, and Y. Yesha. P2P M-Commerce in pervasive environments. In ACM SIGEcom Exchanges, 2003.
5. S. Avancha, A. Joshi, and T. Finin. Enhancing the Bluetooth Service Discovery Protocol. Technical report, CSEE, UMBC, August 2001. TR-CS-01-08.
6. S. Avancha, A. Joshi, and T. Finin. Enhanced service discovery in bluetooth. IEEE Computer, 35(6):96–99, June 2002.
7. P. Bahl and V.N. Padmanabhan. RADAR: an in-building RF-based user location and tracking system. In IEEE INFOCOM, Vol. 2, pp. 775–784, Tel Aviv, Israel, March 2000.

172   F. Perich et al.

8.   H. Bharadvaj, A. Joshi, and S. Auephanwiriyakyl. An active transcoding proxy to support mobile Web access. In Proceedings of the IEEE Symposium on Reliable Distributed Systems, October 1998.
9.   Bluetooth SIG. Specification. http://bluetooth.com/.
10.   C. Bobineau, L. Bouganim, P. Pucheral, and P. Valduriez. PicoDBMS: scaling down database techniques for the smartcard. In Proceedings of the 26th International Conference on Very Large Databases, 2000.
11.   M. Bratmann. Intentions, Plans, and Practical Reason. Harvard University Press, Cambridge, MA, 1987.
12.   D. Brickley and R. Guha. Resource Description Framework (RDF) Schema Specification 1.0 – W3C Recommendation. http://www.w3.org/TR/2000/CR-rdfschema-20000327, 2000.
13.   C. Brooks, M.S. Mazer, S. Meeks, and J. Miller. Application-specific proxy servers as HTTP stream transducers. In Fourth International World Wide Web Conference, pp. 539–548, Boston, Massachusetts, December 1995.
14.   Bukhres, S. Morton, P. Zhang, E. Vanderdijs, C. Crawley, J. Platt, and M. Mossman. A proposed mobile architecture for distributed database environment. Technical report, Indiana University, Purdue University, 1997.
15.   P. Cao and C. Liu. Maintaining strong cache consistency in the world wide web. IEEE Transactions on Computers, 47(4):445–457, 1998.
16.   D. Chakraborty, A. Joshi, T. Finin, and Y. Yesha. GSD: a novel group-based service discovery protocol for MANETS. In Fourth IEEE Conference on Mobile and Wireless Communications Networks (MWCN), pp. 301–306, Stockholm, Sweden, September 2002.
17.   D. Chakraborty, F. Perich, S. Avancha, and A. Joshi. DReggie: a smart service discovery technique for E-Commerce applications. In Workshop at 20th Symposium on Reliable Distributed Systems, October 2001.
18.   D. Chakraborty, F. Perich, S. Avancha, and A. Joshi. DReggie: semantic service discovery for M-Commerce applications. In Workshop on Reliable and Secure Applications in Mobile Environment, SRDS, October 2001.
19.   D. Chakraborty, F. Perich, A. Joshi, T. Finin, and Y. Yesha. A reactive service composition architecture for pervasive computing environments. In Seventh Personal Wireless Communications Conference (PWC), pp. 53–62, Singapore, October 2002.
20.   H. Chen, T. Finin, and A. Joshi. Semantic Web in a pervasive context-aware architecture. Artificial Intelligence in Mobile System 2003, pp. 33–40, October 2003.
21.   M. Cherniak, E. Galvez, D. Brooks, M. Franklin, and S. Zdonik. Profile driven data management. In 28th International Conference on Very Large Databases, August 2002.
22.   R. Chirkova, A. Halevy, and D. Suciu. A formal perspective on the view selection problem. VLDB Journal, 11(3):216–237, 2002.
23.   R. Chirkova and C. Li. Materializing views with minimal size to answer queries. In Proceedings of PODS, 2003.
24.   T.H. Cormen, C.E. Leiserson, R.L. Rivest, and C. Stein. Introduction to Algorithms. Prentice-Hall, Englewood Cliffs, NJ, 2001.

25. S. Czerwinski, B. Zhao, T. Hodes, A. Joseph, and R. Katz. An architecture for a secure service discovery service. In Fifth Annual International Conference on Mobile Computing and Networks (MobiCom'99), pp. 24–35, Seattle, WA, 1999.

26. DARPA. DARPA Agent Markup Language + Ontology Inference Layer (DAML+OIL). http://www.daml.org.

27. J. Demers, K. Petersen, M.J. Spreitzer, D.B. Terry, M.M. Theimer, and B.B. Welch. The bayou architecture: support for data sharing among mobile users. In IEEE Workshop on Mobile Computing Systems & Applications, 1994.

28. K. Dey and G.D. Abowd, editors. Towards a Better Understanding of Context and Context-Awareness, GVU, Georgia Institute of Technology, The Hague, The Netherlands, April 2000.

29. M. Dunham and A. Helal. Mobile computing and databases: anything new? SIGMOD Record, pp. 5–9, 1995.

30. M. Dunham, A. Helal, and S. Balakrishnan. A mobile transaction model that captures both the data and movement behavior. Mobile Networks and Applications, pp. 149–162, 1997.

31. S. Ellis and R.A. Floyd. The roe file system. In Third Symposium on Reliability in Distributed Software and Database Systems, pp. 175–181, IEEE, Clearwater Beach, Florida, 1983.

32. K.P. Eswaran, J. Gray, R.A. Lorie, and I.L. Traiger. The notion of consistency and predicate locks in a database system. Communications of the ACM, 19(11):624–633, December 1976.

33. M. Franklin. Challenges in ubiquitous data management. In Informatics, 2001.

34. T. Gaasterland and J. Lobo. Qualified answers that reflect user needs and preferences. In VLDB, 1994.

35. D. Goodman, J. Borras, N. Mandayam, and R. Yates. INFOSTATIONS: a new system model for data and messaging services. In Proceedings of IEEE VTC'97, Vol. 2, pp. 969–973, 1997.

36. J. Grant, J. Gryz, J. Minker, and L. Raschid. Semantic query optimization for object databases. In ICDE, 1997.

37. E. Guttman, C. Perkins, J. Veizades, and M. Day. RFC 2068: Service Location Protocol, version 2, 1999. ftp://ftp.isi.edu/in-notes/rfc2608.txt.

38. R.G. Guy, P.L. Reiher, D. Ratner, M. Gunter, W. Ma, and G. J. Popek. Rumor: mobile data access through optimistic peer-to-peer replication. In ER Workshops, pp. 254–265, 1998.

39. J. Gwertzman and M.I. Seltzer. World wide web cache consistency. In USENIX Annual Technical Conference, pp. 141–152, 1996.

40. Hofmann-Wellenhof, H. Lichtenegger, and J. Collins. Global Positioning System: Theory and Practice. Springer Berlin Heidelberg New York, 4th edition, May 1997.

41. J. Holliday, D. Agrawal, and A.E. Abbadi. Database replication using epidemic communication. In European Conference on Parallel Processing, pp. 427–434, 2000.

42.   T. Imielinski and B.R. Badrinath. Mobile wireless computing: challenges in data management. Communications of the ACM, 37(10):18–28, 1994.
43.   T. Imielinski, S. Viswanathan, and B.R. Badrinath. Data on air: Organization and access. IEEE Transactions on Knowledge and Data Engineering, pp. 352–372, May/June 1997.
44.   J. Ioannidis, D. Duchamp, and M. Gerald Jr. IP-based protocols for mobile internetworking. In ACM SIGCOMM Symposium on Communication, Architecture and Protocols, pp. 235–243, Z®urich, Suisse, 1991.
45.   D.B. Johnson and D. Maltz. Dynamic source routing in ad hoc wireless networks. In Mobile Computing, 1996.
46.   Joshi. On proxy agents, mobility and Web access. ACM/Baltzer Journal of Mobile Networks and Applications, 2000.
47.   Joshi, R. Weerasinghe, S.P. McDermott, B.K. Tan, G. Bernhardt, and S. Weerawarana. Mowser: Mobile platforms and Web browsers. Bulletin of the Technical Committee on Operating Systems and Application Environments (TCOS), 8(1), 1996.
48.   P. Keleher and U. Cetintemel. Consistency management in Deno. ACM MONET, 1999.
49.   S. Kent and R. Atkinson. IP Encapsulating Security Payload. World Wide Web. http://www.ietf.org/rfc/rfc2406.txt, November 1998.
50.   J.J. Kistler and M. Satyanarayanan. Disconnected operation in the coda file system. In 13th ACM Symposium on Operating Systems Principles, pp. 213–225, Asilomar Conference Center, Pacific Grove, US, 1991. ACM Press.
51.   G. Klyne, F. Raynolds, and C. Woodrow. Composite Capabilities/Preference Profiles (CC/PP): Structure and Vocabularies. World Wide Web. http://www.w3.org/TR/CCPP-struct-vocab/, March 2001.
52.   H. Kottkamp and O. Zukunft. Location-aware query processing in mobile database systems. In Selected Areas in Cryptography, pp. 416–423, 1998.
53.   Lassila and R. Swick. Resource Description Framework. http://www.w3.org/TR/1999/REC/rdf-syntax-19990222, 1999.
54.   S. Lauzac and P. Chrysanthis. Utilizing versions of views within a mobile environment. In Proceedings of the Ninth International Conference on Computing and Information, 1998.
55.   Z.M. Mao, E.A. Brewer, and R.H. Katz. Fault-tolerant, scalable, wide-area internet service composition. Technical report, CS Division, EECS Department, University of California, Berkeley, January 2001
56.   S. Muench and M. Scardina. xslt20req, February 2001. XSLT Requirements. World Wide Web. http://www.w3.org/TR/
57.   M. Oezsu and P. Valduriez. Principles of Distributed Database Systems. Prentice-Hall, New Jersey, 2nd edition, 1999.
58.   F. Perich, S. Avancha, D. Chakraborty, A. Joshi, and Y. Yesha. Profile driven data management for pervasive environments. In 13th International Conference on Database and Expert Systems Applications (DEXA 2002), Aix en Provence, France, September 2002.

59.   F. Perich, A. Joshi, T. Finin, and Y. Yesha. On data management in pervasive computing environments. IEEE Transactions on Knowledge and Data Engineering, 2004. accepted for publication.

60.   F. Perich, A. Joshi, Y. Yesha, and T. Finin. Neighborhood-consistent transaction management for pervasive computing environments. In 14th International Conference on Database and Expert Systems Applications (DEXA 2003), Prague, Czech Republic, September 2003.

61.   F. Perich, A. Joshi, Y. Yesha, and T. Finin. Collaborative joins in a pervasive computing environment. VLDB Journal, December 2004.

62.   F. Perich, J.L. Undercoffer, L. Kagal, A. Joshi, T. Finin, and Y. Yesha. In reputation we believe: query processing in mobile ad-hoc networks. In International Conference on Mobile and Ubiquitous Systems: Networking and Services, Boston, MA, August 2004.

63.   Perkins. RFC 3220: IP Mobility Support for IPv4, 2002. http://www.ietf.org/rfc/rfc3220.txt.

64.   C.E. Perkins and P. Bhagwat. Highly dynamic destination-sequenced distance-vector routing (DSDV) for mobile computers. In ACM SIGCOMM'94 Conference on Communications Architectures, Protocols and Applications, pp. 234–244, 1994.

65.   C.E. Perkins and E.M. Royer. Ad hoc on-demand distance vector routing. In Proceedings of the second IEEE Workshop on Mobile Computing Systems and Applications, pp. 90–100, New Orleans, LA, February 1999.

66.   E. Pitoura. A replication schema to support weak connectivity in mobile information systems. In Database and Expert Systems Applications, pp. 510–520, 1996.

67.   Pullela, L. Xu, D. Chakraborty, and A. Joshi. A component based Architecture for Mobile Information Access. In Workshop in conjunction with International Conference on Parallel Processing, pp. 65–72, August 2000.

68.   J. Rekesh. UPnP, Jini and Salutation – a look at some popular coordination frameworks for future network devices. Technical report, California Software Labs, 1999.

69.   N. Roussopoulos. Materialized views and data warehouses. SIGMOD Record, 27(1), 1998.

70.   P. Roy, S. Seshadri, S. Sudarshan, and S. Bhobe. Efficient and extensible algorithms for multi query optimization. In W. Chen, J.F. Naughton, and P.A. Bernstein, editors, Proceedings of the 2000 ACM SIGMOD International Conference on Management of Data, 16–18 May 2000, Dallas, Texas, USA, pp. 249–260. ACM, 2000.

71.   R. Sessions. COM and DCOM: Microsoft's Vision for Distributed Objects. Wiley, New York, NY, October 1997.

72.   R. Smith. The contract net protocol: high-level communication and control in a distributed problem solver, Readings in Distributed Artificial Intelligence, 1988.

73.   Sun Microsystems. Jini architecture specification. http://www.sun.com/jini/.

74.   Tait, H. Lei, S. Acharya, and H. Chang. Intelligent file hoarding for mobile computers. In Proceedings of the First ACM International Conference on Mobile Computing and Networking – MobiCom'95, 1995.

75.   The OWL Services Coalition. OWL-S: Semantic Markup For Web Services. http://www.daml.org/services/, November 2003.

76.   J. Undercoffer, F. Perich, A. Cedilnik, L. Kagal, and A. Joshi. A secure infrastructure for service discovery and access in pervasive computing. ACM MONET: Special Issue on Security in Mobile Computing Environments, 8(2):113–125, 2003.

77.   UPNP Forum. Understanding Universal Plug and Play: A White Paper. http://upnp.org/download/UPNP_UnderstandingUPNP.doc.

78.   J. Veizades, E. Guttman, C.E. Perkins, and S. Kaplan. RFC 2165: Service Location Protocol, June 1997.

79.   G.D. Walborn and P.K. Chrysanthis. PRO-MOTION: Management of mobile transactions. In Selected Areas in Cryptography, pp. 101–108, 1997.

80.   J.R. Walker. Unsafe at any key size: an analysis of the WEP encapsulation. IEEE Document 802.11–00/362, October 2000.

81.   World Wide Web Consortium (W3C). Ontology web language (owl). http://www.w3.org/

82.   K.J. Worrell. Invalidation in large scale network objects caches. Master's thesis, 1994.

83.   B. Yang and H. Garcia-Molina. Comparing hybrid peer-to-peer systems. In 27th VLDB Conference, 2001.

84.   S. Yi, P. Naldurg, and R. Kravets. Security-aware ad hoc routing for wireless networks. In Second ACM Symposium on Mobile Ad Hoc Networking and Computing, pp. 299–302, Long Beach, California, USA, October 2001.

85.   Y.-C. Hu, A. Perrig, and D.B. Johnson. Ariadne: a secure on-demand routing protocol for ad hoc networks. In Eighth ACM International Conference on Mobile Computing and Networking, pp. 12–23, Atlanta, Georgia, USA, September 2002. ACM Press.

86.   B. Zaslavsky and Z. Tari. Mobile computing: overview and current status. Australian Computer Journal, 30(2):42–52, 1998.

87.   B. Zenel. A proxy based filtering mechanism for the mobile environment. PhD thesis, Department of Computer Science, Columbia University, New York, NY, December 1995.

8 Mobile Agents: The State of the Art

B. Yang[1,2] and J. Liu[1]

1. Hong Kong Baptist University, Kowloon Tong, Kowloon, Hong Kong
2. Jilin University, Changchun, China

8.1 Introduction

This chapter will lead the reader into the world of mobile agents, a promising distributed technology that makes the design, implementation, and maintenance of distributed systems much easier than do traditional development methodologies.

Unlike stationary agents, which run on one host computer during their entire lifecycle, mobile agents can move their code to a new host where they can resume executing. The idea of transporting programs in a network is not new. However, a program whose sole ability is to transport itself from one host to another cannot be properly described as a mobile agent. Generally, mobile agents are a special kind of software – they not only possess basic characteristics (being generally autonomous, reactive, goal driven, and social), but also have the ability to move. Specifically, they can transport themselves from one site in a network to another but are not confined to the systems in which they began to execute.

The ability to travel, which distinguishes mobile agents from other types of agents, allows them to move to a new host and then to take advantage of being in the same environment to interact with each other locally. Lange, the inventor of Aglets, has surveyed the advantages and applications of the mobile agent paradigm [1]. Using mobile agents to develop a distributed system can yield many advantages, such as reducing network load; overcoming network latency; encapsulating protocols; executing asynchronously and autonomously; and adapting dynamically, natural heterogeneity, robustness, and fault tolerance. These advantages lead to improved performance in many distributed applications, and mobile agents are consequently viewed as a general paradigm by which to realize arbitrary distributed applications. These potential beneficiaries include electronic commerce, personal assistance, distributed information retrieval, telecommunication networks services, workflow applications, monitoring and notification, parallel processing, and so on [1].

Many mobile agent systems have been developed to date. These can be classified into two main groups – Java-based and non-Java-based. Aglets [2], Concordia [3], Voyager [4], and Grasshopper [5] are the most famous examples of the former. Telescript [6], Agent Tcl (renamed D'Agent) [7], Ara [8], Messenger [9], and TACOMA [10] are the most widely used non-Java-based systems, using script languages such as Tcl, Python, Perl, or Telescript.

In this chapter, we focus on the kernel technologies required to build a mobile agent system, discussing in detail the facilities, migration and planning, communication and interoperability, and security issues.

8.2 System Facilities

A mobile agent system is a platform that can create, interpret, execute, transfer, and manage agents. The architecture of most existing mobile agent systems is hierarchical, as illustrated in Fig. 8.1. A host can contain one or more of these systems, which themselves are likely to contain a number of places (also called context, location, or environment in some systems), which are the homes of mobile agents and provide various services. To provide security and scalability, the Object Management Group (OMG) introduces the concept of region into mobile agent system architecture [11].

The mobile agent system provides some basic facilities for safely executing local as well as visiting agents. These include naming, lifecycle, serialization/deserialization, code base, transfer, communication and interoperability, security, and management facilities. A stronger system may provide additional useful facilities such as CORBA and event, transaction, yellow page, and domain name services:

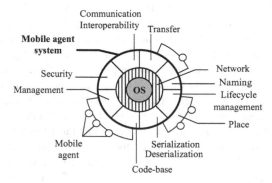

Fig. 8.1. The architecture of mobile agent system

- *Naming facility.* In terms of benefits, a qualified naming facility should at the least be able to (1) generate unique names for agent systems, places, and agents; (2) allow a system to quickly determine whether it can support an incoming agent and (3) enable agents to locate and identify others before communicating with each other by name.
- *Lifecycle facility.* Each mobile agent has its own basic lifecycle model, including some basic behaviors, the implementation and management of which is the responsibility of the lifecycle facility. For example, Aglets

provides a lifecycle facility to manage behaviors such as creation, cloning, dispatching, retraction, activation, deactivation, and disposal [2].

- *Serialization/deserialization facility.* This could be used in circumstances such as creation, moving, activation, and deactivation. OMG defines serialization as the process of storing the agent in a serialized form, and deserialization as the reverse (i.e., the process of restoring the agent from its serialized form [11]).

- *Code-base facility.* The code base is a repository of the codes or classes used by an agent. It can be part of either an agent or a nonagent system such as a Web server, which can be referred to as a code or class provider. In the latter, the agent system must have enough information to locate the code base even if it is distributed in a large network when it creates a new agent.

- *Transfer facility.* The transfer facility is responsible for sending an agent from one place to another across the network using the agent transfer protocol (ATP). As mentioned earlier, it is beneficial for agents to be able to communicate with each other or to access services locally rather than across a network, especially in a low-bandwidth and high-delay wireless network environment. Transferring an agent generally involves certain essential steps, which are described in sect. 8.3.

- *Communication and interoperability facility.* Four types of communication may be involved in applications based on mobile agents: agent/service agent, mobile agent/mobile agent, agent group communication, and user/agent [12]. Existing protocols work well for traditional distributed applications, but they might not be competent in the context of mobile agents. Here, communication issues are mainly addressed in terms of how best to resolve problems resulting from the agent's movements and how to improve its communication performance. As many communication protocols could be used by different mobile agent systems, issues such as interoperability also have to be considered.

- *Security facility.* Before the mobile agent paradigm can become a mainstream software technique for developing commercial applications, the security issues resulting from mobility must be resolved. The security facility is responsible for protecting both hosts and agents. Nowadays, some practical security technologies, such as identity authentication, encryption, integrity verification, authorization, and access control, have been adapted to comprise the security facility. Furthermore, many extensions to these conventional techniques are now available, as are new techniques specifically devised to provide mobile agent security. To date, however, a perfect solution to the security problems has not yet been developed.

- *Management facility.* This permits the administrator to manage the mobile agent system and its component agents via commands or operations provided at the interface, such as creating, suspending, resuming, terminating, and observing the behaviors of an agent. Such resources should be managed for two purposes: accounting and resource control, both of which are prerequisites for commercial applications. Generally the following resources should be managed: CPU time, local network communication, local resource including data information and hard devices, number of created agents, and so on.

According to Rothermel [12], some mobile agent systems draw a strict distinction between mobile agents and the so-called service agents. Service agents are stationary and interface with the services available at particular places. Those services may include system-level services, such as file or directory access, as well as application-level services, such as flight reservation or commodities' delivery. Service agents encapsulate arbitrary services and represent them in the system. From a technical point of view, service agents map the service request expressed in the "agent language" to the individual service interface, which allows legacy systems to be incorporated.

Finally, it is appropriate to examine the deployment issue. Places can be single node or multinode. Typically, a place is located in its entirety at a single host of the underlying network, which is to say that all services associated with a place reside on the same node. In this scenario, more than one place might be implemented on a single host. This does not mean that all the service implementations also have to be located at the place's node. It is conceivable that the place's services might be distributed over the different hosts, so that services can be accessed by a mobile agent not only locally but also remotely, typically via a high-speed LAN. Single-node places are generally cheaper than multinode places during intraplace communication and are simpler to realize.

8.3 Migration and Planning

In this section we present the concepts of migration and planning – two important aspects of mobile agent systems.

8.3.1 Traditional Communication Paradigms

Communication between distributed applications can be supported by various kinds of protocols, such as message passing, remote procedure call (RPC), remote evaluation, mobile code, and so on. The mobility of agents provides a new way to ensure efficient and heterogeneous communication among applications in distributed networks.

Message passing, by explicitly sending and receiving messages, provides a flexible paradigm for communication. However, applications based on message passing are very complex, error prone, and hard to maintain. RPC provides a higher level paradigm in which processes communicate with each other by calling procedures rather than explicitly sending and receiving messages. With RPC, a lot of the hard tasks involved in processing heavy communication become transparent to the developers of complex distributed applications. Based on the RPC paradigm, a famous distributed computing paradigm, client/server (C/S), can be proposed. In the C/S mode, stubs and skeletons, located at the client and server processes, respectively, provide methods for the marshalling/unmarshalling of messages, encoding/decoding in heterogeneous environments, and failure recovery. Obviously, a prerequisite for the effective functioning of RPC or C/S is that the called procedures are available on the corresponding remote node.

In some cases, it may be more efficient to dispatch procedures directly to a remote node and execute them locally. For instance, a filter procedure might be dispatched by its father program to a remote host with a large database to access information locally, without involving heavy traffic in communications channels. Remote evaluation is a flexible communication paradigm in which a process not only passes the parameters of the called procedure but also the code of the procedure itself. Later this paradigm can be generalized to code-on-demand (COD), which supports both "code-pull" and "code-push." For example, Java applets or ActiveX controls are programs that clients pull from servers, while Java servlets are codes pushed to servers by clients.

8.3.2 Mobility

Unlike process migration, agent migration is totally under the control of the agent itself rather than the underlying system (e.g., operating or load balancing). Agents decide when and where to move depending on their reflections on the environment. Consequently, a mobile agent system needs to provide specific statements such as "go" or "move."

When agents are moved, not only their codes but also their state information have to be transferred together to the destination. An agent's state is subdivided into data and execution states. Data states include the agent's global and instance variables, and execution states comprise local variables, program stack, and program counter.

Fuggetta et al. [13] divide mobility into two categories – weak and strong – according to which kind of states should be transported with the agent. Baumann et al., the developers of Mole, use Fig. 8.2 to illustrate the relationship between strong and weak mobility and the other kinds mentioned earlier.

Weak mobility permits the migration of the code and data states. After the migration, the agent is restarted and the values of its attribute variables restored, but its execution starts from the beginning or from a specific procedure (a method in the case of objects). In strong mobility, not only the code and data states but also the whole execution state are all transported, in order to restart the execution from the exact point where it was stopped before migration.

Weak mobility might substantially reduce the size of transferred state information by letting the programmer select the variables making up the agent state. This puts an additional burden on the programmer and makes mobile agent programs more complex because the agent's relevant execution states have to be encoded; the programmer also has to decide where to continue the agent's execution after migration based on the data state information that has been transferred.

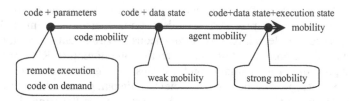

Fig. 8.2. Degrees of mobility concept [Baumann, 1998]

Different mobile agent systems have different ways to transfer agents, although most of these have some basic steps in common. OMG presents a standard procedure of transferring agents, which involve initiating a transfer, receiving an agent, and transferring codes or classes (in the case of object-oriented languages) [11].

Initiating an agent transfer
When a mobile agent prepares for a migration, the following actions will be initiated:
- Suspend the agent.
- Identify the pieces of the agent's state that will be transferred.
- Serialize the instance of the agent.
- Encode the serialized agent for the chosen transport protocol (for example, ATP of Aglets).
- Authenticate the destination agent system.
- Transfer the agent.

Receiving an agent
After it has been agreed that an incoming agent will be inserted into a destination agent system, the following actions will be executed:
- Authenticate source agent system and incoming agent.
- Decode the agent.
- Deserialize the agent class and state.
- Instantiate the agent.
- Restore the agent states.
- Resume agent execution.

Transferring codes
According to OMG there are three possible events that would give rise to a code transfer during the lifespan of a mobile agent [11]. Firstly, the situation where one agent has been created but its codes do not exist at the current system; secondly, where an agent travels to another system within which its codes do not exist at the destination point; and finally, where one agent creates other objects whose codes do not exist in the current system.

Under such circumstances, the following code-transferring strategies can be used [11]:

- Automatic transfer of all possible codes needed.
- Automatic transfer of the agent codes only, with other codes transferred on demand later.
- Transfer of a list of the names of all possible codes with the agent.

8.3.3 Planning

In this section we discuss a further topic of relevance to the world of the mobile agent – the planning system, also called the "navigation system" or "radar system." This endows mobile agents with the ability to deal with dynamic network environments and to search within them for information resources. From the viewpoint of a researcher, planning in the context of a mobile agent includes two main areas where the agent requires assistance (1) a searching problem (finding the information in which the agent is really interested) and (2) a routing problem (choosing the best migration path given the agent's task and the network conditions operating at the time).

As regards the former, most current mobile agent systems use a "directory service" or "yellow page service" to navigate through their agents to search for the information that they want. A directory is usually a single list of resource information. More practical and complex ones may be organized hierarchically, with each entry consisting of either a piece of information about one kind of registered resource or an address pointer pointing to another directory server. Searching mobile agents can access these directories by communicating remotely with directory servers, or by interacting with them locally after having moved on to them. Using these as a guide, searching agents migrate from one host to another until they find the resource that they want. The directory mechanism raises issues, such as how to find new resources and how to keep the information up to date. However, there is as yet no perfect solution to the problem of how to find resources more efficiently; more powerful search mechanisms for mobile agents dealing with more complex and advanced searching tasks are required.

We turn now to the routing problem, which has been formalized as the traveling agent problem (TAP) in Moizumi's Ph.D. dissertation [14]. Moizumi and his colleagues developed a distributed information retrieval application called a "technical-report searcher" based on their mobile agent system D'Agent. In this application, they set out the TAP and design the planning system based on it.

The architecture of the planning system for the TAP is depicted in Fig. 8.3. It consists of three main components: planning, network sensing, and yellow pages' modules. In this system, when a mobile agent is required to search for information, it consults with the planning module. This will find it an optimal path based on the information provided by the other two modules.

The TAP is something like the classical traveling salesman problem (TSP) from graph theory. Formally, it is defined as follows [14]:

"There are $n+1$ sites, s_i with $0 \le i \le n$. Each site has a known probability, $0 \le p_i \le n$, of being able to successfully complete the agent's task, and a time $t_i > 0$, required for the agent to attempt the task at s_i regardless of whether it is successful. These probabilities are independent of each other. Travel times or latencies for the agent to move between sites are also known and given by $l_{ij} \ge 0$ for moving between site i and site j. When the agent's task has been successfully completed at some site, the agent must return to the site from which it started (i.e., site 0). For site 0, $p_0 = t_0 = 0$. TAP is to minimize the expected time to successfully complete the task."

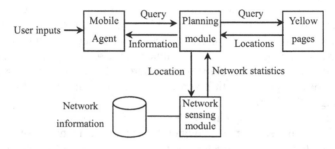

Fig. 8.3. The architecture of the planning system for the TAP [14]

In his dissertation, Moizumi proves that TAP is NP complete, like the traditional TSP. Because of its complexity, he presents a simplified version of TAP with polynomial time, which is described in detail in his dissertation [14].

8.4 Communication and Interoperability

Communication in distributed systems has been widely researched. It remains an open issue and involves a number of fields of study, including low-level communication protocols such as message passing, RPC, RMI in Java, IIOP in CORBA, and all kinds of high-level agent communication languages. In the world of the mobile agent, communication issues have mainly been addressed from the point of view of how best to resolve problems resulting from agent mobility, such as how to enhance reliability and performance, and how to support coordination or collaboration between agents.

8.4.1 Reliability

Unreliability in mobile agent communication is not due to the fault of low-layer network infrastructure, but is a factor of the mere existence of mobility, which extremely complicates the problem of ensuring the delivery of information even in a fault-free network. For instance, as shown in Fig. 8.4, the asynchronous nature of message passing and agent migration may give rise to a situation where a message sent to agent B from agent A chases B forever but never reaches it, since it moves frequently between hosts. Such situations, where information goes missing as a result of agent migration, are referred to as communication failures of the mobile agent.

Existing communication mechanisms for traditional distributed systems do not provide a solution for this problem, because they were not designed with mobility in mind; nor do they enforce continuous connectivity with the message source, which in many cases would defeat the very purpose of using mobile agents.

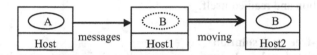

Fig. 8.4. Communication failure of mobile agent

Although the typical use of a mobile agent paradigm is to bypass a communication link and exploit local access to resources on a remote server, remote communication approaches for agents remain indispensable. For example, in the distributed information retrieval system, multiple mobile agents will be generated and roam in networks to search required information. During this process, collaboration requires that agents situated within different hosts interact with each other. Additionally, in scenarios involving commercial interests and secrets, alien mobile agents are not permitted to move directly to the key servers behind company firewalls. In such circumstances, mobile agents can only access such servers by remote communication.

Different approaches have been presented and adopted by existing mobile agent systems in order to solve the issue of communication failure. These can be divided into two main classes – the moving-restricted and moving-free styles – according to their rationales.

The moving-restricted style solution
Since the reason for communication failure is the agent moving while the process is still ongoing, the simplest solution is to restrict agents' movement when communications in which they are involved have not completed. In this scenario, both partners conform to a common promise in which both will stay with the original host and will not leave until the communication is complete. Essentially, in this solution, the behaviors of moving and communicating are taken as mutually exclusive and are executed only sequentially. Because this solution is effective and can be easily implemented it was widely adopted by many early mobile agent systems such as Telescript [6] and Agent TCL [7].

The obvious disadvantage of the moving-restricted style solution is that it restricts the agent's behaviors, or in other words, it violates its autonomy. For example, an agent's moving request will not be responded to for a long time if communication via a low bandwidth wireless network involves too much data transfer, which will continue for a long period. Furthermore, in the case of broadcast communication within a group of agents, any single agent's request to move will not receive a response until all communications links between itself and the other agents have been released. Sometimes the delay to a moving request is dangerous, such as the case where an agent needs to move to another host immediately because it has received a signal that the current one is about to crash.

Some improved solutions place a higher priority on moving behavior. In those cases, if one party to the communication wants to move, it sends the request to the other. Communication stops after the request is accepted and executed, and resumes at precisely the point of interruption after the moving agent has moved to the new location and readied itself.

The moving-free style solution
Moving-restricted style solutions do not work well in most cases because they undermine the autonomy of agents. In contrast, the moving-free style allows agents to move anywhere at any time, rather than wait until the communication is over. Essentially, in this solution, the behaviors of moving and communicating are taken as two mutually independent processes, which can be executed simultaneously, through which autonomy is preserved.

However, a highly desirable requirement for such a solution is the guarantee that the message has actually been delivered to the destination independent of the relative movement of the source and target. Typical delivery schemes suffer from the fundamental problem that an agent in transit during the delivery can easily be missed. To illustrate the issue, two kinds of approaches are widely adopted: broadcast and forwarding.

A simple broadcast scheme assumes a spanning tree of network nodes through which a message may be sent by any node. This node then broadcasts the message to its neighbors, which broadcast the message to theirs, and so on until the leaf nodes are reached. Emerald [15], the precursor of mobile objects, uses a broadcast scheme to forward a message to moving objects. This, however, does not guarantee delivery of the message when an agent is traveling in the reverse direction to the propagation of the message, as depicted in Fig. 8.5a. In this situation, the agent and the message will cross in the channel and the message will be lost. An improved version of the broadcast scheme is presented by Murphy [16]. Here, messages are stored on the nodes through which they pass until they are received correctly by the agent, or they expire.

Forwarding schemes can be divided into forwarding-by-path and forwarding-by-home, depending on the locating mechanism they use.

Some Java-based mobile agent systems such as Mole [17] adopt the forwarding-by-path scheme. Every node in the path traveled by the agent maintains a pointer to its successor node. The message sent to the agent also travels along the path maintained by those pointers until it is correctly received. Sometimes this scheme cannot guarantee whether or when messages are received. For instance, as shown in Fig. 8.5b, the situation could arise where the message is never submitted because the receiver always starts a move to a new location just before the arrival of the message at the previous site.

In contrast, Aglets [2] and Voyager [4] adopt the forwarding-by-home scheme to pass their messages. A simple version of such a scheme maintains a pointer to a server agent at a well-known location, which is called "home." On migration, the mobile agent must inform the "home" of its new location in order to enable further communication. Any message sent to the receiver should be sent firstly to its "home," from where it will be forwarded on according to the most up-to-date information on the receiver's location. However, messages sent between migration and update might be lost, with the agent having, in effect, left before delivery. Even if retransmission to the new location is attempted, the agent can move again and miss the retransmission a second time, as depicted in Fig. 8.5c.

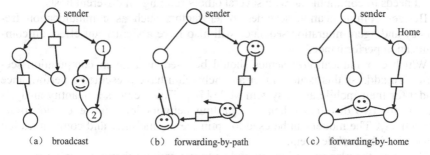

(a) broadcast   (b) forwarding-by-path   (c) forwarding-by-home

Fig. 8.5. Communication failure in both broadcast and forwarding schemes (**a**) Broadcast, (**b**) forwarding-by-path, (**c**) forwarding-by-home

Furthermore, forwarding has an additional drawback in that it requires communication with the "home" location every time the agent moves. In some situations, this may defeat the purpose of using mobile agents by reintroducing centralization. For instance, in the presence of many highly mobile agents spawned from the same host, this scheme may lead to considerable traffic overhead being generated around the "home", and possibly to much slower performance if the latency between the two sites is high.

8.4.2 Performance

Communication performance is one of the most important factors affecting the efficiency of a mobile agent system. Usually two kinds of communication schemes are offered: remote communication, in which two agents running on different hosts communicate using RPC, remote method invocation (RMI), or message passing; and mobile communication, in which one agent moves to the remote host and interacts with the other using local procedure calling or message passing.

In the context of remote communication, the RPC is used to call procedures or methods that are provided by the communication partner (such as a service agent). A classical RPC includes binding to the server; marshalling, transferring, unmarshalling of the request parameters; execution of the request; and marshalling, transferring, and unmarshalling of the reply.

Mobile communication can reduce the network load of intermediate data transfer and enable agents to communicate more reliably in a low-speed, high-delay, and unreliable network environment, but it will increase the cost of transporting agent code, which is already an additional overhead. Besides this, the work performed by agents (such as serializing, authenticating, rebuilding, registering, and so on) can also lead to extra moving costs. So for an agent in any given task, the decision about when to perform remote and when to perform mobile communication will influence the performance of the whole system, especially when the agent needs to communicate with several others running on different hosts.

Besides communication schemes, other factors such as communication frequency and agent migration sequence will also have a significant effect on communication performance.

Which communication schemes should be used in a given computation scenario? To address this issue Straßer and Schwehm have presented a performance model for their mobile agent system Mole [18]. This includes a quantity analysis method for two different schemes regarding network load and execution time, respectively. The model can be used to optimize the mobility and communication behavior of the mobile agent.

However, the planning of an optimal communication scheme for an agent so as to minimize the communication cost of more complex tasks remains a problem without a perfect solution. Traditional optimization techniques for network communication, such as data compression, caching, and media type conversion, are certainly required, but more intelligent techniques need to be used, especially in large-scale intelligent agent systems. Autonomous oriented computation (AOC) [19] is a promising approach to this issue, in which every mobile agent is modeled as an autonomous entity of AOC [20] and has the ability to optimize its moving and communicating behaviors through positive or negative feedback mechanisms provided by AOC [21, 22].

8.4.3 Interoperability

In order to carry out their assigned roles, it is necessary for mobile agents to collaborate and coordinate their activities with those of other entities. Cabri et al. [23] survey the coordination models adopted by existing mobile agent systems. They divide these into four categories on the basis of spatial and temporal coupling, as shown in Table 8.1.

As described by Cabri, spatially coupled coordination models require the entities involved to share a common name space, while spatially uncoupled models

Table 8.1. Mobile agent coordination models [23]

	temporally coupled	temporally uncoupled
spatially coupled	**direct** *Aglets, D'Agent*	**blackboard based** *Ambit, ffMain*
spatially uncoupled	**meeting oriented** *Ara, Mole*	**linda-like** *Jada, MARS*

enforce anonymous interactions. Temporally coupled coordination models imply synchronization of the involved entities, and the converse type achieves asynchronous interactions.

The four coordination models in Table 8.1 can work perfectly to support synchronous, asynchronous, anonymous, and group interactions among mobile agents. However, they are not suitable for the more complex applications, such as distributed optimization problem solving (DOPS), that have recently begun to emerge. DOPS describes the optimization problem in large-scale, open, and dynamic distributed environments. These have more complicated attributes such as stochastic and dynamic evolving, information and control localizing, asynchronous updating of network state, and so on, which make them more difficult to resolve than traditional optimization problems. Resource management and task allocation in the computation grid [24], QoS group-cast routing in multimedia networks [25], and performance optimization in agent-based e-commerce (ABEC) [26] are all typical distributed optimization problems. Because of its extraordinary complexity, traditional optimization methods are not suitable for DOPS.

A mobile agent-based approach seems to be a promising way to deal with DOPS since its advantages match most of its requirements. So far, however, existing mobile agent systems have not performed well with DOPS mainly because of their poor coordination models, which are unable to provide a suitably efficient solving paradigm for optimization, even in traditional central optimization problems.

AOC is a new computation paradigm presented by Liu et al. [20] for solving hard computational problems and characterizing the behaviors of a complex system. It differs from related studies of major complex systems such as artificial life, simulated evolution, and multiagent systems in that it is not solely intended to replicate complex behavior, emulate evolution, or coordinate the functioning of many interacting agents: it emphasizes the modeling of autonomy in the entities of a complex system and their self-organization to achieve a specific goal.

In the AOC-based mobile agent coordination model, every agent has a fitness value, which is evaluated by its fitness function according to its behaviors. During the moving process, the agents interact with their local network environments and might release some information, such as pheromones, into them. The higher a fitness value an agent has, the more pheromone it will release. When agents move to a crossroad, they will preferentially select the path with a denser concentration of pheromone. A group of mobile agents will solve the DOPS collectively through a positive feedback mechanism: agents that can find optimal solutions will have a higher fitness value; their routes will have denser pheromone levels, attracting more agents to choose them; and bad agents with a lower fitness value will adjust their direction of travel (or other behaviors) by following the good agents. Eventually, after a period of evolution controlled by positive feedback, the entire system will reach an equilibrium state corresponding to the desired optimal solution.

In this model, changes to agents' fitness value embody their self-adaptive behaviors as single entities, while the positive feedback system embodies the self-organized behaviors of multiple agents.

8.5 Security

With code migration, the mobile agent paradigm brings increased performance and flexibility to distributed systems. On the other hand, the ability to move in itself brings significant security threats, to both agents and hosts. Only a perfect solution to these serious security problems would enable the mobile agent paradigm to become the mainstream software technique for constructing large-scale distributed commercial applications.

8.5.1 Issues and Countermeasures

Two main types of threat need to be addressed: agent-to-system and system-to-agent attacks. Jansen et al. [27] present a good survey of the threats faced by the mobile agent paradigm and the corresponding countermeasures.

The agent-to-system category includes the kind of threats in which agents exploit security weaknesses to attack an agent system. This group mainly comprises masquerading, denial of service, and unauthorized access. Conversely, the system-to-agent category includes threats in which systems attack agents that are situated within them. Again, masquerading and denial of service form part of this group, as additionally do eavesdropping and alteration.

Many conventional security techniques used in traditional distributed applications such as identity authentication, encryption, integrity verification, authorization, access control, and so on are also useful as countermeasures within the mobile agent paradigm. There are also several extensions to these conventional techniques and new methods devised specifically to control mobile agent security. Jansen et al. [27] survey some recently developed security techniques. Countermeasures aimed at platform protection include software-based fault isolation, safe code interpretation, signed code, authorization, and attribute certificates, state appraisal, path histories, and proof carrying code. Countermeasures for agent protection include partial result encapsulation, mutual itinerary recording, itinerary recording with replication and voting, execution tracing, environmental key generation, computing with encrypted functions, and obfuscated code.

8.5.2 Facility

In this section we present a concrete mobile agent security facility (MASF), which we have ourselves developed, in order to illustrate some of the threats and countermeasures discussed earlier from a more practical and implementation-oriented point of view [28].

Issues

The security threats that may occur over the whole lifecycle of a mobile agent come from both malicious agents and the hosts to which agents migrate. Malicious mobile agents may access and modify data to which they should not have access or attempt to interfere with the execution of their hosts. The potential threats, from both the agent and host points of view, can be:

- *Before migration.* Threat A: During mobile agent storage, the repository might be invaded and the code or class for the mobile agent changed before initiation.
- *During migration.* Threat B1: When a mobile agent migrates across networks are not controlled by sender or receiver, while in possession of confidential data, disclosure of this information could be fatal. Threat B2: The execution logic of the mobile agent might also be changed by the interrupter, which might cause damage to the destination host.
- *After migration.* Threat C1: the supposed "destination" might in fact be a counterfeit, created by a business rival to steal important information being carried by the mobile agent. Threat C2: even if the destination is correct, the agent may still be deceived by a malicious host. For example, it might not receive the contracted services or resources, or might even be maliciously changed before going for another hop. Threat C3: At the same time, the landing host of the mobile agent should also be sure that the incomer is from the correct service contractor and will not cause it any damage. Threat C4: even if the mobile agent does come from the correct peer, the host still needs to keep itself informed about its behavior in case the agent does something that goes beyond its contract or its rights on the system.

Countermeasures

To address such threats, a MASF must provide the following features:

- *Authentication.* This involves checking whether or not an agent comes from a trustworthy source. This can involve asking for the authentication details to be sent from the site where the mobile agent was launched or from which it last migrated. At the same time, authentication also enables the mobile agent to be aware of the real identity of the receiver, which should be the proper service level agreement (SLA) contractor. Authentication is mainly used to solve threats C1 and C3 as described earlier. It can also be used to check on users who want to access the mobile agent repository, which also involves threat A.

- *Confidentiality.* When a mobile agent transports confidential data, the transmitted agent must be encrypted while in transit. This makes it useless to any host, which does not know how to decrypt it (which should only be the designated server). Confidentiality, implemented by encryption/decryption, can cope with the potential data disclosure of threat B1, and can prevent the repository from attack (threat A).

- *Integrity.* On reception, the mobile agent must be checked against any modification or corruption due to network transmission errors or intentional invasion. If the integrity check fails, the receiver can ask the client to repeat the transmission. This can protect the mobile agent from the code modification attack outlined in threat B2.

- *Authorization.* This determines the mobile agent's access permissions to host resources. It is intended to protect those resources from unauthorized or overused access. It indicates, for example, how many times a resource can be accessed or how much it can be used, and what type of access the agent can perform. For instance, one agent on behalf of a network administrator may be able to read, write, and modify a given resource and have unlimited access to it, whilst another agent representing a normal user may only be able to read the resource and access it a limited number of times. Authorization mainly deals with the runtime actions of the mobile agent. Usually this is achieved through an access control policy that grants access to system resources based upon different levels of trust. Authorization, empowered by access control, can defeat threat C4.

- *Logging.* This is a mechanism to keep track of any events relevant to security, such as an agent trying to access system resources or the system itself, as well as authentication failures. These events should be logged to a file for later analysis. Logging can, to some degree, detect and therefore prevent a mobile agent being deceived by the host, as described in threat C2.

Architecture

The implementation of these features, for the protection of both mobile agent and host, is achieved in the MASF, the architecture of which is illustrated as Fig. 8.6. MASF architecture is functionally divided into two layers, the higher being a function layer and the lower a base service layer. The components or services in the latter are common functionalities used by the former.

Obviously, many services of the function layer depend on cryptographic functions based on either symmetric or asymmetric keys to encrypt/decrypt and sign data. Therefore, MASF has a cryptography library integrated in its base service layer.

The key management service enables users to administer their own public/private key pairs and associated certificates for use in self-authentication or data integrity and authentication services, using digital signatures. The authentication information includes both a sequence (chain) of X.509 certificates, and an associated private key, which is usually referenced as "alias".

To achieve security, the MASF framework supports flexible security policies to govern the interactions of agents with each other and with the available resources in the execution sites. This function is implemented by the policy management service in the base service layer. The definition and enforcement of appropriate security policies can only proceed after a precise identification of the principals (i.e., the roles that can be authenticated).

Security logging service fulfils the logging requirement mentioned earlier. Although not specific to MASF, the location service is sometimes used by MASF to identify the user.

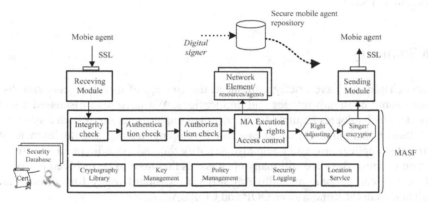

Fig. 8.6. Architecture of mobile agent security facility

Workflow of the MASF
All the mobile agents' classes or codes are stored in digitally signed archive files. Whenever an administrator, or the software on his or her behalf, wants to fulfill some tasks using mobile agents, the appropriate signature must firstly be verified before access can be granted to these agents, which are stored in a protected repository. The administrator then signs the agent to show the initiator, for instance, the first agent system. He or she can also supply the agent with the necessary rights.

If a mobile agent system receives an agent from the communication network via agent transport protocol (ATP), it decrypts it and tests the integrity of the data received by checking the signature that the sender has appended. After successfully passing the integrity check, the next step is authentication. The mobile agent system verifies the signature and certificates attached to this mobile agent and obtains further information such as who wrote it and who sent it (either originally or from the intermediate locations). The information can be further used for authorization and access control. This step will involve the security database.

Once authenticated, MASF authorizes the agent, which means that it attaches rights to it or determines rights based on security policies, which have been defined in advance, probably via a SLA.

The mobile agent can then be executed with care of access control to implement its assigned task. When the mobile agent has finished its work and wants to migrate to another location, the system stops the agent's execution and packs it with its current state, as normal. Depending on the agent's task, the rights' adjusting module may be called at this moment to adjust its current rights, for example, to increase those to be granted at its next location.

Next, the signer/encryptor module is called by agency to sign the mobile agent to confirm the execution or any change of agent. Encryption may also be applied by this module.

Finally, agency opens a communication channel to the target mobile agent system and sends the agent. The channel can be a secure one enhanced by secure socket layer (SSL).

8.6 Summary

In this chapter we have briefly introduced the concept of mobile agents and discussed some of its advantages and applications. We have also discussed some important technologies required for the detailed implementation of such a system.

Although this paradigm could ease the developing, testing, and deployment of distributed applications, and could also simplify the understanding and sustaining of such systems, there are still many open issues that need to be resolved perfectly before this can become an industrial software standard ready for commercial applications in the same way as OOP and CORBA.

Besides issues such as planning, communication, performance, and security, as discussed earlier, there is the important question of standardization. OMG MASIF (mobile agent system interoperability facility) [29] and OMG MAFS (mobile agent facility specification) [11] are good initial efforts to address this issue. However, the mobile agent community must take further steps to develop an industrial standard for this paradigm, just like the one in use in the field of distributed objects.

Furthermore, technologies and theories of artificial intelligence fields should be integrated into the mobile agent paradigm so as to enable mobile agents to become smarter and more competent in highly complex tasks such as distributed optimization problems in truly distributed, large-scale, open, and dynamic environments such as the Internet.

Fortunately, more and more new techniques are now being explored, and current work is promising enough that, within 10 years or even sooner, the mobile-agent paradigm will be widely used in many distributed and intelligent applications, especially in the ubiquitous computing environment.

Ubiquitous computing is said to be the third generation of computation after the mainframe and personal computer (PC) eras. In this, the user is surrounded by lots of invisible small computers or sensors, connected by ad hoc or wireless networks. Ubiquitous computing mainly aims at developing new models and technologies to construct the ubiquitous society (U-society), which can offer anywhere and anytime services, delivered through any devices, as required to support an individual's daily life. In order to adapt to the dynamic requirements of different people, the U-society requires personal information such as profiles, preferences, likes, and habits. Since people often move around, such personal information has to be sent to the current location. Bagci et al. [30] present two possible approaches: either the user carries the relevant information on devices with him or her, or the ubiquitous system takes care of storing and sending it. Obviously, the latter situation, in which a mobile user is always accompanied by a ubiquitous agent, which serves as a virtual reflection of the user and can provide the services, is preferred.

Existing mobile agent systems for Internet applications such as Aglet, More, Grasshoppers, and D'Agent are very heavyweight and are not suitable for ubiquitous computing. Bagci et al. [30] discuss the requirements for the ubiquitous agent paradigm: ubiquitous agents could use both wired and wireless media for communication and migration; the system should be platform independent, since software and hardware are heterogeneous in the U-society; agents should be lightweight so that they work not only on powerful PCs but also on battery-operated and memory-restricted PDAs, wearable computers, or tiny sensors; agents could use different access mechanisms and protocols for accessing information provided by heterogeneous ubiquitous devices; agents should be context sensitive; and security, such as privacy protection, is also an important requirement.

Multiagent teamwork has been widely studied in the fields of distributed artificial intelligence. With the emergence of ubiquitous computing, ubiquitous agent teamwork becomes a new challenge. The ubiquitous agent community (UAC) is a promising approach to the organization of agents into a jointly functioning team. The significant aspect of such a community is that it will always have one goal that will motivate and drive its members to fulfill their individual tasks and functions. UACs with different structures have different functions, and these structures will evolve autonomously according to the collective interactions of their members. Liu et al. [31] present one community structure, called the ubiquitous agent community for rational competition and cooperation in the U-society.

A UAC is essentially an intelligent infrastructure that enables agents to look ahead to plan and deliver what a user wants. It works just like a personal agency. For instance, it can help a user to effectively manage tedious daily routine activities such as processing emails, placing orders, making meeting arrangements, downloading news, and so on. A UAC can interact with users in various ways. For instance, as a person uses a smart hand-held device to enter a subway station on the way to work, a UAC can seamlessly upload list of things to be done to that device. Along with each of the things listed, the information provided by the UAC can also include the corresponding tasks required. Thus, inside the moving subway train, the user will be able to go through each of the recommended task items and further verify and delegate certain jobs, such as forwarding a report or making a meeting appointment, to a community agent within the UAC. Besides planning and executing the items on a calendar, the user can also receive other personalized services based on his or her profile, which may include sports news, urgent emails, and specific documents prepared for the day's meetings. Figure 8.7 gives an illustrative example of personal services that can be provided by a community of competing and cooperating agents.

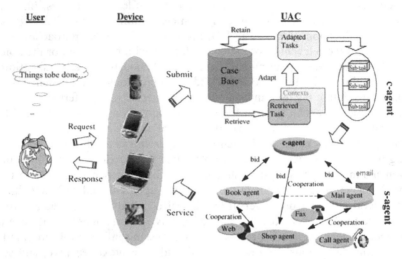

Fig. 8.7. Schematic illustration of an UAC [31]

A UAC contains two types of agents: c-agents and s-agents. The former makes task plans as well as contracting decisions on what and where some tasks will be carried out, whereas the latter performs the delegated tasks. A c-agent carries out such functions as task planning, task delegation, and result evaluation, while an s-agent is responsible for task execution, competition, and cooperation. In the illustrative example in Fig. 8.7, suppose a user writes a few words on his or her PDA regarding what he or she plans to do. A c-agent in the distributed UAC will recognize the user's intention and find similar service cases from its case base. Thereafter, it will execute task planning based on the similarity between the tasks at hand and the previous tasks. Once the c-agent completes this process, a cluster of s-agents will be called upon to distribute and carry out the planned subtasks. Each s-agent will have distinct role(s) and will coordinate its actions with those of other s-agents in a UAC. For instance, a mail agent will be responsible for managing emails, involving three distinct roles: editing, sending, and receiving. As the mail agent works, it will also take into consideration the work status of related s-agents. In other words, it will decide, after communicating with other s-agents, when to receive or send emails and what content to include.

Because many ubiquitous agents have been devised for different services and functions in the U-society, a solution for clustering them is necessary in order to summon these heterogeneous agents roaming across the entire U-society and quickly aggregate them into a seamless community, such as the UAC, which will complete user-specified tasks. However, this is a nontrivial challenge, requiring as it does an automatic, decentralized, and incremental UAC clustering algorithm rather than one which is manual, centralized, and offline.

References

1. D.B. Lange, M. Oshima. Seven good reasons for mobile agents. Communications of the ACM, 1999, 42(3): 88–89.
2. D. Lange M. Oshima. Programming and Deploying Mobile Agents with Aglets, Boston, MA: Addison-Wesley, 1998.
3. D. Wong, N. Paciorek et al. Concordia: An infrastructure for collaborating mobile agents. In K. Rothermel and R. Zeletin, editors, Mobile Agents: First International Workshop MA'97, LNCS 1219, 1997, 86.
4. ObjectSpace Inc. ObjectSpace voyager core package technical overview, 1997, http://www.objectspace.com/voyager/whitepapers.
5. C. Bäumer, T. Magedanz. Grasshopper – A mobile agent platform for active telecommunication. In Proceedings of the Third International Workshop on Intelligent Agents for Telecommunication Applications, LNCS1699, 1999, 19–32.
6. J.E. White. Telescript Technology: The Foundation for the Electronic marketplace. White Paper, General Magic, Inc., 1994.
7. R.S. Gray, G. Cybenko, D. Kotz et al. D'Agents: Applications and performance of a mobile agent system. Software Practice and Experience, 2002, 32(6): 543–573.
8. H. Peine, T. Stolpmann. The architecture of the Ara platform for mobile agents. In K. Rothermel and R. Zeletin, editors, Mobile Agents: First International Workshop MA'97, LNCS 1219, 1997, 50–61.
9. L.F. Bic, M. Fukuda, M. Dillencourt. Distributed computing using autonomous objects. IEEE Computer, 1996, 29(8): 55–61.
10. D. Johansen, R.V. Renesse, F. Schneider. An introduction to the TACOMA distributed system. Technical Report 95–23, University of Tromso, 1995.
11. Object Management Group, Inc. The Mobile Agent Facility Specification, 2000, 6.
12. K. Rothermel, M. Schwehm. Mobile agents. In Encyclopedia for Computer Science and Technology. New York: Dekker, 1998.
13. Fuggetta, G. Picco, G. Vigna. Understanding code mobility. IEEE Transactions on Software Engineering, 1998, 24(5): 352–361.
14. K. Moizumi. The Mobile Agent Planning Problem. [PhD Thesis] Thayer School of Engineering, Dartmouth College, 1998.
15. E. Jul, H. Levy, N. Hutchinson, A. Black. Fine-grained mobility in the Emerald System. ACM Transactions on Computer Systems, 1988, 6(2): 109–133.
16. A.L. Murphy, G.P. Picco. Reliable communication for highly mobile agents. In P. Spring and D. Milojicic, editors, Proceedings of the First International Symposium on Agent Systems and Applications. New York: IEEE Computer Society, 1999, 141–150.
17. J. Baumann et al. Communication concepts for mobile agent systems. In K. Rothermel and R. Zeletin, editors, Mobile Agents: First International Workshop MA'97, LNCS 1219, Berlin Heidelberg New York: Springer, 1997, 123–135.

18. M. Straßer, M. Schwehm. A performance model for mobile agent systems. In Proceeding of the International Conference on Parallel and Distributed Processing Techniques and Applications, 1997, 2: 1132–1140.

19. J. Liu, X.L. Jin, K.C. Tsui. Autonomy Oriented Computing. Dordrecht: Kluwer, 2005.

20. J. Liu, X. Jin, K.C. Tsui. Autonomy oriented computing (AOC): Formulating computational systems with autonomous components. IEEE Transactions on System, Man and Cybernetics. Part A:System and Humans (in press).

21. J. Liu, J. Han, Y.Y. Tang. Multi-agent oriented constraint satisfaction. Artificial Intelligence, 2002, 136(1): 101–144.

22. J. Liu, Y.Y. Tang. Adaptive segmentation with distributed behavior based agents. IEEE Transactions on Pattern Analysis and Machine Intelligence, 1999, 21(6): 544–551.

23. G. Cabri, L. Leonardi, F. Zambonelli. How to coordinate Internet applications based on mobile agents. Proceedings of the 1998 seventh IEEE International Workshop on Enabling Technologies: Infrastructure for Collaborative Enterprises, WET ICE, IEEE Computer Social Press, 1998, 104–109.

24. H. Casanova, J. Hayes, Y. Yang. Algorithm and software to schedule and deploy independent tasks in grid environments. In Proceedings of the Workshop on Distributed Computing, Meta-computing, and Resource Globalization, Aussois, France, 2002.

25. K.S. Teng, M. Maheswaran. Limited scope probing: A distributed approach for QoS-based routing. In IEEE International Symposium on Network Computing and Applications (NCA'01), Cambridge: Massachusetts, 2001, 350–354.

26. M. Moses. Agents in e-commerce. Communications of the ACM, 1999, 42(3): 79–91.

27. W. Jansen, T. Karygiannis. Mobile agent security. NIST Special Publication, 1999, 800–819.

28. B. Yang, K. Yang, D.Y. Liu. Mobile agent security facility for network management. Journal of Software, 2003, 14(10): 1761–1767.

29. D. Milojicic et al. MASIF: The OMG mobile agent system interoperability facility. In Proceedings of the Second International Workshop on Mobile Agents, LNCS 1477, Berlin Heidelberg New York: Springer, 1998, 50–61.

30. F. Bagci, J. Petzold, W. Trumler. Ubiquitous mobile agent system in a P2P-Network. UbiSys-Workshop at the Fifth Annual Conference on Ubiquitous Computing, Seattle, 2003.

31. J. Liu, C. Yao. Rational competition and cooperation in ubiquitous agent communities. Knowledge-Based System, 2004, 17: 189–200.

9 Multiagent Communication for e-Business using Tuple Spaces

H.F. Li, T. Radhakrishnan, and Y. Zhang

Department of Computer Science and Software Engineering
Concordia University, Montreal, Canada H3G 1M8

9.1 Introduction

9.1.1 Motivation

The growth in Web-based applications, distributed computing, and agent-based software technologies has created abundant interest in various aspects of e-business. One such application supported by these technologies is e-commerce in which online transactions between a buyer and a seller are supported in various stages of their trading (Gutman et al., 1998). E-commerce application systems have to deal with a large number of interacting autonomous tasks using heterogeneous information sources. These interactions have a need to be well coordinated and coordination requires efficient communication among the entities. The dynamic and complex nature of e-commerce requires a flexible technological infrastructure to support business processes more easily and effectively.

Agent-based software technology has become the subject of much research in a wide range of fields, especially in distributed system design. Multiagent systems are often used in a dynamic environment with autonomous problem solving entities cooperating and coordinating with each other. A typical software agent has the characteristics of autonomy, reactivity, proactivity and sociality, or structured interactions with other software agents. This makes the multiagent systems a natural candidate choice for implementing e-commerce applications.

Business processes in e-commerce may be considered as a kind of coordinated multiagent system in which the software agents perform various market activities under dynamic partnerships. With the increasing complexity of these applications, we need programming models to deal with the coordination of a large number of concurrently active entities. Thus, an infrastructure for coordination is needed to meet the complex and dynamic requirements. Tuple space that supports inter-agents coordination is an attractive solution.

For this purpose, our research focuses on tuple space-based agent coordination and tuple space-based agent programming framework (TSAF) that effectively supports building agent applications in e-commerce. In the rest of this chapter, we discuss multiagent interactions through tuple space, presenting how tuple space facilitates the dynamic couplings among agents. We also present an agent programming model called TSAF, which provides not only agent architecture in abstraction, but also an easy-to-use programming environment for implementing the resulting design. The incorporation of role models derived from object-oriented methodologies into the design of agent behaviors supports the analysis and design of multiagent systems from the perspective of agent-oriented software engineering. In the implementation level, TSAF also supports tuple space-based agent coupling mechanism. The benefits of this framework are illustrated through a case study in e-commerce.

9.1.2 Agent Coordination in Multiagent System

Agents in a multiagent system have a general need to communicate amongst themselves, coordinate their activities, and negotiate once they find themselves in conflict. Coordination models for multiagent systems can be broadly classified into direct coordination model and indirect coordination model. Direct coordination means that agents explicitly initiate a communication via message passing and explicitly name the involved partners in their messages. In indirect coordination, agents interact via a shared space, like blackboard, where messages are posted and retrieved. A blackboard approach uncouples agent-to-agent interactions in time and space. This suits many application scenarios where agents do not know or care about the address of the collaborators. The tuple space-based coordination model promotes dynamic information sharing, so that information is available to any intended agent and every authorized agent can modify the information on the tuple space. The tuple spaces free the designer from the burden of keeping track of explicit or at least implicit addressing knowledge in agent couplings. Finally, the "reactive tuples" [1] of tuple space can support event-driven coordination among agents by triggering the reactions associated with such tuples. These reactions are normally defined based on the different roles that an agent plays. In addition, reactions can adapt the semantics of the interactions to the specific agent environment, thus simplifying the agent programming.

9.2 Computation and Tuple Spaces

A typical approach in designing multiagent systems is the use of "role models" (Bauer, 2001) [2] that capture the different functionalities in the underlying application. The roles are assigned to different agents. An agent can be assigned multiple roles so that it can cooperate with other agents to complete different missions simultaneously or at different times in its lifeline. Cooperation requires interactions. The traditional form of interaction is through message communication. An agent sends mission-specific messages to other agents involved in the same mission at "opportune times" in order to complete the common mission properly. When viewed globally, a mission involving multiple agents can be represented by the set of interaction protocols executed by these agents together. Generic agent communication language (ACL) protocols can be found in the FIPA library [3], which support the agent application designs.

Message communication is one of the mechanisms for supporting agent interactions. Agents can exchange and share information by sending messages to each other. This form of interaction usually inherits two basic restrictions (1) the receiver must be known to the sender and (2) the information obtained by the receiver reflects only the knowledge of the sender at the time when the message was sent. The first restriction often leads to more static designs. For example, the group of agents involved in the mission may not change dynamically in the middle of an occurrence of the mission. The second restriction leads to the knowledge of an agent to be space-time restricted. An agent causally acquires its knowledge of the world by receiving messages from other agents. Such knowledge may not be up to date and may indeed lead to inconsistent views among cooperating agents, if the interaction protocols do not take care of synchronization properly. The former restriction affects the flexibility of the application design. The latter restriction affects the ease with which a correct design can be constructed and eventually implemented.

9.2.1 Basics of a Tuple Space

Abstractly, a tuple space stores an arbitrary set of entities (tuples) that are shared by a community of agents. Each entity is identified by a tag (template). Conflicts in tags are allowed. The pioneering ideas were developed in Linda [4]. Three essential access primitives are associated with a typical Linda-based tuple space. Insertion of a tuple can be achieved using out (tuple_tag). Removal of a tuple can be achieved using in (tuple_tag), and nondestructive read out of a tuple can be performed using read (tuple_tag). Figure 9.1 demonstrates this use in a tuple space that stores items on sale in an electronic market shared by multiple merchants.

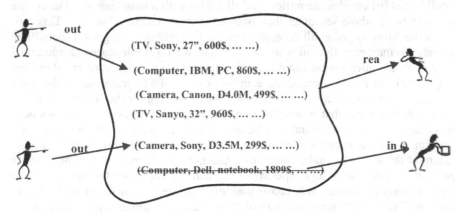

Fig. 9.1. Tuple space with animated items

In Fig. 9.1, the tuple space window contains two TVs, two or three computers, and two cameras, each entity can be made distinct with brand name and other attributes (such as merchant, price).

A tuple space represents a globally consistent space shared by all agents instantaneously at all times. The correctness semantics of a tuple space is the same as other forms of shared memory, i.e., sequential consistency [5]. Stated simply, the state of the tuple space at any time must be as if the accesses from the agents are served in some interleaved (total) order consistent with the local order of the accesses from each agent. As a result, as each agent progresses in its lifeline and changes its knowledge about the tuples in the tuple space, the global changes in the tuple space are kept consistent with the instantaneous knowledge of each agent at all times. Hence all relevant knowledge needed by an agent to advance is up to date when a tuple space is used. By accessing the tuple space, an agent can acquire globally consistent information in a single access.

A tuple space differs from conventional shared memory in two important aspects. (1) It is an associative memory. Tagging provides flexibility of access by association rather than by location address. Tolerance of tag conflicts provides flexibility in storing a set of arbitrary size rather than a singleton at all times. Hence a set of entities fitting the same description (tag) can be presented in a tuple space. (2) It allows destructive readout. Hence agent coordination can be made easy when producer–consumer or mutual exclusion synchronization is required among cooperating agents. Since these are the common forms of relationship between functions performed by agents, tuple space is a natural medium for coordinating multiagent activities.

Extensions of Tuple Primitives and Reactive Tuples
In addition to the basic primitives, several extensions have been reported [6–8]. Collectively, these extensions provide additional flexibilities in tuple accesses. A "bulk" read [9] enables the retrieval of all tuples with a matching tag. Hence one can retrieve a whole set rather than one (arbitrary) element of the set. This provides flexibility to gather all necessary information without going for it in multiple rounds. To maximize flexibility in coordination, WCL [7] introduces an additional type of input called nonblocking (asynchronous) tuple access, represented as "inp (tuple_tag)". In the nonblocking case, in the absence of a matching tuple, the agent is freed to continue with its future access without waiting for the "eventual" return of a matching tuple that is inserted into the tuple space later. This mimics nonblocking message passing and may be used for the purpose of enhancing the performance. But, it requires a proper synchronization in the use of the "future" return of the access yet to be completed. Another notable extension of tuple space primitives is the use of logic operators. An "and" or "or" operator can be used to conjunctively or disjunctively access multiple tuple spaces for matching tuples. In the "and" case, each tuple space must contribute a matching tuple, while in the "or" case, at least one tuple space must return a matching tuple to the access. This provides flexibility in using multiple tuple spaces for separate purposes (such as

different markets), rather than a single tuple space with a possible degradation in performance.

Reactivity of a tuple space is considered in MARS [6] by introducing the notion of reactive tuples. An agent can program the tuple space to react to an event stimulus, such as the retrieval of some tuple. Upon occurrence of the event, a reaction is triggered, leading to a change of the tuple space, such as insertion or modification of a tuple. The reaction is atomic with respect to the stimulus. Hence, it is possible for the read to return a tuple that is modified by the reaction. Similarly in out (tuple), if it triggers a reaction, then the outcome may be a modified tuple that is inserted into the tuple space. In a slightly different manner, JavaSpace provides reactivity by incorporating a notify primitive so that an agent may be notified by the tuple space when some specific event has occurred. The notification is asynchronous. As a result, it is possible upon reaction; the agent may not find the cause (such as the tuple) that triggers the reaction in the tuple space any more.

9.2.3 Implications in Using Tuple Space

Tuples provide a higher-level abstraction that is more powerful and convenient to use than point-to-point message communication. In cooperative problem solving, a tuple space acts like a global bulletin board that can be flexibly searched and updated by all participants without resorting to message exchanges that are more private and local. What must be consistently shared can be maintained by the "runtime system" automatically without explicit programming effort on the side of the application developer. The tuple space abstraction is easier to work with in application design. For example, when the behavior of an agent depends on some global condition of the entire system, the dependency can be resolved and the agent advances forward by examining the shared tuple space. In turn, if the action of an agent may affect the progress of some other agents, it may simply modify the shared tuple space to reflect the consequence of its action already performed. The agent does not have to ask around about the condition in the first case in order to advance its behavior, nor does it have to tell everyone of its action. This avoids redundant push or pull of information among the agents and what must be done is done via the rather strict forward tuple access primitives. In general, the programmability (ease of program development) of the platform based on tuple spaces is improved with the support of this shared medium. Further demonstration of this will be provided in the following sections.

There is also a price to be paid with the use of tuple spaces. The consistency requirement of a tuple space has certain performance implication in its runtime system. To maintain consistency, it is difficult to exploit locality by replicating tuple spaces in a distributed system. But with a single tuple space serving the entire system, a bottleneck effect may arise. Hence tuple space does come with a price at runtime. In other words, to support tuple-based interactions efficiently at runtime, the design of the tuple space requires an efficient underlying protocol that can promote concurrency in accesses by distributing tuples across the physical network and manage them correctly, with or without selective replications of tuples. Otherwise, a tuple space can form a central bottleneck in the progress of the agents attempting to access it simultaneously.

9.3 Examples of Agent Coordination in e-Commerce

This section describes a few scenarios of agent coordination in e-commerce that is facilitated with the use of tuple spaces. It should be noted that since tuple space is a higher level abstraction and is actually implemented via message communication in the runtime system, the significant return in using tuples in agent coordination lies on its ease of use in both the application design and program development. It is also envisioned that tuple space provides global information sharing that often leads to better results in applications as consistent and instantaneous knowledge can be acquired directly among the sharing agents.

9.3.1 Dynamic Public Auction

Existing auction protocols such as the standard FIPA protocols for English and Dutch auction [10] involve a fixed set of participating agents. A dynamic auction in real life may involve a dynamically changing set of participants. Participants can join and leave an auction any time in the auction period, provided outstanding obligations remain committed. Such an auction can be easily implemented using tuple space, as depicted in Fig. 9.2a, b.

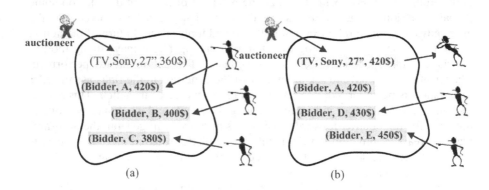

auctioneer

(TV,Sony,27",360$)

(Bidder, A, 420$)

(Bidder, B, 400$)

(Bidder, C, 380$)

(a)

auctioneer

(TV, Sony, 27", 420$)

(Bidder, A, 420$)

(Bidder, D, 430$)

(Bidder, E, 450$)

(b)

Fig. 9.2.

Figure 9.2a shows an animated auction involving a tuple space that holds an animated tuple consisting of a painting and the current highest bid price announced by the auctioneer, and a few newly submitted bids (tuples) from participants A, B, C. Figure 9.2b shows a future round with updated tuples and participants A, D, and E. Obviously, participants have changed. B and C give up in the auction, while D and E are newcomers beating the current highest bid price ($420), which may be the bid price of A.

As can be observed in Fig. 9.2, part of the tuple space has served as the physical auction medium for conducting the auction. The fact that this medium is globally consistent and up to date with respect to all participants makes it easy and extremely user friendly in application design. Note that reactive tuples such as those supported by MARS can make these even simpler by allowing new bids to update the highest bid atomically and conveniently in a single tuple access.

Shopping in Multiple Markets

A single electronic market can be visualized to be supported by a tuple space. To promote market efficiency, different tuple spaces can be formed to support different markets. As a result, it is possible that the tuple space servers can operate concurrently without creating a server bottleneck. This follows the principles of concurrency and locality of interaction in managing system performance. However, it is also conceivable that a client agent may be interested to shop across multiple markets at the same time and decide its purchases simultaneously. When implemented using message passing, this client agent will have to communicate to various market agents, conduct negotiations through separate protocols, and eventually decide on its purchases. Meanwhile, consistency and persistence of availability and pricing information must be maintained in the participants, and the overall coordination involving multiple parties and multiple sites of purchases may lead to complications in synchronization that ultimately affect the market performance.

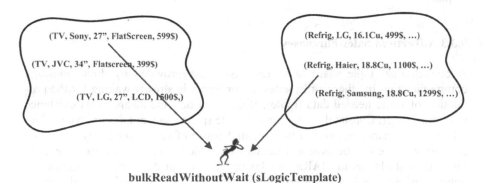

bulkReadWithoutWait (sLogicTemplate)

Fig. 9.3. Logical template

When supported by tuple spaces, a simple extension of tuple access involving logical tags will significantly simplify the interactions required and potentially improve the market efficiency. This extension is implemented in our experimental framework detailed in Sect. 9.4. Conceptually, the client agent can issue a logic_template_in() access. This access will enable him to retrieve, in a single step, multiple sets of tuples from one or more markets. In other words, he may choose to retrieve TVs and refrigerators that satisfy certain criteria from one or all of the markets (tuple spaces) specified in his access operation. Figure 9.3 illustrates such a use scenario. It is obvious that programming effort required to do so is significantly reduced while global consistent information in collected or consumed.

In Fig. 9.3, there are two markets (tuple spaces: tsId1 and tsId2), each of which contains few different types of TVs and refrigerators. A buyer agent wants to retrieve product information from the two markets. From market1, he is interested in the TV product with the fields of "TV," "Sony," and "FlatScreen" in a search tuple; from market2, he wants to know the information of refrigerators with the fields of "Refrig," "Haier," and "18.8Cu" in another search tuple. First, it constructs a search tuple with search requirements. Then it constructs two search templates (template1 and template2) for searching the product from each of the tuple spaces. A logic template combining the two templates is created using logic operator "and." Finally, a bulk synchronous access operation is used to perform the actual search. The returned future object contains a set of tuples.

```
//constructs different search templates for different tuple spaces
Template template1 = new Template (tsId1, search_tuple);
Template template2 = new Template (tsId2, search_tuple);
//constructs a logic template
LogicTemplate sLogicTemplate = new LogicTemplate();
sLogicTemplate.and (template1, template2);
//searches the logic tuples through bulk primitive
MultipleTupleSet multiTSet = myAgent.bulkReadWithoutWait sLogicTemplate);
```

9.3.3 Advertised Sales/Purchases

A conventional tuple space lacks responsiveness provided by direct message communication. In other words, unless a consumer is already waiting for the production of some needed data (tuple), it may not become aware of its existence until much later. Constantly sampling the tuple space using nondestructive readout affects performance because of the potential waste of time. To remedy this, reactive tuple space has become a necessary extension. Reactive tuples have been implemented also as in MARS and JavaSpace. In our experimental framework detailed in Sect. 9.4, a slightly different reactive tuple is implemented. Unlike MARS, the reaction in our case is a sub-behavior of the agent that registers itself with the tuple space. Upon the occurrence of the stimulus, atomically or non-atomically, the reactive behavior of the agent will be triggered and performed by the agent. This can be put to use in advertised sales or purchases. In an advertised sale, a "shopping agent" may register itself with the market (tuple space) so that when a corresponding tuple is inserted into the tuple space by a "seller agent," the shopping agent can immediately react and respond to the state change.

9.4 A Tuple Space-Based Framework for Agent Communication

9.4.1 Reactive Tuple Space

This section presents some details of our experimental reactive tuple space [11] implemented on the JADE platform. Java agent development framework (JADE) is a framework that facilitates the development of multiagent systems. It defines an agent model from which a software developer can extend to include specific business logic. We further extended JADE [8, 12] to reactive tuple space for the support of agent interactions. Figure 9.4 shows the overall architecture of the JADE platform.

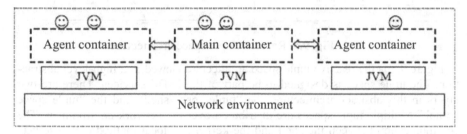

Fig. 9.4. JADE architecture

The JADE platform is composed of several containers. Every container runs on a Java virtual machine and can host zero or more agents. The platform can be actually distributed across several hosts, and an agent will not have to know the existence of the underlying network as JADE provides the high-level abstraction called 'container' to hide the complexity of distribution. In JADE, there are two kinds of interfaces to an agent. The first kind is called "internal interface," which is defined by the container to provide system services of life cycle management, message service, mobility support, and resource allocation. An agent accesses the system services through its container. The container then delegates these service requests to the corresponding manager. The second kind is known as the "callback interface." This interface includes hooks that will be implemented by an agent developer and called back by the container at runtime. The callback interfaces can be further classified into two subcategories: system oriented vs. application oriented. The system-oriented interfaces allow an agent to customize the system service, while the application-oriented interfaces help an agent to program its business logic. The application-oriented interfaces are captured by the agent behavior model in JADE, which illustrated in Sect. 9.4.2.

An agent is an active object and follows "a thread-per-agent concurrency model." It means that there is a single Java thread per agent to execute all its tasks concurrently. JADE also provides an "agent behavior model" in the form of abstract classes to support concurrent execution of agent behaviors. An agent may have multiple behaviors to model the underlying tasks. At runtime, the embedded scheduler inside each agent will schedule and execute the various behaviors in a round-robin manner. JADE provides message passing to support agent interactions. It supports FIPA ACL specification to create messages.

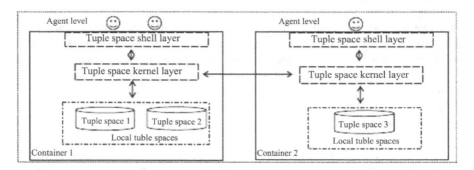

Fig. 9.5. Reactive tuple space architecture

Figure 9.5 is the reactive tuple space architecture viewed in a high-level abstraction. The tuple space is designed to be part of the JADE services. There are two layers in this abstract architecture: the "tuple space shell" and the "tuple space kernel." Multiple tuple spaces are distributed over the network environment. The communication between the shell and the kernel is a local method call. The kernels located inside different JADE containers communicate with each other through RMI. The shell is in the agent level and supplies stable interfaces for agents. In addition, there is a connector in the shell. The connector performs the exchange and transformation of data between an application agent and the kernel level. The kernel processes tuple accesses from the shell locally or remotely, and returns appropriate responses. If the required tuple space is located in a remote container, the kernel forwards the request to the (tuple) kernel in the remote container. The kernel also includes a framework to support agent reactive behaviors. This framework provides the reactive programmable interface called IReactive for agents and will trigger (execute) these reactive behaviors when the specified events occur. The kernel uses replication to make the system efficient.

Our design follows the principle of minimal change to the JADE source code. The first change is to extend the interfaces of the JADE Agent class so that an agent can access tuple spaces. The second is to handle agent mobility so that when an agent migrates from one container to another container, reactive behavior registration information can be updated by the reaction manager. Thus, it can keep location transparency for agent reactions. Finally, the initialization and termination handling of JADE are modified so that tuple space services can start and stop properly.

9.4.2 Tuple Space-Based Agent Interaction Primitives

Some of the tuple primitives are already highlighted in earlier sections. In this section, we present the full taxonomy of primitives that are incorporated in our design.

The set of primitives supported through tuple space can be classified into three categories: synchronous, asynchronous, and reactive (notification) primitives. In addition, in order to facilitate programming as well as improve the resulting system performance, we extend each synchronous or asynchronous primitive into three subcategories (1) single (tuple) access, (2) bulk (tuple) access, and (3) logic-template-based access. Bulk access allows multiple tuples to be retrieved in a single operation. Logic-template-based access provides associative search of tuples via a logic-template to improve the flexibility of agent collaboration protocols. Figure 9.6 outlines the set of primitives that we have implemented in Java.

In the following, selective explanation is offered for some of the primitives shown in Fig. 9.6.

```
interface TupleSpaceService
{
  public TupleSpaceID TSCreate(String name);
  public TupleSpaceID TSFind(String name);

//synchronous single tuple access
  public Tuple   in(TupleSpaceID tsId, Tuple atemplate);
  public Tuple   in(TupleSpaceID tsId, Tuple atemplate, long timeout);
  public Tuple   read(TupleSpaceID tsId, Tuple atemplate);
  public Tuple   read(TupleSpaceID tsId, Tuple atemplate, long timeout);

//asynchronous single tuple access
  public void     asynOut(TupleSpaceID tsId, Tuple atuple);
  public Future   asynIn(TupleSpaceID tsId, Tuple atemplate);
  public Future   asynRead(TupleSpaceID tsId, Tuple atemplate);

// synchronous bulk primitives, which manipulate more than one tuple at a time
  public int   move(TupleSpaceID ts_source, TupleSpaceID ts_dest, Tuple atemplate );
  public int   copy(TupleSpaceID ts_source, TupleSpaceID ts_dest, Tuple atemplate );
  public TupleSet bulkInWithoutWait(TupleSpaceID tsId, Tuple atemplate);
  public TupleSet bulkReadWithoutWait(TupleSpaceID tsId, Tuple atemplate);

// asynchronous bulk primitives, which manipulate more than one tuple at a time
  public Future asynMove(TupleSpaceID ts_source, TupleSpaceID ts_dest, Tuple atemplate );
  public Future asynCopy(TupleSpaceID ts_source, TupleSpaceID ts_dest, Tuple atemplate );
  public Future bulkAsynIn(TupleSpaceID tsId, Tuple atemplate);
  public Future bulkAsynRead(TupleSpaceID tsId, Tuple atemplate);

// logic-template-based asynchronous access
  public Future   asynIn(LogicTemplate alogic_template);
  public Future   asynRead(LogicTemplate alogic_template);

// reactive primitives
  public AgentRegisterID  register(TupleSpaceID tsId, Tuple atemplate, IReactive ref);
  public AgentRegisterID  register(TupleSpaceID tsId, EventChecker checker, IReactive ref);
  public void deregister(AgentRegisterID  register_id);

//for replication purpose
  public void subscribeForReplication(TupleSpaceID tsId, Tuple atemplate);
}
```

Fig. 9.6. Interaction primitives

1. *TSCreate(String name)*. This primitive enables an agent initially to create a tuple space and share with its group members. The group members will access the tuple space by name. The location of tuple space created is transparent to agents.

2. *TSFind(String name)*. It finds an existing tuple space by the given name. This primitive enables an agent to join a group of agents if it is aware of the name of the tuple space.

3. *in(TupleSpaceID tsId, Tuple atemplate)*. It has the same semantics as Linda-like in primitive [4]. It retrieves (destructive read-out) a tuple that matches with the template atemplate from tuple space tsId. Since the primitive is synchronous, the agent will block until a matching tuple is available.

4. *in(TupleSpaceID tsId, Tuple atemplate, long timeout)*. It retrieves (destructive read-out) a tuple that matches with the template atemplate from tuple space tsId. Since the primitive is synchronous, the agent will block until a matching tuple is available or timeout is triggered. This primitive can simulate the probing Linda primitive inp.

5. *read(TupleSpaceID tsId, Tuple atemplate)*. It has the same semantic as in(tsId,atemplate) primitive except that the matching tuple is not removed.

6. *asynIn(TupleSpaceID tsId, Tuple atemplate)*. It asynchronously retrieves a tuple that matches with the template atemplate from tuple space tsId. The primitive is asynchronous and the agent will not be blocked. It returns a tuple-holder object (called future). The agent can check the future object to see if the matching tuple has become available and fetch it from the future object locally. This enables an agent to asynchronously interact with another agent without stalling when the latter is not ready. For example, a buyer agent may look for an item yet to appear in the market.

7. *move(TupleSpaceID ts_source, TupleSpaceID ts_dest, Tuple atemplate)*. It moves all the tuples that match template atemplate from tuple space ts_source to tuple space ts_dest. In fact, it consists of two operations: one is to retrieve tuples from source tuple space, and the other is to write these tuples into the destination tuple space. It returns an integer as the number of tuples that has been moved. This primitive enables an agent to manage the shared tuples according to its roles. For example, a warehouse manager can move selected items from one warehouse to another easily.

8. *bulkInWithoutWait(TupleSpaceID tsId, Tuple atemplate)*. It retrieves all the tuples that match with template atemplate from tuple space tsId and gets a TupleSet object that contains all the matching tuples immediately. If there is not even one matching tuple, an empty tuple set is returned. As demonstrated earlier, this primitive is useful for collecting items that match a requirement together as a set.

9. *asynRead(LogicTemplate alogic_template)*. This primitive reads those tuples that match with the logic template alogic_template asynchronously.

This primitive enables an agent to read tuples across multiple clusters of collaboration simultaneously. To clarify logic-template, its syntax in BNF notation is given here. Suppose that EXP represents the logic-template:

<EXP> ::= <OP>(<ARGS>)
<ARGS> ::= <ARG> | <ARG>,<ARGS>
<ARG> ::= (tsId, template)| <EXP>
<OP> ::= and | or

The semantics of and operator is that it supports retrieval of tuples from the tuple spaces identified by both the left and the right statements. The semantic of or operator is that it supports retrieval of tuples from the tuple spaces identified by either the left or the right statements.

10. *register(TupleSpaceID tsId, Tuple atemplate, IReactive ref)*. It registers a reaction to tuple space tsId. The primitive returns a register identifier register_id. At runtime, if a tuple that matches the template atemplate becomes available in tuple space tsId, the reaction that implements IReactive interface is triggered. If more than one agent registers the same template, all registered reactions will be triggered. This primitive enables the reactive parts of an agent to sense stimulus from other agents passively. Meanwhile, the tuple space manager takes over the responsibility of detecting the stimulus. Reaction is introduced to model agent reactive behaviors and support agent asynchronous couplings. A reaction is defined through the reactive interface called Ireactive, which has only one method reactTo (AgentReactionEvent ev). It is modeled as a serializable object collocated with the agent. The parameter AgentReactionEvent provides the event and its source agent. An event is a tuple. For a programmer, defining a reaction is to implement the Ireactive interface, and corresponding code implements the agent's reaction. At runtime, the kernel keeps track of agent location and knows where the notification should be sent.

9.4.3 TSAF – Agent Framework

This section presents an agent model and the associated framework that we have implemented [13]. Agent-oriented programming relies on the assumption that a complex distributed software system can be programmed as a set of interacting software entities, called (software) agents. Generally, agent-oriented methodologies include agent architecture and agent programming frameworks that support analysis, design, and implementation of agent applications at different levels. Agent architecture is in the abstract level of agent model, while an agent programming framework is in the implementation level and supports building practical agent applications in software engineering sense. Our TSAF is such an agent-oriented framework that includes the agent architecture in the abstract level and an agent programming support in the implementation level for building multi-agent systems. Besides, TSAF supports tuple space-based agent coupling mechanism. The structure of TSAF is shown in Fig. 9.7.

Even though different approaches to the construction of multiagent systems impose different requirements on the individual agents, an agent is generally defined as an autonomous, collaborative, and adaptive computational entity with reactive and proactive behaviors. Many early researches on agent architecture combine the psychological and behavioral studies of humans, and describe agent models to exhibit cognitive behaviors [14, 15]. In this view, an agent has three basic parts: sensory part, communication part, and decision part, whose actions are compatible with the basic action–perception cycle of cognitive brain functions shown in Fig. 9.8. The sensors perceive information from the environment, the effectors affect the environment through activities, and the part of central processing makes decisions of what actions will be taken by the effectors according to the acquired information through sensors.

This agent architecture is based on the AI perspective, which describes agents as entities with knowledge for reasoning in a human-like way. Agent-oriented software engineering is centered on the design of autonomous, active, and interacting agents. It mainly cares about how to design flexible and interactive entities

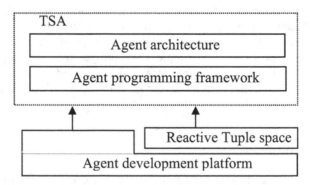

Fig. 9.7. Structure of TSAF

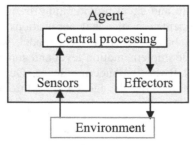

Fig. 9.8. Basic action–perception cycle

with clear definitions of agent's behaviors and their interaction protocols. In multiagent-based applications, the uncertainty of the dynamic environment, the complexity of coordination among autonomous agents, and the multiple roles played by each agent further necessitate the agent architecture to simplify the process of development. In TSAF, we aim at these requirements of a software engineering process to provide different agent architecture. The following section elaborates this architecture in detail.

As an agent-programming model, the primary goal of TSAF is to provide a means for building agent applications to facilitate analysis, design, and implementation of software agents in a relatively rapid and easy way. The agent architecture of TSAF is shown in Fig. 9.9. Based on the basic agent model of action–perception cycle, the communication part and central processing part are still included in the architecture; however, they are deliberated in different ways from the traditional layered architecture for ease of building a software agent.

The sensory part includes agent sensory behaviors that periodically sense the changing environment where the agent lives. The adaptability of agents enables them to readjust themselves to adapt to the environment. In this case, we assume that an agent often knows quite a bit about its environment and knows how to adapt to its environment. For example, a mobile information agent in an e-commerce application may need to sense its operating environment to decide whether to move away from some sites. Meanwhile, it also keeps sensing the status of local data resource. If it knows that the accessed data sources are problematic, it may stop the searching activity immediately and move to other places.

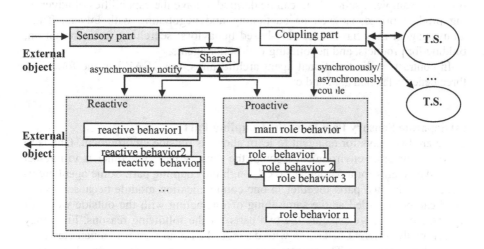

Fig. 9.9. Agent architecture of TSAF

The reactive part includes reactive behaviors that can be regarded as stimulus–response pattern. The stimulus may be from the external objects sensed by the sensory part or from the other agents' notifications through the coupling part. Therefore, the reactive behaviors are divided into two different types. One type includes simple behaviors that are triggered by other behaviors of the agent. For example, they may be triggered by the sensory behavior to react to the external environment or by the proactive behaviors to react to some internal results. The other type is as asynchronous listeners to other agents to perform collaborations with other agents. The latter can be realized through reactive tuples.

A reactive behavior is a precise and deterministic action without long-term proactive protocols needed to interact with other agents. It may be a simple activity starting at once, like stopping some actions, sending alarm signals or just triggering an agent's proactive behavior. For example, in e-market application, a seller agent as an auctioneer may have three reactive behaviors. One may be triggered by an abort event of a buyer agent to stop all transactions with the buyer agent. The second may be triggered by a change of a price level of a product in the market to readjust its selling price for this product. The third may be triggered by a new bidding request from a buyer agent to activate an auction behavior.

Proactive part includes the agent's proactive behaviors. Such behaviors are task initiative behaviors that do not merely act in response to their environment but are able to exhibit goal-directed behaviors to perform some intended tasks. Collaborations with other agents to perform such tasks are often needed. An agent may have to play multiple roles. As a result, each role-based behavior can be defined to perform a specific task. The "main role behavior" is a proactive behavior that runs periodically as a dispatcher of other role-based behaviors. In the e-market application, for example, a seller agent can be defined to have the capabilities of advertising product prices, as well as auctioning and negotiating with buyers. Thus, a buyer agent may have three role-based behaviors: searching for information, bidding for products, and negotiating with seller agents.

In contrast to the traditional agent architectures, our TSAF has the following three benefits labeled a, b, and c:

(a) Separate Sensory Part from the Coupling Part

There are two ways for an agent to learn about its outside environment. One is to sense the dynamic environment through the sensory part. The other is to interact with other agents for a particular task through the coupling part. Some agent architecture put the two parts together in one communication module because both of them can be regarded as the same thing of interacting with the outside world of agents. However, we separate the two parts for the following reasons. First, they reflect totally different behaviors with distinguished issues, so it is much clearer to model them separately. The sensory part performs the works of periodically perceiving the environment for some specific parameters and keeping them in the internal shared database for successive stages of decision-making or reactions. On the other hand, an agent still faces one or more tasks to be solved through collaborating with other agents. The coupling part just performs this work to provide unified interfaces for couplings among a group of agents. Moreover, the sensory part and coupling part may often lead to concurrent behaviors. While an agent couples with other agents, it may sense the environment at the same time. The independence of the two parts reflects the natures of agents' behaviors. Therefore, their separation simplifies the underlying implementation of the two parts and facilitates the design of the reactive behaviors and proactive behaviors of agents.

(b) Separate Reactive Part from the Proactive Part
Generally, an agent may combine aspects of both reactive and proactive behaviors so that it can make use of the best features of both behaviors. Some agent architectures process the two types of behaviors in the same workflow. In the layered architecture, for example, any event, no matter what behaviors it will cause, is in turn sent to each layer and is processed by each layer. In TSAF, however, we separate the reactive part from the proactive part, define them separately, and activate them concurrently if necessary.

First of all, the separation of the two parts simplifies the design process because it supports the concurrent execution of the two types of behaviors. In traditional architectures, the actions of reactive or proactive behaviors are started by a "central scheduler." This is in fact a sequential mechanism that is not suited for the nature of agent's behaviors. Separating reactive behaviors from proactive behaviors allows a developer to manage different behaviors simply, and results in a better structured design with explicit concurrency that is more easily implemented in an agent. This is a fundamental aspect of our TSAF framework.

Second, when designing a software agent, it is important for agents to be as easily configurable and scalable as possible. Therefore, it must be easy to create a new agent through behavior definition, and it must be simple to add new role-based behaviors to scale up the agent when it plays additional roles. The separation of reactive behaviors from proactive behaviors makes it easy to change/add/delete different role-based behaviors without interfering with other components in the architecture.

Finally, from the perspective of the life cycle of an agent, reactive behavior and proactive behavior have different effects on the state transition of an agent. Figure 9.10 shows a typical life-cycle model of an agent [8], where an agent has a basic life cycle with six states (Initiated, Active, Waiting, Suspended, on the Move, and Unknown). To build a complete agent, it is necessary for the agent architecture to support the state transitions very well. Proactive behaviors can change the agent's state according to its role-based protocols. However, to avoid directly affecting the on-going execution of a proactive behavior, a reactive behavior may inform the proactive behavior its intention through the shared object rather than directly change the agent's internal state. For example, in an e-market application, when a buyer agent moves to the location of a local market, the local market is down. In this situation, a reactive behavior is activated immediately to inform the proactive behavior, which then may decide to wait for the market recovery or move to another market. The different influences of reactive behaviors and proactive behaviors on agent state transition make it necessary to separate them in agent architecture.

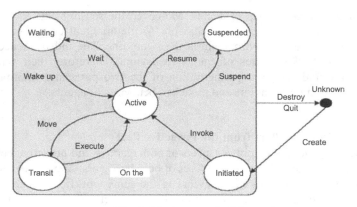

Fig. 9.10. An agent's life cycle

(c) Support Definition of Role-based Behaviors

In agent-based systems, a role model identifies and describes a structure of inter-acting entities in terms of roles that will be played by agents. The capabilities of roles represent a set of actions that are needed for an agent to achieve its tasks. In the agent architecture, the proactive behaviors are role-based behaviors that are defined according to the responsibility of roles. The start of role-based behaviors is based on couplings with the environment or other agents. Each role-based behavior can be modeled as a sequence of tasks related to a role. It involves a partial order of tasks and is mapped to one thread when running.

Using role model in the analysis and design of agent proactive behaviors is an essential part of agent-oriented software engineering. In the analysis stage, an agent is defined to play one or more roles in applications. In the design stage, each proactive behavior is defined separately in accordance with the role-related tasks. In the implementation stage, when creating an agent playing a set of roles, the cor-responding predefined role-based behaviors are simply assembled into an agent class. Therefore, the definitions of role-based behaviors make the development of agent systems faster and clearer than otherwise.

9.4.4 Agent Programming with TSAF Framework

TSAF is built on top of JADE. JADE provides a complete agent class for creating and defining JADE agent in a multiagent application. In JADE agent class, there is a set of attributes to describe an agent properties and a number of methods to define the agent actions, especially a set of FIPA-compliant ACLs that are embed-ded in the sets of agent methods. Moreover, the JADE scheduler kernel supports concurrent execution of agent behaviors and provides an abstract class of agent behaviors as an interface called action. Here, we adopt all the definitions in a JADE agent class but make extensions in the following two aspects:

1.   We add coupling interfaces of all the tuple space-based services introduced earlier in JADE agent class, through which the agent can perform any tuple space-based coupling actions with other agents. These interfaces can be useful complementary methods with message passing-based communication in agent coordination. They are implemented by tuple space services.

2.   We extend the agent behavior class with three types of "specific agent behaviors" as discussed earlier: sensory behavior, reactive behavior, and (proactive) role behaviors. In these agent behaviors, we provide different behavior mechanisms that facilitate the application development.

Figure 9.11 is the class diagram of an agent in TSAF. The class of the shared data is used in the couplings among the behaviors within an agent, while the coupling class facilitates the couplings between the agents.

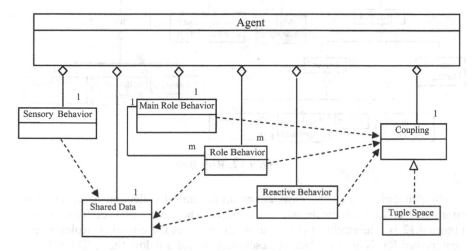

Fig. 9.11. Agent class diagram

9.5 A Case Study in e-Commerce Using Tuple Spaces

In this section, we introduce a hypothetical electronic market (e-market) and its simulation to bring out the use and benefits of TSAF. The e-market has several sellers and buyers.

9.5.1 Analysis and Specifications of the Requirements on the e-Market

The e-market comprises single buyers as well as groups of buyers where their buying needs are grouped together. Similarly, the sellers are organized as an individual seller or as a group in an electronic mall. The transactions in the e-market involve: dynamic information sharing, collaboration among the participants, and dynamic relationships among the participants. For example, in online auction, the number of bidders in an auction is not fixed before the start of an auction. A bidder can join and quit from the auction dynamically. A similar situation can be conceived in a group buying where a buyer can decide to join a group at any time. With complex trading activities, an e-market can face unexpected events. Unexpected events include changes in the external environment, resource problems, buyer/seller failure, etc. The e-market supports a reactive mechanism to sense and to react to these unexpected events properly without affecting the rest of the community in conducting their businesses.

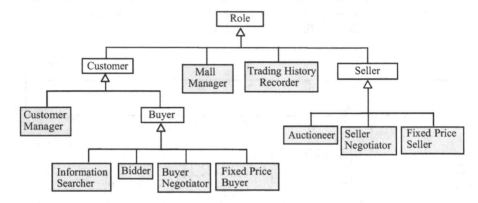

Fig. 9.12. Role tree

The simulation views the e-market as an organized collection of agents that coordinate and communicate with each other. The agents play different roles. Figure 9.12 is a hierarchical depiction of the roles in the e-market. Roles in the nonterminal levels are the abstract description of roles below them. The roles at the terminal nodes are the roles that ultimately emerge to be separately mapped to agents. Each role is described by its responsibilities, knowledge, and its collaborators. On the buyer or customer side, two roles are involved: (a) the customer manager is responsible for management of the coordinated buying tasks and (b) buyers perform the actual buying tasks. On the market side, two roles are involved: (a) a role of trading recorder and (b) a role of mall manager providing services to all the participants (buyers and sellers). On the sale side, the role of sellers is in charge of selling products to buyers.

Once the roles in an application are captured, the relationships among the roles are analyzed. We identify two types of relationships: static relationships and dynamic relationships. The latter can change at runtime. For example, a seller has a static relationship with a mall manager when it registers in the market, on the other hand, the relationship between a buyer and a seller may be established dynamically according to their trading needs. Figure 9.13 shows the dynamic relationships among roles. The interactions between roles may be relations of one to one, one to many, many to one, or many to many. The arrows show the initialization direction of interactions.

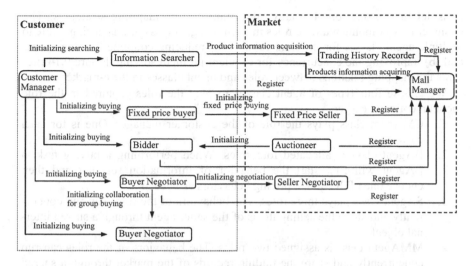

Fig. 9.13. Interactions between roles

9.5.2 Software Architecture

Role models help in the design of agent systems. The proactive behaviors of agents are role based, and can be defined based on the individual roles, knowledge, and the protocols involved. When mapping the roles to agents [2, 16], we

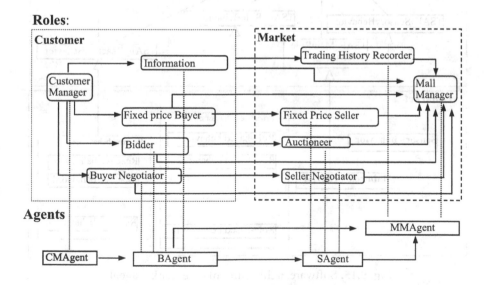

Fig. 9.14. Mapping relations between roles and agents

consider one-to-one, one-to-many, and many-to-one mapping strategies. The designer may combine multiple roles in a single agent class or map a single role to multiple agent classes for different reasons (a) reducing couplings among agents and (b) improving the concurrency for efficient problem solving. Figure 9.14 presents the mapping relations between roles and agent classes in the e-market.

We choose four types of agent classes to play the roles captured in the role model mentioned earlier.

1. CMAgent class plays the role of the customer manager. One is for each customer.
2. BAgent class is allocated four roles. When performing a buying task, a BAgent will first start the behavior of information searcher and then choose one of the online pricing behaviors as needed.
3. SAgent class plays three roles. The behaviors of the roles can run concurrently and share the selling items of the seller agent through a shared internal object.
4. MMAgent class is assigned two roles. The behaviors of the roles can run concurrently and share the trading records of the market through a shared internal object. One MMManager for each mall uses its own tuple space.

Based on TSAF, each type of agents in the e-market is designed consisting of different behaviors. In TSAF, the sensory behavior and proactive behaviors are

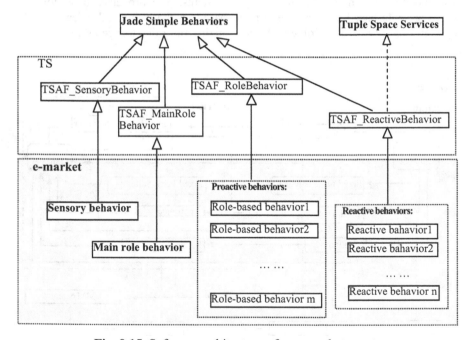

Fig. 9.15. Software architecture of an e-market agent

inherited from SimpleBehavior of JADE, and the reactive behaviors are implemented by tuple space services. Figure 9.15 presents the software architecture of an e-market agent.

9.5.3 Agent Behavior

Dynamic information sharing occurs in many scenarios of the e-market. The case of public special sale is a representative use of dynamic information sharing, where all the buyer agents share the "special sale" information. The buying actions of the buyer agents are concurrent and nondeterministically modify the shared 'product tuples.' Agent behaviors can be formally described using Coloured Petri Nets. More details on this are found in [13].

In many transactions, the relations among agents are dynamic and can be changed at runtime. In what follows, we present the collaboration among agents in an English auction protocol as an example. The tuple space is created by a mall manager agent and it is shared by all its participants. In our case, bidders are allowed to enter or quit an auction dynamically and the auctioneer does not know the participants in advance. When a bidder agent (ABuyer) decides to buy a product in our case, it may read the current price from the tuple space, analyze it, and plan the next step. It can propose a higher bidding price or it can decide to give up and move out. If the bidder agent proposes its bidding price, it can obtain an auction commitment and become the winner, or fail to become a winner.

Tuple space-based coordination model provides reactive tuples that allow an agent to react to asynchronous notifications from other agents as part of the collaboration with other agents. This type of protocols is easily implemented under TSAF. For example, during the "Public Special Sale," a seller agent may register a reaction by means of "a reactive tuple." When a buyer agent buys a product through that "Public Special Sale," it will write into the tuple space to which the seller agent will react by activating its relevant registered reaction to respond to the seller.

TSAF simplifies the design of such e-market applications. In particular, role analysis and role mapping to agents provide the designer clear separation of concern in designing efficient collaboration protocols among agents. At the same time, the availability of tuple space as an interaction medium facilitates the dynamic information sharing and the nondeterministic progress. As nondeterminism promotes performance (relative to static scheduling), the resulting e-market can achieve results not obtainable by static synchronous protocols.

9.5.4 Implementation of the e-Market Application

Figure 9.16 is a graphical representation of the system architecture. It is a distributed multiagent system where agents are separate entities running concurrently, and are possibly distributed on different nodes in a network of computers.

A CManager is a mediator between consumers and buyer agents. It receives purchase requests from consumers, assigns buying tasks to buyer agents, and returns the purchase results to the consumers. Each CManager has its own tuple space shared with all its registered buyer agents. In the e-market, stores basic unit represented by seller agents (ASeller). Some stores are located in the same location called "mall" to give buyers more convenience of searching and buying. A MManager is responsible for such a mall (local market). As a participant of more than one mall, an ASeller may register with more than one MManager.

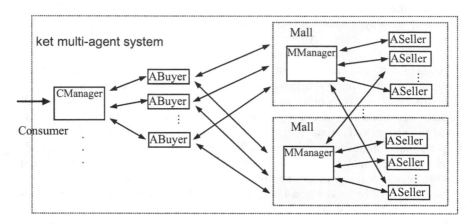

Fig. 9.16. System architecture

Logically, as a shared space, one tuple space would suffice. However, the e-market is viewed as a distributed system, where multiple agents execute concurrently in different nodes, and there are different sets of tuples shared by different group of agents. Hence, physically more than one tuple space may help to improve the concurrency and enhance the efficiency of matching the associated tuples.

In the e-market, four types of agents are created. The different behaviors of each e-market agent are listed in Table 9.1.

A sensory behavior of e-market agents can be implemented by extending the abstract class of TSAF_SensoryBehavior. Figure 9.17 describes how to create a sensory behavior of a seller agent via TSAF. A seller agent senses the external environment through checking an environment file. If it senses that an exception will cause an abort, it will trigger a reaction to stop all its transactions and inform other agents of this situation.

TSAF simplifies the implementation of the sensory behavior. A sensory behavior is a special behavior because of its periodicity of running. Without TSAF, the management of its execution must be considered explicitly. Application programmers only need to code the functions of sense and reactions in the method of "myaction()."

Table 9.1. Behaviors of e-market agents

agent name	Functionality	proactive behaviors	reactive behavior	sensory behavior
CM Agent (customer manager agent)	responsible for the management of buying tasks of consumers and the registration of buyer Agents	main role behavior assign task	agent register task assign buyer agent abort task result	sensory behavior
MMAgent (mall manager agent)	responsible for the management of local market and the registration of the participants of the market place	main role behavior history recorder	agent register price info seller transaction buyer agent abort seller agent abort	sensory behavior
BAgent (buyer agent)	as a representative of consumer, responsible for buying products through interacting with seller agents	main role behavior compete for task direct search english auction group auction group buying negotiation public special sale	buyer agent abort customer abort market abort seller abort	sensory behavior
SAgent (seller agent)	as a representative of a vendor, responsible for selling products through interacting with buyer agents	main role behavior english auction negotiation	buyer agent abort market abort group auction negotiation request public special sale	sensory behavior

```
public class Seller_SensoryBehaviour extends TSAF_SensoryBehaviour{
public Seller_SBehaviour(Agent a, long p) {// creates a new instance of Seller_SBehaviour
  super(a,p);
  myAgent=(SellAgent)a;
}
public void myaction() { //supplied by application programmers
              sense (); //senses the environment object of the seller agent
  // triggers a reaction to stop all its transactions if it will abort,
  If (abortName.equals(myAgent.getLocalName())&&abortType.equals("abort"))
  {
  // deals with the exception
          ... ...
  }
  //checks other environment parameters
  ... ...
  }
}
```

Fig. 9.17. Code fragment of a sensory behavior of a seller agent

```
public class Buyer_PBehaviour_DirectSearch extends TSAF_ProactiveRoleBehaviour{
  /creates a new instance of Buyer_PBehaviour_DirectSearch
public Buyer_PBehaviour_DirectSearch(Agent a, int i, String taskname) {
super(a);
myAgent=(BuyerAgent)a;
index=i;
currentTaskName=taskname;
}
public void myaction() { //supplied by application programmers to perform the search task
... ...
}
... ...
}
```

Fig. 9.18. Code fragment of a role-based behavior of a buyer agent

In TSAF, two types of proactive behaviors are created for each e-market agent (a) one main-role behavior and (b) a set of role-based behaviors. The role-based behaviors perform role-related tasks, while the main-role behavior is responsible for dispatching the role-based behaviors. In the e-market, a buyer agent plays seven roles (listed in Table 5.1), each of which performs different role-related tasks coded in the method of "myaction()" of each behavior class. Figure 9.18 describes a code fragment of a role-based behavior (Buyer_PBehavior_DirectSearch).

The reactive behaviors of an agent are specific behaviors that support the asynchronous notifications from other agents. TSAF provides an abstract class TSAF_ReactiveBehavior for creating reactive behaviors. In Fig. 9.19, we describe how to create a reactive behavior of a seller agent in "group auction." The seller agent first registers a reactive tuple and its intended reactive behavior in a tuple space. Whenever a buyer agent writes the reactive tuple in that tuple space, the specified reactive behavior (Seller_RBehavior_GroupAuction) is triggered.

Performance Aspects

The implemented e-market was exercised with sample test data to study its performance aspects. On the one hand, we have claimed that the tuple space approach to system development is simpler than that based on agent-to-agent message communication. On the other hand, we needed to know how much the performance would suffer because of the tuple space approach. The simulation involved the creation of three types of test data (1) Consumers' task data, (2) supplier product data, and (3) e-market place running data. The tasks of consumers are abstracted as purchase requests that include: task name, product information (requests), buying strategy, quantity, permitted high/lower price, and expired date. These data are generated automatically for the simulation test in different ways. The supplier product data are the basis for any transactions in the e-market system. Each seller agent sells product items that may belong to different suppliers. In the simulation test, we put all the suppliers' data into one data source that include all the products sold in the e-market. The data of each seller agents can be generated based on the suppliers' data source, which includes item name, product information, sell strategy, lower limit price (LLP), available number, the expired date, and the group-buying strategy. Before the system runs, a set of "configuration run" data must be determined for system initialization purposes. These data are system wide (1) random distribution of markets (malls) and agents across the physical nodes and (2) random logical distribution of sellers registered in different markets.

Application performance represents the performance of the entire market that includes high level of user satisfaction, and maximizing efficiency and productivity of the whole market. From the point of view of consumers, the response time is the main factor to evaluate the e-market. In the simulation test, we select two parameters to express the satisfaction quality of consumers (1) average waiting time for consumers to get the final purchases and (2) possible successful number of transactions within a period of time. From the point of view of suppliers, the

```
public class Seller_RBehaviour_GroupAuction extends TSAF_ReactiveBehaviour {
    //creates a new instance of Seller_RBehaviour_GroupAuction
public Seller_RPBehaviour_GroupAuction(Agent a) {
super(a);
myAgent=(SellerAgent)a;
}
public void myaction() {//reactions supplied by application programmers
    if (reactiveTuple!=null) {
    // reads the content of the reactive tuple
    ... ...
    //changes the current bid price and the remaining quantity of the product in PrinceInfo
    ... ...
} //if
}
}
```

Fig. 9.19. Code fragment of a reactive behavior of a seller agent in group auction

whole market sale is what we have considered as a measure. It is the actual revenue and successful number of transactions within a period of time.

Test Results and Analysis
In the simulation, we considered centralized market place, distributed market
places, and group purchases to study how the tuple space and message passing
affect the application performance as the number of buyer agent changes. In each
of these cases, three types of application performance (response time, number of
transactions, and market revenue within a specified period of time) are obtained as
the number of buyer agents was increased.

Case 1: Centralized Market Place
Test Data
Market size: 500 items
Number of physical nodes (machines): 8
Number of seller agents: 10
Test Results [shown in Fig. 9.20]
(ACL: message passing based Agent Communication Language, TS: Tuple Space)

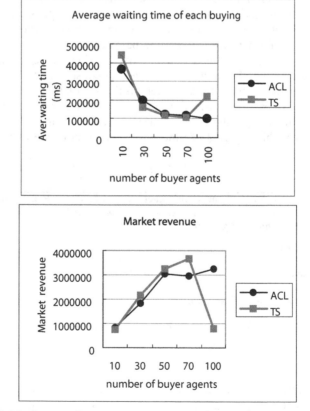

Fig. 9.20. Curves of performance in centralized market place with small
market size

Comments. In the case of message passing, all the agents in a container share one sending buffer, which needs to be synchronized when they send messages. When the number of buyer agents is small (smaller than 20), the couplings among agents tend to favor sequential process, in which message passing has more advantage than tuple space. When using tuple space, all the agents in one container can access the tuple space concurrently. In addition, the bulk tuple match and reactive tuples features of TSAF improve the concurrent couplings among agents. When the number of agents lies in a proper range (20–70), the application performance of using tuple space is better (better around 13%). However, tuple space needs to synchronize the concurrent accesses from agents. When the number of buyer agents is increased to the limit (70), the number of synchronized accesses of tuples also increases. In turn, this causes a longer waiting time. As a result, the performance with tuple spaces is not as good as the message passing.

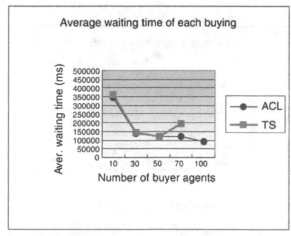

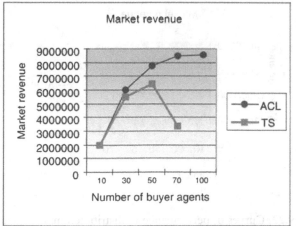

Fig. 9.21. Curves of performance in centralized market place with large market size

Case 2: Same as Case 1 but market size increased to 3,000:
The same test data are applied with the market size is increased to 3,000 items. Figure 9.21 shows the test results.

Comments. When the market size is large, the ACL always performs better than the TS (better around 6%). The difference between the two performances is more pronounced as the number of buyer agents increases. The time spent on synchronized access to tuple space is the main factor that counteracts the tuple space's positive effects. The market size also affects the breakpoint at which the tuple space performance would start to decrease. The breakpoint is at 70 (number of buyer agents) when the market size is 500, whereas the breakpoint is lowered to 50 when the market size is 3,000. This result is attributed to the increases of templates in the tuple space when the market size increases. Distinct templates lead to distinct entities to be matched and this may increase the associative search time.

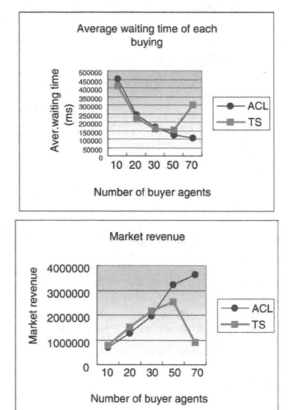

Fig. 9.22. Curves of performance in distributed market places

Case 3: Distributed Market Places
Test Data
Number of physical nodes (machines): 8
Number of seller agents: 10
Number of distributed market places: 4

Comments. Refer to Fig. 9.22. When the number of buyer agents is not large (less than 50), the application performance of tuple space is not worse than that of ACL. As we already know that, in message passing, agents in one container send their messages sequentially. In the case of using distributed tuple spaces, the agents in a container can access the different tuple spaces concurrently. This provides real concurrent activities of agent couplings. When the number of buyer agents exceeds 50, the performance of tuple space becomes worse because more synchronized access to the distributed tuple spaces block the accessing processes. Distributed market place seems to result in a lower breakpoint (from 70 to 50 compared with centralized market place). This may be attributed to the behavioral pattern of agents in the use of these markets and the actual concurrency that is achieved.

Case 4:Group Purchase
Test Data
Number of physical nodes (machines): 8
Number of seller agents: 10
Number of distributed market places: 4
Total number of buyer agents: 30

Comments. Refer to Fig. 9.23. Tuple space supports agent collaborations more efficiently than message passing in all cases of group buying. When the group size increases, more buyer agents join the group in buying. Once the group relationship is established, communication loads between agents decrease as a much less number of buying transactions are involved. As a result, the performance gets better. Moreover, the characteristics of tuple space (global information sharing, bulk template match, and reactive tuples) introduced in TSAF seem to have a strong positive impact on agent collaborations.

From this comparison, though not very exhaustive, we observe that using tuple spaces as the coupling medium does not produce worse application performance. In cases where distributed tuple spaces exist and agents require tighter coordination as in group buying, tuple space has a performance advantage over message passing. However, when heavily synchronized communication is involved, there is a breakpoint, beyond which the load increase induces sharp decline in performance due to the associative semantics of the tuple space. This should be viewed in light of the fact that application system development is relatively simpler as TSAF supports features that naturally occur in applications like e-business. The TSAF framework will be made available for researchers from a Concordia Website soon.

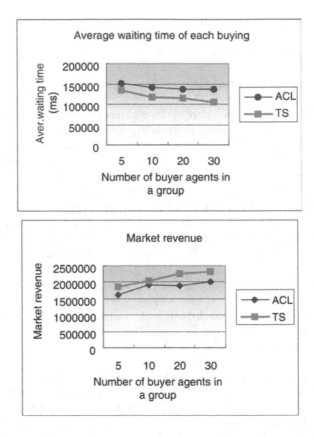

Fig. 9.23. Curves of performance in a group purchase

9.6 Summary

The use of the agent technology in building e-business applications seems to have several advantages. In this effort coordination among multiple agents is the central issue. In this chapter we have promoted the role that "tuple spaces" can play in the coordination and information sharing among multiple agents. Dynamic relations among the roles played by the agents and proactive as well as reactive responses can be well supported in a natural way when tuple spaces are used. The advantages of simplicity and flexibility provided by such an approach, we believe, would outweigh the extra overhead that might occur in certain circumstances as shown in the case study.

References

1. N. Carriero, D. Gelernter. Linda in context. Communication of the ACM, vol. 32, no. 4, pp. 444–458, April 1989
2. E.A. Kendall. Role model designs and implementations with aspect-oriented programming. In Proceedings of ACM Conference on Object-Oriented Systems, Languages, and Applications, Denver, Colorado, United States, 1999, pp. 353–369
3. FIPA-1. Publicly Available Implementations of FIPA Specifications: http://www.fipa.org/
4. D. Gelernter. Generative communication in Linda. ACM Transactions on Programming Languages and Systems (TOPLAS), vol. 7, pp. 80–112, 1985
5. G. Girard, H.F. Li. Evaluation of two optimized protocols for sequential consistency. In Proceedings of the 32nd Annual Hawaii International Conference on System Sciences, January 1999
6. G. Cabri, L. Leonardi, and F. Zambonelli. MARS: A programmable coordination architecture for mobile agents. Internet Computing, vol. 4, no. 4, pp. 26–35, 2000
7. Rowstron. WCL: A co-ordination language for geographically distributed agents. World Wide Web Journal, vol. 1, no. 3, 1998, pp. 167–179
8. JavaSpaces: http://www.cdegroot.com/cgi-bin/jini/JavaSpace JADE, http://sharon.cselt.it/projects/jade/
9. J. Snyder, R. Menezes. Using logical operators as an extended coordination mechanism in Linda. In Proceedings of Coordination 2002, York, England, April 2002
10. FIPA-2. Interaction Protocol Specifications: http://www.fipa.org/repository/ips.php3
11. Y. Li. Reactive tuple space for a mobile agent platform. Master Thesis, Dept. of Computer Science, Concordia University, Montreal, 2004
12. G. Rimassa. Runtime support for distributed multi-agent systems, Ph.D. Thesis, University of Parma, January 2003
13. Y. Zhang. A tuple space based agent programming framework. Master Thesis, Dept. of Computer Science, Concordia University, Montreal, 2004
14. H.A. Mallot. Behavior-oriented approaches to cognition: Theoretical perspectives, Theory in Biosciences. Vol. 116, 1997, pp. 196–220
15. G. Wagner. A Logical and Operational Model of Scalable Knowledge-and Perception-Based Agent. In Proceedings Seventh European Workshop on Modeling Autonomous Agents in a Multi-Agent World: Agents Breaking Away, Einhoven, The Netherlands, 1996, pp. 26–41
16. G. Cabri. Role-based infrastructures for agents. Eighth IEEE Workshop on Future Trends Distributed Computing System, Bologna, Italy, 31 October–2 November 2001
17. T. Dierks, C. Allen (1999) The TLS protocol version 1.0. http://www.ietf.org/rfc/rfc2246.txt
18. J. Schiller (2000) Mobile Communications. Addison-Wesley, New York.

19.   U. Hansmann, et al. (2001) Pervasive Computing Handbook. Springer, Berlin Heidelberg New York
20.   C. Sharma (2001) Wireless Internet Enterprise Applications. Wiley, New York
21.   Y.B. Lin, I. Chlamtac (2001) Wireless and Mobile Network Architectures. Wiley, New York
22.   Dornan (2001) The Essential Guide to Wireless Communications Applications. Prentice-Hall, New York

10 Mobile Payment

Y. Liu[*], X. Cao[*], and L. Dang[*]

[*] ISN National Key Lab, Xidian University, P.R. China

10.1 Introduction

Mobile payment is defined as "paying for goods or services with a mobile device such as a phone, personal digital assistant (PDA), or other such device [1]." Mobile payment is the next innovative step in the business world; it can be used in a variety of business situations. The user selects to make a mobile payment, by connecting to a server via the mobile device to execute authorization and authentication, and is presented with confirmation if the transaction is completed.

Mobile payment is regarded as the next big innovation that will enhance existing e-commerce and m-commerce efforts to unleash the potentials of mobile business. Mobile payment has been dramatically developing in recent years, and although it is still considered to be fairly new, it brings great promise and hope to the mobile industry.

In this chapter, we discuss the characteristics of mobile payment, the mobile payment agents, and the security for mobile payment.

10.2 Characteristics

10.2.1 Various Methods

For mobile payment, the mobile devices include mobile phone, tablet PC, PDA, and any mobile payment terminal or device.

Mobile telecommunications continue to be unbelievably successful, with estimations of around one billion mobile subscribers at the end of 2002. The success of NTT DoCoMo's i-mode service in Japan, which currently has 34 million data subscribers, exemplifies the desire for persuasive mobile data services. In Europe, the uptake of short messaging (SMS) has demonstrated the huge demand for non-voice services. According to the GSM Association, there were over 30 billion SMS messages sent in 2001.

In 2004, it was estimated that 60 million mobile payment users generated sales of US $50 billion, according to Celent, a financial services research and consulting firm. A joint survey by Visa International and Boston Consulting predicted that combined e-commerce and m-commerce volumes grew from US $38 billion in 2002 to US $128 billion in 2004.

As more refined devices are developed, new applications are rising to benefit from the new color screens, keyboards, and longer battery life. These new applications include enhanced messaging (EMS) and multimedia messaging (MMS), which enable the downloading of images, streaming video, and data files. Also, the proposed Federal Communication Commission's directive mandating the addition of global positioning (GPS) in mobile phones will enable location-based m-commerce.

Meanwhile, there is further enthusiasm surrounding proximity payments, a method of sending data between devices within a certain range with no physical contact. There are a number of wireless technologies and standards that will enable consumers to send transaction data from a mobile device to a point of sale terminal without manually swiping a card through a reader. These include:

- Bluetooth
- 802.11
- Infrared
- RFID and contactless chip

Mobile payments are extensive and can vary, and are determined by regional differences and individual market dynamics. For example:

- In Japan, the success of mobile Internet services can be attributed to a high population density in cities, long transportation times, consumer comfort with small electronic devices, and the lack of a fixed-line Internet infrastructure.
- In Europe, prepaid phone services are popular.
- In individual markets in Asia Pacific, Europe, and the USA, there is a drive to implement proximity payments in places such as road tolling, fast food drive-through, and service stations.

Despite these regional differences, there is a shared requirement for payment to be secure and easy to use.

10.2.2 Standardization

Public concerns relating to security, privacy, and facile use of the system are restricting the growth of mobile payment. Research from Forrester Research indicates that over half of surveyed consumers consider credit card security to be the major inhibitor to the growth of m-commerce. The challenge for the mobile and the payment industry is to convince the majority of consumers to embrace mobile payments by addressing these concerns.

For example, Forrester also indicated that fewer than 15% of consumers feel completely comfortable sending their payment card details over mobile networks and over 65% claim to be "averse" to sending confidential information. If the industry tackles this concern to ensure that both the actual security and perceived security are strong, then the potential of mobile payments will be more readily accepted. There are also a number of other technical issues to be overcome. These include providing standards that are mutually developed, agreed upon, and supported by mobile operators, merchants, payment associations, and financial institutions.

Mobile payments, whether executed via a mobile network or a proximity-based protocol, must be subject to the same level of standardization that governs payment cards such as credit cards, in order to be perceived as familiar and secure. Attempts to introduce proprietary payment schemes in addition to the existing array of networks, devices, and operating systems, can be confusing and difficult, which can ultimately hinder growth.

The four main parties involved in a mobile payment transaction – the user, network operator, financial institution, and merchant – share many of the same concerns that need to be addressed by a mobile payment standards' body. However, not all these concerns are given equal weight by each party. For example:

- Consumers are mostly concerned with security, ease of use, and privacy. They also require any payment scheme to work across multiple devices, including mobile phones, PDAs, wireless tablets, and handheld computers.
- Mobile operators' principal concerns revolve around standardization and interoperability. Operators want payment to be seamless, allowing them to compete on services and applications.
- Financial institutions, meanwhile, are primarily concerned with ensuring the integrity of the payment system and reducing the risk of fraud.
- Merchants or content providers want the payment process to be transparent to the user, as this encourages greater usage and/or propensity to complete a purchase. They also want any payment scheme to facilitate swift and easy completion to ensure they get paid on time.

Besides the four parties involved in any given payment card transaction, a network is also an integral part of the transaction flow (see Fig. 10.1). The issuer provides the user with the ability to make payments by providing a credit link or a direct link to a checking or savings account. The validity of the user's payment credentials is contained on the piece of plastic in the form of an account number, hologram, and expiration date. Further payment credentials are encoded in the card's magnetic strip or chip. Once the transaction is initiated, the merchant requires transaction credentials from the user in the form of a signature or PIN, and this is verified against information stored centrally at the user's issuer.

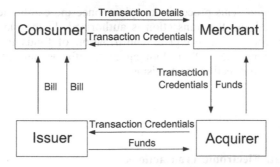

Fig. 10.1. The four parties of mobile payment

Once the transaction is complete, the funds are transferred from the issuer to the acquirer to the merchant, and the cardholder is billed for the goods purchased.

In the mobile environment, the transaction dynamics are similar, although the form of factor that contains the transaction credentials is different. In addition, in the case of remote payments, the transport of payment details will involve a mobile network operator and use either a browser-based protocol, such as WAP or HTML, or a messaging system, such as SMS or unstructured supplementary service data (USSD). Alternatively, the transport of payment details could be via Bluetooth, infrared, RFID, or contactless chip in the case of proximity payments.

In order to understand the challenges facing mobile payments, it is important to explore the user experience within the card transaction flow described earlier. For the user, the card transaction contains four concurrent steps:

Set-up and configuration. The first phase of the payment lifecycle is the configuration of the payment mechanism. In the mobile payment environment this could be the installation of an applet or application on a mobile device, such as a mobile wallet, or the issuance of a new mobile device and/or new SIM card. The set-up and configuration of the payment instrument usually takes place only once.

Payment initiation. Payment initiation for mobile payments will involve transferring payment information (PI) over a network or wireless protocol to the merchant. The Mobile Payment Forum (MPF) is considering the requirements for form fill standards, and developing best practices with regard to the transmission of PI and device wallet requirements [2].

Authentication. The authentication of the user is one of the most important elements of any payment transaction. The MPF is looking at two-way messaging authentication and SAT (SIM Alliance/Application Toolkit) authentication applications. In the case of two-way messaging, this involves defining a universal interface for requesting an authorization. SAT authentication standardization includes defining a set of minimum requirements for authenticating the user based on the SIM on a GSM handset.

Payment completion. This process takes place once the cardholder's details have been authenticated and the transaction is authorized. In the physical world this involves the printing of a receipt as confirmation of funds transferred. In the mobile environment, the MPF is looking at the format and storage of digital receipts as well as redirection mechanisms.

10.3 Agents

10.3.1 Automate Electronic Transactions

In real life, people can turn to a few agents or agencies for buying air tickets and notebooks, renting or buying a house, or even shopping for groceries. They can choose a satisfactory one from multiple provided plans. Similarly, the introduction of autonomous agents acting on behalf of end consumers could reduce the effort required from users to conduct e-commerce transactions by automating a variety of activities: looking for and filtering online shops selling the specified products, asking offers, negotiating with shops, and even completing transactions.

Mobile software agents are programs that act on behalf of a user or another program and, for a specified mission, are able to migrate from host to host on a network. Compared to the conventional client–server paradigm, mobile agents provide fast and efficient interaction with a remote service, and save network bandwidth.

Numerous applications could benefit from mobile agent technology, such as Internet information retrieval and network management. However, the greatest potential for mobile agents has been e-commerce applications in which the agents automate and facilitate the phases of brokering, negotiation, payment, and delivery of a transaction. Agents are now being used to further automate the purchase processes.

In the brokering phase, an agent roams the Web, evaluates available products, and decides what to buy and from whom to buy, based on a purchaser's requirements and preferences. In the next phase, agents could negotiate deals autonomously according to a set of user constraints and strategic guidelines. In the payment and delivery phase, an agent may automatically fill out a form to place an order, process the order, and track the shipment of the product. So far, the final service and evaluation phase is the area least explored for mobile agent applications. Nevertheless, mobile agents may find a promising future in this phase.

10.3.2 Accounting Architecture for Agent Frameworks

To identify the participating agents let us take a look at a conventional transaction. For example, you buy a meal at your favorite restaurant. Two parties are obvious: you, the paying customer, and the selling restaurant owner. The third party in the interaction is a banking service that provides the guarantee for the payment used. When paying cash this is the central bank of a country that guarantees the value of your bank notes; for credit card payment this is the credit card company; and when paying by check this will be the bank that issued the check. Either way there is always a third party involved that both parties must recognize and trust. This means that within the agent framework three independent components are needed. One for the provider, one for the customer, and a third that represents a banking service.

- The service agent represents the business side and deals with requests from the outside. It holds the information about the pricing of offered goods and available subscriptions to its services.
- The accounting agent can be the bank within the system. It keeps track of the payments made toward the service providers. It will also notify them when a transaction in their favor has been booked.

- An agent within the system is associated with the customer. It keeps the user's preferences about handling payments for the requested services. It will typically be a companion of the user's personal assistant; however, this is not strictly necessary and therefore the personal assistant is not considered part of the accounting system. This also helps minimize adjustments in existing personal assistants and greatly enhances the reusability of the accounting system.

So far only the components of the system have been described. What is essential, though, is the interaction of those components. The main interaction of the system is issuing a request to the service agent. Therefore, we shall have a closer look into this interaction.

All three parties cooperating in a purchase need control over the transaction. In particular every single agent needs some sort of veto capability to be able to stop the transaction.

A circular information processing path becomes apparent: Consider a shopping trip with your credit card. First you will ask the clerk for whatever you want to buy. He will then tell you the price and you can choose you think it is appropriate. If it is, you will hand him your credit card and he will try to get the conformation from your card company that this transaction is valid and booked. Unless you have exceeded your limit, the clerk will get this verification and hand you your merchandise.

Figure 10.2 shows the simplified object model with additional information about information flow. Steps 1–5 define the normal flow of information for a "service" use case. That is, if the request is completed and carried out – the primary scenario.

In step number 1 the user agent (customer) issues a request for service by contacting the respective service agent. The service agent will then send a payment request to the user agent (step 2), which in turn forwards this request to its accounting agent (step 3). After the transaction is booked the service agent is informed (step 4). Finally the service is carried out (step 5). One must note that the actions of contacting the service provider and getting the results have no numbers in this sequence. This is due to the fact that they can indeed happen at just about any time desired. A closer look reveals are two cases that are of interest:

- The request (e.g., a query to a database) is very cost intensive. The service agent then will not start the actual request to the provider until the expenses for it are covered. In this case the request to the provider will happen after the account agent has notified the service agent of the completed transaction (immediately before step 5). This lazy evaluation is always the preferred option by the provider since operating costs are kept to a minimum.
- The results of the query might be needed, however, to calculate the price for this request. This applies for all pricing models that use "per hit" as a factor. In this case the entire request has to be carried out by the time the payment request to the user agent is issued (between steps 1 and 2).

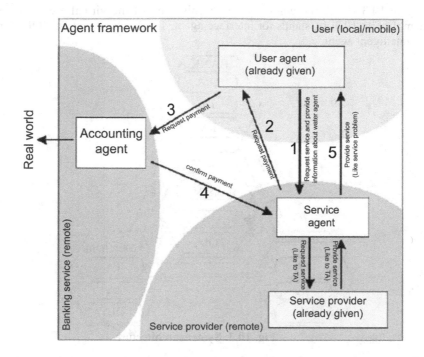

Fig. 10.2. Information flow in the simple object model

At this level of abstraction it is concluded and assumed that all communications reach their respective recipients and that the agents work properly. But during any time of the transaction, any party may choose to stop the transaction.

The most common reason for the user agent to stop a transaction is that it concludes that the price exceeds the limit set by the user. It could also mean that the agent has gotten a better offer from another service provider.

Another reason is that the bank can abort the transaction. Typically this happens when the accounting agent finds that a user has surpassed his/her credit limit. It can also happen when the user agent is not registered at the accounting agent (i.e., has no account).

10.3.3 Application of Intelligent Agent in Payment Security in e-Commerce

An intelligent agent is receptive, practical, and social, meaning that there can be automatic interaction between agents. This contributes to payment security in e-commerce in an immense fashion because the authentication function can be implemented, along with encryption function, decryption function, and many other functions with all kinds of intelligent agents.

Figure 10.3 shows the whole system architecture of the virtual e-commerce system. In Fig. 10.3, IA stands for interface agent, TA for task agent, and OIA for other intelligent agent.

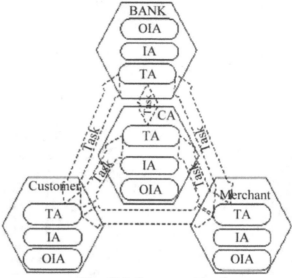

Fig. 10.3. System architecture

There are two types of intelligent agents in the system: interface agent (IA) and task agent (TA). IAs interact with the user by delivering results and receiving specifications. They obtain user preferences to perform system collaboration to help facilitate the user's tasks. TAs help users perform tasks by forming problem solving plans and carrying out these plans through communicating with other task agents.

Our payment security system is mainly composed of three kinds of intelligent agents: handshake agent, authentication agent, and payment agent. After the user provides an order online, the interface agent transmits the proper information format to the handshake agent. And then the payment procedure begins.

The whole payment procedure of one transaction is carried out as follows. Firstly, the client, bank, and merchant exchange the electronic certificates through the handshake agent. Secondly, the client, merchant, and bank identify each other through an authentication agent. If any of the three identifications fails, then the transaction is void and revoked. Thirdly, the client submits his/her order along with additional information, and the payment agent divides the information into two parts: order information (OI) and user payment instruction. The payment agent will then automatically communicate with the payment agent in the bank server with the user payment instruction, and the payment agent in merchant server with the OI. After authenticating the user's credit card, the bank server will do corresponding computing task and send the approved information to the merchant server if it succeeds. Thus the merchant can confirm the user order and prepare for the commodity delivery.

The guideline to get the favorable performance is to do the operations as few times as possible and only do the necessary operations. That is, reducing the encryption time to the least and accelerating the speed of these operations at the same time. This encryption takes a lot of time and reduces the performance in a way. There is no question that we should keep the PI secret to avoid some unexpected troubles. But as to the OI, we have different opinions. Just imagine the scene when we do shopping in a mall in real life. There are so many people who can see what we are purchasing, but we do not mind that. The same rule can be used to conduct purchase on Internet. People are concerned more about whether their OI is juggled than keeping it invisible to others. Therefore, the major goal of this procedure is to encrypt the PI. As to OI, we only do the authentication. Figures 10.4 and 10.5 exhibit the encryption and the authentication procedures.

Legends:

C: Customer, B: Bank
M: Merchant
PI: Payment information
OI: Order information
H: Hash function
E: Encryption
$K_{X,Y}$: The key share by X and Y
$EK_{X,Y}[M]$: Use the $K_{X,Y}$ encrypt the M: Connection

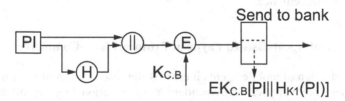

Fig 10.4. Encrypting process of PI

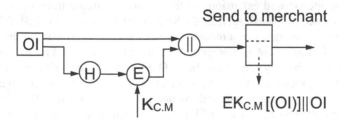

Fig. 10.5. Process of OI

These two processes are implemented in a special task agent, the payment agent. Figure 10.6 shows the payment procedure of the payment agent.

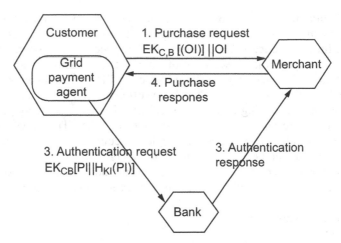

Fig. 10.6. Payment procedure of the payment agent

The three figures (Figs. 10.4–10.6) exhibit our scheme for the payment messages. We only encrypt the message digest of OI via the key that belongs to customer and merchant. It can reduce the encryption burden, for the message digest is far less than the whole message. Through this way, we can also implement the authentication for OI. It not only satisfies the demand of security, but also the demand of convenience.

10.3.4 Several Agent-assisted Payment Protocols for e-Commerce

The introduction of mobile agents increases the risk in terms of security, particularly when they carry critical/confidential information (e.g., credit card information), sign contracts, or make payment on behalf of the consumers since the agents and their carried sensitive data will be exposed to potentially hostile environments.

Several agent-based extensions of the secure electronic transaction (SET) protocol have been proposed, such as the SET/A, SET/A+, and LITESET/A+, aiming at utilizing the autonomy of a mobile payment agent while ensuring the security of payments. But in SET/A+, a pregenerated signature is carried by the agent, which can be abused by any merchant. In LITESET/A+, some critical arguments are exposed to the merchant who can regenerate the cardholder's secret signature key.

Recently, a new agent-assisted secure payment protocol LITESET/A++ has been proposed. The goal of LITESET/A++, which is based on SET, is to enable a mobile agent to automatically and autonomously make final transactions and payment with the "best" merchant without interacting with the consumer after performing all kinds of tasks, including looking for offers and negotiating with merchants. This requires the capability of the agent in the protocol to dynamically sign with the "best" merchant, who cannot be determined in advance, and pass the PI to the payment gateway (PG), which can be determined only after the interaction with the "best" merchant according to the brand of the credit card. Hence encrypting everything in advance is not possible while asking the agent to carry any key for encryption is certainly a risk. In LITESET/A++, by adopting the signature-share and signcryption-share schemes, the agent can sign contracts and pass the PI to the PG in corporation with the trusted third party (TTP) without the possibility of disclosing any secret to any participants.

In LITESET/A++, signature-share scheme is adopted for passing securely the information on OI to the merchant, while signcryption-share scheme is adopted for passing the PI to the PG and a temporarily session public key pair is used to encrypt the PI. The dispatched agent does not carry its shared private signature key. Instead it only carries two half-shared signatures signed on the OI and PI, respectively, by the cardholder that should be sent to the merchant and PG accordingly. The shared signature key is kept by the cardholder. The other two half-signatures are generated with the assistance of TTP. The merchant can verify the OI and check the data integrity. Meanwhile the PG can not only decrypt the PI but also check the data integrity after obtaining the shared signatures from the agent and TTP, respectively. This is better than using a symmetric key only as in SET, SET/A, SET/A+, and LITESET/A+. Additionally, nonrepudiation property of LITESET/A++ is significantly improved.

In LITESET/A++, the agent in the transaction period is more of a messenger. Most of the encryption and signing work are done by the TTP. What the agent should do is to communicate with different participants sending relevant messages to them.

LITESET/A++ corrects the security flaw in LITESET/A+ so that it is not possible for the merchant to regenerate the private signature key of the cardholder. Meanwhile the flexibility for the agent to "sign" on behalf of the cardholder and make a deal with the merchant remains unchanged. Moreover, with the involvement of TTP, the agent in LITESET/A++ does not need to do any encryption and decryption. In contrast, in SET/A+ and LITESET/A+, the agent executes at the merchant's server and completes encryption operations. In LITESET/A++, both the signature-share scheme and signcryption-share scheme are used. For the first one, it is similar to LITESET/A+. The signcryption-share scheme is used to pass the session secret key to the PG while no participant but PG can decrypt PI and check the data integrity. Moreover, as the cardholder's signature is dynamically generated with the assistance of TTP, LITSSET/A++ avoids the flaw in SET/A+ using a pregenerated signature that can be abused by any merchant causing loss to the cardholder. In addition, the nonrepudiation properties in SET/A, SET/A+, and LITESET/A+ are all weak.

In comparison with other agent-based secure payment protocols, LITSSET/A++ can prevent the replay attack and has improved the nonrepudiation property.

10.4 Security for Mobile Payment

The evaluation of mobile services enables us to enjoy the convenience of mobile payment. The payment method has progressed from seashells of the remote ancient times to coins, from paper notes to electronic cash. Mobile payment revolutionizes the traditional payment method and is bound to be the dominant way of payment in the future. However, there are still many factors that prevent the wide acceptance of mobile payment by all customers. According to the study by the MPF [2], consumers focus mainly on the security-related issues such as security of credit card and privacy, and sometimes the ease of use. The challenge for the mobile payment industry is to convince the "conservative majority" of consumers to embrace mobile payments by addressing these concerns.

Regardless of the bright future of mobile payment, convincing the conservative majority is not an easy job in terms of security. Many groups and organizations make endless effort to settle down the issues which calls for the cooperation of experts and scholars from a wide range of fields because mobile payment is based on different infrastructures and technologies, e.g., wireless network, authentication, smart card, electronic cash, mobile telecommunication, and so on. In this section, we attempt to give an overview of the security-related issues in mobile payment.

10.4.1 Basic Requirement

Regardless of the adopted technologies, all the mobile payment applications have the same procedures, which are defined by MPF as lifecycle. Secure requirements in face origin from the procedures of lifecycle, which include the execution of mobile payment procedures.

Lifecycle
There are four steps in a complete lifecycle of mobile payment, including:
- Device set-up and configuration
- Payment initiation
- Authentication
- Set-up and configuration
- Payment completion

Device set-up and configuration. The set-up of the payment mechanism in the mobile environment could take place over a mobile network, the Internet, or physically when the mobile device is purchased. It may take place in the form of mutual authentication between the home network and the holder of the mobile device. The home mobile network records the identity information of the holder and authorizes it by delivering it the authorized certificate, which denotes the holder is a legal customer of the network. This process requires that both the network and the holder make sure the peer's identity is in accordance with what was claimed.

Payment initiation. If the customer decides to execute payment via a network or a wireless protocol, it initiates a payment and exchanges information with the intended merchant. The secure requirements include the requirements for form fill standards and developing best practices with regard to the transmission of PI and device-wallet requirements.

Authentication. For any secure protocol including mobile authenticity of payment, authentication is of paramount importance for it ensures the information being transferred between the "correct" peers. Authentication-secure requirements consist mainly of two-way messaging authentication and SAT authentication applications. In the case of two-way messaging, this involves defining a universal interface for requesting an authorization. SAT authentication standardization includes defining a set of minimum requirements for authenticating the user based on the SIM in a GSM handset.

Payment completion. When the cardholder's identity has been authenticated and the transaction authorized, this process takes place. In the physical world this involves the printing of a receipt as confirmation of funds transferred. In the mobile environment, the mobile payment protocols should ensure a suitable way of the format and the storage of digital receipts as well as redirection mechanisms.

Properties

The lifecycle of mobile payment determines that a mobile payment system satisfy the following security properties so that the electronic transaction can be conducted successfully.

Authentication. As mentioned earlier, authentication is the most important property in almost all the secure protocols. Before the detailed information is transferred, the participating entities themselves must be sure of the identity of the communication peer. This service prevents an unauthorized third party from masquerading as one of the legitimate parties. With proper technologies and standards of protocol construction, authentication can be achieved.

Data confidentiality/secrecy. In an e-business transaction, it is assumed that only the sender and intended receiver(s) will be able to comprehend the transmitted messages in cleartext. Data confidentiality guarantees that the confidential information can only be obtained by authenticated parties rather than eavesdroppers or interceptors. It is usually accomplished using computer-based cryptographic encryption and decryption computation.

Data integrity. The message may be replaced wholly or partly without data integrity protection even if it is perfect authenticated or encrypted. One must pay attention to the integrity and freshness of the date. Because of the way the cryptographic algorithm functions, a malicious attacker would maintain the fresh identifier, e.g., the nonce or time stamp, while replacing the confidential information following the fresh identifier by an old message. Data integrity should be treated with enough care and distinguished form freshness. With this security feature, an interceptor is not able to fool the receiver by modifying the content of a message in transmission.

Nonrepudiation. This property is badly needed in business-related applications. Mobile payment is an official business deal; neither the sender nor receiver should be able to deny the existence of a legitimate transaction afterward. More specifically, the customer has no way to deny the reception of the item he/she purchased while the merchant receives the money. This property can be guaranteed via signature scheme with the acknowledgement of the likely result, because in some cases, effort is made to prevent its existence.

Availability. The availability of a mobile payment system ensures that legitimate users can access the business service reliably and securely. The realization of this property can minimize the impact of the notorious denial-of-service (DOS) attack, which causes the waste of computation resource of a certain participating entity. A guarantee of this property could be the deployment of network security devices such as firewalls and configuring them along with associated protocols properly.

However, due to the action of attackers and eavesdroppers, the design of a mobile system satisfying these properties has proven to be quite a troublesome task, and any mobile payment system should undergo careful examination before it is put into practice.

10.4.2 Infrastructure

Wireless Wide Area Network and Security
Mobile payment is often performed on handset devices and messages are transmitted via wireless networks, thus cellular wireless network is one of the most important technologies.

Cellular system users can conduct m-commerce operations through their mobile phones or handset devices. Cellular systems have undergone a fast development and evolved from the voice-only first generation to the highly integrated third generation. Originally designed for voice-only communication, now they have evolved from analog to digital, and from circuit-switched to packet-switched networks, in order to accommodate m-commerce (data) applications. Table 10.1 lists the classifications of standards in first-generation (1G), second-generation (2G, 2.5G), and third-generation (3G) wireless cellular networks.

Nowadays, most of the mobile systems adopt the 2G or 2.5G standards, but due to the technology advantages of 3G standards over the current ones, 3G standard is likely to dominate tomorrow's communication market. 3G standard also can accelerate the realization and promotion of mobile payment system. There are three main 3G standards namely Wideband CDMA, CDMA2000, and TD-SCDMA proposed by China. The core technology of 3G standard includes the direct sequence spread spectrum (DSSS) and a 5-MHz bandwidth. 3G standards have advantages of wide bandwidth, high QOS, satisfying stability, low transmission power, rich endpoint functions and protocols, and the integration of data transfer together with the voice service. Universal mobile telecommunications system (UMTS) is the 3G mobile communication system standards proposed by 3GPP, with the principle of separating RAN from core network. In a wireless cellular system, radio transceivers are connected with core networks via a radio access network (RAN). Two examples of existing RAN architectures are UMTS Terrestrial Radio Access Network (UTRAN) (UTRAN overall description, 1999) and

IOS (MSC to BS interface inter-operability specification, 1999). UTRAN is the new radio access network designed especially for 3G UMTS. It can be seen from various cases that an ideal scheme is where GSM evaluates toward WCDMA gradually and the security of both GSM and UMTS would be introduced here.

Table 10.1. Major cellular wireless networks

generation	radio channels	switching technique	standards (examples)
1G	analog voice channels digital control channels	circuit switched	AMPS TACS
2G	digital channels	circuit switched	GSM TDMA
		packet switched	CDMA
2.5G	digital channels	packet switched	GPRS EDGE
3G	digital channels	packet switched	CDMA2000 WCDMA

GSM security

The subscriber identity module (SIM) in the GSM comprises the subscriber's authentication information, e.g., the secret keys, and a unique identifier called international mobile subscriber identity (IMSI). The SIM always takes the form of a smart card with a limited ability of computation and storage. The GSM network's authentication center (AC) and home location register (HLR) also store the same set of the subscriber's authentication key and IMSI, respectively. In GSM, short messages are stored in the SIM and calls are directed to the SIM rather than to the mobile terminal. This feature allows GSM subscribers to share a terminal with different SIM cards. The security features provided between GSM network and mobile station include IMSI confidentiality and authentication, user data confidentiality, and signaling information element confidentiality. One of the security weaknesses identified in GSM is the one-way authentication. That is, only the mobile station is authenticated while the network is not. This can pose a security threat, as a compromised base station can launch a "man-in-the-middle" attack without being detected by mobile stations.

UMTS Security

UMTS is designed to reuse and evolve from existing core network components of the GSM/GPRS and fix known GSM security weaknesses such as the one-way authentication scheme and optional encryption. UMTS has the following security features: the realization of mutual authentications between subscriber and network by the additional feature of subscriber's authentication to the network; encryption is mandatory rather than optional between mobile terminal and RNC; an integration protection to signaling and data is added; the secret key has a length of 128 bits in UMTS; the cryptographic algorithm is public and has undergone an overall and objective evaluation in terms of security; the encryption algorithm of the UMTS is Kasumi algorithm and no flaw is discovered that can be a result in possible attacks; a mechanism of key agreement is induced in UMTS, allowing the terminal and the network function together to determine the session key. Still additional space is left in UMTS for the future cryptographic algorithm. The UMTS security is evolving from version R99 to R6. R99 focuses on the security of access network and defines a mandatory security protection, an optional encryption protection, and the realization of Kasumi algorithm. R4 improves the secure framework and function of R99 by an added protection to core network SS7 signaling and the signaling based on IP. R5 defines the IMS secure mechanism. R6 defines the secure mechanism of generic authentication architecture (GAA) and multimedia broadcast/multicast service (MBMS). The target of GAA is to provide a universal authentication scheme applicable to both old and new services, thus avoid providing every emerging service with a unique authentication mechanism.

Security of PKI and WPKI

Public key infrastructure (PKI) is an integrated secure platform based on asymmetric encryption, its combination with wireless network technology leads to the wireless PKI (WPKI). WPKI optimizes the traditional PKI and applies it to the wireless environment. The optimization includes the format of certificate and the adoption of ECC rather than traditional RSA, which improves the computation efficiency as well as the length of the secret key.

10.4.3 Mobile Payment Protocols

As mentioned earlier, the design of mobile payment protocols is proven to be error prone. Some of seemingly good mobile payment protocols are found to be not perfect in application; however, due to their importance we still give them a brief description. This section gives an introduction of protocols in practical use.

SET protocol. SET is a protocol produced under the joint effort of two international credit card corporations, MasterCard and Visa. This protocol provides identity authentication, confidentiality, integration, and nonrepudiation of the transaction data. The SET features the merchant's invisibility to sensitive information such as the customer's account number and the bank's invisibility to the customer's transaction information. Also, the SET allows the authentication of the card owner to prevent certain kinds of possible attack.

Electronic Cash. Electronic cash simulates hard cash of the real world; the digital signature scheme is used to provide the unforgeability and reliability of electronic cash. Most of the e-cash protocols feature swiftness, offline transaction, and security. It is however applicable only to micropayment.

Electronic Check. Electronic check payment system is used mainly in the private network of banks. By digital signature and payment commitment, it acts as a paper check in virtual world. It is advised by the Financial Services Technology Consortium and programmed by FSML. The current typical e-check system includes NetBill, E-check, NetCheque, and so on.

Micropayments. Micropayment is usually used in the obtaining of information products and merchandises with a low price and a low transaction charge. This system tries to achieve maximum speed and efficiency with certain security requirements. In this case, the current e-business protocols such as SET and SSL are no longer suitable. Specific micropayment protocol has been developed, including CyberCash and Millicent.

10.4.4 Security

There are now two methods, SMS and WAP, for subscribers to use in their mobile payment.

SMS

SMS is the most popular data service in mobile telecommunication. By dividing service data into multiple groups with limited length, SMS center transfers short messages between cell phone and service provider. The current SMS defines two types of PTP services: MO SMS (initiated by mobile phone) and MT SMS (takes the mobile phone as terminal). When the mobile payment is settled by SMS, the communication channel in use is mainly wireless channel, SS7 channel of network, and the IP transmission channel, all of which have an excellent reliability. However, due to the switch of the short message via SMS center and its limited transfer capability to run IP protocols, it is impossible to realize the mutual transmission between the customer and the server, which poses risk to security.

The security risks that short message data package faces come mainly from wireless channel and network, because GSM network does employ A5 algorithm that is defined by GSM standard to encrypt voice, data, and signaling. The short messages are transferred in cleartext in wireless channel, which enables interception. What is worse, the transmission protocol with which to transfer short messages in signaling channel does not define secure measures of any forms. So the SM data packets are transferred in cleartext in control channel. However, core network is an internal network and can provide the security of the data to some extent. As a result, it is necessary to define a secure point-to-point authentication encryption protocol. Due to the limited storage and computation ability of mobile phone, symmetric encryption should be employed.

WAP

While Chap. 4 had a detailed description of the WAP protocol, we deal mainly with the security of WAP here.

WAP is another way for a subscriber to conduct mobile payment. With the development of 3G technologies, WAP is bound to become the primary method of mobile payment. The security of WAP is realized by wireless transport layer security (WTLS) protocol, whose origins are based on transport layer security (TLS), and can provide security, integration, and mutual authentication in wireless communication environment. One security problem, known as the "WAP gap" is caused by the inclusion of the WAP gateway in a security session. That is, encrypted messages sent by end systems might temporarily become cleartext on the WAP gateway when messages are processed. One solution is to make the WAP gateway resident within the enterprise (server) network (Ashley et al., 2001), where heavyweight security mechanisms can be enforced.

10.4.5 A Case Study

Figure 10.7 shows a model of system that uses short messages to implement mobile payment. It consists mainly of the following parts:

- *Subscriber.* He/she proves to the GSM network his/her legal identity and obtains the transaction secret key provided by the service provider
- *Wireless network, SMS center, and short message gateway.* Responsible for the secure transmission of short messages
- *Service provider.* Provides charged services to subscriber who has individual account in the bank and pays for the services obtained by the PG of the bank
- *Payment gateway.* It is the most important part of mobile payment, responsible for the transmission between bank network private protocols, the IP protocol, and the process of the payment requirement.
- *Bank.* Trusted financial party participates in the payment.

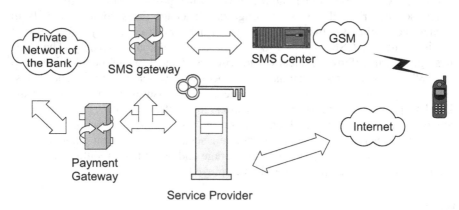

Fig. 10.7. Model of a mobile payment system employing SMS

Mobile payment system based on SMS provides secure mechanism of two categories, including security between the bank and the service provider together with that between the subscriber and the service provider.

Security mechanisms between subscriber and service provider can adopt the synchronous identity authentication protocol based on HMAC, which can provide integrity, security, and authentication.

Both service provider and bank are connected on a network, which gives them a great computation power. Thus they have the ability to use complicated and more secure payment protocols. Also, the asymmetric encryption can be used, so can the current CA certificate. The bank may choose to set up a special online bank to backup the application of mobile payment.

Lots of security solutions for mobile payment are commercially available, the primary tendency and choice of practical application include:

- *Encryption*. This is necessary because there are many flaws in the current encryption technologies of GSM and GPRS. This solution functions in the current system of wireless service provider and can be controlled by subscribers. Such solutions include IPSec, WTLS, and TPKDP.

- *Personal firewall*. The equipment connected to an always-on-line network need stronger security to prevent unauthorized access. However, due to the limitation of power, some handset devices cannot use this solution.

- *Strict subscriber authentication*. In some cases such as business transaction, strict authentication is required. Double-key authentication is strongly recommended in which the authentication is based on what you know and what you own. Traditional double-key technology such as TAN code can be used in wireless environments, the substitutes include time-based cipher generator used in handset devices and smart card based on challenge–response mechanism

- *WPKI*. The perfect point-to-point security, secure subscriber authentication, and trusted transaction can be realized by WPKI. It uses the asymmetric encryption and open standards to construct trusted secure framework, which can promote the transaction and secure communication in public wireless networks. A trusted PKI also contributes to realizing the non-repudiation; thus the participating entities have no means to deny the conducted transactions.

- *Authentication*. The access of user can be limited if necessary. There are two ways to implement authentication: authentication based on functions (according to the information that the subscriber needs in a certain transaction) and that based on ACL (according to the transaction information for the subscriber to use).

10.5 Summary

With the increasing deployment of wireless networks and the widespread popularity of handheld devices, m-commerce is growing. Mobile payment is essential to mobile commerce. This chapter provide a review of mobile payment technologies, including mobile payment methods and standardization, mobile payment agents, security, and WAP technology.

Mobile payment has not been adopted on a scale large enough to make it viable. It is ultimately the users who will determine the level of success of mobile payment technology through their adoption. However, when mobile payment issues, such as wireless network security, standardization of protocols, and user interface design, are addressed at a satisfactory level, when the handset, network operator, and vendor infrastructure are in place; and when mobile payment becomes an easier and cheaper approach to transact business than conventional methods; massive adoption of mobile payment will arrive.

References

1.   http://en.wikipedia.org
2.   http://www.mobilepaymentforum.org
3.   Stamatis Karnouskos, Fraunhofer FOKUS, Mobile Payment: A Journey through Existing Procedures and Standardization Initiatives http://www. comsoc.org/livepubs/surveys/public/2004/oct/KARNOUSKOS.html
4.   Mobile payment forum, Mobile Payment Forum White Paper, http://www. mobilepaymentforum.org/pdfs/mpf_whitepaper.pdf
5.   Durlacher Research Ltd, Mobile Commerce Report, http://www.durlacher. com
6.   J. Zhao, T. Blum, Next-Generation E-Commerce: XML + Mobile Agent + Trust
7.   Y. Wang T. Li, LITESET/A++: A new agent-assisted secure payment protocol, Proceedings of the IEEE International Conference on E-Commerce Technology, 0-7695-2098-7/04 $20.00, 2004
8.   S. Fonseca, M. Griss, and R. Letsinger, Software Technology Laboratory, HP Laboratories Palo Alto, An Agent-Mediated E-Commerce Environment for the Mobile Shopper, HPL-2001-157, 21 June 2001
9.   R. Rockinger, and H. Baumeister, Institut fur Informatik Universitat Munchen, BABSy: Basic Agent Framework Billing System
10.   H.-Z. Shen, J. -di Zhao, Institute of System Engineering, Shanghai Jiao Tong University, Application of Intelligent Agent in Network Payment Security
11.   S.-U. Guan, S.L. Tan, and F. Hua, Department of Electrical & Computer Engineering National University of Singapore, A Modularized Electronic Payment System for Agent-based e-Commerce

11 Mobile Content Delivery Technologies

Y. Yang and R. Yan

IBM China Research Laboratory

11.1 Introduction

Content delivery in the mobile computing world is different from what we have in the stationary computing world. Mobile devices have their special needs because of design and usability limitations. Their power supply is limited, processors are weaker, storages and displays are smaller, user interfaces are not so convenient, and wireless network connections are usually slow and unreliable. Beside the basic voice communication functions, the earliest content delivery service for digital mobile phones was the short message service (SMS), which supports peer-to-peer exchange of short text messages. Since its inception in 1992, SMS has become the most popular mobile information exchange service and plenty of value-added services (VAS) are based on it. Multimedia message service (MMS) extends the capability of SMS to support more media types such as images, audio clips, video clips, and more. In addition to the non-realtime, nonconnected content delivery that message services provide, online content delivery such as World Wide Web browsing is also making its way into mobile computing world through services such as general packet radio service (GPRS). Beside the infrastructure support of mobile data communication, the contents themselves also need to fit in with the special requirements of the mobiles device. These devices may support limited content formats, and contents that require large storage and high computing power are certainly not welcome. Transcoding is the technology that can be applied to adapt/convert the original contents and let them comply with the special requirements of mobile devices.

In this chapter, we start with an introduction to messaging services and then turn to a survey of existing transcoding technologies. Section 11.2 introduces the SMS, while Sect. 11.3 covers MMS. In Sect. 11.4, we give a survey of existing transcoding technologies of image, video, audio, and Web pages.

11.2 Short Message Service

This section gives an overview of SMS. The huge commercial success of SMS owes to the universally accepted business model and wide deployment. So in Sect. 11.2.2 SMS business model and applications are first introduced, which is followed by a top-down technical discussion in Sect. 11.2.3 which refers to the content from the architecture of SMS deployment to two basic SMS service

(SM MT/SM MO) introduction. This is followed by the SMS protocol stacks and the structure of one piece of message in Sect. 11.2.4. Sect. 11.2.5 focuses on deployment of MS, while in Sect. 11.2.6, the protocols used in communication between mobile stations and terminal equipments are discussed. Finally, an application-level extension of SMS, called EMS, is introduced, which brings to SMS more market opportunities actually. SMS and EMS are simple messaging technologies that do not require complex rendering capabilities in mobiles, so they make messaging services suitable in all mobile devices, from the very low-cost to the high-cost handset.

11.2.1 SMS – "Service of Most Success"

The SMS is a non-realtime delivery system. It allows the exchange of text messages among subscribers. The text can comprise words, numbers, or alphanumeric combinations. The first SMS was sent in 1992 from a computer to a mobile phone on the global system for mobile (GSM) network in UK 2002 marked 10 years of SMS in Europe. Now, SMS is supported by all GSM/GPRS mobiles and by most GSM/GPRS networks, as well as code division multiple access (CDMA) mobiles and networks. Messages of limited size are sent from and to GSM/GPRS/CDMA mobiles as well as from a variety of other sources, e.g., speech, telex, or facsimile.

SMS is currently the most popular mobile data service for peer-to-peer communication and VAS on mobile phones. It generates over 10% of revenues for mobile operators. About 30 billion short messages are sent every month, with the average mobile phone user exchanging 30 SMS per month [1]. The SMS market in North America has seen slow and steady growth in recent years. In 2002, SMS crossed 1 billion messages a month mark [2]. Now, the Asian SMS market is booming. China is becoming the world's largest SMS market. The Chinese market reached RMB 9 billion in 2002, RMB 17 billion in 2003, and is expected to achieve RMB 30 billion in 2004 [3]. China's mobile phone users sent 90 billion short messages in the year 2002, accounting for about a quarter of the world's total. According to a survey conducted in 2003 by Kongzhong.com, a value-added mobile service provider based in Beijing, about 40% of users between 18 and 60 years have used the SMS service. Approximately 57% use SMS to chat and play online games, making it rank first among all applications. The increase in the rate of the Chinese SMS market is expected to be 76.5% for 2004, 50% for 2005, and 22.2% for 2006 [3].

11.2.2 Business Model and Applications

The commercial success of SMS comes from both its wide deployment by operators/mobiles and its universally accepted billing model.

The standard SMS billing model is pay-per-message that occurs among operators and mobile phone users, especially for peer-to-peer communication. To attract more customers, the operators work with service/content providers to develop

VAS that run on a revenue-sharing model like premium SMS. In the premium SMS model, the charge is often for special VAS or content. Many attractive applications have been developed based on these business models, which can be categorized as consumer applications and business applications [4].

The main consumer applications based on SMS are:

- *Person-to-person messaging* is the most popular method of two-way communication because of its low price. Such messages usually originate from mobile station (MS).
- *Voice and fax mail notifications* is to notify mobile phone users by a short message that there is a new voice or fax mail in the mailbox.
- *Internet email alerts* is to send a short message to mobile phone users to notify the arrival of a new email. The message provides information on the sender of the email, subject field, and first few words of the email message.
- *Unified messaging* tries to provide mobile phone users a single interface to access all kinds of messaging, e.g., email, message fax, and voice message. Usually users receive a notification short message and are guided to read the message in a unified message box. The message includes an indication of the type of new message, such as fax, email, or voice mail.
- *Ringtones' downloading* is a very popular SMS service. Ringtones are the tunes that the phone plays when someone calls. Users use unique ringtones to distinguish their own mobile phones from others.
- *Chat* is an emerging application for SMS. It enables people to chat, communicate, and discuss by means of short messages. Commercial chat services will let participants select the message sender. Chat can be distinguished from general information services because the source of the information is a person, whereas it tends to be from an Internet site for information services.
- *Information service* is to deliver a wide range of information to mobile phone users by a short message, e.g., share prices, sports scores, weather, flight information, news headlines, lottery results, jokes, and horoscopes. Essentially, any information that fits into a short message size can be delivered by SMS.

The main business applications based on SMS are:

- *Corporate email notifications* are similar to Internet email notifications. Users are given information over the wireless network whenever an email sent to the corporate email address.
- *Electronic commerce* involves using SMS for financial transaction purposes, such as transferring money between accounts and paying for purchases. Related issues of security and integration with the retail and banking hardware and systems, must be considered.
- *Customer service* is to provide account-related information to mobile phone users by SMS. It avoids expensive person-to-person voice calls to customer service centers.

- *Vehicle positioning* is to send position information by a short message to tell people where they are. This application must be deployed by integrating satellite positioning system.
- *Job dispatch* is to use SMS to assign and communicate new jobs from office-based staff to mobile field staff.
- *Remote point of sale* uses SMS in a retail environment for credit card authorization. A mobile phone is connected to a point-of-sale terminal such as a credit card swipe and keypad. The credit card number is sent to a bank for authorization. The authorization code is then returned as a short message to the point-of-sale terminal.
- *Over-the-air* capability gives mobile network operators, service providers, and corporate sales managers some remote control of mobile phones for service and subscription activation, personalization, and programming.
- *Remote monitoring* is to use SMS to manage machines in a remote monitoring environment. Valuable information is transmitted by short messages from a remote site when something occurs. Examples of remote monitoring applications include remote meter reading, sending computer system fault information to mobile phones, and notifying companies about empty vending machines.

11.2.3 Architecture and Basic Services

The SMS technical specs were created by the European Telecommunication Standard Institute (ETSI) as part of the GSM phase 1 standard, which include standards of SMS point-to-point service (SMSPP) and SMS cell broadcast service (SMSCB). SMSPP deals with exchanging SMS messages to or from a mobile phone, and SMSCB with SMS messages broadcasting onto mobile phones. This is now taken over by third generation partnership project (3GPP). The 3GPP technical specifications on SMS are listed in Table 11.1. We now discuss techniques that enable the SMSPP.

The GSM SMS Architecture

Fig. 11.1 shows the architecture of an SMS-enabled GSM network. SMS center (SMSC) and email gateway are the additional GSM network elements to enable SMS [5]. However, an element called short message entity (SME) is not presented in Fig. 11.1. It can send and receive short messages and may be located in a fixed network, a MS, or an SMSC [6]. Service Center (SC) or SMSC manages the relaying of short messages between SMEs and storing/forwarding short messages. The message can even be sent from an SME in one network to an SME in another network, which is known as SMS roaming, as long as there is mutual agreement between network operators to allow the exchange of messages; at the same time all involved mobile networks support SMS. The email gateway is to connect the

SMSC with the Internet. It converts the message format between SMS and email as well as relay messages between SMS and Internet domains.

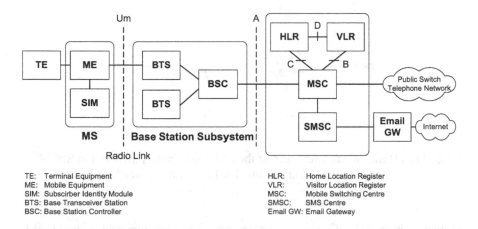

TE: Terminal Equipment
ME: Mobile Equipment
SIM: Subscirber Identity Module
BTS: Base Transceiver Station
BSC: Base Station Controller

HLR: Home Location Register
VLR: Visitor Location Register
MSC: Mobile Switching Centre
SMSC: SMS Centre
Email GW: Email Gateway

Fig. 11.1. SMS-enabled GSM network architecture

Basic Services

We further abstract the SMS architecture from GSM network architecture for two kinds of basic SMS services, i.e., short message mobile terminated (SM MT), short message mobile originated (SM MO), which are presented in Fig. 11.2.

Fig. 11.2a presents the SM MO procedure. It denotes the capability of the SMS system to transfer a short message submitted from the MS to an SME via an SC, and to provide information about the delivery of the short message either by a delivery report or a failure report. The message must include the address of that SME to which the SC will eventually attempt to relay the short message. Here, interworking MSC for SMS (SMS-IWMSC) is the function of an MSC capable of receiving a short message from within the public limited mobile network (PLMN) and submitting it to the recipient SC [6]. This process is also known as message sending.

Fig. 11.2b denotes SM MT transmission process where a short message is transferred from the SC to MS, and provides information about the delivery of the short message either by a delivery report or a failure report with a specific mechanism for later delivery. The gateway MSC for SMS (SMS-GMSC) is the function of an MSC capable of receiving a short message from an SC, interrogating a home location register (HLR) database for routing information and SMS info, and delivering the short message to the MSC of the recipient MS [6]. This is also called message delivery.

The process can be described in simple words: an SMS sender types the text of the message and sends it to the addressee by keying in his mobile phone number. The message is first is sent to the SMSC of the sender's mobile operator. SMSC stores the message in a queue and records the transaction in the network billing

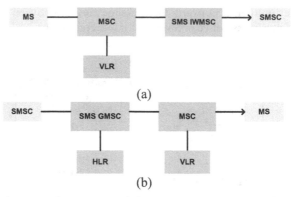

Fig. 11.2. Basic network structure of the SMS. (**a**) Entities involved in SM MO procedure. (**b**) Entities involved in SM MT procedure

system. It is an SM MO transmission process. The short message is then sent to the addressee. The SM MO becomes SM MT once it reaches the SMSC of the addressee's mobile operator. The recipient SMSC holds the message in a queue and tries to locate the message recipient via the HLR. If the addressee is reachable, the message is sent to him. Otherwise, the message is stored in the SMSC for a period of time and delivered as soon as the user becomes reachable.

There are several services elements related, e.g., validity-period, service-center-time-stamp, protocol-identifier, more-messages-to-send, priority, messages-waiting, and alert-SC. Validity-period give a information on how long the SC or SMSC shall guarantee the existence of a short message in its memory before delivery is performed; Service-center-time-stamp is the time of arrival of the short message at SC/SMSC; Protocol-identifier is used to indicate the protocol being used; More-messages-to-send is to inform the MS that there is one or more messages waiting in SC/SMSC to be delivered; priority is provided by an SC/SMSC or SME to indicate whether or not a message is a priority message; messages-waiting, only used in the case of previous unsuccessful delivery attempt(s) due to temporarily absent mobile or MS memory capacity exceeded, is to inform MS that there is a message in the origination SC/SMSC waiting to be delivered to it; and alert-SC is to inform the SC that a delivery attempt to an MS has failed because the MS is not reachable or because the MS memory capacity was exceeded.

11.2.4 Protocols and Structure

The protocol layers of the SMS are, as shown in Fig. 11.3, the application layer (SM-AL), the transfer layer (SM-TL), the relay layer (SM-RL), and the link layer (SM-LL) [6].

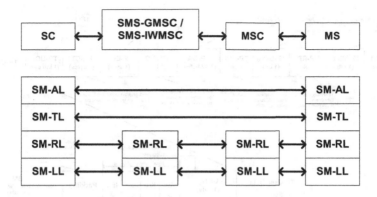

Fig. 11.3. Protocol layer overview for the SMS

The SM-TL services the SM-AL and enables two SMEs to exchange messages that may be separated into many pieces at sender side, while concatenated at receiver side; each segment is an organized sequence of bytes known as transport protocol data unit (TPDU). All transactions at SM-TL are ackowledged between the MS and the network so that message loss can be controlled. The SM-RL conveys the TPDUs via the SM-LL among various network elements, as described in Sect. 11.2.3, where the SM-LL will protect the message with low-level channel errors and the short message will be transported over the SS7 signaling channels [7].

There are six types of TPDU, which correspond to the six types of transactions between an SME and the SMSC/SC [6].

- SMS-DELIVER conveys a short message from the SMSC/SC to the MS;
- SMS-DELIVER-REPORT conveys (a) a failure cause (if necessary) and (b) information as part of a positive or negative acknowledgment to an SMS-DELIVER or SMS-STATUS-REPORT;
- SMS-SUBMIT conveys a short message from the MS to the SMSC/SC;
- SMS-SUBMIT-REPORT conveys (a) a failure cause (if necessary) and (b) information as part of a positive or negative acknowledgment to an SMS-SUBMIT or SMS-COMMAND;
- SMS-STATUS-REPORT conveys a status report from the SMSC/SC to the MS;
- SMS-COMMAND conveys a command from the MS to the SMSC/SC.

If we do not consider the case of concatenation, a piece of short message maps to one TPDU with a size limitation of 140 bytes. Each type of TPDU has specific elements and its own layout. We use SMS-DELIVER as an example in Fig. 11.4.

Using the IEI allows sending and receiving concatenated short messages. The IED field contains all necessary information to reassemble the message. The IEI and associated IEI length and IEI data will be present in every segment of the concatenated SM.

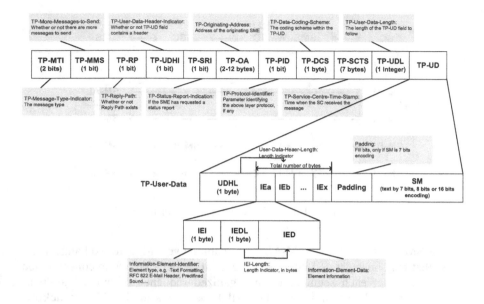

Fig. 11.4. Structure of SMS-DELIVER TPDU

11.2.5 Deployment of MS

Today, all mobile phones in the market have integrated the SMS standard. Received messages can be stored on the mobile equipment or on the SIM card. Usually the SIM card is with limited storage capacity and mainly stores subscriber information, while SIM toolkit (STK) provides an application layer that enables the storage of additional information and offers value-added services on the SIM card itself. The STK defines the mechanisms for communication between the SIM card and the network, as well as the mobile equipment. The specification on STK is defined in 3GPP TS 31.111 as listed in Table 11. 1.

11.2.6 Submission Protocols

Besides MS, users can submit a short message from a terminal equipment (TE) such as a personal digital assistant and so on. Usually, the TE is connected to an MS via a cable, and the interface protocols for short messages' transfer between an MS and a TE are specified in 3GPP TS 27.005 as shown in Table 11. 1. When sending the short message via the TE, TE always controls the transaction, while the MS is the "slave." There are three different modes for SMS submission:

Table 11.1. 3GPP technical specifications of SMS

3GPP technical specification	Title
3GPP TS 23.011	technical realization of supplementary services
3GPP TS 23.038	alphabets and language-specific information
3GPP TS 23.039	interface protocols for the connection of short message service centers (SMSCs) to short message entities (SMEs)
3GPP TS 23.040	technical realization of the short message service (SMS)
3GPP TS 23.041	technical realization of cell broadcast service (CBS)
3GPP TS 23.042	compression algorithm for text messaging services
3GPP TS 24.011	short message service (SMS) support on mobile radio interface
3GPP TS 24.012	cell broadcast service (CBS) support on the mobile radio interface
3GPP TS 27.005	use of data terminal equipment-data circuit terminating equipment (DTE-DCE) interface for short message service (SMS) and cell broadcast service (CBS)
3GPP TS 29.002	mobile application part (MAP) specification
3GPP TS 31.111	USIM application toolkit (USAT)
3GPP TS 43.047	example of protocol stacks for interconnecting service center(s) (SC) and mobile-services switching center(s) (MSC)

- *Block mode* is a binary protocol including error detection. It is suitable for use when the link between the MS and the TE is subject to errors. In this mode, the application has to construct a binary string, including a header and the SM-TPDU.
- *Text mode* is a character-based protocol built on the basis of "AT" command, where AT stands for ATtention. It is suitable for application software built on command structures like those defined in ITU V25ter.
- *PDU mode* is also a character-based protocol similar to the text mode. The difference is that the TPDU is built by the application. This mode allows binary data to be transmitted, and not just character.

11.2.7 Enhanced Messaging Service

Enhanced messaging service (EMS) is an application-level extension of SMS for mobile phones available on GSM/GPRS and CDMA networks. 3GPP defines two sets of EMS features in 3GPP TS release 99/4 and release 5/6. EMS now allows users to send text messages containing sounds, pictures, and animations. EMS messages that are sent to devices that do not support it will be displayed as SMS transmissions.

EMS messaging is based on standard mechanisms in GSM SMS messaging. There are two kinds of mechanisms involved, viz. user data header (TP-UDH) and concatenation [6]. In TP-UDH, each information element (IE) identifies an object to be transferred. It contains a byte that identifies the absolute position of the object within and from the beginning of the SM data. If users want to send a message longer than 140 bytes, the message will be divided into several segments. Up to 255 messages of 140 bytes each can be concatenated so that one long message is up to about 38k bytes.

There are different types of EMS IEs, e.g., text formatting, predefined sound, user defined sound, predefined animation, large animation, small animation, large picture, small picture, and variable picture. An IE named user prompt indicator is used when download service is provided. The RFC 822 e-mail header indicates the existence of an RFC 822 Internet e-mail in the data part of the message. The extended object IE allows an extended code range for format types. The Extended Object may cross segment boundaries of a concatenated message and its type is also defined in [6], e.g., iMelody, 6bit color bitmap, polyphonic melody, and so on. The same type may occur more than once in a single message of one segment of a concatenated SM.

11.3 Multimedia Messaging Service

As an extension of SMS, MMS provides longer text messages, and the sending of music and pictures. Sect. 11.3.1 first gives a simple introduction of MMS and prospects its market growth. Then MMS applications are described in Sect. 11.3.2 before explaining MMS architecture and its interface in Sect. 11.3.3. The standard work of MMS is introduced in Sect. 11.3.4. MMS transactions and protocol framework are discussed in Sect. 11.3.5; we use MM1 WAP implementation for further discussion in Sect. 11.3.6. To comprehend the multimedia messages more, the structure of MMS is discussed in Sect. 11.3.7, and the media and file format it support in Sect. 11.3.8. Sect. 11.3.9 is about the MMS client issues.

11.3.1 MMS – Shore up the Future Messaging Service

MMS, just like SMS, is a non-realtime delivery system [8]. It allows subscribers to send and receive messages of the entire gamut available today, e.g., text, images,

audio, and video while it also makes possible to support new content types whenever they become popular. An MMS message is a combination of one or more
different media elements in a multimedia presentation [9]. MMS provides a store-
and-forward usage paradigm just like many messaging systems in use today, e.g.,
traditional email system available on the Internet and wireless messaging system
such as paging or SMS, and interoperates with such systems [8].

The commercial introduction of MMS was launched in March 2002 [5]. Market
analysis [10] shows its recent growth. The research group, IDC, expects the strong
growth in camera phones to help drive a strong growth in MMS subscribers. IDC
forecasts a 178% compound annual growth rate through 2007 in the number of
wireless MMS subscribers, reaching 67 million MMS subscribers with camera
phones and 29 million MMS subscribers without camera phones. Some analyses
[11] show that the overall messaging market will begin to slow from 2006, while
the growth in multimedia messaging revenues will shore up the overall mobile
messaging market and will start to grow strongly from late 2004. The worldwide
annual revenue of MMS is expected to reach nearly US$11 billion by 2008. Multi-
media messaging in Western Europe will grow steadily and will reach US$5.5
billion by 2008. However, MMS is likely to take off later and grow more slowly
in North America, and the annual revenue is expected to reach US$700 million in
2008. The Chinese/Indian market is the engine of growth; the revenue from them
is expected to grow to US$455 million in 2008.

11.3.2 Applications

Unlike SMS, MMS is a new messaging service yet to be accepted by the mass
market. The critical success factor for MMS is the attractive portfolio of MMS
applications, both consumer and business. The expected applications of MMS are:

Person-to-person messaging is always closely associated with the availability
of multimedia devices such as the camera or the camcorder. The most popular
content of such person-to-person multimedia message is private pictures [12]. Subscribers can capture still images and video sequences to be inserted in multimedia
messages, which is known as photo messaging. Besides, they can select, edit, and
send personalized postcards via multimedia messages. Also, music, cartoons, and
jokes are popular content that can be sent.

Content-oriented messaging is another application of MMS. The typical uses
are download service, where subscribers can get ringtones, picture messages,
wallpapers, screensavers, and operator logos by downloading; news and information
service, where subscribed news, advertisements, and any other kind of information
will be delivered onto the MMS-enabled mobile phone; voicemail push allows
subscribers to leave voice messages along with some graphical and textual
elements in voicemail servers; and so on. The involving of multimedia in these
applications enhances the experience of subscribers and makes the application
more attractive.

Ancillary applications include VAS and these more complex services need
MMS as a building block. VAS provide services based on MMS. The VAS provider

needs to establish a service agreement with the MMS provider to specify how the revenue generated by the VAS is shared between them. Uses, for example, are interactive quiz games, mobile photo albums, chat, streaming, and so on. Some more complex services also need MMS. For example, immediate messaging is often seen as the combination of two concepts: presence and messaging. Presence refers to the availability of some information related to the state of a subscriber such as whether he is connected, where he is, what is his situation(e.g., in a meeting or a coffee break). The MMS is considered as one of the suitable candidates for messaging aspect.

11.3.3 Specifications

Till now, three main organizations were involved in developing MMS specifications. 3GPP is the main authority to define the entire architecture and high-level requirements to the interfaces between system components. Wireless application protocol forum (WAP Forum) addresses the protocol implementation of the particular interface. Mobile multimedia drafting committee (MMDC), which is one of the two "multimedia" groups, MMDC and multimedia expert group (MMEG), in WAP Forum, produced the first version of WAP MMS specification suite. Now, the work of WAP Forum is taken over by the open mobile alliance (OMA) and the OMA MMS specifications are based on WAP MMS specifications. It is currently working on testing, interoperability, and the user agent profile for WAP-based MMS. Table 11.2 lists MMS specifications from 3GPP/WAP/OMA, while Fig. 11.5 shows the 3GPP/OMA specifications.

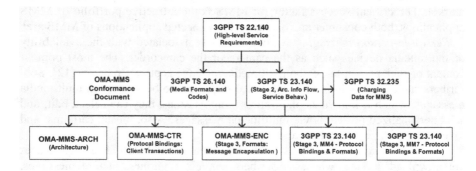

Fig. 11.5. Positioning of 3GPP/OMA MMS specifications

Besides, the third-generation partnership project 2 (3GPP2) is working on 3GPP2 MMS specifications based on 3GPP/OMA documents, pulsing additional protocol, codec, and format options [13]. This book will not address 3GPP2 MMS specifications.

Table 11.2. MMS specifications

specification	Title	Scope
3GPP TS 22.140	multimedia messaging service (MMS); stage 1	defines stage 1 description of the non-real time MMS. It defines the set of requirements that will be supported for the provision of non-real time MMS, seen primarily from the subscribers' and providers' points of views
3GPP TS 23.140	multimedia messaging service (MMS); functional description; stage 2	defines stages 2 and 3 description of the non-real time MMS. It identifies the functional capabilities and information flows needed to support the service described in stage 1
3GPP TS 26.140	multimedia messaging service (MMS); media formats and codecs; stage 2	specifies the media types, formats, and codecs for the MMS within the 3GPP system
3GPP TS 32.235	charging management; charging data description for application services	specifies, for MMS, the structure and content of the charge data record (CDR) and the interface protocol that is used to transfer them to the collecting node
WAP-205-MMSArchOverview-20010425-a	WAP^{TM} MMS architecture overview	defines application-level protocol activities that take place to realize the MMS service within the WAP environment
WAP-206-MMSCTR-20020115-a	WAP^{TM} MMS client transaction	defines the operational flow of the messages that transit between the MMS client and the MMS proxy-relay
WAP-209-MMSEncapsulation-20020105-a	wireless application protocol; MMS encapsulation protocol	defines the message encapsulation, i.e., the message structure and encodings for the multimedia messaging service
OMA-MMS-ARCH-v12-20031217-C	multimedia messaging service; architecture overview; version 1.2	based on "WAP-205-MMSArchOverview-20010425-a"
OMA-MMS-CTR--v1_2-20031215-C	multimedia messaging service; client transaction; version 1.2	based on "WAP-206-MMSCTR-20020115-a"
OMA-MMS-ENC-v1_2-20040323-C	multimedia messaging service; encapsulation protocol; version 1.2	based on "WAP-209-MMSEncapsulation-20020105-a"
OMA-MMS-CONF-v1_2-20040219-C	MMS conformance document 1.2	defines the minimum set of requirements and guidelines for end-to-end interoperability of MMS handsets and servers. It further serves as a baseline for MMS interoperability testing

11.3.4 Architecture

MMS is an application-level service that fits into the current WAP architecture. The basic concept of sending an MMS message is exactly the same as that of SMS. The originator addresses the receiver, the message is first sent to the MMS center (MMSC) associated with that receiver, then the MMSC informs the receiver and attempts to forward the message to the receiver. If the receiver is unreachable, MMSC stores the message for some time, and if possible, delivers the message later. If the message cannot be delivered within a certain time frame, it is eventually discarded. In fact, it is a much more complicated process. To enable this service, a set of network elements is organized as shown in Fig. 11.6 [14].

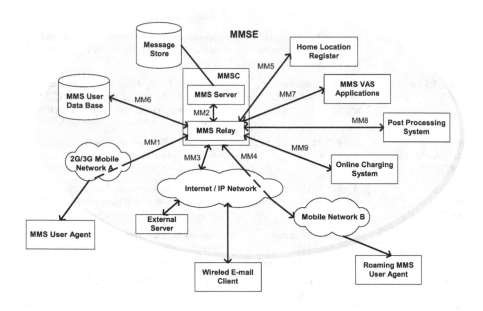

Fig. 11.6. MMS architectural elements

The whole MMS environment (MMSE) encompasses all necessary service elements for delivery, storage, and notification. The elements can be located within one network, or across several networks or network types. In the case of roaming, the visited network is considered a part of that user's MMSE. However, subscribers to another service provider are considered to be a part of a separate MMSE.

The MMS relay and MMS server may be a single logical element or may be separate. These can be distributed across different domains. The combination of the MMS relay/server is the MMSC. It is in charge of storing and handling incoming/outgoing messages and is responsible for the transfer of messages among different messaging systems. It should be able to generate charging data for MMS and VAS provider-related operations.

MMS user database contains user-related information such as subscription and configuration.

MMS user agent is an application layer function that provides the users with the ability to view, compose, and handle multimedia messages. It resides on the user equipment (UE) or on an external device connected to the UE or MS.

MMS VAS applications provide VAS to MMS users. They can be seen as fixed MMS user agents but with some additional features like multimedia message recall between MMS VAS applications and MMSC. MMS VAS applications should be able to generate the charging data when receiving/submitting multimedia messages from/to MMSC.

External servers may be included within, or connected to, an MMSE, e.g., e-mail server, SMSC, and fax. MMSC would integrate different server types across different networks and provide convergence functionality between external servers and MMS user agents.

In MMSE, elements communicate via a set of interfaces [14].

MM1 is the reference point between the MMS user agent and the MMSC. It is used to submit multimedia messages from MMS user agent to MMSC, to let the MMS user agent pull multimedia messages from the MMSC, let the MMSC push information about multimedia messages to the MMS user Agent as a part of a multimedia message notification, and to exchange delivery reports between MMSC and MMS user agent.

MM2 is the reference point between the MMS relay and the MMS server. Most MMS solutions offer a combined MMS relay and MMS server as a whole MMSC. This interface has not been specified till now.

MM3 is the reference point between the MMSC and external messaging systems. It is used by the MMSC to send/retrieve multimedia messages to/from servers of external messaging systems that are connected to the service provider's MMSC. To provide flexible implementation of integration of existing and new services together with interoperability across different networks and terminals [14], the MMS makes use of the protocol framework depicted in Fig. 11.7. In this framework the MMSC communicates with both MMS user agent and external servers. It can provide convergence functionality between external servers and MMS user agents, and thus enables the integration of different server types across different networks.

MM4 is the reference point between the MMSC and another MMSC that is within another MMSE. It is in charge of transferring messages between MMSCs belonging to different MMSEs. Interworking between MMSCs will be based on SMTP according to IETF STD 10 (RFC2821) [15] shown in Fig. 11.8.

MM5 is the reference point between the MMSC and the HLR. It may be used to provide information to the MMSC about the subscriber to the MMSC.

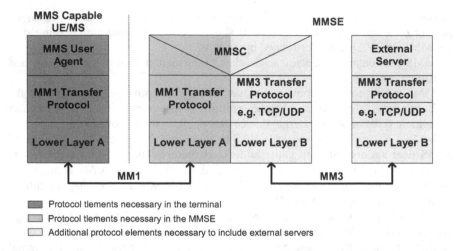

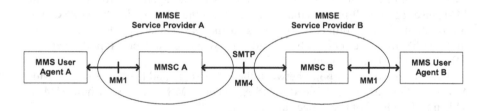

Fig. 11.7. Protocol framework to provide MMS

Fig. 11.8. Interworking of different MMSEs

MM6 is the reference point between the MMSC and the MMS user database.

MM7 is the reference point between the MMSC and the MMS VAS applications. It allows multimedia messages transferring from/to MMSC to/from MMS VAS applications. This interface will be based on SOAP 1.1 [16] and SOAP messages with attachments [17] using an HTTP transport layer.

MM8 is the reference point between MMSC and the postprocessing system. It is needed when transfering MMS-specific CDRs from MMSC to the operators in the postprocessing system.

MM9 is the reference point between MMSC and online charging system. It is used to transfer charging messages from MMSC to the online charging system.

11.3.5 Transactions

There are four typical MMS transactions:

- *Mobile-originated (MO) transaction* is originated by an MS. The multimedia messages are sent directly to an MS or possibly to an e-mail address. If some sort of processing/conversion is needed, the multimedia messages are first are sent to an application that does the processing/conversion, and then to the destination.
- *Mobile-terminated (MT) transaction* sends the messages to an MS. The originator of such messages can be another MS or an application.
- *Application originated (AO) transaction* is originated by an application and terminated directly an MS or another application. Before the multimedia messages are sent to the destination, they can be processed in one or more applications.
- *Application-terminated (AT) transaction* is terminated at an application and originated by an MS or another application. As noted in MO transaction, the multimedia messages can be sent to an application that does the processing/conversion, so it is actually an AT transaction.

Based on these four types of transactions, transactions for each interface are realized that can be described in terms of abstract messages. The abstract messages can be categorized into transactions consisting of "requests" and "responses." To label the abstract message, the transactions for a certain interface are prefixed by its name, e.g., the transactions for MM1 are prefixed with "MM1." Besides, "requests" are identified with ".REQ" as a suffix and "responses" are identified with the ".RES" suffix.

Each abstract message carries certain IEs, which may vary according to the specific message. All messages carry a protocol version and message type, so that the MMSE components are able to properly identify and manage the message contents. The mapping of abstract messages to specific protocols is not necessarily a one-to-one relationship. Depending on the MMS WAP implementation, one or more abstract messages may be mapped to a single lower layer PDU and vice versa. The following clause uses MM1 WAP implementation for further discussion.

11.3.6 WAP Implementation of MM1

As noted earlier, WAP addresses the protocol implementation of the particular interface. Now, MMS activities of the WAP Forum have been integrated to OMA. There are two different configurations of the WAP architecture and protocol stacks for implementation of MMS as shown in Fig. 11.9 and Fig. 11.10.

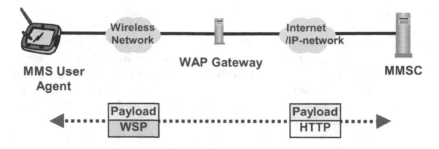

Fig. 11.9. Implementation of MM1 interface using WAP 1.x gateway

Fig. 11.9 shows the WAP 1.x architecture with two links. The first is between the wireless MMS user agent and the WAP gateway, and the messages are normally transferred using a wireless transport such as WSP. The second link connects the WAP gateway and the MMSC. In the WAP architecture the MMSC is considered as origin server. Messages transit over HTTP from the WAP gateway to the MMSC. The WAP gateway provides a common set of services over a variety of wireless bearers by using "WAP stack," which includes WSP invocation of HTTP methods; WAP PUSH services; OTA security; and capability negotiations (UAProf). The "Payload" represents the MMS application layer protocol data units (PDUs), which is carried by WAP and HTTP. The structure of PDUs is described later.

Fig. 11.10 shows a different architectural configuration. HTTP is used to carry MMS PDUs directly between the MMS user agent and the MMSC, and a gateway is only needed for push functionality. A gateway is omitted in Fig. 11.10.

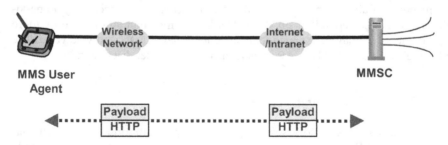

Fig. 11.10. Implementation of MM1 interface using HTTP-based protocol stack

An example of end-to-end transactions that occur between the MMS user agent and the MMSC is depicted in Fig. 11.11.

The transactions on MM1 interface utilize a variety of transport schemes, e.g., abstract messages. The MMS user agent issues a multimedia message by sending an M-Send.req to the MMSC using a WSP/HTTP POST method. This operation transmits the required data from the MMS user agent to the MMSC as well as provides a transactional context for the resulting M-Send.conf response. The MMSC uses WAP PUSH technology to send the M-Notification.ind to the MMS user agent to inform the availability of multimedia message for retrieval. The URI of the multimedia message is also included in the data. In the URI, the MMS user agent uses the WSP/HTTP GET method to retrieve the message. The fetching of the URI returns the M-retrieve.conf, which contains the actual multimedia message to be presented to the user. The M-Acknowledge.ind passed from the MMS user agent to MMSC is to indicate that the message is actually received by the MMS user agent. And the MMSC is responsible for providing a delivery report back to the originator MMS user agent again utilizing the WAP PUSH technology with the M-Delivery.ind message.

Each abstract message may be mapped to one or more lower layer PDUs, which is discussed in the following.

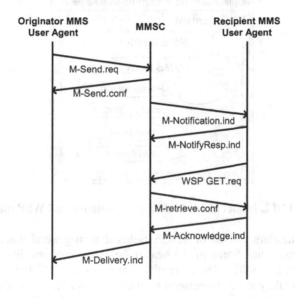

Fig. 11.11. Example of MMS transactional flow in WAP

11.3.7 Structure

In the earlier transaction, most messages are sent as MMS PDUs. An MMS PDU may consist of MMS headers and MMS body; also it can include only headers. The MMS PDUs are, in turn, passed in the content section of WAP or HTTP messages, and the content type of these messages is set as application/vnd.wap.mms-message.

Fig. 11.12 is an example of how multimedia content and presentation information can be encapsulated to a single message and be contained by a WSP message [18].

The MMS headers contain MMS-specific information of the PDU, mainly about how to transfer the multimedia message from the originating terminal to the recipient terminal. The MMS body includes multimedia objects, each in separate part, as well as optional presentation part. The order of the parts has no significance. The presentation part contains instructions on how the multimedia content should be rendered on the terminal. There may be multiple presentation part, but one of them must be the root part; in the case of multipart/related, the root part is pointed from the Start parameter. Examples of the presentation techniques are synchronized multimedia integration language (SMIL) [19], wireless markup language (WML) [20], and XHTML.

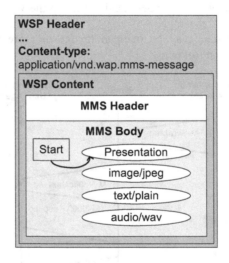

Fig. 11.12. Model of MMS data encapsulation and WSP message

The MMS headers consist of header fields that in general consist of a field name and a field value. Some of the header fields are common header fields and others are specific to MMS. There are different types of MMS PDUs used for different roles, and they are distinguished by the parameter "X-Mms-Message-Type" in MMS headers. Each type of message is with a kind of MMS headers with particular fields.In the earlier example, the M-Send.conf message contains an MMS header only and it includes several fields listed in Table 11.3.

11.3.8 Supported Media and File Formats

Multiple media elements can be combined into a composite single multimedia message using MIME multipart format as defined in RFC 2046 [21]. The minimum support media types should comply with the following selection of media formats:

Table 11.3. M-Send.conf message

field name	field content	description
X-Mms-Message-Type	Message-type-value = m-notifyresp-ind	mandatory specifies the PDU type
X-Mms-Transaction-ID	Transaction-id-value	mandatory identifies the transaction started by M-Notification.ind PDU
X-Mms-MMS-Version	MMS-version-value	mandatory the MMS version number. According to this specification, the version is 1.2
X-Mms-Status	Status-value	mandatory message status. The status retrieved will be used only after successful retrieval of the MM
X-Mms-Report-Allowed	Report-allowed-value	optional. Default: Yes. indication of whether or not the sending of delivery report is allowed by the recipient MMS client

- *Text.* plain text must be supported. Any character encoding that contains a subset of the logical characters in unicode can be used.
- *Speech.* the ARM codec supports narrowband speech. The ARM wideband (ARM-WB) speech codec of 16-kHz sampling frequency is supported. The ARM and ARM-WB is used for speech media-type alone.
- *Audio.* MPEG-4 AAC low complexity object type with a sampling rate up to 48 kHz is supported. The channel configurations to be supported are mono (1/0) and stereo (2/0). In addition, the MPEG-4 AAC long-term prediction object type may be supported.
- *Synthetic audio.* The scalable polyphony MIDI (SP-MIDI) content format defined in scalable polyphony MIDI specification [22] and the device requirements defined in scalable polyphony MIDI device 5-to-24 note profile for 3GPP [23] are supported. SP-MIDI content is delivered in the

structure specified in standard MIDI files 1.0 [24], either in format 0 or format 1.

- *Still image.* ISO/IEC JPEG together with JFIF is supported. When supporting JPEG, baseline DCT is mandatory while progressive DCT is optional.
- *Bitmap graphics.* GIF87a, GIF89a, and PNG bitmap graphics formats are supported.
- *Video.* The mandatory video codec for the MMS is ITU-T recommendation H.263 profile 0, level 10. In addition, H.263 Profile 3, Level 10, and MPEG-4 Visual Simple Profile Level 0 are optional to implement.
- *Vector graphics.* For terminals supporting media type "2D vector graphics" the "Tiny" profile of the scalable vector graphics (SVG-Tiny) format is supported, and the "Basic" profile of the scalable vector graphics (SVG-Basic) format may be supported.
- *File format for dynamic media.* To ensure interoperability for the transport of video and associated speech/audio and timed text in a multimedia message, the 3GPP file format is supported.
- *Media synchronization and presentation format.* The mandatory format for media synchronization and scene description of multimedia messaging is SMIL. The 3GPP MMS uses a subset of SMIL 2.0 as the format of the scene description. Additionally, 3GPP MMS should provide the format of XHTML mobile profile.
- *DRM format.* The support of DRM in MMS conforms to the OMA DRM specifications [25]. DRM protection of a multimedia message takes precedence over message distribution indication and over MM7 content adaptation registration from REL-6 onward. The protected files are in the format of OMA DRM content format (DCF) for discrete media and OMA packetized DRM content format (PDCF) for packetized (continuous media [26].

11.3.9 Client-Side Structure

The general model of how the MMS user agent fits within the general WAP Client architecture is depicted in Fig. 11.13 [18].

The MMS user agent is responsible for the composition and rendering of multimedia messages as well as sending and receiving multimedia messages by utilizing the message transfer services of the appropriate network protocols. The MMS user agent is not dependent on, but may use, the services of the other components shown in Fig. 11.13, i.e., the common functions, WAP identity module (WIM) [27] and external functionality interface (EFI) [28].

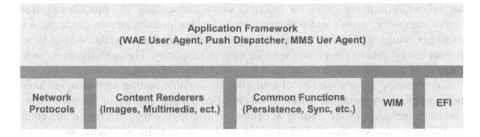

Fig. 11.13. General WAP client architecture

11.4 Transcoding Techniques

In this section, we focus on progresses in content transcoding techniques. We introduce the prevailing status and give details of some transcoding techniques with different media types. As an application and enhancement of content transcoding, we also introduce some progresses in adaptive content delivery and scalable content coding.

11.4.1 Transcoding – The Bridge for Content Delivery

Because of the various mobile computing technologies involved, multimedia content access on mobile devices is possible. While stationary computing devices such as PCs and STBs had multimedia support long before, mobile devices have special features that make them different from stationary computing devices. Due to limitations of design and usability, mobile devices normally have lower computing power, smaller and lower resolution display, limited storage, slower and less reliable network connections, and last but importantly, limited user interaction interfaces. As a result, only specially tailored contents can have the best user experiences on these devices. In this case, content creators may choose to produce contents specifically for mobile devices. However, large quantities of multimedia contents and documents have already been created for stationary computing devices with high bandwidth and processing capabilities. Converting these existing contents to fit the special requirements of the mobile devices is another more cost-effective and reasonable approach. The process that does this conversion is called transcoding.

Generally speaking, we can define transcoding as the process of transforming contents from one representation format or level of details to another one. In some cases, transcoding can be trivial and can take place when the contents are being served, while in many cases, for example video transcoding, the process requires heavy computing power and offline process. For multimedia stream contents, for example, audio and video, a specific transcoding scenario exists, which is to reduce the bit rate to meet some specific channel capacity. This specific process is commonly referred to as transrating.

To eliminate the complexity of transcoding, scalable coding technologies have been adopted. In common, different layers of detail and quality of the same contents are included in the coding schemes. These layers may represent different spatial/temporal resolutions and/or different bit rates/qualities. Higher quality or resolution layers may depend on lower quality or resolution layers. Typical examples are the scalable coding schemes in MPEG-2 and MPEG-4 video [29]. Transcoding requirements such as transrating and spatial resolution change thus become simple selections among different layers.

With the increasing diversity and heterogeneity of contents, client devices and network conditions combined with individual preferences of end users, mere transcodings cannot handle the complexities. Adaptive content delivery is the system solution that meets the requirements. Contents are generated, selected, or transcoded dynamically according to factors, including the user's preferences, device capabilities, and network conditions. In this way, it allows better user experience under the changing circumstances.

In the following sections, we first give an overview of existing transcoding technologies for different media types. Then details of some transcoding algorithms regarding different media types are discussed. Later, we introduce the progresses of adaptive content delivery and scalable content coding technologies.

11.4.2 Overview

Transcoding can be applied to different content such types and formats. In this section, we focus on commonly used content types as video, audio, image, and formatted document, and our discussions are limited to some specific content formats. Table 11.4 gives a summary of typical transcoding methods that are frequently used in producing contents for mobile devices. Some people consider the techniques to add more redundant information for error resilience and recovery with error-prone wireless network channels as transcoding. In our opinion, we would rather prefer to treat them as robust content coding and channel coding techniques.

11.4.3 Image Transcoding

Before video was incorporated into the digital media era, images were the most important 2D visual media types for computer users. From the exchange of GIF pictures on UseNet, to the booming of World Wide Web, images occupy a large portion of Internet contents. With the increased digital imaging capabilities of devices like mobile phones and infrastructure supports such as MMS, images are also becoming an important content type on mobile devices.

Basically, there are two classes of images. One is bitmap, the other is vector graphics. The contents created with 2D digital imaging devices and painting applications are normally bitmap images. The basic unit of the bitmap images is pixel. A pixel is a single point or dot on the bitmap image. A bitmap image is composed of a 2D matrix of pixels. Each pixel has a value that either represents a color or an index to some color palette. This value can be from 1 bit to 64 bits or more depending on the bitmap types and color resolutions. Bitmap images are also called raster images because they can be directly mapped to raster graphics displays that we commonly use. Vector graphics take a different road. The basic units of vector graphics are geometrical elements such as lines, curves, shapes, fills, etc. Some vector graphic formats also allow embedding of bitmap images. Both bitmap and vector images have their pros and cons. For example, bitmap images are superior in representing nature scenes and can be rendered to the raster graphics displays we commonly use. In case of geometrical transformations such as scaling, rotating, and deforming, bitmap images normally suffer from quality losses because of the interpolations used to map the pixels to different locations. On the contrary, vector graphics can represent high resolution artificial drawings and can be transformed without losing information. But they are weak in representing nature scenes, and displaying vector images on the raster display devices requires rasterizing processes.

There are many image file formats in use. Some commonly used formats are listed in [30]. In Web contents, the recommended image file formats are GIF, JPEG, PNG, and SVG. Since support of vector graphics such as SVG in browsers and drawing applications is yet to come, we limit our following discussion to bitmap images.

Image Format Conversion

Image format conversion with bitmap files may simply be done by some applications that could support loading and saving of image files in different formats. One example of such applications is ImageMagick (http://www.imagemagick.org), which claims to support over 89 file formats. There are, however, some special cases where more thorough studies show improvements. In [31], a method to improve the performance of GIF to JPEG-LS conversion is discussed. GIF uses the LZW [32] compression for generic string compression, while JPEG-LS benefits from the continuous tones in adjacent areas of photos. The approach attacks the optimization by reordering the palette index of GIF to emulate a continuous tone neighborhood for pixels. Thus it can be handled better by JPEG-LS. With the special reordering, JPEG-LS outperforms GIF in general.

Color Space Conversion

We live in a colorful world. Naturally so are the images. Limited by the device capabilities, file formats, and storage requirements, images may need to be converted to different color representations. For example, true color images convert to palette images or gray scale ones. There are different methods to convert true color images to gray scale ones and each method results in different visual styles. The most commonly used approach with RGB colors is the color space conversion matrix borrowed from NTSC TV standards as shown by the following equation.

$$Y = 0.299 * R + 0.587 * G + 0.114 * B \qquad (11.1)$$

Table 11.4. Content types and transcoding methods

source type	Transcoding method	result type	Examples
video	encoding format conversion	video	MPEG-1 to MPEG-4
	Transrating	video	5 Mbps DVD to 1 Mbps MPEG-4
	spatial resolution reduction	video	CIF to QCIF
	temporal resolution reduction	video	30 fps to 10 fps
	key frame extraction	image	summary of typical scenes
audio	sound track extraction	audio	film sound track
	encoding format conversion	audio	CD audio to MP3
	transrating	audio	320 kbps MP3 to 128 kbps
	channel down mix	audio	5.1 channels surround to 2 channels stereo
	sampling rate change	audio	44.1 kHz to 8 kHz
	sampling resolution change	audio	16 bits to 8 bits
	audio summary	audio	sample clips
	speech detection	text	speech recognition
image	encoding format conversion	image	PNG to JPEG
	transrating	image	JPEG requantization
	spatial resolution redution	image	XGA 1024×768 to VGA 640×480
	color space conversion	image	color to gray scale
	sampling resolution change	image	24-bit RGB to 16-bit 565RGB
	ROI detection	image	part of original image as region of interests
	representation format conversion	image	bitmap to vector or vice versa
document	format conversion	document	HTML to WML
	text to speech	audio	screen reader
	screen rendering	image	presentation slides to PNGs on Web

To convert a true color image to the limited colors of a palette image, there will certainly be loss of visual quality. For example, a 24-bit RGB image can represent $2^{24} = 16,777,216$ colors, while an 8-bit palette image can only represent 256 colors. In order to keep mimic visual quality, techniques such as color quantization and dithering are used. Color quantization is the process to select a suitable color palette and map each pixel of the original image to an index of the palette. With the limited number of colors a palette represents, the mismatching pixels may cause significant visual artifacts especially in the area of continuous tone changes. Halftone technique [33] is then used as a remedy. Generally speaking, it is the process of transforming images of continuous tones to images of limited tones with simulated continuous tones. At some distances, human vision systems will tend to perceive the halftone images as images of continuous tones. Fig. 11.14 gives an example of image quantization and dithering.

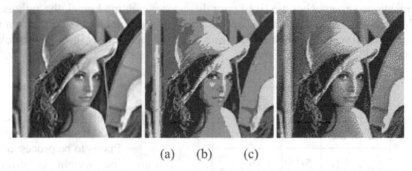

(a)   (b)   (c)

Fig. 11.14. Example of image quantization and dithering. (**a**) Original, (**b**) quantization to four levels, and (**c**) dithered result

Regarding color quantization, there are many methods. The Color Maker of Tom Boyle and Andy Lippman in late 1970's uses a popularity algorithm. They quantize the 24-bit RGB image first to 15-bit RGB with each color component in 5 bits. This will allow the computing to be reasonable for hardware at that time while still preserving bearable quality losses. Then the densest clusters of pixel distribution in the $2^5*2^5*2^5$ color space cube will be chosen as the palette and all other unmatched colors are remapped to these. In [34], the media cut algorithm is proposed. The palette is chosen under constraints of making each entry cover an approximately equal number of pixels in the image. The algorithm does this by dividing the color cube into smaller rectangular boxes until the number of boxes equals that of palettes. Each division makes sure that the number of pixels in the two parts is equal. Thus each box will finally contain similar number of pixels. The author of [35] proposes to start the initial palette from the most popular entries in the color value histogram and then optimize it iteratively by applying the Linde–Buzo–Gray algorithm [36]. A hierarchical binary tree splitting based method is discussed in [37]. The color clusters are formed on the leaves of the tree generated by iteratively splitting nodes, with each leaf corresponding to one palette entry.

Halftone has been in practice for over a hundred years in the printing industry. A detailed review of the history of halftones techniques can be found in [33]. With advances in digital imaging technologies, many new halftone methods have been developed. Dithering was introduced first by Floyd and Steinberg [38]. Their original technique is still largely in use even today. The basic idea is to diffuse the errors between original pixels and resulting pixels to neighboring pixels in the resulting images. The diffusing is done in a weighted way as shown in Fig. 11.15. The calculations are carried out in scan lines. Each pixel will diffuse its errors to four neighboring pixels. Later on, many researchers have made more detailed study of the dithering algorithms, including those proposed by Jarvis, Judice and Ninke in [39], and Stevenson and Arce in [40]. In [41], a detailed study of the dithering theory and a comparison of different methods is given. While the earlier mentioned approaches use fixed error diffusion weighting kernel, the authors of [42] take a different approach by using adaptive weighting kernel and performing the dithering in separated color components. Their subjective tests show the improvements over FloydSteinberg approach.

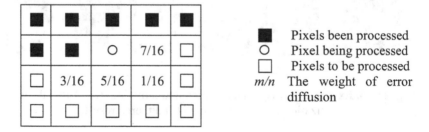

Fig. 11.15. Floyd–Steinberg dithering

Traditionally, color quantization and dithering has been done sequentially. While in this way, the dithering step may change the optimal distributions the quantizer tries to attain, the result may not be optimal. To address the problem, some researchers take the approach of performing joint color quantization and dithering. Some examples are given in [43] and [44]. However, due to limitation of space, we do not cover them in this book.

11.4.4 Video Transcoding

Video is different from other media types because it contains extremely rich information and requires much higher computing power. In uncompressed state, digital video contents require very huge storage and transport capacities. For example, an hour of typical standard NTSC resolution YUV 4:2:2 digital video stream needs 720 (horizontal) * 480 (vertical) * 2 (2 bytes per pixel) * 30 (fps) * 3600 (s) $\approx$ 70 GB of storage to handle and a bandwidth of 720 (horizontal) * 480 (vertical) * 16 (16 bits/pixel) * 30 (fps) $\approx$ 158 Mbps to transfer in realtime. These requirements exceed the capabilities of most mobile devices. Thus, in most cases the video contents are stored and transferred in compressed formats and will only be uncompressed during play back. The most commonly used video coding standards are MPEG-1/-2/-4 serials from ISO/IEC and H.261/262/263/264 from ITU. These standards utilize inter/intra frame prediction and transformation domain lossy compression with entropy coding to reduce the storage requirements of digital video contents while still maintaining reasonable visual quality. Typical compression ratios are between 20 and 200 due to different compression standards used and quality factors selected. Higher quality and compression ratio normally require more advanced and complex algorithms.

Basics of MPEG Video Compression Fig. 11.16 illustrates the flow of typical MPEG video compression algorithm. Each video frame is divided into a set of macroblocks (MBs), each MB consisting of luminance block (16×16 or four 8×8) and related chromatic blocks as Cb and Cr (8×8). There are two types of frame coding methods. One is intraframe coding, the other is interframe coding. Intraframe coding utilizes the data only from current frame, thus the result can be decoded without referring to previously decoded frames. Interframe coding benefits from the similarities between succeeding video frames. Each MB is searched in previous frames (reference frames) to find the most similar matching (motion estimation). Then only the differences between the matching results are coded (motion compensation, MC) together with the displacement information (motion vector, MV). In the MC process, one or two reference frames can be used accordingly for unidirectional and bidirectional predictions. With intraframe coding, each 8×8 block in one MB is transformed by discrete cosine transform (DCT) first, then vector quantization (VQ) is applied to the DCT results (this is where the loss comes from). Afterward, the resulting 8×8 blocks are scanned in a zigzag manner and encoded using variable length entropy coding algorithms (VLC). For interframe coding, as mentioned earlier, the result of MC is used instead of the original MB, and MV of each MB is also encoded. The coded unidirectional predicted frames are called P-frame and bidirectional predicted frame B-frame. Because the compression is lossy, to eliminate the propagation of errors, reference frames are actually reconstructed from compression results. Recent MPEG coding standards have made improvements in many cases, the block size of DCT may change to 4×4 and each smaller block may also have their own MVs. MC may be based on interpolation of reference frames called subpixel level MC. ITU H.26x uses similar methods of MPEG with minor differences.

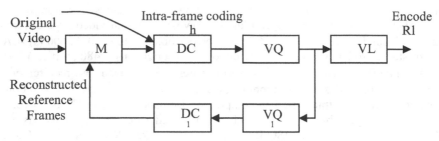

Fig. 11.16. MPEG encoding flow diagram

Video Transcoding in General

Common video transcoding requirements for mobile content access include compression format conversion, bit rate reduction, spatial resolution reduction, and temporal resolution reduction. Each of these transcoding requirements targets the limitations of mobile content access in different aspects. For example, format conversion faces limited support for compression formats in devices; bit rate reduction addresses the bandwidth limitation, lower storage capacities etc. For each transcoding requirement, different methods have been proposed. Many of them are covered in the review [45].

Because of the compression methods applied, coded video streams are normally not meant to be handled directly. To carry out video transcoding, the most straight forward approach is shown in Fig. 11.17. It is also called cascade pixel domain transcoder (CPDT). The compressed video stream is decoded first into a sequence of frames, then necessary intermediate operations are carried out (for example, frame resizing), and the resulting frame sequence is recompressed finally. With the application of proper decompression and compression methods, this approach gives the highest quality results with the best flexibility. On the contrary, it demands the heaviest computing power and may require special hardware accelerators in the case of realtime processing. The authors of [46] show how to utilize Intel's MMX technology for doing realtime transcoding. For dedicated hardware chips, vWeb vw2010 [47] is a good example. The chip is capable of simultaneously encoding and decoding in MPEG-1, -2, and -4 with interlaced, full-screen (D1) resolution. And its internal data path allows transcoding between these formats in realtime.

Under specific usage scenarios, the complexity of CPDT can be optimized. By carefully analyzing the internal flow and connections of video encoding and decoding process, researchers have proposed different approaches to improve the performance of video transcoders. Some of them are compressed domain transcoder (CDT), partial decoding, motion information reuse, etc. We introduce the details in the following paragraphs.

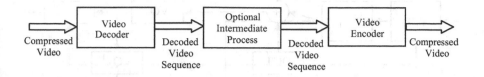

Fig. 11.17. The cascade pixel domain transcoder

Transrating

The target of transrating is to shape the video stream to fit in some channel requirement while still maintaining the highest quality possible. Early researches of video transrating in compressed domains take a very simple approach as shown in Fig. 11.18. Their methods are to directly requantize or truncate the DCT results of MBs to more coarse ones and thus the bit rate is lowered. As the process does not utilize any feedback, these methods are also called open-loop transrating. The first two methods mentioned in [48] and also in [49] belong to this category. Because succeeding predictions are used during the encoding procedure, without feedback, errors in requantization of previous frames will propagate into later frames. This error propagation can cause the "drifting" visual alias. The approach of [50] makes some improvements by dropping DCT coefficients selectively based on minimization of potential errors in each MB.

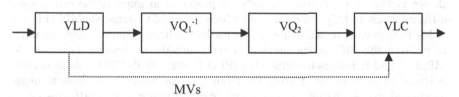

Fig. 11.18. Direct quantization video transrating approach

Contrary to the open-loop solutions, there are closed-loop transrating methods such as those introduced in [51]. As shown in Fig. 11.19, the key difference in open-loop approach is that an extra residue feedback loop is used to compensate the errors caused by the requantization. Thus the accumulation of errors in succeeding predictive frames is minimized. Further improvement of the closed-loop approach is possible by doing the motion compensation in compressed domain based on the methods proposed in [52][53][54][55]. In this way, the extra IDCT/DCT steps in the feedback loop can be eliminated.

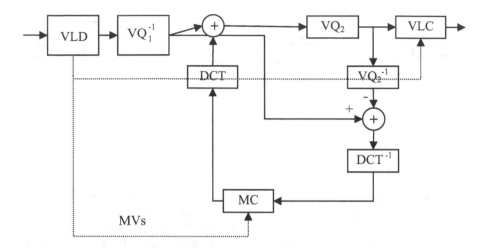

Fig. 11.19. Closed-loop video transcoding approach

Video Stream Format Conversion

Conversion of video encoding formats is needed when either the target device cannot support the current encoding format or when there are some special content access requirements. For example, in nonlinear editing applications, random access to each video frame is expected. Thus frame-based encoding methods such as motion-JPEG are commonly used. Compared to the simple CPDT approach shown in Fig. 11.17, several methods are proposed to improve the efficiency in different cases. In [52], the authors introduce a method to transcode MPEG I video to M-JPEG in compressed domain. This method utilizes a similar technique in [53] to perform the MC in compressed domain directly to convert the intercoded MPEG P and B frames to intracoded JPEG frames. With CPDT, there is also a potential to improve by utilizing the motion vector information reuse technique mentioned in [54]. More improvements can be made with platform-specific optimizations. One example is [46] that makes heavy use of Intel's MMX. The authors of [57][58] propose a hybrid spatial and frequency domain method to transcode MPEG-4 FGS video stream [29] to MPEG-4 simple profile for delivering devices that do not support FGS decoding. In [59], an interesting method to transcode Macromedia Flash^{TM} animations to MPEG-4 BIFS streams is proposed. The method is based on the object description capabilities of both formats. However, lack of the script-based interaction capability in MPEG BIFS does limit the usability of this approach.

Spatial and Temporal Resolution Reduction

Because of the popularity of DVD, broadband network, and digital TV broadcast, most of the existing contents are encoded in higher spatial and temporal resolutions.

On the other hand most of the mobile devices have limitations in display resolutions, processing capabilities, connection speed, and storage. Beside significant technology and infrastructure improvements, these existing contents can only be delivered to mobile devices by reducing the spatial and temporal resolutions.

Because motion estimation is one of the most computing intensive stages in video coding, motion information reuse becomes a key point of improvement regarding CPDT. In [49] the authors analyze the performance of three MV remapping methods in spatial reduction of H.263 coded video. In [56] the problem of transcoding MPEG-2 to MPEG-4 with both temporal and spatial resolution reduction is discussed, and MV re-estimation under different cases is studied. Their work also shows that a limited range of MV refinement after MV remapping will give good results. In [60] the problem of MV refinement is discussed in detail.

Contrary to CPDT, CDT improves the efficiency of transcoding largely with some limitations. The authors of [61][62][63] give examples of spatial reduction in a factor of 2 in the compressed domain. Their methods reduce the four 8×8 blocks in each MB to one 8×8 block. One type of approach utilizes bilinear filtering. The 2:1 bilinear interpolation operation in spatial domain is decomposited to matrix multiplications and what reflects in the DCT domain is multiplication of the DCT results of the interpolation matrix in the DCT domain [61]. Since the DCT of the bilinear interpolation matrix is only computed once, the interpolation in DCT domain costs similar to that in spatial domain. Another method is DCT decimation. The low-frequency 4×4 coefficients in the 8×8 DCT coefficients of each MB are used to reconstruct a 4×4 spatial image by IDCT, and then the four 4×4 blocks are combined to get the 8×8 block [62]. This method is reported to have better performance than that of bi-linear filtering approach. And in CDT, the technique of MC in the compressed domain [56][57] is also needed. The authors of [64] introduce an intrarefresh by selectively converting some intercoded MBs to intracoded ones to reduce the drifting alias in compressed domain spatial reduction.

Temporal resolution reduction is normally done together with spatial resolution reduction in a hybrid way [56][61], and it shares many of common techniques such as motion information reuse and compressed domain MC.

We have discussed some typical video transcoding schemes separately. However, in real world cases, the different schemes are actually bundled together to balance the final video quality [65][66]. Also there are ongoing proposals for new video transcoding methods. For example, [67] introduces the concept of content-based transcoding. The authors of [68] introduce the transcoding technique to facilitate trick play modes.

11.4.5 Audio Transcoding

Unlike the visual information, audio represents another important perceptual information source for humans. It has been observed that most people could hear audio frequency ranges only from 20 Hz to 20 kHz. Thus most of the audio equipment are designed around this frequency range. According to Shannon's sampling theory, for digital audio, a sampling rate higher than 40 kHz would be enough to restore the full audible ranges. In reality, some margins are needed to ease the design of output filters. As an inheritance of audio compact disc (Red-book CD), the most commonly used digital audio format is stereo (dual channel) 16-bit PCM sampled at 44.1 kHz. Compared to previous generations of analog audio reproduction technologies, with proper equipment, CD audio can reproduce very high-quality audio signals, which the layman accepts as high fidelity (hi-fi). The most recent advances of digital audio such as DVD-audio can provide even high fidelity audio with multichannel 24-bit PCM at a sampling rate of 96 kHz. For speech signals, there are two common classes: one is defined in telephony systems that sample at 8 kHz with bandwidth from 200 Hz to 3.4 kHz; another is for wideband speech applications that samples at 16 kHz with bandwidth up to 7 kHz.

Without compression/coding[1], one hour of CD audio requires 16 (bits) * 2 (channels) * 44,100 (Hz) * 3600 (s) $\approx$ 4.9 Gb $\approx$ 606 MB of storage and $16*2*44,100 \approx 1.4$ Mb s^{-1} bandwidth. A standard 12-cm CD stores 74 min of non-compressed audio, which equals 747 MB of data. For mobile content accesses, compression is apparently a must. There are two types of audio coding methods. The lossless coding [69] keeps all subtle information in the digital audio signals with the cost of lower compression ratios typically between 1.5 and 2. The lossy coding benefits from the perceptual limitations of human auditory systems and thus could attain compression ratios larger than 10 with minimal perceptual audio quality losses that even the "golden ear" experts could hardly distinguish (aka transparent). Since the early 1990s, the most popular lossy audio coding standard for Internet music contents is ISO/IEC MPEG I/II audio layer 3 or what is commonly known as MP3. Only recently, alternatives such as Real Audio, MPEG AAC, Ogg Vorbis, and Windows Media Audio have become popular. In the field of digital movie contents, AC-3 and DTS are commonly used along with MPEG audio layer 1/2. For speech coding, ITU G.7xx and GSM coding algorithms are the most popular ones. To get more details of different audio coding techniques, readers may refer to [70][71][72].

Audio transcoding is carried out generally in a cascade manner by decoding the compressed stream first, then doing the manipulation operations, and encoding again. Works regarding compressed domain transcoding of audio stream have rarely been reported. In [73], three methods are introduced to do bitrate scaling of MPEG audio in compressed domain by way of band limitation and requantization. Some quality loss have been reported, compared to the decoding and then encoding approach. The authors of [74] present a method to perform channel mixing and bit rate scaling of MPEG 1 layer II audio in compressed domain. And in [75] methods for gain control, mixing, and equalization on MPEG audio streams are studied.

---

[1] Coding is the more preferred term when referring to audio and speech compression among researchers of audio and speech technologies.

Sampling rate conversion is one of the most common audio transcoding requirements. As delineated Shannon's sampling theorem, the signal to be resampled must be low-pass filtered to a bandwidth of less than half of the new sampling rate. Otherwise it introduces alias distortion. An efficient approach is the bandwidth limited interpolation that does resampling and low-pass filter in one pass. The author of [76] gives a very detailed analysis and also provides a software implementation of the algorithm.

For sampling bit-resolution reduction, the most commonly used one is the conversion from 13-bit linear PCM to 8-bit A-law or μ-law PCM. Both A-law and μ-law use nonlinear quantization steps, enlarging with signal levels. The result is a larger dynamic range and better small signal resolution with some resolution loss of high amplitude signals.

Channel down mixing is used to convert multichannel audio, for example, movie surround sound tracks to stereo or monolithic audio used with Internet streaming contents. A down mixing can be as simple as addition of the signals from the channels to be mixed. The addition can be weighted for different channels and clipping must be applied to avoid sampling range overrun. There are more advanced down mixing methods, for example, virtual surround sound as Dolby Headphone, Sensaura Headphone Theater, Yamaha Silent Cinema and SRS Headphone. With these advanced methods, multichannel surround sound like Dolby Digital 5.1 could be down mixed to two channels while the listener could still have some level of the surround sound experiences. Basically the technology behind these is head-related transformation function (HRTF), which emulates the response of human mind and auditory sense to audio signals from different directions. Some introduction of HRTF can be found in [77][78]; we do not go into the details here.

11.4.6 Webpage Transcoding

The World Wide Web has become one of the most important information sources today. Most of the data on Web are available in the form of Web pages and are encoded in markup languages like HTML. Normally these Web pages are designed to be best viewed on PCs with high resolution display and flexibly interaction capabilities. For mobile devices, special markup languages such as WML are designed to take care of the limited display and interaction capabilities of mobile devices. But the quantity of existing WML contents is far smaller than that of HTML contents, though there are some mobile devices with browsers that support HTML rendering, for example, Windows CE with Pocket IE. However, due to the limited screen size and slow wireless network connection, only specially composed HTML pages can be best viewed. Developing similar contents for multiple platforms is the ideal solution, but the cost increase is to be considered too. Therefore, automatically transcoding existing Web contents to fit the special requirements of mobile devices would be more cost effective.

Generally speaking, transcoding of Web pages requires some semantic information of the Web pages. Only by knowing which parts of the Web pages contain important information, can the transcoders generate more meaningful results. HTML, as it evolved, contains mixed presentational and structural tags.[2] Even worse, misuse of structural tags for layout purposes is quite common. We may not easily distinguish authors' purposes only from the tags used in Web pages. Because of this reason, Web page transcoding approaches that are based only on structural tags may not work effectively with real world Web contents. In [80], a method to extract the semantics of Web pages based on layout cues is proposed. The result is then tested in a Web page transcoding proxy for pocket PC devices.

Since each Internet content provider (ICP) has its own specific content organization styles, transcoding of Web pages can be done in an ICP-specific way. For a client-side solution, an example is the now-defunct Web Clipping technology for 3Com's Palm VII. It requires ICPs to provide special content filter applications running on the Palm VII device to filter their pages extracting important contents. A more popular approach is to run the content filter service on a Web proxy. For example, TranSend [81], ProxyNet ProxiWare, SpyGlass Prism Server, and OnlineAnywhere FlashMap use proxy servers to adjust Web pages to fit the display of small devices based on some heuristic rules and special content filters designed for specific Websites to extract the most important contents from HTML pages. Similar approaches are reported in [82][83][84]. Instead of specific rules and filters, these methods use semantic annotations of the Web pages to help extraction of important information. The annotations, however, still need to be prepared manually according to the content organization styles of each specific ICP or Web page.

As XML is becoming popular, more and more contents are prepared in the XML format. With the strict separation of semantic and presentational capabilities in the XML world, contents could be transcoded easily to different formats by using XSL. The transformation rules and templates are defined by XSLT, and those parts of documents to be referred to are given by XPath. This approach is used in IBM's WebSphere Transcoding Publisher together with the annotation-based methods.

With the increased demands of heterogeneous Web access, W3C has also started a work group to drive the development of device independent Web access technologies (W3C, Device Independence Working Group). Their focus is on:

- Methods by which the characteristics of the device are made available for use in the processing associated with device independence.
- Methods to assist authors in creating sites and applications that can support device independence in ways that allow it to be widely employed.

With this effort, the boundary of Web content creation and transcoding will be blurred. This opens the door to the adaptive content delivery techniques that we introduce next.

---

[2] In the first version of HTML most of the tags were for structures. But many layout and presentation tags were added on into following versions and are widely used today. Some of the historical aspects can be found in [79]

11.4.7 Adaptive Content Delivery Techniques

Content transcoding techniques only target at the specific requirements of transforming contents with some prerequests. With the increasing diversity and heterogeneity of client devices and network conditions combined with individual preferences of end users, simple transcoding processes cannot handle the changing situations. Adaptive content delivery [85] is a technique that extends content transcoding and delivery techniques to support the changing content access requirements in dynamic ways. For example, assume a user who subscribes to some news service and some important event occurs; when he is in an area where the operator provides only SMS service, the news can be delivered to him only in pieces of summarized text; when he roams to another network where GPRS service is enabled, a detailed report with pictures is then possible; and when he comes near a WiFi access point, video clips regarding that event are available. With the help of adaptive content delivery, this usage scenario is quite possible.

The block diagram of a typical adaptive content delivery system is given in Fig. 11.20. The center of the system is the decision engine. It is where delivery plans are made. Appropriate contents and types, the set of transcoders, and layout templates are selected based on knowledge of system resource usage, network conditions, device types, and user preference factors. The result is normally a complex optimization of some QoS factor under these constraints. While some constraints such as network conditions dynamically change when contents delivered, the decision engine may also adjust its results accordingly to reflect the changes. Another important part of the system is the profile discovery module where factors like network condition, user preferences, and device capabilities are detected or learned either automatically or through user/device interactions. To improve the system performance, caches can be used to temporarily store the transcoding results for future reuse. The decision engine can then take caching into consideration. Suboptimal cached results may be preferred in the case of high system load. A data analysis and mining utility can also be included in the system to help find hidden user preferences and typical usage scenarios. And last but not least, the content authoring tools should the adaptive content delivery requirements and create contents accordingly.

Research of adaptive content delivery is becoming popular with the booming of Internet and World Wide Web. Early commercial applications like Intel's Quickweb and Spectrum Information Technologies' FastLane are focused on providing faster Web page downloads for narrow bandwidth connected users (like dialup and mobile access). Most of them just accelerate the download by reducing embedded image file sizes with aggressive lossy compression. The constraints are the lowest acceptable quality factors and maximal wait times specified by the users. Lossless text compression is also utilized to reduce the transmission time of HTML pages. The TranSend [81], Digestor [86], and Mowgli [87] touched some aspects of content adaptation for different situations by re-authoring the Web pages. Companies like ProxyNet (based on TranSend technology), SpyGlass and OnlineAnywhere provide proxy servers to adjust Web pages to fit the display of small devices. Their

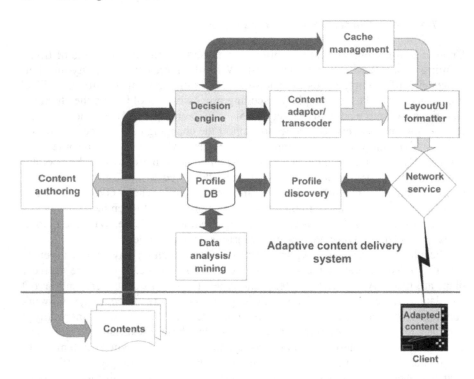

Fig. 11.20. Architecture of a typical adaptive content delivery system

technologies are based on heuristic rules and special content filters designed for specific Websites that are used to extract the most important contents from Web pages. Besides the similar features introduced earlier, IBM's WebSphere Transcoding Publisher also supports XML + XSL-based approach. The contents are prepared in XML formats and a set of XSLs are designed for different situations. The content adaptation is done by applying the best-fit XSL to transform the original XML materials according to the prevailing situation. While the solution has an elegant style, composing XSLs for different situations and applications is not a trivial task.

In the case of better optimization of the content adaptation system, Han et al. [88] study an adaptive image transcoding application that can provide maximized image quality under some delay time constraint or minimized delay at some fixed image quality. [89] tells a similar story. The study in [90] improves that by also considering the balance of compression quality and image spatial resolution. Similar work is reported in [91]. Ma et al. [92] improve this idea in many aspects and their work is extended in [93]. To address the relationship between multiple media content types and adaptation strategies, structurized content models are proposed. For example, Smith et al. give the InfoPyramid content transcoding model in [94][95][96]. The authors of [80][97][98] utilize a tree-like abstract document model in an adaptive Web content delivery test system. Web contents are analyzed based on layout factors and are automatically converted to the document model. The tree model is then used in making delivery plans. Similar works can be found in [99][100].

Considering the special requirements of mobile devices, the European Telecommunication Standards Institute has proposed the universal mobile telecommunication system [101], which is oriented to mobile-aware adaptive content services. One of their usage scenarios is CityGuide, which is a navigation system based on device location information. An other is online Web access with adaptive filtering based on a QoS trading of client/network situations and user-preferred maximum wait time.

There are also some standard works that target applications of adaptive content delivery. W3C's Device Independence WG does many works. Among them, CC/PP (Composite Capability/Preference Profiles) establishes a standard method to describe device capabilities and user preferences. With the help of HTTP/1.1 content negotiation capability (IETF conneg WG) and CC/PP, the infrastructure of adaptive Web content delivery has already come to a shape. The metadata of structurized contents such as MPEG-7 and JPEG 2000 can also help content adaptation. Some examples are given in [102][103].

Scalable media coding technologies provide more chances for adaptive content delivery. Since MPEG II, MPEG video coding standards have started to support some coarse levels of scalabilities, including SNR scalability, spatial scalability, and temporal scalability. Video contents are coded into different layers. The base layer contains a low resolution or low-quality video contents. Enhancement layers contain incremental details to construct higher quality video and are encoded into separate streams. Scalability is supported by adding/removing higher layers. Since there are a limited number of layers, the control of scalability can only be done in a coarse level. In the case of network transport, the coarse control may not be able to fully utilize the dynamic changing bandwidth to get the maximum quality possible. MPEG-4 FGS is a proposal to address the problem of fine granularity control of scalability. Interested readers can refer to [29] for more details. For still picture compression, the newly standardized JPEG 2000 supports the capabilities of multiple resolutions, and progressive and regional-based decoding. Part 9 of JPEG 2000 (JPIP) specifies the interaction protocols to access different picture resolutions and regions. Regarding the specific situation of wireless application, the mechanism to support error protection and correction is defined in Part 11 (JPWL). Metadata such as region of interest (ROI) are also supported. Thus it will be possible to view JPEG 2000-coded pictures according to client-side requirements of region, resolution, and quality in a flexible manner.

Adaptive content delivery techniques are still in the evolving stages. What we list here is only part of the being done. Some of the techniques are already incorporated in commercial products. For example, newer versions of streaming applications from Microsoft and RealNetworks are capable of delivering streaming media contents adaptively based on user's network connection situation; Apple's QuickTime streaming server has the capability to select an effective starting bandwidth automatically by negotiating with client software. However, for the idea of universal content accessing capability, there is still a large gap. Researches are still being carried out in different directions as system architecture [104][105], server scheduling, communication channel characteristic discovery, content semantic description [106], content model, user preference collection, generic decision making framework, integration of heterogeneous content types, etc.

11.5 Summary

Mobile content delivery technologies, at present, are still in their growing stages. New technologies, customer requirements, and business opportunities are coming out as fast as bamboo shoots. When SMS was introduced a decade ago, nobody would have anticipated its current popularity. With the follow up of MMS, we all know that it will create large business opportunities. Transcoding technologies, as they were developed before the increasing needs of mobile content delivery, serve as an important bridge between the worlds of mobile and stationary computing. In this chapter, we focused our attention on these existing technologies. The new ones are still held in the hands of their innovators. Only one thing is clear: With the development of technologies, the gap between mobile and stationary computing will finally blur.

Reference

1. Netsize (2003) European SMS Guide. http://www.gsmworld.com
2. "SMS in North America crosses 1billion messages a month mark", http://www.mobileyouth.org/news/mobileyouth454.html
3. Market report, http://www.iresearch.com.cn
4. What is SMS, http://www.gsmworld.com/technology/sms/intro.shtml
5. G.L. Bodic, Mobile Messaging Technologies and Services: SMS, EMS and MMS", Alcatel, France, ISBN 0470848766
6. 3GPP TS 23.040. Technical Realization of the Short Message Service (SMS), March 2004

7. C. Peersman, S. Cvetkovic, P. Griffiths, and H. Spear (2000) The global system for mobile communications Short Message Service. IEEE Personal Communications 7(3):15–23

8. OMA-MMS-ARCH-V1_2-20031217-C. Multimedia Messaging Service, Architecture Overview, version 1.2. December 2003

9. 3GPP TS 22.140. Multimedia Messaging Service (MMS) Stage 1 (Release 6). March 2004

10. Photo Phones Everywhere – MMS future looks bright, http://www. the3gportal.com/essentialreading/archives/002943.php

11. The future of mobile messaging, http://www.cww.net.cn/Near3G/Article. asp?id=9364

12. T. Wolf (2002) MMS-Shooting Star for 2.5G and 3G, http://www. gsmworld.com/technology/mms/mms_presentations.shtml

13. 3GPP2 MMS arch, www.3gpp2.org

14. 3GPP TS 23.140. Multimedia Messaging Service (MMS); Functional description; Stage 2 (Release 6). March 2004

15. IETF; STD 0010 (RFC 2821). Simple Mail Transfer Protocol. http://www.ietf/rfc/rcf2821.txt

16. W3C Note 8 May 2000. Simple Object Access Protocol (SOAP). http://www.w3.org/TR/SOAP

17. W3C Note 11 December 2000. SOAP Messages with Attachments. http://www.w3.org/TR/SOAP-attachments

18. OMA-MMS-ENC-v1_2-20040323-C. Multimedia Messaging Service Encapsulation Protocol Version 1.2. March 2004

19. W3C Recommendation 7 August 2001. Synchronized Multimedia Integration Language (SMIL 2.0). http://www.w3.org/TR/smil20/

20. WAP Forum™, WAP-191-WML. Wireless Application Protocol, Wireless Markup Language Specification, Version 1.3. http://www. openmobilealliance.org

21. IETF RFC 2046. Multipurpose Internet Mail Extensions (MIME) Part Two: Media types

22. MIDI Manufacturers Association. RP-34. Scalable Polyphony MIDI Specification. http://www.midi.org/about-midi/abtspmidi.htm, 2002

23. MIDI Manufacturers Association. RP-35. Scalable Polyphony MIDI Device 5-to-24 Note Profile for 3GPP. http://www.midi.org/about-midi/abtspmidi. htm, 2002

24. MIDI Manufacturers Association. RP-001. Standard MIDI Files 1.0, 1996

25. OMA-DRM-DRM-V2_0-20040420-D. DRM specification v2.0. http://www. openmobile.org

26. OMA-DRM-DCF-V2_0-20040420. DRM Content Format v2.0. http://www. openmobile.org

27. WAP Forum™, WAP-260-WIM. Wireless Application Protocol, Wireless Identity Module. http://www.openmobilealliance.org

28. WAP Forum™, WAP-231-EFI-20050511-a. EFI framework. http://www. openmobile.org

29.   W. Li (2001) Overview of fine granularity scalability in MPEG-4 video standard. IEEE transaction on Circuits and Systems fro Video Technology 11(3):301–317

30.   The Internet FAQ Archive. Graphics File Formats FAQ. http://www.faqs.org/faqs/graphics/fileformats-faq

31.   N. Memon, R. Rodila (1997) Transcoding GIF images to JPEG-LS. IEEE Transactions on Consumer Electronics 43(3):423–429

32.   T.A. Welch (1984) A technique for high-performance data compression. IEEE Computer, 17(6):8–19

33.   R. Ulichney (2000) A review of halftoning techniques. Color Imaging: Device-Independent Color, Color Hardcopy, and Graphic Arts V, Proc SPIE, vol. 3963, January 2000

34.   P.S. HeckBert (1980) Color image quantization for frame buffer display. Bachelor of Science Thesis, MIT. http://www-2.cs.cmu.edu/~ph/ciq_thesis

35.   G.W. Braudaway (1986) A procedure for optimum choice of a small number of colors from a large color palette for color imaging. In: Proceedings of Electronic Imaging '86 – International Electronic Imaging Exposition and Conference, pp. 75–79

36.   Y. Linde, A. Buzo, R.M. Gray (1980) An algorithm for vector quantizer design. IEEE Transactions on Communication 28(1):84–95

37.   M. Orchard, C. Bouman (1991) Color quantization of images. IEEE Transactions on Signal Processing 39(12):2677–2690

38.   R.W. Floyd, L. Steinberg (1976) An adaptive algorithm for spatial grey scale.Proceedings of the Society of Information Display 17:76–77

39.   J.F. Jarvis, C.N. Judice, W.H. Ninke (1976) A survey of techniques for the display of continuous tone pictures on bilevel displays. Computer Graphics Image Processing, 5:13–40

40.   R.L. Stevenson, G.R. Arce (1985) Binary display of hexagonally sampled continuous-tone images. Journal of the Optical Society of America A. 2(7):1009–1013

41.   R.A. Ulichney (1988) Dithering with blue noise. Proceedings of the IEEE 76(1):56–79

42.   L. Akarun, Y. Yardımcı, A. Enis Cetin (1997) Adaptive methods for dithering color images. IEEE Transactions on Image Processing 6(7):950–955

43.   L. Akarun, D. Ozdemir, O. Yalcin (1996) Joint quantization and dithering of color images. Proceedings of International Conference on Image Processing 1:557–560

44.   D. Özdemir, L. Akarun (2001) Fuzzy algorithms for combined quantization and dithering. IEEE Transactions on Image Processing 10(6):923–931

45.   A. Vetro, C. Christopoulos, H.F. Sun (2003) Video transcoding architectures and techniques: an overview. IEEE Signal Processing Magazine 20(2):18–29

46.   H. Kalva, A. Vetro, H. Sun (2003) Performance optimization of the MPEG-2 to MPEG-4 video transcoder. Proceedings of SPIE Conference on VLSI Circuits and Systems 5117:341–350

47.   vWeb vW2010 MPEG codec chip, http://www.vwebcorp.com/mall/c110/s3066/Products/VW2010%20CODEC.html

48.   H. Sun, W. Kwok, J. Zdepski (1996) Architectures for MPEG compressed bitstream scaling. IEEE transaction on Circuits and Systems fro Video Technology 6(2):191–199

49.   N. Bjork, C. Christopoulos (1998) Transcoder architectures for video coding. IEEE Transactions on Consumer Electronics 44(1):88–98

50.   A. Eleftheriadis, D. Anastassiou (1995) Constrained and general dynamic rate shaping of compressed digital video. Proceedings of the 1995 IEEE International Conference on Image Processing, vol. 3

51.   H. Sorial, W.E. Lynch, A. Vincent (2000) Selective requantization for transcoding of MPEG compressed video. Proceeding of IEEE International Conference on Multimedia and Expo 1:217–220

52.   S. Acharya, B. Smith (1998) Compressed domain transcoding of MPEG. In: Proceedings IEEE International Conference on Multimedia Computing and Systems, pp. 295–304

53.   S.F. Chang, D.G. Messerschmidt (1995) Manipulation and compositing of MC-DCT compressed video. IEEE Journal of Selected Areas in Communication 13(1):1–11

54.   J. Wang, S. Yu (1998) Dynamic rate scaling of coded digital video for IVOD applications. IEEE Transaction on Consumer Electronics 44(8):743–749

55.   P. Assunção, M. Ghanbari (1998) A frequency-domain video transcoder for dynamic bit-rate reduction of MPEG-2 bitstreams. IEEE Transactions on Circuits and Systems fro Video Technology 8(12):953–967

56.   J. Xin, M.T. Sun, K. Chun (2002) Motion re-estimation for MPEG-2 to MPEG-4 simple profile transcoding. Proceedings of Packet Video. http://amp.ece.cmu.edu/packetvideo2002/final_program.htm

57.   Y.Q. Liang, Y.P. Tan (2002) Methods and needs for transcoding MPEG-4 fine granularity scalability video. Proceedings of IEEE International Symposium on Circuits and Systems 4:719–722

58.   Y.C. Lin, C.N. Wang, T. Chiang, A. Vetro, H. Sun (2002) Efficient FGS to single layer transcoding. In: Proceedings of IEEE International Conference on Consumer Electronics (ICCE), pp. 134–135

59.   A. Lee, M. Bourges-Sevenier, G. Rajan (2001) Converting macromedia FlashTM shockwave to MPEG-4 BIFS. In: Proceedings of Workshop and Exhibition on MPEG-4, pp. 9–12

60.   J. Youn, M.T. Sun, C.W. Lin (1999) Motion vector refinement for high-performance transcoding. IEEE Transactions on Multimedia 1(1):30–40

61.   W. Zhu, K.Yang, M. Beacken (1998) CIF-to-QCIF video bitstream down-conversion in the DCT domain. Bell Labs Technical Journal 1998(3):21–29

62.   T. Shanableh, M. Ghanbari (2000) Heterogeneous video transcoding to lower spatio-temporal resolutions and different encoding formats. IEEE Transactions on Multimedia 2(2):101–110

63.   Y.R. Lee, C.W. Lin, C.C. Kao (2002) A DCT-domain video transcoder for spatial resolution downconversion. Lecture Notes in Computer Science: Recent Advances in Visual Information Systems 2002(3):207–218

64.   A. Vetro, C.W. Chen (2002) Rate-reduction transcoding design for wireless video streaming. Proceedings of 2002 International Conference on Image Processing 1:29–32

65.   Y. Yu, C.W. Chen (2000) SNR scalable transcoding for video over wireless channels. Proceeding of IEEE Wireless Communications and Networking Conference 3:1398–1402

66.   P.F. Correia, V.M. Silva, P.A. Amado Assuncao (2003) A method for improving the quality of mobile video under hard transcoding conditions. Proceedings of IEEE International Conference on Communications 2:928–932

67.   Y.Q. Liang, Y.P. Tan (2001) A new content-based hybrid video transcoding method. Proceedings of International Conference on Image Processing 1:429–432

68.   Y.P. Tan, Y.Q. Liang, J. Yu (2002) Video transcoding for fast forward/reverse video playback. Proceedings of IEEE International Conference of Image Processing 1:713–716

69.   R. Whittle (2003) Lossless Compression of Audio, http://www.firstpr.com.au/audiocomp/lossless/

70.   Gersho (1994) Advances in speech and audio compression. Proceedings of the IEEE. 82(6):900–918

71.   D. Pan (1995) A tutorial on MPEG/audio compression. IEEE Multimedia 2(2):60–74

72.   P. Null (1997) MPEG digital audio coding. IEEE Signal Processing Magazine, 14(5):59–81

73.   Y. Nakajima, H. Yanagihara, A. Yoneyama, M. Sugano (1998) MPEG audio bit rate scaling on coded data domain. Proceedings of the 1998 IEEE International Conference on Acoustics, Speech, and Signal Processing 6:3669–3672

74.   P. De Smet, T.V. Stichele (2001) Subband based MPEG audio mixing for internet streaming applications. In: Proceedings of ICASSP'01. Also available at http://mti.xidian.edu.cn/multimedia/2001/supp/icassp2001/MAIN/papers/pap1881.pdf

75.   M.A. Broadhead, C.B. Owen (1995) Direct manipulation of MPEG compressed digital audio. In: Proceeding of the Third ACM International Conference on Multimedia, pp. 499–507

76.   J.O. Smith III (2004) The Digital Audio Resampling Home Page. http://ccrma-www.stanford.edu/~jos/resample/

77.   F. Filipanits Jr. (1994) Design and Implementation of an Auralization System with a Spectrum-based Temporal Processing Optimization. http://alumnus.caltech.edu/~franko/thesis/thesis.html

78.   Center for Image Processing and Integrated Computing, University of California. HRTF Database. http://interface.cipic.ucdavis.edu/CIL_html/CIL_whatis.htm

79.   D. Siegel (1997) The Web is Ruined and I Ruined It. http://www.xml.com/pub/a/w3j/s1.people.html

80.   Y.D. Yang, H.J. Zhang (2001) HTML page analysis based on visual cues. In: Proceedings Sixth International Conference on Document Analysis and Recognition (ICDAR '01), pp. 859–864

81. A. Fox, S.D. Gribble, Y. Chawathe, E.A. Brewer (1998) Adapting to network and client variation using infrastructural proxies: Lessons and perspectives. IEEE Personal Communication 5(4):10–19

82. R. Schaefer, A. Dangberg, W. Mueller (2002) Fuzzy rules for HTML transcoding. In: Proceedings of the 35th Annual Hawaii International Conference on System Sciences, pp. 1385–1393

83. Z.Y. Shao, R. Capra, M.A. Perez-Quinones (2003) Transcoding HTML to voiceXML using annotation. In: Proceedings of 15th IEEE International Conference on Tools with Artificial Intelligence, pp. 249–258

84. J. Maeda, K. Fukuda, H. Takagi, C. Asakawa (2003) WebDigest: layout-preserving visually enhanced Web pages. In: Proceedings of 2003 Symposium on Applications and the Internet, pp. 418–421

85. H.J. Zhang (2000) Adaptive content delivery: A new research area in media computing. In: Proceedings of the 2000 International Workshop on Multimedia Data Storage, Retrieval, Integration and Applications, pp. 13–15

86. T.W. BickMore, B.N. Schilit (1997) Digestor: Device-independent access to the World Wide Web. In: Proceedings of the sixth International World Wide Web Conference, pp. 655–663

87. M. Liijeberg, H. Helin, M. Kojo, K. Raatikainen (1996) Enhanced services for World Wide Web in mobile WAN environment. Report C-1996–28, University of Helsinki Finland. http://www.cs.helsinki.fi/research/mowgli/mowgli-papers.html

88. R. Han, P. Bhagwat, R. LaMaire, T. Mummert, V. Perret, J. Rubas (1998) Dynamic adaptation in an image transcoding proxy for mobile Web browsing. IEEE Personal Communications 5(6):8–17

89. A. Gaddah, A. El-Shentenawy, T. Kunz, R. Hafez (2002) Image transcoding proxy for mobile Internet access. In:Proceedings of IEEE 56th Vehicular Technology Conference 2:24–28.

90. S. Chandra, C.S. Ellis, A. Vahdat (2000) Application-level differentiated multimedia Web services using quality aware transcoding. IEEE Journal on Selected Areas in Communications 18(12):2544–2565

91. K. Lee, H.S. Chang, S.S. Chun, H. Choi, S. Sull (2001) Perception-based image transcoding for universal multimedia access. Proceedings of 2001 International Conference on Image Processing 2:475–478

92. W.Y. Ma, I. Bedner, G. Chang, A. Kuchinsky, H.J. Zhang (2000) A framework for adaptive content delivery in heterogeneous network environments. In: Proceedings of MMCN2000

93. H.J. Zhang, W.Y. Ma (2004) Adaptive content delivery on mobile internet across multiple form factor. In: Proceedings of 10th International Multimedia Modelling Conference

94. J.R. Smith, R. Mohan, C.S. Li (1998) Transcoding Internet content for heterogeneous client devices. Proceedings of the 1998 IEEE International Symposium on Circuits and Systems 3:599–602

95. R. Mohan, J.R. Smith, C.S. Li (1999) Content adaptation framework: bringing the Internet to information appliances. Proceeding of Global Telecommunications Conference 4:2015–2021

96.   J.R. Smith, R. Mohan, C.S. Li (1999) Scalable multimedia delivery for pervasive computing. In: Proceedings of ACM Multimedia '99

97.   Y.D. Yang, J.L. Chen, H.J. Zhang (2000) Adaptive delivery of HTML contents. In: WWW9 Poster Proceedings, pp. 24–25

98.   J.L. Chen, Y.D. Yang, H.J. Zhang (2000) An adaptive web content delivery system. In: Proceedings of International Conference on Adaptive Hypermedia and Adaptive Web-based Systems (AH-2000)

99.   T. Phan, G. Zorpas, R. Bagrodia (2002) An extensible and scalable content adaptation pipeline architecture to support heterogeneous clients. In: Proceedings of 22nd International Conference on Distributed Computing Systems, pp. 507–516

100. W.Y. Lum, F.C.M. Lau (2002) A context-aware decision engine for content adaptation. IEEE Pervasive Computing 1(3):41–49

101. B. Kreller, A.S.B Park, J. Meggers, G. Forsgren, E. Kovacs, M. Rosinus (1998) UMTS: A middleware architecture and mobile API approach. IEEE Personal Communication, 5(4):8–17

102. P. van Beek, J.R. Smith, T. Ebrahimi, T. Suzuki, J. Askelof (2003) Metadata-driven multimedia access. IEEE Signal Processing Magazine 20(2):40–52

103. J.H. Kuo, C.C. Ho, J.L. Wu (2003) Building MPEG-7 transcoding hints from intrinsic characteristics of MPEG videos. In: Proceedings of IEEE International Conference on Consumer Electronics, pp. 34–35

104. F.T. Abdelzaher, N. Bhatti (1999) Web content adaptation to improve server overload behavior. In: Proceedings of the Eighth International World Wide Web Conference, pp. 485–499

105. J. Guo; F. Chen; L. Bhuyan, R. Kumar (2003) A cluster-based active router architecture supporting video/audio stream transcoding service. In: Proceedings of International Parallel and Distributed Processing Symposium, pp. 44–51

106. B. Knutsson (2003) Server Directed Transcoding—a short overview. In: First Swedish National Computer Networking Workshop, http://winternet.sics.se/workshops/sncnw2003/proceedings.html

12 Mobile Services Computing

L. -J. Zhang[1], B. Li[2], and Y. Song[3]

[1]IBM T.J. Watson Research Center
[2]Department of Computer Science and Engineering, Arizona State University
[3]MathWorks, Natick, MA

12.1 Web Services Overview

The World Wide Web Consortium (W3C) [1] defines a Web service [2] as a software system designed to support interoperable machine-to-machine interaction over a network. The emergence of Web services is the result of the Internet progress and the reuse requirement of the large amount of legacy IT systems. The widely used Internet techniques make it possible for organizations and persons to connect through a unique way, i.e., HTTP (hypertext transfer protocol) [3] and XML (eXtensible markup language) [4]. Meanwhile, there are a huge number of legacy systems among those organizations and persons. To tie the separate parts together, the technology of Web services is proposed. With its support, each legacy system is wrapped with a standard interface, Web services description language (WSDL) [5]. Therefore, a legacy system is regarded as a standard computing unit over the Internet, a Web service. Moreover, there exists a standard connection among those Web services so that communication among them can be carried out. The connection, called simple object access protocol (SOAP) [6], is based on the Internet communication protocol, HTTP, and the standard data description format, XML. Via SOAP, Web services can be invoked by others and it is possible for multiple Web services to work collaboratively. For the convenience of publishing and retrieving Web services, a registration server, universal description, discovery, and integration (UDDI) [7], has been established. According to the information in UDDI servers, consumers of Web services are able to obtain essential knowledge so as to ensure that the services meet their requirements.

12.2 Extending Web Services to Mobile Services

The technology of Web services is initially designed for the desktop computing world, which relies on fixed and reliable Internet access. With the rapid progress of mobile computing [8], and increased need for information and services on the go, it is natural to extend Web services to mobile services [9, 10]. Although the fundamental ideas of mobile services are the same as those of Web services, there are also significant differences between them. It is necessary for managers and developers to be aware of the unique challenges of mobile services.

12.2.1 Mobility

First of all, mobility is one distinct feature of mobile services that differs from ordinary Web services. Traditionally, Web services reside at a static physical location, such as a Web server, which supports HTTP invocation and XML message transmission. A fixed universal resource locator (URL) [11] is assigned so that a particular Web service is accessible through the address. The address is retrievable from a UDDI server. After obtaining a Web service, it can be integrated into an application in order to be consumed at a static location, such as a Web browser. Finally, end users utilize integrated Web services in a static environment too, such as buying a book using a desktop PC.

On the contrary, mobile services are a totally different story. The three major roles in mobile services, namely the terminal, the user, and the service, are all movable. To access a mobile service, there are a lot of candidate devices, for example, pocket PC, cell phone, camera phone, and personal digital assistant (PDA). These devices are connected to the Internet through wireless techniques, such as Bluetooth [12], Wi-Fi [13], and 3G [14]. Since these devices are small and light-weighted, it is convenient for users to hold them in hand and access a mobile service while on the move. In addition, it is possible that a service is not located at a static location. The main purpose of making a service movable is to adapt to the more complicated computing environment for mobile services. For example, to use a PDA to access driving direction information, the service must be located somewhere near the PDA. Otherwise, the service may fail because of low-quality wireless connections. To reach the goal, the same service has to be deployed to multiple locations to ensure service quality.

12.2.2 Security

Given the mobility of the devices, users, and services, wireless communication is involved. Unlike signals carried by optical or electrical wires, radio signals are much more susceptible to eavesdropping and malicious interfering. Security measures must be taken on different layers of the system, possibly from the physical layer all up to the application layer. Especially for the sensitive m-commerce [15, 16], encryption [17], authentication, and authorization are all critical issues. The tradeoff of security and efficiency must be resolved, based on the particular application. Mobile services require stronger protection than regular Web services.

12.2.3 Context Sensitivity

The context [18, 19] here specifies the ever-changing computing environment that affects service content. Mobile service providers must ensure that the design of mobile services adapts to the different scenarios at runtime or even each time when a service is started.

In general, ordinary Web services providers do not need to consider the issue because it is assumed that a stable computing environment is available. Each time when a Web service is invoked, there is no need to collect the computing environment information. Meanwhile, during the service procedure, it is not required to detect any changes on the client's computing environment at runtime except those data related to business logic.

However, as a successful mobile service, it should not only take care of completing the business logic, but also detecting the changes of mobile devices environment in order to provide more effective and efficient services. Sometimes the context information is the key to the success of mobile services. The primary context information includes locations, resources, environments users reside in, and so on. That information could be very rich and depends on specific applications heavily. For example, a weather forecast service must know where the service requester is located before sending the relevant weather information. A car dealer service must also learn the service requester's location before providing any information. Payment for a particular mobile service may depend on the location of the service consumer, or even how fast the consumer (mobile device) is moving. Additional possible cases are airplanes, ships deep in ocean, spacecrafts, or vehicles in a highway.

12.2.4 Multimodality

Multimodality [20] is another important feature that is different from regular Web services. This feature is caused by the large number of mobile devices and the specific characteristics of each of them. Here, multimodality specifies the different access tiers for a unique service. The wireless and mobile world is simply much more diversified than the desktop computing world. There is no unified or dominant standard, both in hardware and software. It is a constantly evolving situation, due to business interests of all parties involved, including many telecom equipment manufacturers, consumer electronics and software vendors, as well as government agencies.

For regular Web services, SOAP is the major approach to access them. In essence, SOAP is an XML message transmission approach over HTTP. It is assumed that HTTP is always available at the service client end and that XML message can be processed there when Web services are being consumed.

However, it is inappropriate for mobile services to assume this scenario. There exist multiple communication protocols in the wireless Internet world. A mobile service must be able to handle complicated communication situations so as to build the connection between the specific client and itself. Furthermore, it is necessary to consider that a mobile device may not be able to process XML messages from the service because of the limited resources available. Therefore, providers of mobile services have to transmit data in specific formats to specific devices at the worst situations.

12.2.5 Resource Limitations

For regular Web services, due to the rapid progress in the manufacture of hardware, it is usually unnecessary to consider the issue of resource availability at client side. It is assumed that sufficient resources are always available for the types of computing demanded, such as audio and video applications.

Mobile devices all have physical constraints of size, weight, etc. which lead to limited computing resources [21] such as CPU power and installed memory. Therefore, this assumption cannot be made for mobile services. This will significantly affect the implementation of mobile services, since almost all devices that consume mobile services are classified as thin clients. For example, as the standard language for Web services, XML was designed without considering the resource issue. It is quite redundant and not nearly as efficient as some existing binary message formats. The display of mobile devices is much smaller than that of desktop monitors where rich graphical interfaces are already standardized. Designers must be highly creative to make mobile applications useful and usable. Another issue is that compared with wired channels, wireless communication channels suffer from much more severe defects such as multipath fading. The communication capacity and quality can change dramatically, and cannot possibly match that of wired communication, which is the foundation of regular Web services. This leads to constantly varying quality of service (QoS) [22] of mobile services. It is a challenge to satisfy a large number of users.

12.2.6 Peer to Peer

Since mobile services depend on context information, a particular device is usually required to provide such context information before a service is invoked, or during the process when a service is being consumed. At this time, the device itself resembles a service. This means each mobile device is capable of providing some functionalities, i.e., it is possible to build connections between two mobile devices and either of them works not only as a Web service but also as a client to consume the counterpart's service. This is a peer-to-peer computing mechanism.

Physically, the peer-to-peer computing [23] among mobile devices is built on techniques such as Bluetooth, 802.11 [24], wireless application protocol (WAP), [25] or general packet radio service (GPRS) [26]. The key challenge of such a mechanism is software design, i.e., each device is in an equal situation to the other. To implement this architecture, devices are published in a registry server (UDDI) to be accessed. A lot of interesting applications are built based on it.

12.3 General Architecture of Mobile Services

The general architecture of mobile services is constructed according to the important features of mobile services. Figure 12.1 illustrates the architecture, which is composed of two major parts, the mobile service server and the mobile client. Besides   those two parts, there is an integration manager on the server side.

12.3.1 Mobile Service Server

The mobile service server consists of the regular Web services, and the modules that support mobile features, such as multimodal adaptor, context adaptor, and context information collector. It provides service consumers with business logic, i.e., the real service. It works like a server end that waits for requests from a client and sends the corresponding response to the client.

Multimodal Adaptor

This module is used to adapt to specific mobile devices' requirements so as to build a communication channel between the mobile service and the mobile client. To fulfill its task, the multimodal adaptor must be able to access the mobile client's profile, which contains the specific device information. According to the profile, the multimodal adaptor configures the communication approach for the corresponding mobile service, to enable the service to receive requests from the specific client and to send responses to it.

Context Information Collector

As discussed earlier, to make a mobile service work, it is essential to collect the mobile device context information, which is completed by the context information collector. It works not only before the service is started but also during the process of the service invocation.

Context Adaptor

Once the context information is collected, the mobile service is made available to the particular mobile device. This module makes it possible for mobile service to accommodate changes of the mobile context.

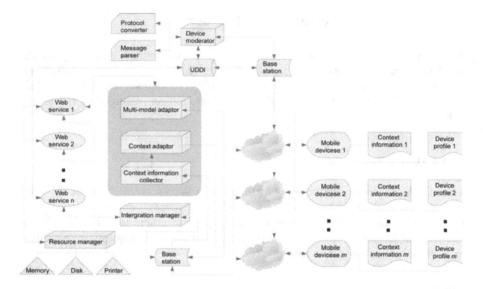

Fig. 12.1. General architecture of mobile services

Device Moderator

To implement peer-to-peer computing for mobile devices, a device moderator is designed to support communications between them. The moderator is responsible for protocol conversions and message parsing. Since any specific device may transmit data via a different protocol, it is necessary to have such a protocol converter, which makes it possible to exchange information between different mobile devices. Another issue is semantic and syntax concerns about transmitted messages. Since software on mobile devices may be implemented by many different developers, it is inevitable that message formats encounter field's meaning or syntax misunderstanding. A message parser is used to solve this problem.

Resource Manager

As a matter of fact, mobile devices are always resource limited even though hardware techniques keep making rapid progresses. This acts as a barrier to carry out complicated computing that requires a large amount of resources. To solve this problem, it is possible to build a resource manager, which provides virtual resources for mobile devices that lack necessary resources in order to continue the computing or services. These virtual resources may contain memory, disk, IO devices, etc.

12.3.2 Mobile Client

Another essential component of the architecture is the mobile client. Different from a regular Web services client, a mobile client must provide context information and a profile that describes its device-specific information and environment. The design is proposed to adapt to the large number of mobile devices available nowadays and in the future.

Device Profile

Device profile is the static data that must be adapted by mobile services. Since there are so many differences among the large number of mobile devices, it is impossible to implement a mobile service that supports all devices. The reasonable approach is to design an adaptive service that is capable of providing services according to changes in the field. Therefore, a device profile is the data that must be provided before a specific device consumes any mobile services. In general, the device profile consists of device resource information, communication protocols, message formats, and access address.

Context Information

On the other hand, context information is the dynamic data that must be adapted by mobile services. The context information is also proposed because of the features of mobile computing, even though for the same requests from the same device, mobile services might have different responses due to context information at runtime or non-runtime. As a matter of fact, location is one of the most important pieces of information in the context. Beside that, specific context information must be required for the services and devices. For example, a temperature-sensitive service must update the current temperature before a service is provided.

12.3.3 Integration Manager

One of the major advantages of Web/mobile services is that it provides an approach to integrate legacy systems [27, 28]. It is possible that none of the available mobile services in the UDDI meets the user's requirements. Under this condition, integrating available services and provisioning them together is a good solution to the problem. An integration script can be created and uploaded to the integration manager, which interprets the scripts, invokes corresponding services, ensures state consistency, and sends responses to a specific mobile device.

12.4 Two General Approaches to Develop Web/Mobile Services

To develop Web/mobile services, there are two major approaches, namely, the induction [29] and deduction [30].

12.4.1 Induction

Using the induction approach, the starting point is to implement all the details and then combine them together as a final Web/mobile service. Developers have to be clear about all the implementation details besides the business logic. For Web/mobile services, those implementation details contain programming methodologies, HTTP, XML, WSDL, SOAP, UDDI, Web server, and databases. In fact, developers have to learn a lot before starting a Web/mobile service implementation. Business logic of the service has to be involved in the implementation details. The development process is tedious and inefficient.

12.4.2 Deduction

The deduction approach is a straightforward one to develop an application that contains too many technical details. Using this approach, those details are transparent to developers, so they can focus on the business logic descriptions.

However, a framework must be built for developers to work on, in which the implementation details are contained. Developers can then follow a certain format to describe business logic and then the business logic is combined with techniques provided by the framework. As a matter of fact, the development process starts from high-level descriptions instead of a low-level detailed implementation. That is why this approach is called deduction.

By using an induction approach, because all the implementation details are taken care of by developers, the Web/mobile services typically have better quality than the deduction one. In general, applications generated by a framework are not as good as the ones that are created manually.

12.5 Case Study – WAS (Wireless Alarm System)

At present, a typical car alarm system does not utilize any information technology. This section describes a novel car alarm system that is supported by advanced technologies, one of which is the mobile services discussed so far.

12.5.1 Scenario

A car is parked in a parking lot, and the owner of the car gets off and walks somewhere. Before he gets off the car, he turns on the alarm system. The owner carries a cell phone with him, with the phone connected to a wireless alarm system (WAS) in the car. WAS has sensors that detect whether the car is touched by someone. If the car is touched, the WAS sends an alert to the owner's cell phone. Thereafter, the owner sends a command to the WAS to protect his car from being stolen. Based on the thief's reaction, different requests/commands are sent to the WAS and the WAS gives feedbacks to the thief until the car engine is locked finally. The WAS works based on not only the owner's commands, but also context information, such as the time, thief's attempt, and resources available.

The complete scenario of the WAS is shown in Fig. 12.2 and is explained as follows:

- A thief touches a car.
- The detector (sensor) of the car gets the information and sends it to the owner's cell phone.
- The owner of the car sends an alert invocation command to the WAS.
- The WAS gives a speech-based alert to the theft, and the volume of the alert is determined by time: if it is daytime, the volume may be higher; otherwise, it is lower.
- The thief continues to tamper the car.
- The detector gets the information, sends it to the owner's cell phone, and prompts that the alert does not take effect.
- The owner sends a picture-taking alert command to the WAS.
- The WAS sends a speech-based alert that a picture will be taken if the theft continues.
- The thief still continues to tamper the car.
- The detector gets the information, sends it to the owner's cell phone, and prompts that the taking-picture alert did not take effect.
- The owner sends a picture-taking command to the WAS.
- The WAS invokes the corresponding service and a picture is taken of the thief and a speech alert is broadcast; if the disk space is not enough to save the picture, the resource manager is invoked and virtual memory is added.
- The thief continues to tamper the car.
- The detector gets the information, sends it to the owner's cell phone, and prompts that the picture-taking did not take effect.
- The owner of the car sends a command to the WAS to lock the engine.
- The WAS invokes the service to lock the engine.
- Hopefully the thief leaves the car alone.
- Optionally, the WAS can also connect to police either automatically or based on the owner's instruction, at any stage, to report the case.

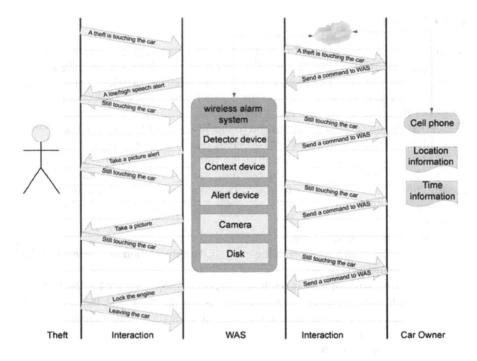

Fig. 12.2. Scenario of WAS

12.5.2 Solution

The architecture of the WAS is shown in Fig. 12.3. This is an example of a typical context-sensitive mobile service. Four services are available in the WAS, namely detector service, context service, alert service, and camera service. Since media data (pictures) must be saved, a resource manager is designed in case that there is no adequate disk space. It is also possible that different types of cell phones are used in the WAS so that a device moderator is designed to support communications between cell phones and mobile devices.

In this implementation, the service is provided by a small device that is connected to the car. In general, HTTP protocol is not supported by it. So a specific communication protocol must be used, for example, 802.11. In addition, the cell phone might be connected to the Internet by GPRS. Therefore, a multimodal adaptation is required. The cell phone must have the capability to detect location and the current time, since this information is the context that supports the mobile service. In summary, each mobile device satisfies the basic requirements of mobile services, i.e., multimodal adaptor, context adaptor, and context information collector are included in each of them.

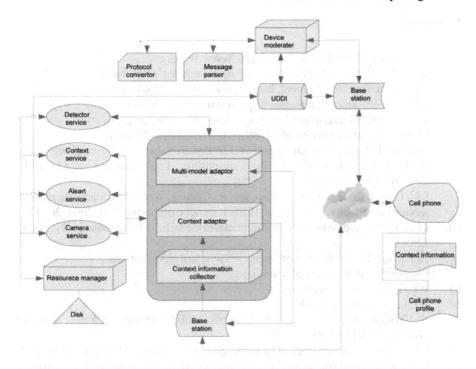

Fig. 12.3. The architecture of WAS

12.6 Summary

Web service is an effective technique for improving business efficiency by automating the collaboration of heterogeneous information systems. Its potential application in the real world is limitless and has been enthusiastically embraced by the IT industry. By extending it to the wireless and mobile world, much more people can be connected to the enormous Web of information and services, anywhere and anytime. The scope and effectiveness of those information services will transcend to a new level, where unlimited new business opportunities exist. Some examples are mobile entertainment, mobile enterprise, and mobile law enforcement. Particularly, mobile Web service is an important approach for realizing m-commerce, which is expected to become increasingly popular, following successful desktop e-commerce. Mobile service is the next direction of Web service. Unique technical challenges lie ahead, if mobile services are to be as successful as regular Web services.

References

1. World Wide Web Consortium, http://www.w3.org
2. W3C, "Web Services Architecture," http://w3.org/TR/ws-arch/
3. Hypertext Transfer Protocol, http://www.w3.org/Protocols/
4. eXtensible Markup Language, http://www.w3.org/XML/
5. Web Services Description Language, http://www.w3.org/TR/wsdl
6. Simple Object Access Protocol, http://www.w3.org/TR/soap/
7. Universal Description, Discovery and Integration, http://www.uddi.org/
8. IEEE Transactions on Mobile Computing, Los Alamitos, CA: IEEE Computer Society, 2002
9. S.N. Chuang, A.T.S. Chan, J. Cao, and R. Cheung, Actively deployable mobile services for adaptive web access, IEEE Internet Computing 8(2), 2004, 26–33
10. J.F. Huber, Mobile next-generation networks, IEEE Multimedia 11(1), 2004, 72–83
11. Universal Resource Locator, http://www.w3.org/Addressing/
12. Bluetooth, https://www.bluetooth.org/
13. Wi-Fi, http://www.wi-fi.org/
14. 3G, http://www.3g.co.uk/
15. U. Varshney, R.J. Vetter, and R. Kalakota, Mobile commerce: A new frontier, Computer 33(10), 2000, 32–38
16. J.A. Senn, The emergence of m-commerce, Computer 33(12), 2000, 148–150
17. S. Schwiderski-Grosche, and H. Knospe, Secure mobile commerce, Electronics & Communication Engineering Journal 14(5), 2002, 228–238
18. B.N. Schilit, D.M. Hilbert, and J. Trevor, Context-aware communication, IEEE Wireless Communications [see also IEEE Personal Communications] 9(5), 2002, 46–54
19. J.-Y. Pan, C.-P. Tan, W.-T. Lee, Context-aware service protocol, Wireless Communications and Networking, 2003, WCNC 2003, 2003 IEEE, volume 3, 16–20 March 2003, pp. 2058–2063
20. G. Niklfeld, M. Pucher, R. Finan, and W. Eckhart, Mobile multi-modal data services for GPRS phones and beyond, multimodal interfaces, 2002. Proceedings of Fourth IEEE International Conference on 14–16 October 2002, pp. 337–342
21. P.D. Le, B. Srinivasan, V. Malhotra, and N. Mani, Resource and load sharing in mobile computing environments TENCON '98, 1998. IEEE Region 10 International Conference on Global Connectivity in Energy, Computer, Communication and Control, volume 1, 17–19 December 1998, pp. 82–85
22. G. Le Grand, J. Ben-Othman, and E. Horlait, Providing quality of service in mobile environments with MIR (mobile IP reservation protocol), networks, 2000 (ICON 2000). Proceedings of IEEE International Conference on 5–8 September 2000, pp. 24–29
23. D. Barkai, Peer-to-Peer Computing: Technologies for Sharing and Collaborating on the Net, Hillsboro, OR: Intel Press, 2001

24. 802.11, http://grouper.ieee.org/groups/802/11/
25. Wireless Application Protocol, http://www.w3schools.com/wap/
26. R.J. Bates, GPRS: General Packet Radio Service, New York: McGraw-Hill, 2002
27. I.-R. Chen, N.A. Phan, and I.-L. Yen, Algorithms for supporting disconnected write operations for wireless web access in mobile client–server environments, IEEE Transactions on Mobile Computing 1(1), 2002, 46–58
28. M. Berger, M. Bouzid, M. Buckland, H. Lee, N. Lhuillier, D. Olpp, J. Picault, and J. Shepherdson, An approach to agent-based service composition and its application to mobile business processes, IEEE Transactions on Mobile Computing 2(3), 2003, 197–206
29. E. Cerami, Web Services Essentials, Beijing, Sebastopol, CA: O'Reilly, 2002
30. B. Li, W.-T. Tsai, L.-J. Zhang, Building e-commerce systems using the semantic application framework, International Journal of Web Engineering and Technology 1(3), 2004, 297–319

13 Location-Aware Services and its Infrastructure Support

Y. Chen and D. Liu

IBM China Research Laboratory

13.1 Introduction

With advances in wireless Internet and mobile computing, location-based services (LBS) have emerged as a key value-added service for telecom operators to deliver personalized location-aware content to their subscribers using its wireless infrastructure. Besides telecom operators, more and more service providers, such as public wireless LAN (PWLAN) providers, enterprises, etc. are developing and deploying location-aware services for consumers and employees to gain more revenue and productivity. These location-aware services providers (LASPs) are facing both technical and social challenges, such as positioning in various environments using different locating mechanisms, location tracking, information delivery models, privacy protection, and developing innovative LBS applications to achieve more business impact and value, among others. It has been realized that a flexible and resilient middleware should be built as the enabling infrastructure to support different players, so that service provider can efficiently and effectively develop and deploy LBS applications, and support innovative location-aware applications quickly. The location-aware infrastructure should address key challenges in location-aware computing as identified in [1], such as technology-independent location sensing, end-to-end control of location information, tracking and predication, and other research challenges involving geospatial information processing and human interaction with these information.

To address these challenges from a middleware infrastructure point of view, a location operating reference model (LORE) is developed to capture the location operation semantics from a layered perspective, where richer location operation semantic is modeled at a higher layer. The presented location operation semantics addresses many issues, for example, how to retrieve the location data, how the location data are modeled, how to fuse location from different location sources, how to query the location data, how to use tracking mechanism to deliver intelligent location-aware notification, etc. In addition to the semantics, two other important dimensions in location-aware computing, privacy protection and management, are also covered by the LORE model. Based on the LORE model, different components of the location-aware infrastructure are built to meet the requirements of different layers and expose APIs to developers to build other components that could plug into the model. In the following sections, several key components of the LORE infrastructure are introduced to show how issues of the location-aware computing addressed and how the composition of components could facilitate the development of various location-aware services.

The chapter is organized as follows. In Sect. 13.2 the LORE model and the infrastructure are presented. Three key components of the infrastructure, location server with common adapter framework (CAF), moving object database (MOD), and spatial publish/subscribe engine are introduced in Sects. 13.3, 13.4, and 13.5, respectively. Section 13.6 outlines the related works, while Sect. 13.8 summarizes our studies and presents future directions.

13.2 Location Operating Reference Model and Infrastructure

Figure 13.1a illustrates the LORE model proposed to capture the semantics and management issues required by building location-aware services. The LORE model includes four domains: operation semantics, management, privacy and security, and agent.

13.2.1 Operation Semantics Domain

The operation semantics domain includes layered components that, from bottom to top, are positioning, modeling, fusion, query, tracking, and intelligent notification. The layered components explicitly describe the dependencies among components, i.e., the upper component uses the functionalities exposed by lower components to build more advanced functionalities. The overall functionalities provide the capabilities for location-aware applications requiring rich location operating semantics.

The *positioning component* addresses the issue of technology-independent location sensing, i.e., how to get the location information of target objects via specific positioning mechanisms. Technical neutral positioning requires that the positioning component interface with heterogeneous positioning equipment and expose a uniform virtual positioning mechanism for other components. The component has to deal with two different modes of positioning: server based and client based. In server-based mode, the location of the target object is measured and calculated on the server side, for example, the GSM networks could determine the subscriber's position by the cell where the mobile phone is being served. In client-based mode, the device does self-positioning, e.g., a device with GPS can determine its location. The major difference between the two modes is how the positioning component retrieves the location information. In the server-based mode, the component pulls the location from server by accessing the location interface (e.g., LIF [2] interface) exposed by the server. In the client-based mode, the device always pushes the location to the positioning component, because it is difficult for client to have a location interface. Two positioning modes require the positioning component to support both push and pull models.

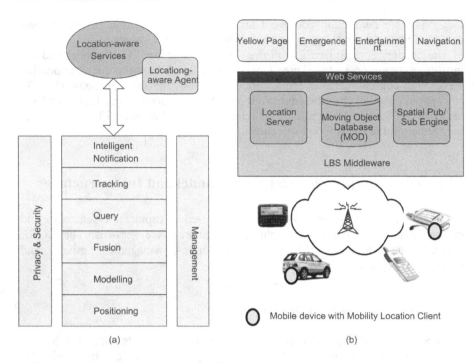

Fig. 13.1. (a) Location operating reference model. **(b)** Infrastructure supporting location-aware services

The *modeling component* describes the semantics of location information. As it comes from different positioning mechanisms, the location data show great heterogeneities in syntax, name, type, and metric system. For example, the LIF exposes location data in XML format, while GPS exposes the location data in compact binary format. GPS can provide velocity information, while most GSM positioning approaches cannot provide such data. The modeling component integrates heterogeneous location data by providing a uniform location model that facilitates the development of flexible services. The location model captures enough information on location, including coordinates, time, velocity, error, and other related information.

The *fusion component* addresses the issue of how to derive accurate location by fusing location reports from multiple devices for one target object. For example, a person has a cell phone, a notebook computer with wireless card, and a GPS receiver, all these devices can be positioned and their location reports are sent to the fusion component for determining the precise location. The fusion component derives the precise location based on predefined rule set, which may define the possibilities of the location accuracy in a different context. There are lot of interesting topics in the location fusion algorithms and rule set to be researched.

The *query component* provides spatio-temporal query interfaces from which applications and end users could get location information of interested objects and issue location-related queries. The query could involve not only current location information, but also historical and/or future location information. A typical location query is *"Please report the location of object X."* Another more complex spatio-temporal query involving historical information is *"Please report the objects that are in zone X at time Y."* The query component uses the positioning and/or fusion components to get the location data. For supporting effective historical and current location information retrieval, the query component employs spatial index to improve the query performance. The spatial index could be R-tree and its variation, grid index, Z-order, and so on. Location predication mechanisms are used by the query component to answer the question about the future location of specific objects.

The *tracking component* plays a key role in LBS in the sense that most of LBS applications require tracking locations of target objects to get the trajectory and provides information based on the location or trajectory. Typical applications include fleet management, taxi dispatch, and road assistance navigation. Tracking puts significant performance impact on the underlying positioning component by positioning the location of the objects continuously or in a specified time interval.

The *intelligent notification component* brings new user experience by sending location-dependent message, including sales promotion, weather and traffic information, nearby events, and so on. A typical application of the intelligent notification is *"Please send me promotion message while I am in zone X."* The key technology behind the intelligent notification is spatial publish/subscription service where users define the events they are interested in, in advance, by specifying spatio-temporal conditions, and then the notification will be delivered to them while the condition is met by taking the users' location information into consideration. When the intelligent notification component is deployed for supporting a large number of users, the spatial pub/sub should also provide scalable mechanism to enable intelligent location-aware services.

13.2.2 Management Domain

The management domain includes all necessary mechanisms to support managing the components in the operation semantics domain except privacy and security issues, such as configuration management, policy management, monitoring and logging, component availability, and so on.

13.2.3 Privacy and Security Domain

Privacy and security play important roles in building location-aware business services where location and the user's private information should be protected from abuse. The privacy and security domain provides a framework to guarantee that the use of location information is under control in the location-aware services environment. In the privacy framework, a user can decide who or which service is able to get his/her location information, and furthermore, the user can define where, when, and why (for what purpose) the information could be retrieved or used. The security framework protects the location information by leveraging proven security mechanisms, such as encryption, digital signature, and secure transportation protocol.

13.2.4 Agent Domain

With advances in mobile computing, mobile devices, such as mobile phone and PDA, get more capabilities in computing, networking, and storage. Taking advantage of the resources in such devices could help build more scalable location-aware services and innovative user experiences. The agent domain introduces the location-aware agent that resides in the mobile device and cooperates with servers to complete the location-aware services. For example, in the tracking service, a self-positioning client, for reducing the network traffic and resource consumption on the server side, could send the location information to server only when the changes of the location is larger than a predefined threshold. The agent domain provides the framework for building service-specific location-aware agent.

13.2.5 Infrastructure Supporting LORE Model

Based on the LORE model, an infrastructure supporting location-aware services is proposed as depicted in Fig. 13.1b. With the support of the infrastructure, location-aware services, such as yellow pages, emergence services, and navigation services, could be created and deployed easily. Three prototypes of the key components in the LBS middleware of the infrastructure are implemented, and all the components in the LORE operation semantics domain are covered.

- Location server provides the positioning, modeling, and fusion components in the LORE operations semantic domain. Also it supports simple query and tracking functionalities. A CAF is introduced to support technology-independent location sensing, which is detailed in Sect. 13.3. The location server supports WAP [3] location API and LIF [2] interface for retrieving and querying location information. Also the location server includes a privacy mechanism to protect the location information from being used without the owner's permission.
- MOD manages the location data collected from the location server and provides the query and tracking components in the LORE operations semantic domain. Continuous, active monitoring engine for location-based services (CAMEL) [4] is built as a MOD prototype which supports queries of both historical and current location information. MOD discussed in Sect. 13.4.
- Spatial pub/sub engine supports the intelligent notification component in LORE operations semantic domain. It provides interfaces for subscribing location-aware message and defining the system wide or

application-specific location information for subscription. The spatial pub/sub is discussed in Sect. 13.5.

Besides the LBS middleware, the infrastructure also includes mobility location client (MLC) that supports the location-aware agent domain in LORE model. An MLC framework based on J2ME is implemented, and it supports the JSR179 specification. The MLC enables the applications in mobile devices leverage local resource and cooperate with a remote server to improve system performance and reduce network traffic.

13.3 Location Server

Location server provides the positioning, modeling, and fusion components of the LORE operations semantic domain, and supports privacy and security domain and management domain in the LORE model. The architecture of location server is depicted in Fig. 13.2. There are three layers in ULS: location APIs, service management framework, and CAF. The location server is designed with three features in mind, flexibility in location API, scalability in command adapter framework, and extensibility in service management.

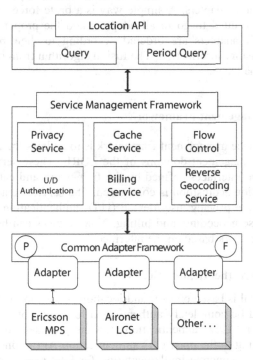

Fig. 13.2. Location server architecture

13.3.1 Common Adapter Framework

CAF provides standard APIs to fetch location information of the target object independent of positioning mechanisms. It defines a common adapter interface intended to shield the details of various positioning systems and provides an adapter implementing this interface for each underlying positioning system. Each vendor-specific adapter focuses only on dealing with transport (HTTP or TCP) and the XML format transcoding. A new adapter is very easily developed and can be plugged into the framework rapidly.

In some specified infrastructures, e.g., in GSM/CDMA wireless network, positioning is a resource- and time-consuming process, CAF provides performance optimization mechanisms, such as connection pools and mobile station identifier (MSID) combination, specified as circle P in the figure. Connection pools are designed to reuse socket connections and restrict the maximum network traffic. MSID combination can bind multiple concurrent location queries to one location query so that the corresponding adapter only communicates to the positioning equipment once and gets location information of multiple MSIDs.

CAF supports multiple adapters simultaneously by various fusion algorithms, specified as circle F in Fig. 13.2. There are many kinds of policy for retrieving location from multiple adapters. A simple way is a brute force solution in which every request is permitted to go to all adapters and the proper one is selected. Another way is all adapters are ordered according to their probabilities and calculated by the history information. The fusion algorithm from multiple adapters is still a research challenge.

13.3.2 Service Management Framework

The goal of the service management framework is to address the issues in privacy and security and management domains of the LORE. These services implement the common service interfaces defined by the framework and can be called prior to or after the location acquisition is configured. The services currently supported by the framework are privacy, user/device (U/D) authentication services, cache, flow control, reverse geocoding, and billing. New services can be developed and plugged to the framework based on the interface.

User/Device (U/D) Authentication Service

Since privacy control is based on user and location acquisition is from device, the pair of U/D should be completely authenticated to avoid potential disclosure of privacy information. U/D authentication service provides the U/D mapping information according to the open U/D authentication API defined in the system. Note that there is no concrete implementation for U/D authentication service in location server. The service is implemented in a domain-specific or solution-specific way. For example, it can be implemented based on the enterprise employee database for an enterprise location-aware system, or on the user profile repository for mobile operators to deploy LBS applications.

Privacy Service

Indiscriminate use of location information for people can infringe people's privacy. Therefore, fine-grained access control to location information is necessary. Privacy service provides the privacy protection mechanism based on role-based access control (RBAC) model with time and location constraints. A user can determine who can access to what location information under which circumstances.

Cache Service

The location acquisition is a time- and resource-consuming process; so the cache service is introduced to accelerate the responsiveness. The goal of cache service is to maximize the usage of available location information under the caching strategy to reduce the consumption of system resource and improve performance.

Flow Control Service

Flow control service prevents location server from traffic congestion and assures a fair play among applications. There are two kinds of constraints: application-independent constraint, such as the maximum concurrence requests' limit, and application-dependent constraint, such as the maximum number of requests allowed within the given period of time and the minimum interval among consecutive successful requests. By supporting effective and efficient flow control, location server could avoid DOS-like (denial of service) attack and resource overspending.

Billing Service

Billing service is a special logging service to facilitate billing for location services. It logs detailed data related to request/response into output files from which necessary information can be extracted by various billing engines to conduct charge and generate billing report.

Reverse Geocoding Service

Reverse geocoding defines the interface to map the raw location data to a normalized and meaningful symbolic address like city, street, zipcode, etc. Consequently, there are two types of reverse geocoding. One is a common process that provides domain-independent reverse geocoding, e.g., at the city or country level, and another is application-specific process, which provides domain-dependent reverse geocoding, such as for an enterprise or office building. The implementation for this service can either be self-developed or a wrapper for third-party reverse-geocoding modules.

13.3.3 Location APIs

Location server addresses the modeling issue by defining a common open location model, including geolocation, address, timestamp, and application-specific information. The location information based on this model adapts to various positioning techniques and covers all information needed by application.

Two kinds of query modes are supported: query and subscription. In the query mode, the location of target object could be sent to the requester immediately. In the subscription mode, the locations of target object are sent to the requester in a specified interval. Two sets of primitive messages' are defined for the modes, the query service primitive messages' set and the subscribe service primitive messages set. Each set includes several primitive messages that describe the interaction pattern between the requestor and the requestee (location server). Based on the two core services and corresponding primitive messages, it is easy to support different industry standard location APIs such as WAP and LIF by mapping them to core services at location server. For example, WAP immediate query service and deferred query service are mapped to query service and subscribe service, respectively.

13.3.4 Positioning Technology

The foundation for LBS is retrieving the location information of the target moving object using various location determination methods. Based on the scope of the moving object, there are two kinds of locating method, indoor positioning for determining location in building and outdoor positioning for determining location out of building. There are lots of indoor positioning methods based on different, mostly proprietary, methods for locating objects, such as using wireless LAN including access points (AP) to which the mobile devices associates, active badge that can be sensed by stationary sensors and positioning based on Bluetooth. Indoor positioning normally achieves more accurate location data than outdoor, the precision of the location positioned by indoor positioning method is normally less than 10 m, even less than 1 m. Traditional outdoor positioning method is global positioning system (GPS), which was developed by the US Navy for military purpose and now is used worldwide for various civil purposes, such as road assistance and air navigation. Normally GPS can achieve 10–30 m accuracy; using differential GPS technology (DGPS) can achieve more accurate location with 1–10 m.

In typical LBS application, mobile users or moving objects are located in a mobile network, e.g., GSM and CDMA, where typical approaches are cell of origin (COO), time of arrival (TOA), angle of arrival (AOA), enhanced observed time difference (E-OTD), and assisted GPS (AGPS). Based on the location of positioning mechanism, there are three modes, handset based, network based, and mixed mode.

In the handset-based mode, the handset or device gets necessary information from the network and calculates the location data, the network-based mode calculates the location data from data collected from network equipment, and the mixed mode depends both on handset and network to estimate the location data.

Cell of Origin (COO)

COO uses the network base station cell area to identify the location of the caller. The accuracy depends upon the cell area and the accuracy can be up to 150 m for an urban area. COO is network based. Although the accuracy is not high and cannot be applied for emergency usage, it is popular amongst the operators as it does not require any modifications in the handset or the network, hence it is comparatively cheap to deploy.

Time of Arrival (TOA)

Here the difference in the TOA of the signal from the mobile to more than one base station is used to calculate the location of the device. This needs synchronization of cellular network using GPS or atomic clock at each base station. The cell sites are fitted with location measurement units (LMUs). By measuring the signal from the mobile phone, the LMUs can triangulate the user's position. TOA is also network based and can achieve more accurate position than COO but it is more expensive because of the large number of LMUs required.

Angle of Arrival (AOA)

This method uses multiple antennas at a base station to determine the incident angle of an arriving signal from the mobile device. The information of two base stations allows to calculate the position of the mobile device. This technique is very sensitive for multipath signals, which have to be accounted for. Installing and aligning antenna arrays on base stations can be a sensitive and costly process. The network-based AOA could achieve the accuracy of 100–200 m.

Advanced Forward Link Trilateration (A-FLT)

This method of location is unique to code division multiple access (CDMA) networks, since they are inherently synchronous in their operation. It measures the phase delay between signals sent to a pair of base stations and then compares this to the same data taken from another pair. Data of three base stations can be used to positively locate a mobile device. The accuracy is from 50 to 200 m.

Enhanced Observed Time Difference (E-OTD)

E-OTD systems operate by placing location receivers, overlaid on the cellular network as a LMU at multiple sites geographically dispersed in a wide area. Each of these LMU has an accurate timing source. When a signal from at least three base stations is received by an E-OTD software-enabled mobile and the LMU, the time differences of arrival of the signal from each BTS at the handset and the LMU are calculated. The differences in time are combined to produce intersecting hyperbolic lines from which the location is estimated. E-OTD schemes offer greater positioning accuracy than COO, between 50 and 125 m, but have a slower speed of response, typically around 5 s, and require software modified handsets. E-OTD is handset based and requires network modification. An example of an E-OTD system is the Cambridge positioning systems (CPS) Cursor™ system.

Observed Time Difference of Arrival (OTDOA)

It is similar to E-OTD but may provide lower yield (percentage of successful position determinations) and operates only on UMTS networks. The accuracy is from 50 to 200 m.

Assisted Global Positioning System (AGPS)

AGPS relies on wireless devices that have an integrated GPS receiver. Assistance data can be transmitted from the network to expedite the GPS signal search and possibly improve sensitivity. The network sends GPS information it has picked up to the mobile handset, which uses this information to detect GPS signals from the satellites. The mobile handset then returns data about the signals it received to the network, where it is used to compute the handset's location. Since the calculation of the exact position is done within the network, the handset does not need to be complex and expensive. The mixed mode-based AGPS can be accurate up to 10 m.

13.4 Moving Objects Databases

CAMEL is a high-performance engine managing location stream to support query, tracking, and intelligent notification components in LORE operation semantic domain. These components are typically from requirements of building next-generation intelligent location-aware services. CAMEL takes a MOD approach that not only stores historical and current location information of mobile users, but also predicts the future locations of a user. In addition, the historical information captured in CAMEL can be used by a data mining tool to discover mobility patterns. Figure 13.3 illustrates the overall architecture for CAMEL. CAMEL is composed of several components that can be physically distributed in different network nodes, which communicate with each other using standard protocols and interfaces such as TCP/IP, HTTP, and JDBC. CAMEL components include location listener (LL), query engine (QE), location filter (LF), trigger handler (TH), data server (DS), database (DB), and admin console (CON). The distributed component based architecture not only makes the system robust but also facilitates the easy deployment of CAMEL in different environments. In this section we briefly introduce the components.

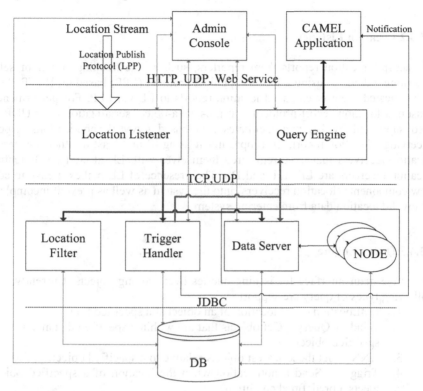

Fig. 13.3. CAMEL – The moving object database architecture

13.4.1 Database

The DB component is the heart of CAMEL, and it serves not only as the location data storage but also as the registry and configuration repository. The registry is used by the system to record component running information, such as host address, port number, and running status. When starting up, each component registers in the registry its host address and port information through which other dependent components can find it. The configuration repository is a central repository for all components to store component-specific parameters. The registry and configuration repositories make the system more flexible and manageable.

Location data of each moving object at checkpoint time are stored in an object checkpoint table (OCT) in the DB. OCT records the historical information of a moving object and is used for historical queries and data mining. For example, the query *"Please give the trajectory of object A from time t1 to t2"* can be answered by functions: *trajectory (select location from OCT, where oid = A and t1 < = t < = t2)*.

13.4.2 Location Listener

LL accepts location reports from reporters, such as the tracking server or self-positioning devices, using a location publish protocol (LPP) based on HTTP. Any authenticated reporter can send location reports to LL via LPP. For performance reason, a location report protocol that uses Java-object serialization over UDP is also supported by LL and facilitates Java-based CAMEL applications. Upon receiving a location report, LL propagates it using IP multicast to other registered location receivers that have registered themselves with LL at start-up. Potential location receivers are LF, TH, and DS. The presence of LL makes it easy to add new components (location receivers) into the system as well as prevent incomplete or invalid location data from entering system.

13.4.3 Query Engine

QE is the main interface for issuing queries over moving objects. Currently, the following types of query are supported:

1. GetLocation – Get location of an object at a specified time.
2. Window Query – Get objects that are within a specified distance from a specified object.
3. KNN – Get the k nearest objects relative to a specified object.
4. Trigger – Send a notification when the location of a specified object meets a predefined condition.
5. Historical query.

The QE exposes its interface using Web services technology and the query supported is represented by WSDL. QE forwards some type of query using TCP to underlying components, such as TH and DS.

13.4.4 Location Filter

A high arrival rate of location reports from location reporters introduces two difficulties: DB insertion of location data may become a bottleneck, and there is a possibility of redundant location data. LF is designed to filter incoming location data to reduce the location stream while guaranteeing its quality. LF is implemented as a location receiver of LL and it writes the filtered location into the OCT DB table. CAMEL implements several filter algorithms that typically reduce the original location stream by 60–80% while maintaining reasonable location accuracy.

13.4.5 Trigger Handler

Spatial trigger is a very important kind of query in a MOD and the base for push-based services in LBS. In CAMEL, trigger Tr is defined by a tuple $Tr = (SP,$ $Sink)$, where SP is a spatial predicate with location variables and $Sink$ is the access point of the notification receiver when the trigger is fired. Currently four $Sink$ types are supported: HTTP, TCP, UDP, and console that only print the notification on the standard output. When a location arrives, TH evaluates it against the defined triggers in the system (binding the location to the predicate) to check if it satisfies any trigger predicate. If one trigger is satisfied, the notification along with the triggered location is sent to the sink defined in the trigger. TH is implemented as a location receiver of LL and it supports trigger operations CREATE TRIGGER and DROP TRIGGER. In Sect. 13.5 we discuss spatial triggers in more detail and how it can support spatial pub/sub engine.

13.4.6 Data Server

As mentioned earlier, CAMEL supports historical, current, and future location queries. In practice, most queries are related to the current location of objects, for example, kNN and window query, and requires real time processing. DS is responsible for processing queries concerning current locations only, which is the most common query in location aware services. To improve the performance of the query related to current location and avoiding access to DB, a main memory snapshot of moving objects is used to manage current locations. More specifically, the snapshot stores the latest locations from reporters instead of current locations of moving objects. The snapshot is organized as a spatial index that accelerates the processing of some queries like window query and kNN query. Meanwhile, the spatial index is required to sustain high-performance updates and lookups because of the high arrival rate of location data. After comparing several spatial index methods, making a trade-off between updating and searching, and taking the main memory characteristic into consideration, CAMEL employs a grid index as its snapshot indexing mechanism. The main reason is that the index scales up well under high update rates and has a clean implementation with good performance in searching in main memory, while an R-tree and its variations suffer from frequent index entry splitting and merging. Dongseop Kwon [5] proposed a lazy update R-tree (LUR-tree) to reduce updates in R-tree. It is, however, based on continuous model that requires predefined moving pattern like speed.

One consideration is whether CAMEL will be set up in a region with a large area, or several small administration regions. An example of the latter is Beijing, a large city composed of several districts. For scalability and load balancing, DS is designed with a distributed architecture where new components, NODEs, are added to handle the moving objects that belong to each region. The use of NODEs brings new issues like distributed query processing and mobile object migration/roaming. In addition, new mechanisms, such as distributed query manager and roaming managers, are also introduced in DS.

13.4.7 Admin Console

CON is a text interface console used to configure and monitor other components in system. The console reads runtime information from the DB and connects to the various components. In addition, the user can use the console to issue queries and use it as a testing tool.

13.5 Spatial Publish/Subscribe Engine

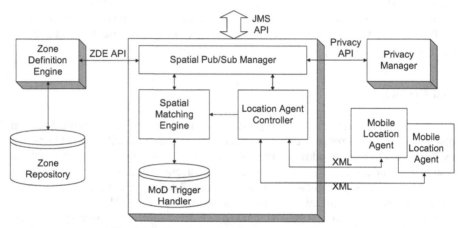

Fig. 13.4. Spatial pub/sub engine architecture

With the support of location server and MOD, LBS could be delivered to support applications such as location-aware yellow pages, road assistance, and tracking. Spatial pub/sub engine brings rich location operation semantic and new user experiences by enabling active messaging push based on users' subscription. In this section, the spatial pub/sub engine to support intelligent notification component of the LORE model is described. The architecture of the engine is illustrated in Fig. 13.4. The engine adopts a novel client-side event processing approach to improve performance by eliminating server side-computing cost. The mobile location agent, cooperating with location agent controller, implements the role of location-aware agent in LORE model. The key components include spatial pub/sub manager, spatial matching engine, zone definition engine, location agent controller, and mobile location agent.

13.5.1 Models

The models adopted by pub/sub engine include spatial event model, spatial subscription model, and notification model.

Spatial Event Model

A spatial event is described by a set of properties specified by name–value (NV) pairs. The three mandatory properties for a spatial event are:

- Object identifier (OID) is a unique identity indicating the owner of the location. The object is a person, a device, or anything that can be located.
- Timestamp (TS) is the time when the object is positioned.
- Location (LOC) is the geographical location specified by predefined spatial reference system (SRS) or textual description of location that could be translated into geographical location via geocoding.

These three properties describe the most important three dimensions pertaining to a spatial event: who, when, and where. Other optional properties could also be introduced to facilitate the processing of spatial events, such as:

- *Uncertainty* (UNC), which describes the uncertainty of the location detected.
- *Location provider identifier* (LPID), which is the provider of the location information.

Besides the predefined mandatory and optional names for properties, other properties could be attached to the spatial event to describe domain- or application-specific information. Usually this information is intended for the subscription application and is not processed by the pub/sub engine.

Spatial Subscription Model

Spatial subscriptions are used by subscribers for expressing their interests on spatial events. In the spatial pub/sub system, a spatial subscription is defined as tuple (*SP*, *ToS*), where *SP* is spatial predicate defined upon location of objects and *ToS* is a type of services that are discussed later. The semantic for a spatial subscription is: *a notification (based on notification model) is sent to a subscriber when an incoming spatial event (based on spatial event model) meets SP and ToS requirement.* Currently two kinds of *SP* are supported in the spatial pub/sub system:

- *Within* predicate has the syntax *(oid-1, oid-2,…,oid-n) within (zone-1, zone-2,…,zone-n)*. The predicate is true if and only if one of the locations of the mobile user (*oid-i*) is within one of the zones (*zone-j*). A zone is used to represent an interested region. Subscription using "within" predicate can be used to support services like "Please send me e-coupon while I am near ABC shopping mall."
- *Distance* predicate has the syntax *(oid) distance (D, oid-1, oid-2, …,oid-n)*. The predicate is true if and only if distance between *oid* and *oid-i* (*1,…,i,….n*) is less than *D*. Subscription using distance trigger can support services like mobile buddy list through which a user can define his buddy list and ask for an alert when any of his buddy is near to him.

The two *SPs* discussed here could meet a large amount of requirement of location-aware applications, and we are investigating other *SPs* for constructing more complex location-aware application. Traditional pub/sub systems are based on the "publish-match-notify" operational cycle, therefore, a spatial event is always sent to subscribers when a spatial subscription is satisfied by the event. In the context of location-aware applications, however, the event filter mechanism could sometimes confuse the user. For example, a user defines a "within" subscription "*(oid1) within (zone1)*", where *zone1* is the predefined area of a shopping mall. When the user (*oid1*) enters the zone (*zone1*), he receives a promotion message. The within subscription is always evaluated to be true when the user stays in the shopping mall, so that he continuously receives the promotion message. Obviously in this case only one promotion message makes sense both to the user and the promotion provider. One-time semantic of subscription specified by *ToS* is introduced to guarantee that the user receives only one promotion message. While the *ToS* is set to once, one-time semantic of subscription is applied by spatial matching engine.

Notification Model

Notification takes the same NV pairs' format as event model and includes two parts:
- Original event part copied from the event information.
- Subscription-specific part derived from the process of matching subscriptions with events.

13.5.2 Spatial Pub/Sub Manager

The pub/sub manager manages event subscription/publish and exposes Java messaging service (JMS) [6] interface. Message selectors from JMS are extended to support spatial subscription whose syntax is based on a subscription model. For a subscription request, privacy check should be done first. Instead of forwarding all subscriptions to spatial matching engine, the pub/sub manager exploits the semantic of the subscriptions and sends "within" subscriptions to a location agent controller. As a result, the workload of spatial matching engine is relieved.

13.5.3 Spatial Matching Engine

The matching engine takes charge of filtering spatial events. For achieving high performance in spatial matching, the engine uses spatial index technique to accelerate the matching process. For "within" predicate, R-tree is employed to index predefined zones based on their minimum bounding rectangle (MBR) and transform subscription evaluation to R-tree searching. Each zone maintains a hash table to record the list of interested users. When a mobile user's location is within a zone and the mobile user is in the hash table of the zone, a notification is sent out. Distance evaluation involves more than one mobile user, and the location cache is provided to store the latest location data of those users and an object trigger graph mechanism is employed to handle the case. Spatial match engine reuses the module called TH from the CAMEL project [4]. The detailed algorithms and performance comparison can be found in [4]. The result shows that the matching engine has good performance and scalability.

13.5.4 Zone Definition Engine

The zone definition engine (ZDE) is used by the system administrator and/or end users to define the well-known zone of interest (ZOI) or user-specific ZOI, which could be a polygon (including rectangle) or a circle. For example, in Beijing, hot places such as Xidan can be predefined in the system as a polygon based on its geographic coordination (latitude, longitude), and each user can define his/her home according to its geographic location. Predefined ZOI can be referred to in a system as a symbol name, like SYSTEM.Xidan or Mike.HOME, where the prefix SYSTEM stands for system defined ZOI, otherwise it can be the name of the user who defines the ZOI. ZDE exposes ZDE API for client applications and spatial pub/sub manager to manipulate zones.

13.5.5 Location Agent Controller

The controller manages all mobile location agents running on intelligent devices. It provides authentication mechanism for these agents, sends related spatial subscriptions to them, receives the matching spatial events from them, and forwards those matching events to the spatial pub/sub manager. When the mobile user involves "distance" predicates, the controller sends a command of periodical location report to the agent, receives locations of the mobile user periodically, and passes them to spatial matching engine. The interface between the controller and the agent is based on XML.

13.5.6 Mobile Location Agent

Running on intelligent devices, the agent focuses on obtaining its location information from embedded positioning modules such as GPS and handling "within" predicates sent by the controller. It evaluates spatial predicates based on the current location of the mobile device. When a spatial predicate is evaluated to be true, the matching spatial event will be sent to the controller. Also mobile location agent can send the location of the mobile device periodically according to instructions from the controller.

13.6 Related Works

There are lots of research and efforts both in academia and industry on location-aware computing. To our knowledge, however, none of them proposes a comprehensive framework on building location-aware services like the LORE model. Several separate works related to partial components or domains in the LORE model are introduced in the following paragraphs.

Much research has focused on developing services architecture for location-based applications. Building on the active badge location technology, researchers at Olivetti proposed and developed the architecture for a distributed location service [7]. The Olivetti system is tied to the specific positioning technology. ULF Leonhardt presents a global general location service to support location-awareness in open distributed systems [8]. He emphasizes the importance of integrating various location techniques and depicts a hierarchical, semisymbolic location model and uses policy-based access control to protect location privacy. Although his effort influences our location model, it is short of abundant auxiliary services to simplify LBS development. The work of Tom Pfeifer et al. [9] has many aspects in common with our work on location server. They introduce a modular location-aware service and an application platform. The platform provides modular, unified access to various services, which are commonly used by multiple applications. Its prototype, however, is based on CORBA, and less effort has been made for privacy control. Privacy is considered to be the critical issue in LBS. Ajith K. Narayanan presents the idea of logical location contexts, which provides enhanced privacy in location-aware mobile computing [10]. His work has helped us to build an advanced privacy control mechanism.

MOD research addresses the issues of storing and processing continuously moving objects arising in a wide range of applications, including traffic control and monitoring, transportation and supply chain management, digital battlefields, and mobile e-commerce [11]. The pioneering work in MOD is from Wolfson at University of Illinois in Chicago. In their DOMINO prototype [12, 13], they proposed the MOST model [14] and FTL query language for modeling and querying moving objects' locations. CAMEL shares the same goal of managing moving objects' locations and also attempts to manage historical locations of moving objects for further use in data mining.

The challenge in MOD is to support dynamic, continuously evolving data and moving queries. As a spatio-temporal DB, MOD manages data with spatial and temporal dimensions. To improve query performance, indexing moving objects is needed. Several methods of indexing moving objects ([15–19]) based on R-trees have been put forward in literature. Two data models are investigated on indexing moving objects:

- *Continuous model.* Moving objects are modeled as points in MOST that start moving from a specific location with a constant velocity vector. Some indexing methods, like time-parametrized R-tree (TPR-tree) [17] and indexing scheme [20], are developed based on this model.

- *Discrete model*. In this model, only the locations of moving object are stored in a DB as (LOC, TS) tuples. Pfoser et al. [16] further developed the model to describe trajectory segments and proposed two access methods based on the model: spatial temporal R-tree (STR-tree) and trajectory-Bundle tree (TB-tree) to index the historical trajectory of moving objects.

The continuous model implicitly requires that moving objects report both their location and velocity to the location management system. This model is feasible in areas like vehicle tracking and digital battlefield where advanced devices equipped with GPS receivers can report the required data to the system. However, in LBS that serve mobile users, a large portion of the potential customers only have cell phones that have no capacity of self-positioning and require assistance from the wireless network to determine their locations. Thus, the velocities of many mobile users are hard to determine directly in real life. For this reason, CAMEL employs a discrete location model instead of a continuous model, and it receives only location information with TSs from a tracking server or from the device itself. The inherent differences between the two models suggest different ways to process queries and to index locations.

Gryphon [21] and Siena [22] are content-based pub/sub systems. Gryphon provided an efficient and scalable filtering algorithm to handle event matching. Siena provided expressive subscription language for subscribers to select interested events. Both of them supported primitive data types while our spatial pub/sub system can handle complicated spatial data type. Ivana Podnar et al. presented the architecture to delivery content to mobile users based on the publish/subscriber paradigm [23]. Their publish/subscribe system can work together with location management to deliver location-aware message to mobile users. However, the spatial pub/sub system proposed in this research focused on spatial-related information matching and performance improvement. An event specification language that can be used to express spatial events is presented in [24]. Semantics of basic spatial events is the same as ours. They paid more attention to event definition and event composition, while we put in great effort on spatial subscription and spatial event matching. Work at Cambridge has investigated services that, based on registration of interest in user locations and proximities, notify clients when changes occur [25]. Their system architecture called CALAIS was based on distributed events technology and a dynamically modifiable R-tree index, fed with a stream of location events, was used to monitor locations and proximities. CALAIS was suitable for the support of context-aware applications operating within a typical indoor, office domain, while our spatial pub/sub system is more suitable for outdoor environment by leveraging intelligent devices to provide a high-performance spatial event processing. A scalable location-aware system Rover [26], developed in University of Maryland, College Park, provided similar function as our eagle demo. Rover focuses on achieving system scalability to very large client sets by introducing an action model concurrent software architecture and our Eagle demo targets high-performance spatial pub/sub mechanisms.

13.7 Summary

This chapter presented the LORE model including domains of location operation semantic, privacy and security, management, and location-aware agent. Based on the LORE model, an infrastructure – LBS middleware-is built to support the rich sets of location-aware applications. Three key components of LBS middleware, location server, MOD, and spatial pub/sub engine, implement the domain components of the LORE model, enable innovative location-aware applications, and bring new user experiences.

There are still some issues in the LORE model to be addressed and integrated to the LBS middleware. How to support fusion component is to be investigated to achieve more accurate location information from multiple location sources. The privacy model and privacy provisioning mechanism should be developed to protect the users' privacy information while they enjoy new services, especially services based on intelligent notification. The LBS middleware requires enhanced and integrated management tools for facilitating the deployment and management of location-aware services aligned with other IT applications in enterprise or computing environment.

In order to make LBS a successful business for all players in the value system that includes location providers, device providers, service providers, end customers, as well as middleware/infrastructure providers, a sound business model, including role and responsibility of each player, B2B processes, etc. has to be defined and refined. In the foreseeable future, wireless operators will continue to play a key role in the LBS value system, and building a value chain around wireless operators should be a technical and business requirement. In the long run, locating capability and connectivity will become ubiquitous, making it possible for semiautonomous LBS value network to grow rapidly.

Acknowledgment

The authors would like to thank James Yeh, Xiao Yan Chen, Xiu Lan Yu, Fang Yan Rao, Ying Li, Xiao Cheng Ding, and Thomas Li for their contribution to our LBS-related research, which is the base of this chapter.

References

1.   C.A. Patterson, R.R. Muntz, and C.M. Pancake. Challenges in location-aware computing. IEEE Pervasive Computing, 80–89, April–June 2003
2.   WAP Location Protocol, http://www.wapforum.org/
3.   Location Inter-operability Forum (LIF), http://www.locationforum.org/
4.   Y. Chen, F. Rao, X. Yu, and D. Liu, CAMEL: A Moving Object

5. D. Kwon, S. Lee, and S. Lee. Indexing the current positions of moving objects using the lazy update R-tree. Proceedings of the IEEE International Conference on Mobile Data Management, Singapore, pp. 113–120, 2002

6. Java Messaging Service, http://java.sun.com/products/jms/

7. Database approach for intelligent location aware services. Proceedings of International Conference on Mobile Data Management, Melbourne, Australia, pp. 331–334, 21–24 January 2003

8. A. Harter and A. Hopper. A distributed location system for the active office. IEEE Network 36(1):62–70, 1994

9. U. Leonhardt. Supporting location-awareness in open distributed systems. PhD Thesis, Imperial College of Science, Technology and Medicine, University of London, 1998

10. T. Pfeifer and R. Popescu-Zeletin. A modular location-aware service and application platform, The Fourth IEEE Symposium on Computers and Communications, ISCC'99, IEEE Computer Society Press, pp. 137–148, 1999

11. A. Narayanan. Realms and states: A framework for location aware mobile computing, Proceedings of the First International Workshop on Mobile Commerce, WMC 01, Rome, Italy, pp. 48–54, 2001

12. O. Wolfson, B. Xu, S. Chamberlaina, and L. Jiang. Moving objects databases: Issues and solutions. Proceedings of Tenth International Conference on Scientific and Statistical Database Management (SSDBM), pp. 111–122, 1998

13. O. Wolfson, A.P. Sistla, S. Chamberlain, and Y. Yesha. Updating and querying database that track mobile units. Distributed and Parallel Databases 7(3):257–387, 1999

14. O. Wolfson, A.P. Sistla, B. Xu, J. Zhou, and S. Chamberlain. DOMINO: Database fOr MovINg Objects tracking. Proceedings of ACM SIGMO International Conference on Management of Data, pp. 547–549, Philadelphia, PA, June 1999

15. A.P. Sistla, O. Wolfson, S. Chamberlain, and S. Dao. Modeling and querying moving objects. Proceedings of 13th IEEE International Conference on Data Engineering, pp. 422–432, Birmingham, UK, April 1997

16. P.K. Agarwal, L. Arge, and J. Erickson. Indexing moving points. Proceedings of Annual ACM Symposium Principles Database System, pp. 175–186, 2000

17. D. Pfoser, Y. Theodoridis, and C.S. Jensen. Novel approaches in query processing for moving object trajectories. Proceedings of the 26th International Conference on Very Large Data Bases, pp. 395–406, 2000

18. S. Saltenis, C.S. Jensen, S.T. Leutenegger, and M.A. Lopez. Indexing the positions of continuously moving objects. Proceedings of the ACM SIGMOD Conference, pp. 331–342, 2000

19. G. Kollios et al. Indexing animated objects using spatiotemporal access methods. TimeCenter Tech. Rep. TR-54, 2001

20. S. Saltenis and C.S. Jensen. Indexing of moving objects for location-based services. Proceedings of the IEEE International Conference on Data Engineering, pp. 463–472, 2000

21. G. Kollios, D. Gunopulos, and V.J. Tsotras. On indexing mobile objects. Proceedings of the 18th ACM Symposium on Principles of Database Systems, pp. 261–272, 1999

22. M.K. Aguilera, R.E. Strom, D.C. Sturman, M. Astley, and T.D. Chandra, Matching events in a content-based subscription system. Proceedings of Principles of Distributed Computing (PODC '99), Atlanta, GA, pp. 53–61, May 1999

23. A. Carzaniga, D.S. Rosenblum, and A.L. Wolf. Achieving scalability and expressiveness in an Internet-scale event notification service, Nineteenth ACM Symposium on Principles of Distributed Computing (PODC2000), Portland, OR, pp. 219–227, July 2000

24. I. Podnar, M. Hauswirth, and M. Jazayeri. Mobile push: Delivering content to mobile users. Proceedings of the 22nd International Conference on Distributed Computing System Workshops (ICDCSW'02), pp. 563–570, 2002

25. M. Bauer and K. Rothermel. Towards the observation of spatial events in distributed location-aware systems. Proceedings of the 22nd International Conference on Distributed Computing Systems Workshops (ICDCSW'02), pp. 581–582, 2002

26. G. Nelson, Context-aware and location systems. PhD Thesis, University of Cambridge Computer Laboratory, 1998

27. S. Banerjee, S. Agarwal, K. Kamel, A. Kochut, C. Kommareddy, T. Nadeem, P. Thakkar, B. Trinh, A.M. Youssef, M. Youssef, R.L. Larsen, A. Udaya Shankar, A.K. Agrawala. Rover: Scalable location-aware computing. IEEE Computer 35(10):46–53, 2002

14 Mobile Commerce and Wireless E-Business Applications

S. Song

IBM China Research Laboratory

14.1 Introduction

From the historical perspective, commerce, and the way people do business have always been affected by the progress in communications and computations and vice versa. The desire of ancient merchants, to reach more and varied customers, motivated them to undertake difficult and hazardous journeys across deserts, oceans, and mountains. This desire resulted in heavy investments in infra-structure and thus the progress in transportation and communication industries.

The continuing interplay of commercial success and communication technology is going to push new means of interaction for rich content and on multiple communication media. In recent times, there has been a dramatic increase in the use of powerful mobile devices. These mobile devices, ranging from pagers to mobile phones, wireless PDAs, and wireless laptops, are changing the way people interact at work, on the road, and at home. The sophistication of the mobile devices and wireless technologies has advanced to the stage of mass-market usage and acceptance. Just as we saw a surge in e-business by PC browser clients, we are now experiencing a similar phenol-menon in mobile commerce and wireless e-business applications by users of these more advanced mobile devices.

Mobile computing, also known as pervasive computing, provides a series of technologies that enable people to communicate in various new ways and accomplish personal and professional tasks using this new class of portable, intelligent, wireless mobile devices. These mobile devices give people access to information at any time and any place. Although some countries have invested more in wireless technologies than others, diverse technologies and systems are implemented in different parts of the world. The capability and number of users in all countries of the world are growing at a tremendous rate.

Wherever you live, mobile computing will, in the very near future, become a prominent means of accessing information on the Internet. Just as the PC browser client market matured from accessing the Internet simply for browsing and gathering information to full-blown e-business and e-commerce, the same is happening for mobile devices.

14.2 Mobile Commerce

14.2.1 What is Mobile Commerce?

Depending on the goals of the user and tools used in the operating, the term *mobile commerce* (or *m-commerce*) can vary widely in meaning. Generally defined, m-commerce refers to the use of mobile devices to partially or completely perform a transaction electronically from a commerce service provider for the exchange of goods or services for monetary consideration. Simply put, m-commerce is defined as any type of transaction of an economic value having at least at one end a mobile terminal via a mobile telecommunications network.

Under this definition, m-commerce represents a subset of all e-commerce transactions, both in the business-to-consumer and business-to-business area. There is a variety of m-commerce scenarios that have different implications for a classical e-commerce infrastructure.

E-commerce (or *electronic commerce*) is a general term for any type of business, or commercial transaction, that involves the transfer of information across the Internet. This covers a range of different types of businesses, from consumer-based retail sites like Amazon.com, auction and music sites like eBay or MP3.com, respectively, to business exchanges trading goods or services between corporations. E-commerce has expanded rapidly over the past 5 years and this growth is forecast to continue or even accelerate. It is likely that in the future the boundaries between "conventional" and "electronic" commerce will become increasingly blurred as more and more businesses move parts of their operation onto the Internet.

M-commerce on wireless Internet is growing explosively. It combines two highly explosive technologies, Internet and wireless communications. M-commerce enables you to do business with your customer at any time and any place without any geographical constraint theoretically.

Unlike e-commerce, m-commerce has four unique characteristics:

1. *Convenience and accessibility.* In an m-commerce world, people are not constrained by time and place.
2. *Diversity.* Web browser assisted with email is the most common e-commerce model. There are various methods to do m-commerce because of the diversity of mobile devices and wireless network services.
3. *Personalization.* Where the PC is often shared across multiple users, mobile devices are typically operated by and configured for a single user.
4. *Limitation.* Because of the device capability, connection reliability and security problems, today's m-commerce is mostly used in B2C and for small- and low-value items.

14.2.2 Benefits

The introduction of m-commerce should bring a series of benefits to consumers, service providers, and telecommunication operators. The typical beneficiaries now include:

1. *For consumers.* Consumers can access on-demand, at the point of purchase, the best prices in the marketplace. This can similarly be done right now via clicking on their mobile device.
2. *For service providers.* M-commerce provides a technology to increase merchants' sales and drive management efficiency for service providers because companies can send product information to customers in time according to their personalized preference via a web page promotion or a mobile alert to increase their willingness to buy a product.
3. *For telecommunication operators.* The more the airtime used by customers, the more the revenue telecom operators can achieve. Furthermore, the operator can get money from fees charged to service providers for each m-commerce transaction.

14.2.3 Requirements and Key Issues

M-commerce creates new business opportunities for different players, including mobile network operators, equipment manufacturers, content providers, solution developers, and system integrators. However, there is still quite a lot of issues that have to be addressed and resolved for different players in order to have general acceptance from mobile users.

Security

Security is one of the critical issues for successful adoption of m-commerce. And, with the innate portability of mobile devices, a higher level of security is required if stolen devices are not to be used to purchase goods or send fraudulent messages. In time, it is expected that mobile devices will support payments, hence the need for security is significant.

To feel confident of trading in this marketplace, both business and individual consumers have to feel sure that the risk of fraud is minimized. There are four main security features that are needed to create a trusted, secure environment for trading electronically:

- *Confidentiality.* Electronic messages that are sent must not be visible to eavesdroppers.
- *Authentication.* Communicating parties must be certain of each other's identity.
- *Integrity.* Communicating parties must know when the data they send have been tampered with.
- *Nonrepudiation.* It must be possible to prove that a transaction has taken place.

Organizations are working together to deliver public key infrastructure (PKI) solutions across wireless solutions. A PKI provides a security framework that tightly binds digital identities to content providers and wireless customers and while securing their associated transactions. With the increase in connectivity between consumers and the Internet, the need for trusted and secure e-business transactions is also projected to increase in both frequency and value. PKI frees up m-commerce growth by letting secure electronic transactions (SETs) take place at any time and any place.

Privacy

Mobile network location-based services offer content and service providers an unprecedented avenue to target consumers based on their physical locale. With location technology steadily improving, it is possible that subscribers could soon be placed with near pinpoint accuracy. Consumer advocates view this to be a threat to personal privacy, with the associated issues of undue surveillance, spam, and profiling.

There are proposals to stave off potential privacy problems such as using low granularity location information when precision is not critical or desirable, obtaining explicit user consent before releasing location details to advertisers, and guaranteeing user anonymity even when data are used by applying only aggregate information without identifying specific individuals. Subscribers ought to stay vigilant by getting acquainted with the privacy policies of their service providers, who in turn should have strict measures in place for securing user profile databases to prevent misuse or abuse.

Wireless Network

The necessary network infrastructure for wireless mobile computing in general combines various wireless networks, including cellular, wireless LAN, private and public radio, satellite services, and paging. As compared with wired networks, wireless radio communications add new challenges.

The handsets in the wireless radio networks do not normally always communicate with the network infrastructure, i.e., they are unreachable. There are numerous reasons for this behavior. First, disconnections may be voluntary, e.g., when the user avoids network access during nightime, or while in a meeting. It is often reasonable to cut the wireless communications with the network to reduce cost, power consumption, or bandwidth use. The handheld devices are very likely not always reachable and can become at any time unreachable if the user wants it.

In case of many wireless networks, communication channels have much less transfer capacity than wired networks. This is caused by the fact that the modulation used and channel allocation schemes designed for voice traffic have rather modest upper bounds. Further, the wireless communications are much more error prone than the wired communications and require much redundancy in the channel coding of the payload. In spite of the redundancy in the channel coding that makes correcting bit errors in large scale possible at the receiving end, retransmission of the data is required more often here than in the wired networks.

Another phenomenon also observable in the wireless world is burst traffic. As found on wired networks, the traffic pattern is burst, and this holds in different time scales.

Mobile Devices

Mobile devices that are of interest to m-commerce can be divided into several categories, such as physical size of devices, screen capability, input method, processing power, memory capability, power consumption, security, network connection, and operating system. Properties of mobile devices can highly impact popularity of m-commerce and also bring high complexity to implement an m-commerce architecture.

Mobile Payment

Mobile payment is one of the major issues of m-commerce applications. Most of mobile users are concerned about payment procedures, and whether payment transactions are secure and there is enough or not.

Credit card payment is the most popular payment method on Internet as its penetration is high enough, and it has been widely adopted on e-commerce via Internet. However, privacy and security should be resolved as mentioned earlier. To further fortify security, credit card companies have implemented authentication systems that verify the identities of transacting parties. Advocated by Visa and MasterCard, the SET system is supported by major banks but has been relatively costly for merchants to implement, delaying its widespread adoption. But the biggest shortcoming of credit card settlement schemes by far relates to the expensive fixed transaction overheads that favor higher value transactions, precluding cost effective use for small value payments.

Mobile payment systems are forced to evolve to accommodate new e-commerce phenomena such as m-commerce conducted on cellular phones and the proliferation of innovative online charging structures such as payment per access by data volume or elapsed time. An ideal system must handle all payment values large and small, cope well with high transaction volume, track billing comprehensively, adapt to sophisticated pricing structures, and interface seamlessly with diverse payment platforms like mobile phones and wireless terminals.

One mobile payment solution is that mobile network operator can act as a trusted third party to their subscribers if the operator can guarantee that the customer pays only if both products are delivered in good condition and are interoperable. The operator is responsible in this case for the whole billing process, thus the mobile users just pay the operator, who is then responsible for distributing the money to the corresponding content, service, or goods providers. This approach is convenient for mobile users because they settle payment to their operator.

14.2.4 M-Commerce Architecture

E-Commerce Architecture

M-commerce is the evolution of e-commerce and its implementation is built on the e-commerce infrastructure, so we first introduce a typical e-commerce architecture, as shown in Fig. 14.1.

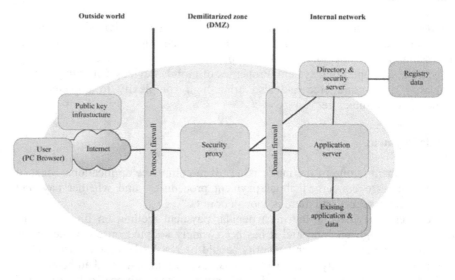

Fig. 14.1. A typical e-commerce architecture

This e-commerce architecture is based on a three-tier architecture where the security proxy is separated from the application server. The security proxy resides in the demilitarized zone and is responsible for redirecting application requests to the web application server. The application server runs the application business logic and communicates with the back-end systems and databases.

The main nodes of the architecture are listedhere.

- The protocol firewall prevents unauthorized access from the Internet to the demilitarized zone. The role of this node is to allow the Internet traffic access only on certain ports and block other ports.
- The security proxy is used to redirect the application requests to the application server node. The advantage of using security proxy server is that we can move the application server and all the application business logic behind the domain firewall. The security proxy has two functions. The first one is to intercept incoming requests, and map or transform user credentials into the format acceptable to the application server that was the original target of the request. The second function is to implement single sign-on between heterogeneous Web application servers.

- The domain firewall prevents unauthorized access from the demilitarized zone to the internal network. The role of this firewall is to allow the network traffic originating only from the demilitarized zone and not from the Internet.
- The application server provides the infrastructure to run the application logic and communicate with internal back-end systems and databases.
- The directory and security server provide information about the users and theirs rights for the application. The information may contain users' IDs, passwords, certificates, access groups, and so on. This node supplies the information to security services, such as authentication and authorization service.
- The existing application and data node depict the back-end systems and databases that are accessible from the Web application.

Mobile Commerce Architectures

Different technical variables, e.g., device, communications network, and protocols, influence how a m-commerce solution is implemented. In general, m-commerce solutions can be divided into four modes: online web, notification, asynchronous, and voice. Apparently these modes do not have to be used in isolation but can be combined within an application design.

Online Web Mode

Like PC users, mobile users access m-commerce applications via a web browser on mobile devices. But different mobile devices may adopt different communication protocols and presentation languages, and have different display characteristics, hence a gateway should be deployed in the m-commerce architecture to support various pervasive devices, as shown in the lower left ellipse area of Fig. 14.2.

A common instance of this topology would be a WAP-enabled device with a cellular network and a gateway that includes the WAP gateway software. The WAP gateway is responsible for transforming a WAP request into an HTTP request to the web application.

There is an important choice for the configuration of the gateway in this topology. It may be configured by the cellular network provider and connected to the public Internet. This is the most common configuration and is denoted as a solid connection. This gateway configuration is important for an ISP providing a set of public services to subscribers.

Alternatively, the gateway can be configured by the e-commerce solution provider, and the mobile network provides a direct connection to that gateway and does not involve the public Internet. This option is shown here as a dotted line. This gateway configuration is relevant for a solution for a service intended only for an enterprise group requiring mobile access to m-commerce services.

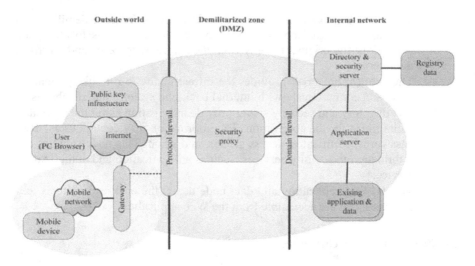

Fig. 14.2. Online web mode

Notification Mode

The notification mode enables e-commerce features such as real-time message alerts on a very small portable device. Additional examples include other appealing services such as:

- Instant messages on Internet
- SMS/MMS messages on a GSM/GPRS cellular network

In order to be effective, the notification mode requires that the mobile network be "always-on." Figure 14.3 shows how the notification mode can be employed in an m-commerce solution. A message gateway is installed to offer different messaging communication stacks, and perform message queue management, and notification event management.

Asynchronous Mode

The asynchronous mode of operation is highly prevalent with the current generation of PDAs, irrespective whether they have occasional network connectivity or are only connected to a PC for synchronization in the office or base location. The mode enables users to download content to mobile devices and operate the content offline without network requirement, so it could greatly enhance the user experience for m-commerce especially when the wireless network bandwidth is slow or the quality of the wireless signal is poor. The range of content that can be considered under this mode includes:

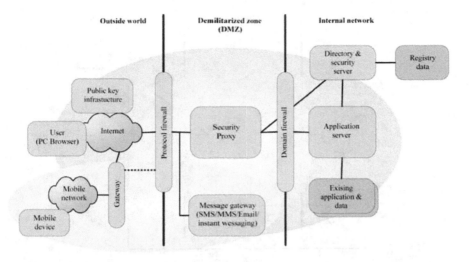

Fig. 14.3. Notification mode

Personal productivity data. Calendar, to-do lists, memos, e-mails, documents
- Web content
- Database forms' input
- Application messaging

Figure 14.4 depicts the architecture of the asynchronous mode.

The mobile device can synchronize with the sync gateway based on IP connectivity to a sync server, or if that gateway is on a PC, using a serial cable, USB, Bluetooth, or infrared connection. The sync gateway can connect the device to a range of content-not only to a database in the case of forms' input, but also to personal productivity data.

For Web content, the sync gateway allows the mobile device to synchronize personalized Web content. The personalized selection is determined using the synchronous mode, usually through a PC. The user selection can be associated with a profile in the Directory service.

Voice Mode

With the limited keypad space and screen size of mobile devices, voice technology promises enhanced input and output functionality for m-commerce. Technologies that enable voice interaction with applications have matured to the point where it can be used intelligently by application designers both for command input and for system response.

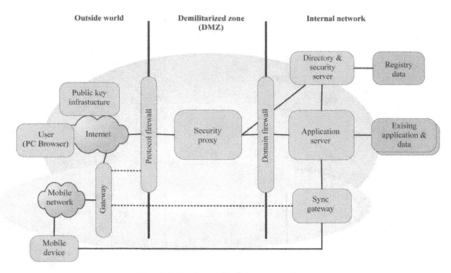

Fig. 14.4. Asynchronous mode

The voice mode of interaction with an application requires speech recognition and text-to-speech synthesis (TTS) technology. In principle, either of these transforms can occur on either a client or a server. However, unlike personal computers, the current generation of mobile devices does not have the processing power to perform these transforms, and so we assume in the following that they are performed on a voice server. We further assume that the range of input commands is constrained so that a personalized voice recognition function is not required.

As shown in Fig. 14.5, a voice server is installed to act as a proxy client to the web application server. The web application server provides dynamic content in an XML format known as VoiceXML. The voice server renders VoiceXML into speech. VoiceXML also contains dialog tags that prescribe possible inputs. The user's vocal response can be matched to one of the allowed responses and the voice server transmits this as a new request to the web application server.

14.3 Wireless e-Business Applications

Wireless e-business applications are sometimes called mobile applications. Mobile applications give people the convenience to access relevant information and to act on that information at any time and any place. In the context of e-business, it translates into increased sales, better customer service, and lower transaction costs.

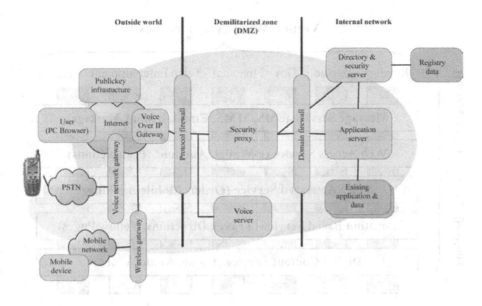

Fig. 14.5. Voice mode

Just like e-business, there are two types of wireless e-business applications, horizontal and vertical. Horizontal applications are those used across a broad selection of end users. Vertical applications, on the other hand, are optimized for a specific target market. Figure 14.6 illustrates the basic categories for mobile applications.

14.3.1 Horizontal Applications

Messaging Services

Since 1992 short messaging service (SMS) has been providing the ability to send and receive text messages to and from mobile phones. Each message can contain up to 160 alphanumeric characters. After finding it tough going in the GSM market, SMS suddenly started to explode since the year 1998. About 90% of SMS messages are voice mail notifications or simple person-to-person messaging. The rest is mobile information services, such as news, stock prices, sport, weather, horoscope, jokes, etc. Additionally, SMS e-mail notification, SMS chat, and downloading of ringing tones have been offered recently. SMS is an ideal technology for pushing information from one-to-one or one-to-few. It is expected that SMS will show further rapid growth, with the number of messages doubling every six months. Many mobile applications have been initiated using SMS as a platform. In some countries, SMS is also used as a certification and payment method in e-commerce.

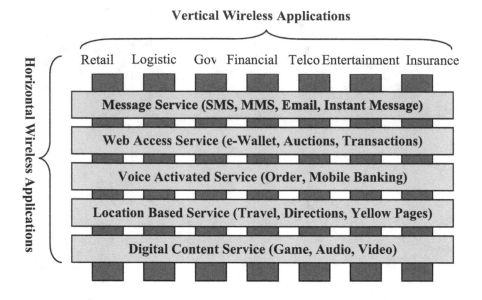

Fig. 14.6. Vertical and horizontal mobile applications

Multimedia messaging service (MMS) is a new global messaging standard that enables a wide range of different media elements (including text, pictures, audio, and video) to be combined and synchronized in messages sent among mobile devices. MMS is designed to be used on 2.5G, which includes general packet radio service (GPRS), and 3G with the experience being richer as the network, bearer, and device capabilities permit. For device users, MMS enhances personal connectivity and productivity through a more immediate exchange of rich content – for instance, while on the road, users can receive a localized city map; or while at a conference, an up-to-the-minute graph or layout. For network operators, MMS promises additional revenue as a result of increased air time, heavier all-around usage, service differentiation, and customer loyalty. By deploying MMS today, operators can secure a strong market position early in the personal multimedia era.

Web Access Services

Web access is one of the most popular mobile applications. Typically there are two kinds of Web access for mobile applications. One is online, the other is offline. The online mode is analogous to the wired browsing. The only differences are wireless connection and mobile browser.

The offline mode is based on synchronization. The content is synchronized between the mobile device and back-end services before it is used or processed. A synchronization service helps synchronize the user's desktop or back-end server and mobile device, keeping both devices updated. Users can automatically transfer their websites, files, contacts, and calendar events into their mobile devices before leaving the office or when there is a need.

Voice-Activated Services

The strength of a good mobile application implementation lies in how well it deals with natural human behavior. Hence voiceXML technology is proposed to bring voice control to websites, enabling voice response paradigms to navigate websites and general speech recognition interfaces.

Currently, customers dialing into an automated voice-menu-driven phone system have to go through a series of complex commands and inputs to get to their goal. The "Please press 1 for..., 2 for..." approach is not the easiest one to follow, forcing the customer to remember the required option after listening to all of the options on the voice menu or more often than not repeating the menu choices. This system is not expected to work well for mobile applications. A possible solution is a voice interface driven by predefined questions and comments. In such a system, mobile users might ask mobile application services questions such as "What is my account balance?" or "When is the next showing of Troy at Century?" Mobile application services can then recognize common voice inputs and respond to them accordingly.

Location-Based Services

The ability to locate the position of a mobile device is a key to providing geo-graphically specific value-added information that simulates mobile applications. Mobile location services may either be terminal or network based. The largest push for this technology is coming from the USA. There, mobile telephone operators had been forced by the FCC to provide emergency 911 services by October 2001 in such a way that the location of the caller could be determined within a radius of 125 m in 67% of all cases.

Until now, location information has been the monopoly of the carriers and network operators themselves. In the future, this may not be the case. For example, Bluetooth or WiFi can contribute to location determination in that a network fixed devices may constantly communicate with mobile devices over a Bluetooth network or wireless LAN. In such a solution, a mobile device can request its own location relative to that of the fixed device because the fixed device already knows its location.

Location-sensitive information becomes a key in mobile applications. Knowing the location of the user drives the service and application offering to a level that creates significant value to the user. Users need local information about their normal local environment. Location-specific information is even more valuable in new environments, when traveling.

Digital Content Services

The higher data bandwidth afforded by 2.5G and 3G networks will be a boon to mobile applications in the field of interactive multimedia entertainment. In particular, the distribution of multimedia content such as computer games, audio, and video will be wireless and on demand.

14.3.2 Vertical Applications

Entertainment

Mobile users will be able to download different programs, products, or services to their devices, such as MP3 files, videos, or games. They will also be able to play games and listen music online via mobile devices.

Financial Applications

The volume of transactions that customers conduct with their financial institutions, as well as the importance of these transactions, creates an important source of value. Users will be able to pay bills and transfer money from different accounts.

Enterprise Applications

Through their wireless devices, employees will be able to fill out forms, read and download files, send and receive messages that are important to their business. This will improve productivity by decreasing the amount of time that employees spend looking for different information. For example, workflow can now be extended to mobile devices, ensuring not only that the right people are always involved in the process but also that processes are not delayed due to an individual being out of office.

14.3.3 Wireless E-Business Application Architecture

A typical wireless e-business system includes the components shown in Fig. 14.7:

Wireless Handheld devices

Mobile devices are portable physical devices, which sense and collect information and transmit the data wirelessly, ranging from pagers to mobile phones, wireless PDAs, and wireless laptops. There are a large variety of ways through which wireless handheld devices, which cover GSM, GPRS, CDMA, CDPD, WiFi, infrared, and Bluetooth, send and receive information.

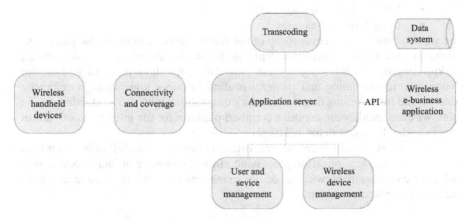

Fig. 14.7. Wireless e-business system components

Connectivity and Coverage

From the end user point of view, the mobile device is used to access a local cell tower (or access point). The cell tower is responsible for sending the data to a base station. From the base station point of view, the data are delivered to a mobile switching center that connects all the base stations.

There are two types of data transmission: circuit switched and packet switched. Circuit-switched transmission entails a dedicated circuit for communication between two dedicated devices. Its duration is the length of the entire communication. Packet switching does not require a dedicated line between the sender and recipient. This method enables the data to be divided into a number of packets and to be sent to their intended destination using different paths.

Wireless Middleware

The main goal for the wireless middleware is to help alleviate the problems inherent to delivering content and applications to mobile devices. As we know, most of today's Internet applications and services are designed for the desktop client like browser, email, etc. How to expand the existing Internet applications to the wireless application and service domain with minimum modifications on them is the major challenge for the wireless middleware. For example, wireless middleware could let you link Internet content and applications to the wireless Web without rewriting the application, database interfaces, or HTML site.

Usually, the wireless middleware components provide the following benefits:
- Multiple mobile devices' support
- No effort or minimum effort to rewrite the existing applications
- Wireless user and service authentication, and authorization
- Continuous wireless access to content and applications

- Mobile device management
- Long-term cost savings

The wireless middleware eases many of the functions that can otherwise plague the conversion of a corporate system to wireless. It can ease the process of transforming markup languages, delivering content and data, providing protocol and device recognition, incorporating and properly routing business logic through enterprise systems, and transforming data formats for compatibility with different databases. In short, wireless middleware creates a common platform for the integration of various sources under diverse systems and displays.

The wireless middleware system often comprises the following common modules: gateways, application processing engine, content handling module, user and service management, wireless device management, and interfaces to the back-end legacy application system.

Gateways

Wireless e-business application is dominated by a variety of non-IP network protocols, which are either proprietary or specific to a particular industry. As soon as devices want to access the Internet or other computer networks a protocol conversion is required. This task is done by a connectivity gateway. Gateways are the point of entry into a server network. They isolate the individual communication channels and their specific requirements from the rest of the back-end systems. Gateways, like a WAP Gateway or a Palm Webclipping Proxy Server, convert TCP/IP to protocols optimized for wireless data transmission.

Gateways can either be hosted by a service provider offering wireless access to his customers or an enterprise environment providing wireless access to the enterprise data to his employees.

Application Server

A web application server is the base component in the e-business application environment. It is the foundation of a comprehensive business solution. Technically, an application server is always referred to as a container. This means that web-based applications are deployed, then reside and run in this container. In the wireless e-business application environment, an application server must have more functionalities, for example, an application server might provide message queuing, thus ensuring that data- and content-requested transactions to and from wireless devices are delivered only once. This is particularly important in financial transactions, where a transfer request should not be performed twice.

In addition, an application server might participate in the intelligent transformation of Web-based application interfaces. As previously explained, intelligent transformation is more than a process of simple data conversion. An intelligent transformation system – wireless middleware combined with an application server – "understands" content and so can break HTML into menus and submenus suitable to the handheld device.

Intelligent transformation limits the size of files delivered to mobile devices, thus improving the transfer rate. This benefits users by sparing them content that is both too expensive and too unwieldy to be accessed by a handheld device such as video clips, large images, and large subsets of data.

The wireless application server can use common device characteristics to display the data. Using these standards helps productivity in development. User IDs and handheld device IDs are stored in the database at the application server level. Once a login request is received, the application server accesses the database. The middleware database is used to prepare and format the data for the device requesting the login. The application server will also compare the registered device ID to the user ID for additional security verification. The application server communicates with the gateway server for the specific device that initiates the request. The gateway then pushes the information to the handheld device based on the connectivity platform being used (e.g., CDPD, SMS, Mobitex, or CDMA).

The application server must accommodate different handheld platforms such as thin-client devices (IP-based devices), two-way paging, SMS messaging, and smart phones. It must then deliver data formatted for that specific device, end-to-end, in a reliable and secure manner.

Content Handling Module

Besides transport protocol conversion done by the connectivity gateways, content should also be adjusted for specific classes of devices. Traditionally, there are two ways for accomplishing this task. One is that the back-end application is responsible for generating the appropriate content layout and formats to adapt the various mobile clients. The other is by using transcoding technology in the middleware. Transcoding is one such kind of content adaptation technology, which tailors information for a specific device by transforming its format and representation.

The purpose of transcoding is obvious: When the content providers deliver content to various mobile clients, they need to accommodate device specific constraints such as limited memory, slow data transmission, and small screens. Transcoding automatically translates content into different representations for each class of receiving client systems. This simplifies authoring, deployment, and maintenance dramatically. An arbitrary multimedia web page can be provided to Internet TVs, handhelds, and WAP phones without change. It is even possible to adapt content from legacy systems into a standardized Internet representation, or transcode Web pages to the proprietary format of a specific client device.

Transcoding is the process of formatting the content (data) according to the handheld device request using XML, XSL stylesheets, and DTD files, as shown in Fig. 14.8. This method enables end users to access data universally regardless of the device type.

Once a request from a handheld device is initiated, the application server intercepts the request to identify the device type and capture the content. Using

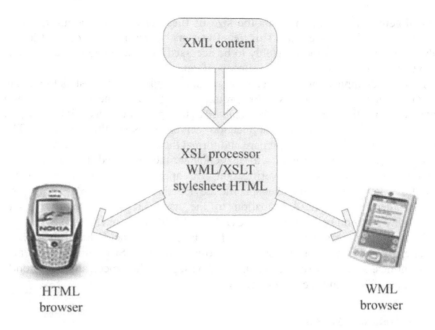

Fig. 14.8. Transcoding process

several logical processes, the application server engine processes the data into an XML document, which can be communicated to the back-end system via the API connection. The result is then transcoded (processed) using XSL stylesheets and reformatted for the handheld device that made the initial request. The application server engine selects the correct screen template, formats the data for the handheld device, and delivers the data requested. XSL is used for data transformation definitions, where the API will exchange messages between the back-end system and the application server. XSL and XSLT stylesheets are mainly used to manage the presentation of the data, whereas XML handles the data itself.

User and Service Management

User management module provides the wireless e-business administrator to add a new user or delete an existing user. Service management module is to help the wireless service administrator to deploy and manage the service with more ease. It usually provides tools for the administrator to install, activate or inactivate, monitor, stop, and uninstall the wireless e-business applications. Wireless middleware also takes care of the access control for both the wireless users and wireless services.

In the wireless e-business deployment phrase, the wireless middleware could help the administrator to specify the allowed user groups correspond to the deployed wireless e-business applications. In the runtime phrase, the middleware is responsible for mapping the wireless device ID to the user ID, then check out if such a user is allowed to access the requested service. Only the authorized wireless user's request could be passed through to the back-end service. If the back-end service initiates the request to push the information to one wireless user, the wireless middleware will check if the target recipient belongs to this service. Any out-range recipient will be filtered by the middleware to help reduce the problems raised by wireless content spam.

Mobile Device Management

With the growth of high-end wireless handheld device market and the realistic needs for the wireless e-business applications, the wireless device management has become one of major concerns for both service providers and enterprise IT managers. Different from PC clients that are consistently tethered to a LAN and protected behind a firewall, wireless devices such as PDA and smart phones are, by nature, far more difficult to manage. The following five aspects are important for the wireless device management:

- Software deployment
- Asset and configuration management
- Fault management
- Device control and data security
- Back-up and restore

Pushing and Pulling model

Pull technology is when the handheld device initiates the communication using its gateway to request data. The data are then pulled from the application server down to the handheld device. The dominant paradigm of communication on the World Wide Web and in most distributed systems is this request–reply model.

Push technology is when the application server is in control over the handheld device. The application server makes basic content decisions and pushes data to the handheld device without waiting for the client's request. Push model is usually adopted when the back-end applications attempt to overcome the deficiencies of pull model by allowing the information producer to "push" the information to the user without the user initiating the request first. A typical push application, for example, could be the news alert. After the news subscriber specifies the news category that interests him to the news service provider, the back-end agent would intelligently deliver the corresponding news content via MMS to the wireless end users.

In either method, authentication must take place first. Under the pull model, the gateway transfers the handheld's request to the application server. The application server usually needs to map the device ID to the user ID. After confirming that the wireless request user has the access right to the back-end application, the application server will translate the wireless device request into the application-specific request by complementing parameters like user ID, user request data, device type, etc. This information is then sent to the back-end application system using the API between the application server and the back-end system. The application server receives the reply information from the back-end system and reports it to the handheld device. The reply data are formatted into screens appropriate to the device that requested the data either via transcoding module or by the back-end application itself. The push model is often used in event-based applications. When some specific even happens, the back-end application initiates a push request. The application server will check if this application has the authorization to push the data to the wireless user to avoid the push spam. Then the application server will help to deliver the push content to the wireless user via the gateway modules.

In general, the pull model is often applied to the client–server/browser–server model, which provides an architectural approach for organizing the software for distributed platforms. The basic scheme is that clients initiate the request to the servers, then servers respond to the client request. It is suitable for real time and session-based applications. The push model is often applied to the event-based model. The architecture is more loose connected. The basic scheme is peer-to-peer communication and server-to-client communication. The store and forward functionality is also the basic function module in the model, which is used to temporally store the data in case the push recipient does not retrieve the push data in time. There are several common channels available for push model like SMS, MMS, etc.

Both pull model or push model have their benefits. In the pull model, the client presentation capability is more powerful in providing the complex user interface dialog, while the push model provides the flexible notification mechanism helping the back-end application initiate the information delivery to its end users. How to combine these two mechanisms to improve user experience is one of the interesting research topics and challenges in the wireless e-business applications (Fig. 14.9).

14.4 Case Study

14.4.1 IBM WCS M-Commerce Solution

IBM provides a wide range of e-commerce solutions for customer business needs. Within the IBM WebSphere brand, IBM has enabled an e-commerce product suite to support m-commerce: IBM WebSphere Commerce Suite (WCS) V5.1.

Architecture Overview

This product suite is very versatile and can be used for B2C, B2B, and auction e-commerce websites. WCS V5.1 provides a pure Java programming model that is conducive to supporting mobile clients. Features have been added to WCS V5.1 to provide integration and support for mobile devices.

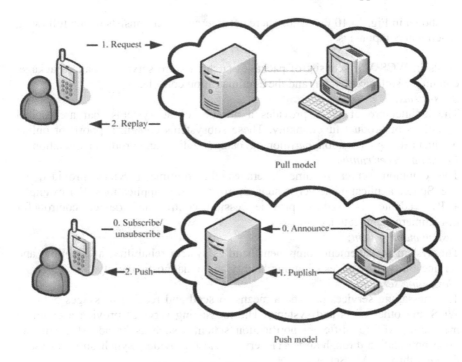

Pull model

Push model

Fig. 14.9. Pull and push model

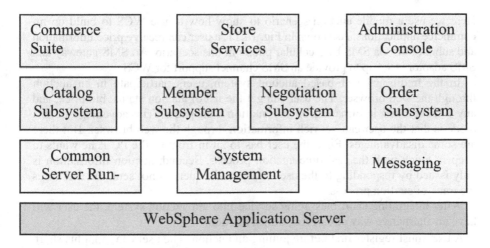

Fig. 14.10. WebSphere commerce server

As shown in Fig. 14.10 the WebSphere commerce server consists of the following functional components:

Tools:

Tools in WCS V5.1 consist of packages such as store services, loader package, commerce suite accelerator, and the administration console.

Subsystems:

The architecture of WCS provides a number of subsystems that are logical groupings of product functionality. These subsystems contain support for online product catalog navigation, partitioning, categorization, and product association.

Common server runtime:

The common server runtime leverages the runtime services provided by WebSphere application server to support m-commerce applications. For example, a PvC adapter is used to provide session control and device control for m-commerce applications.

System management:

The system management component handles system reliability, availability, and serviceability. It provides a logging facility and a diagnostic facility.

Messaging services:

The messaging services provide a means to send and receive messages between WCS and other users and systems. The messaging services provide a common messaging API for different notification schemes such as broadcast email and order notification through an SMTP server. It also provides asynchronous message delivery through MQSeries.

Mobile Auction Scenario

Here we use a mobile auction scenario to show how to use WCS to build up m-commerce applications. As shown in Fig. 14.11, a user can receive price information and submit bids via SMS by a cellular phone in this scenario. An SMS gateway and SMS adaptor is set up to provide an SMS channel support for WCS.

In the traditional web-based auction system, users participate in an auction through the web browser. The user can get the list of auction status, bid price, and any other related information on the auction web pages. The advantage of this mode is that the user can get rich information through the web browser. But there are some disadvantages. First, the user has to sit in front of the PC if he wants to keep in touch with the real-time auction process. Second, auction information is only issued by responding to the user request. If a query is not sent, the user loses the track of auction process.

After integrating short messaging service into the auction system, the user will have an alternative way of carrying out an auction.

A user must register first before joining an auction. The user can input his short message-enabled phone number on the WCS user registration web page. The user does not need to stay in front of a PC. If another user submits a higher price to the

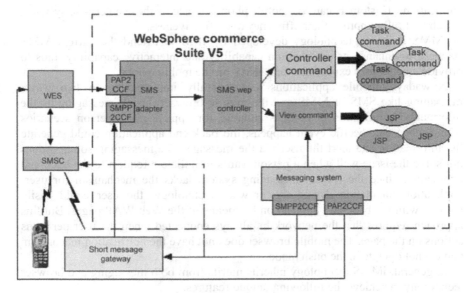

Fig. 14.11. A mobile auction scenario

same item, a short message notification will be sent to all the users who have bid the item. The short message notification carries the new bid price. The receiver can modify the price and send it back to the WCS server if he wants to make another bid. After that, a server-side confirmation will be sent back to inform whether the new request has been successfully submitted or has failed to be accepted.

14.4.2 Interactive MMS (iMMS)-Based Mobile Workflow Solution

Workflow is a means of automatically routing work based on business rules and assigning work based on a person's position or functional role in an organization. Because workflow can help in faster work completion, gaining productivity, and improving the quality of process management, workflow becomes one of most important applications in an enterprise. For example, it is widely used in office automation systems.

Currently most workflow applications can only be accessed by PC via browser or other client. If a user is not using a PC, he/she cannot use the system via a mobile device. In order to deal with this problem, an iMMS-based mobile workflow solution is being developed by IBM, which provides a mobile workflow middleware and software development kit (SDK) to provide mobile supports by integrating with existing workflow applications or developing new workflow applications. Customers can use mobile phones to access these enterprise systems, which will fully improve their efficiency and effectiveness.

iMMS is a new technology developed by IBM to extend the current MMS standard to enhance its presentation capability and interactive capability, thus to provide a better user experience than MMS on the mobile phone.

Nowadays, mobile applications are generally implemented in two ways: messaging like SMS or MMS and the mobile browser. Using messaging as the information notification channel is suitable for application-to-person scenarios where when the specific event happens, the back-end application could generate the information and alert the user via the message. The messaging solution does not solve the issue well when a person wants to initiate a request to the back-end application since the current messaging system lacks the mechanism for user-application interaction. Using the browser technology, the user could easily interact with the back-end application by means of the Web/WAP pages. But this approach requires that the network be always connected when the user performs actions on the page. The mobile browser does not have the notification mechanism and cannot operate in the push mode.

In general, iMMS technology inherits merits from both messaging and browser technology to achieve the following unique features:

Guaranteed message delivery: Since the MMS center has the MMS store and forward capability and guarantees the message delivery, the back-end application can have freedom from message loss incidence.

Notification – Push mode.

Interactive messaging capabilities – Pull mode

Offline operation and client side management – Offline mode

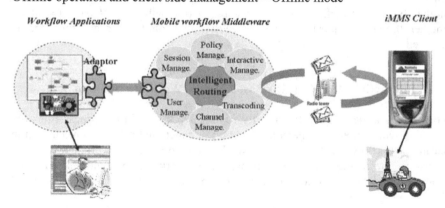

Fig. 14.12. iMMS workflow solution

As illustrated in Fig. 14.12, there are three main three components in the mobile workflow solution:

    1.   *iMMS client.* Runtime container of iMMS messages on mobile device. Its functions include (1) iMMS message's presentation and management and (2) local interaction support between mobile user and iMMS messages.

2. *Workflow adaptor*. A plug-in for workflow engine. Its main functions include (1) monitoring and delivering information of workflow activeties to mobile workflow middleware and (2) controlling workflow engine and business processes according to the commands of mobile workflow middleware;

3. *Mobile workflow middleware*. Bridge of workflow applications and mobile users. Its main functions include (1) transcoding workflow activities into iMMS messages and routing to corresponding mobile users and (2) unwrapping incoming iMMS messages and controlling workflow applications (via workflow adaptor) on behalf of mobile users.

When there is an urgent business mobile workflow task, an iMMS message is sent to the iMMS client of the mobile user. This iMMS message includes both the task information and the possible actions on that task, and the iMMS client allows the mobile user to view the workflow task content on the mobile devices. The iMMS message contains the control elements such as check box, form, button, etc. to help people to interact with the back-end application efficiently. Therefore the mobile solution allows the mobile user to accomplish the workflow tasks in offline model. Mobile users can save the related workflow in processing data in their mobile devices and retrieve them when needed. Once they submit the "send message" request, all the work for data transmission is handled by the iMMS client. Because the iMMS client guarantees the delivery of the iMMS message, the user does not need to worry about the network connection status and other issues.

The target users of the solution are enterprise mobile employees. This solution can improve enterprise productivity by enabling mobile users to handle their workflow activities easily and reliably at any time and any place by using mobile phones only, even in conditions where wireless network performance is poor.

14.5 Summary

This chapter provided an overview of m-commerce and wireless e-business applications, including wireless networks, security issues such as single sign-on and privacy, location-based services, notification services, mobile payment, short message, multimedia messages, content handling, mobile user management, mobile device management, and a variety of architecture issues. In addition, we provided a case study to present wireless applications such as interactive mobile workflow management (iMMS) solution.

References

1. W. Hu, C. Lee, and W. Kou, (2004), Advances in Security and Payment Methods for Mobile Commerce, Idea Group Publishing

2. WAP Location Protocol, http://www.wapforum.org/
3. IBM (2004), Pervasive computing and wireless technology, http://www.ibm.com/software/pervasive
4. National Institute of Standards and Technology (2000), Digital Signature Standard, FIPS Publication 186-2, February 2000. Available at http://cstc.nist.gov/fips

Glossary

Application Programming Interface (API)
A set of the specific methods, services, or instructions prescribed by a computer program by which a programmer writing an application program can make reqests of the computer program.

Authentication
Providing assurance that the entity (user, host, and so forth) reqesting access is the entity that it claims to be.

CDMA2000 1x
CDMA2000 1x operates in various freqency bands of 450, 800, 900, 1700, 1800, 1900, and 2100 MHz, and is fully backward compatible with IS-95.

Certificate
A digital credential in a public-key cryptography system, which contains the certificate holder's name and public key, a serial number, the expiration date of the certificate, and the digital signature of the certificate authority that issued the certificate.

Certificate Authority (CA)
A trusted entity that is part of a public key infrastructure (PKI) and that creates, issues, and manages certificates for PKI users.

Certificate Revocation List (CRL)
A list of certificates issued by a certification authority (CA) that are no longer valid. The CRL is maintained and published by the CA.

Code Division Multiple Access 2000 (CDMA2000)
CDMA2000 is an evolution from IS-95 and is able to support high-rate data over the air interface. CDMA2000 is currently under the standardization of Third-Generation Partnership Project 2 (3GPP2) and is a family of standards.

Common Adapter Framework (CAF)
It provides a standard API to fetch location information of the target object independent of positioning mechanisms. It defines a common adapter interface intended to shield the details of various positioning systems and provides an adapter implementing this interface for each underlying positioning system.

Context Awareness
Context awareness refers to the capabilities of a computational system to understand the situation and adjust its behavior accordingly.

Cookie
A file sent by a Web server to a browser and stored by the browser. The cookie includes a destination address as a URL, possibly with wildcards. When the browser sends any request to a Web server corresponding to the destination address, the browser attaches the cookie to the request. Cookies are used to identify the consumer, especially for repeat access to the same site.

Denial-of-Service Attack (DoS Attack)
In the running of a given protocol, some malicious clients initiate numerous requests for the connections with se rver, which include numerous stateful cookies'for a server to maintain. As a result, the computation and storage of the server are seriously taken up, the request from good'clients may be refused, and the server system may even break down.

Destination-Sequential Distance Vector Routing Algorithm
A table-driven algorithm based on the BellmanFord routing mechanism.

Digital Cash
An electronic form of cash in a cash-like e-payment system with which a person can make online payment for goods or services purchased over the Internet.

Digital Check
An electronic form of a check in a check-like e-payment system where the check can be conveyed across computer networks.

Digital Signature
A digital string produced by applying a cryptographic algorithm with the private-key information on a message/document to authenticate the message/document.

Dynamic Source Routing Algorithm (DSR)
A source-initiated on demand-routing protocol-an alternative to table-driven routing algorithms. DRS creates a route only upon an explicit source-initiated request.

Elliptic Curve Cryptography
Elliptic curve cryptography is a branch of public-key cryptography proposed by Victor Miller and Neal Koblitz in the mid-1980s. It is an alternative method to the older RSA system and offers the relative advantage of higher performance in terms of speed and space usage. This makes it especially suited for implementation on devices with limited computation capability, storage area, battery power, and communication bandwidth.

Enhanced Messaging Service (EMS)
It is an application-level extension of SMS for mobile phones available on GSM/GPRS and CDMA networks. EMS now allows users to send text messages

containing sounds, pictures, and animations. EMS messages that are sent to devices that do not support it will be displayed as SMS transmissions.

ETSI
European Telecommunication Standards Institute

General Packet Radio Service (GPRS)
GPRS is part of ETSIs GSM Phase 2-development to support packet switching within GSM. It can be upgraded from GSM without extra infrastructure.

Heterogeneity
A remarkable trait of future computing environments. The range of computing devices is widening continuously, and they dramatically differ in computing capabilities, including storage, processing power, screen size, networking, to name a few. Such devices would seamlessly interact and coordinate to fulfill a users reqirement. Heterogeneity in this sense is a double-edged sword. On the one hand, specialties of various devices provide alternatives for different user preferences; on the other, the challenge to bridge those devices becomes imperative.

HyperText Transfer Protocol (HTTP)
Standard transfer protocol used in the Internet, which defines how messages are formatted and transmitted, and what actions Web servers and browsers should take in response to various commands. For example, when entering a URL in a browser, one actually sends an HTTP command to the Web server and instructs it to fetch and transmit the reqested Web document.

International Mobile Subscriber Identity (IMSI)
In GSM, the user identity is represented by IMSI and is stored in the subscriber identity module (SIM) card. The identity of the MS is represented by the international mobile station eqipment identity (IMEI). The IMEI is allocated by the eqipment manufacturer and registered by the network operator. SIM card can be transferred between mobile stations, user service only relates to the SIM card and is not dependent on a particular MS.

Interactive MMS (iMMS)
iMMS is a new technology developed by IBM to extend the current MMS standard to enhance its presentation capability and interactive capability, and thereby provide a better user experience than MMS on the mobile phone. It provides a mobile workflow middleware and software development kit (SDK) to provide mobile supports by integrating with existing workflow applications or developing new workflow applications.

Internet Protocol Security (IPSec)
A set of security functions and options available at the IP level.

Internet Service Provider (ISP)
A company that provides users with access to the Internet. For a monthly fee, the ISP provides users with a software package, user ID, password, and access phone number. Some ISPs also provide users with a modem to enable users to access the Internet.

IS-95
IS-95 was standardized by the USA. IS-95 is also known as CDMA One. IS-95 has two substandards: IS-95 A and IS-95 B. IS-95 A is a 2G technology and is mainly designed for voice communication. IS-95 B can provide higher data rates by simultaneously using multiple code channels for each user

ITU
International Telecommunication Union

Key
A small piece of data used in conjunction with an algorithm to encrypt or decrypt (a) messages/data of arbitrary size (see also PKI), or (b) an attribute whose value serves to identify a uniqe record in a   database/table (e.g., employee ID number may be the primary key used to locate and identify a specific employees personal data, such as name, address, telephone number, salary).

Lightweight Mobile Code System (LMCS)
LMCS handles strong mobility of mobile code and caters to various modes of mobility

Location-Based Services (LBS)
A key value-added service for telecom operators to deliver personalized location-aware content to their subscribers using its wireless infrastructure.

Location Operating Reference Model (LORE)
It is developed to capture the location operation semantics from a layered perspective, where richer location operation semantic is modeled at a higher layer.

Media Access Control (MAC)
A layer that is responsible for the management of packet transmission.

Message Authentication Code (MAC)
A fixed-size binary code obtained by applying a shared-key cryptographic algorithm to an arbitrary amount of data to serve as an authenticator of the data.

Micropayment
A payment of small amounts, close to or below the minimal credit card fees (of about 20 US cents).

Micropayment System
A system allowing merchants to charge many payments of small amounts (micropayments) from customers over open data networks such as the Internet by using one or more payment service providers (PSPs).

Mobile Switching Center (MSC)
MSC which monitors the signaling between the mobile station (MS) and the core network, and performs switching between the base transceiver station (BTS) and core network. It is also responsible for resource management for each BTS.

Multimedia Message Service (MMS)
It extends the capability of SMS to support more media types such as images, audio clips, video clips, and more.

NetBill
A payment system where the digital check is used to sell and deliver low-priced information goods.

NetCheque System
A distributed accounting service supporting the creditdebit model of payment.

Nonrepudiation
A proof that the consumer approved a particular action, usually a payment.

Offline Payments
Payments between the consumer and the merchant that do not reqire communication with other parties such as the PSP.

Order Information (OI)
Information included in a SET transaction to describe the transaction.

Payment Approval
A process where the customer agrees to a particular payment.

Payment Authorization
A process where the PSP takes responsibility for a payment, in particular by indicating that there are funds to cover the payment.

Payment Gateway (PG)
Entity in a SET transaction that handles credit card verification and authorization of transactions.

Payment Order (PO)
A message indicating payment to the merchant.

Payment Routing Table (PRT)
A message sent by a PSP to a merchant or another PSP, indicating the terms under which the PSP sending the PRT is willing to receive payment orders issued by other PSPs.

Payment Service Provider (PSP)
An entity that maintains a long-term relationship with customers and merchants, receiving payments of aggregated (large) amounts from customers, and passing aggregated payments to the merchants.

Penalty Payment
A payment by a merchant who has had too many disputes and/or chargebacks.

Personal Identification Number (PIN)
A security method whereby a (usually) four-digit number is entered by an individual to gain access to a particular system or area.

Physical/Physiological Biometric
A biometric that is characterized by a physical characteristic rather than a behavioral trait (in contrast with behavioral biometric).

Private Key
In public-key cryptography, this key is the secret key. It is primarily used for decryption and also used for encryption with digital signatures.

Public Key
In public-key cryptography, this key is made public to all. It is primarily used for encryption but can be used for verifying signatures.

Public-Key Cryptography
Cryptography based on methods involving a public key and a private key.

Public-Key Infrastructure (PKI)
Structure used to issue, manage, and allow verification of public-key certificates. PKI is a security framework for messages and data, based on the notion of a pair of cryptographic keys (i.e., one public and one private) and used to facilitate security, integrity, and privacy.

Pull Technology
It is when the handheld device initiates the communication using its gateway to reqest data. The data are then pulled fr om the application server down to the handheld device. The dominant paradigm of communication on the World Wide Web and in most distributed systems is this reqestreply model.

Push Technology
It is when the application server is in control over the handheld device. The application server makes basic content decisions and pushes data to the handheld device without waiting for the clients reqest. The push model is usually adopted when the backend applications attempt to overcome the deficiencies of pull model by allowing the information producer to push"their information to the user without the user initiate the reqest first.

Quality of Service (QoS)
QS reqirements are vastly different among all types of applications and should be considered in the GPRS network.

Radio Frequency Identification (RFID)
The use of radio waves to facilitate wireless (contactless) communication with a chip or device.

Response Time/Processing Time
The time period reqired by a biometric system to return a decision on the identification or verification of a biometric sample.

Secure Electronic Commerce
A form of commerce conducted via electronic means, but designed with security in mind to enable identification, authentication, authorization, or payment processing.

Secure Electronic Transaction (SET)
A protocol for secure payment processing over the Internet in which credit card information (e.g., Visa, MasterCard) is not read or stored by a merchant. The protocol links many parties, including the customer, merchant, acqirer, and certification authorities. The protocol is designed to emulate card-present transactions.

Secure Electronic Transaction (SET) Protocol
SET is a protocol produced by MasterCard and Visa. This protocol provides identity authentication, confidentiality, integration, and nonrepudiation of the transaction data.

Secure Sockets Layer (SSL)
A protocol originally introduced by Netscape to secure communication between Web servers and Web clients, supported by most Web browsers and servers, and superceded by TLS.

SemiOffline Payments
Payment protocol where most transactions are offline (involving only communication between the consumer and merchant, not with the PSP), but sometimes communication with the PSP is necessary.

Short Message Services (SMS)

It is a non-realtime delivery system. It allows the exchange of the text messages between subscribers. The text can comprise words, numbers, or alphanumeric combinations.

Simple Object Access Protocol (SOAP)

SOAP is the major approach to access regular Web services. In essence, SOAP is an XML message transmission approach over HTTP. It is assumed that HTTP is always available at the service client end and that XML messages can be processed there when Web services are being consumed.

Smart Card

A plastic card with an embedded chip to enable payment processing or digital identification. A typical smart card chip includes a microprocessor or CPU, ROM (for storing operating instructions), RAM (for storing data during processing), and EPROM (or EEPROM) memory for nonvolatile storage of information.

Soft Handoff

Soft handoff means a mobile station (MS) can connect to more than one base station (BS) during the handoff process, and the MS can select the link with the best connection qality. Further, soft handoff allows an MS to have continuous connection with the BS so that the connection is never interrupted.

Software Agent

A computer program that acts autonomously on behalf of a person or an organization to accomplish a predefined task or a series of tasks.

Subscriber Identity Module (SIM)

SIM in the GSM comprises the subscriber's authentication information, e.g., the secret keys, and a uniqe identifier called international mobile subscriber identity. The SIM always takes the form of a smart card with a limited ability of computation and storage.

Third-Generation Partnership Project (3GPP)

A set of the specific methods, services, or instructions prescribed by a computer program.

Time Division Multiple Access (TDMA)

A digital signal transmission technology, which is the foundation of the current D-AMPS and GSM. A TDMA frame lasts for 4.615 ms and is divided into eight time slots, corresponding to a slot time of 576.9 µs. The gross data rate of a frame is 271 kbps, or 33.9 kbps for a slot. This data rate is eqivalent to 156.25 bit periods in a time slot. There are five types of time slot burst:normal, freqency correction, synchronization, access, and dummy slot.

Time Stamp (TS)
The time when the object is positioned.

Transmission Control Protocol (TCP)
Internet protocol, which manages message exchanges at the transport level.

Transport-Layer Security (TLS)
An Internet engineering task force (IETF) standard protocol to secure communication between Web servers and Web clients, supported by most Web browsers and servers;the previous version was called SSL.

Trusted Third Party
An organization or entity that is impartial to both the customer and the merchant (or buyer and seller), is trusted by both, and whose testimony is accepted as valid evidence in a court of law.

Universal Mobile Telecommunications System (UMTS)
The UMTS is the most widely supported third-generation mobile communications system. ITU started the process of defining the standard for third-generation systems, referred to as International Mobile Telecommunications 2000 (IMT-2000). ETSI was responsible for UMTS standardization. In 1998 3GPP was formed to continue the technical specification work. A UMTS network consists of three interacting domains: core netw ork (CN), UMTS terrestrial radio access network (UTRAN), and user eqipment (UE).

Uniform Resource Locator (URL)
URL specifying the uniqe address of a Web document.

Validation
The process of demonstrating that the system under consideration meets the specification of that system in all respects.

Wireless Application Protocol (WAP)
A specification that allows users to access information instantly via handheld wireless devices such as cellular phones, pagers, and personal digital assistants (PDAs) through wireless communication networks and the Internet. WAP includes wireless application environment (WAE), wireless session protocol (WSP), wireless transaction protocol (WTP), wireless transport layer security (WTLS), and wireless datagram protocol (WDP).

Wireless Datagram Protocol (WDP)
A datagram protocol for non-IP wireless packet data networks. WDP specifies how different existing bearer services should be used to provide a consistent service to the upper layers of the WAP architecture framework.

Wireless Markup Language (WML)
An XML-based markup language for wireless handheld devices, including cellular phones, pagers, and PDAs.

Wireless Public Key Infrastructure (WPKI)
WAP Forum established the WPKI framework not as a new PKI standard but as an extension of the traditional PKI to the wireless environment. It utilizes two approaches to satisfy the mobile devices requirement (1) It makes use of elliptic curve cryptography, and (2) It reduces certain fields within the X.509 certificate to cut down on the total length. The specifics are illustrated more clearly in Sect. 3.2.1. Aside from those differences, WPKI is also a certificate-based infrastructure.

Wireless Session Protocol (WSP)
A protocol family derived from the HTTP version 1.1 standard with extensions for wireless data applications. WSP provides WAP applications with a consistent interface for session services.

Wireless Telephony Applications (WTA)
A framework for integrating wireless data applications with voice networks. WTA is a collection of telephony-specific extensions for call and feature control mechanisms that make advanced mobile network services available to the mobile users.

Wireless Transaction Protocol (WTP)
A protocol operating on top of a secure or insecure datagram service. WTP is an extremely lightweight reqestresponseacknowledge transaction protocol.

Wireless Transport-Layer Security (WTLS)
A security protocol based on SSL and adapted to wireless networks and datagram transports.

About the Editors

Weidong Kou is the chief architect and senior manager at IBM Software Group in Great China Group, and adjunct professor of Xidian University. He was the director of ISN National Key Laboratory of China and dean of the School of Computer Science and Technology at Xidian University, China.

Prof. Kou is the Laureate of 2004 Friendship Award of China, the most prestige award and the highest honor from the National Government of China.

Prof. Kou also serves as adjunct professor, honorary professor, or guest professor in more than a dozen of universities, including the University of Maryland, the University of Hong Kong, and Shanghai Jiao Tong University.

Prof. Kou has authored/edited seven books in the areas of e-commerce, security, and multimedia technologies, and published over 80 refereed papers. He has also authored nine issued patents from US and Canada. He has served as a guest editor of special issues on e-commerce for the *International Journal on Digital Libraries*, an associate editor of *International Journal on Education and Information Technologies*, and a member of Editorial Review Board of *Journal of Electronic Commerce in Organizations*. Prof. Kou was the general chair of 2004 IEEE International Conference on e-Commerce Technology for Dynamic E-Business.

Prof. Kou has over 20 years of IT industrial experience, including 12 years of experience in the software development and management in North America. From 1997 to 2000, Prof. Kou was the principal investigator at the IBM Center of Advanced Studies in Toronto, Canada. From 1995 to 1997, he was an architect of a major B2B e-commerce project at the IBM Canada. Before joining IBM in 1995, he was the chairman of the Imaging Committee at the AT&T Imaging Systems Division. Prior to joining AT&T in 1991, he was a Senior Software Engineer at Siemens in Toronto, Canada. He received various invention achievement and technical excellence awards from IBM, AT&T, and Siemens.

Prof. Kou was the associate director of the E-Business Technology Institute (ETI) at the University of Hong Kong from 2000 to 2003.

Prof. Kou served as the industrial co-leader of a major project of the CITR (Canadian Institute of Telecommunications Research, a Canadian National Center of Excellence), *Enabling Technology for Electronic Commerce*, for more than three years. He served as a member of American National Standard Committees, ANSI X9B9 (Financial Image Interchange) and ANSI X3L3 (JPEG and MPEG), for more than four years.

Prof. Kou received his Ph.D. degree in Electrical Engineering in 1985 from Xidian University, and M.S. degree in applied mathematics in 1982 from Beijing University of Posts and Telecommunications, respectively. He was a postdoctoral fellow at the University of Waterloo, Canada, from April 1987 to February 1989.

Prof. Kou is a Senior Member of IEEE, and a member of the Advisory Committee of W3C. He was elected as a member of the New York Academy of Sciences in 1992.

Yelena Yesha received the B.Sc. degree in computer science from York University, Toronto, Canada in 1984, and the M.Sc. and Ph.D degrees in computer and information science from The Ohio State University in 1986 and 1989, respectively.

Since 1989 she has been with the Department of Computer Science and Electrical Engineering at the University of Maryland Baltimore County, where she is presently an Exceptional Research Professor. In addition, from December, 1994 through August, 1999 Dr. Yesha served as the Director of the Center of Excellence in Space Data and Information Sciences at NASA.

Her research interests are in the areas of distributed databases, distributed systems, mobile computing, digital libraries, electronic commerce, and trusted information systems.

She published over 140 refereed articles and also 13 books in these areas. Dr. Yesha has received a substantial amount of research funding as PI or Co-PI from NASA, NSF, NIST, NSA, DHMH, Aether Systems, Cisco, Fujitsu, Nokia and IBM.

She is a member of the editorial board of the Very Large Databases Journal, and the IEEE Transaction on Knowledge and Data Engineering, and is editor-in-chief of the International Journal of Digital Libraries. She served a general chair and program chair of several major international conferences, and recently served as the general chair of ACM SIGMOD 2005.

During 1994, Dr. Yesha was the Director of the Center for Applied Information Technology at the National Institute of Standards and Technology.

Dr. Yesha is a senior member of IEEE, Fellow of IBM CAS and a member of the ACM.

Contributors

Nalini Belaramani received her Master of Philosophy in computer science from the University of Hong Kong in 2002. During her study, she designed the Facet programming model for the Sparkle project. She is now a Ph.D. student at the University of Texas at Austin. Her current interests include distributed systems and autonomic computing. Contact her at nalini@cs.utexas.edu.

Ying Chen is a research staff member of IBM China Research Lab. His research interests include distributed computing, grid computing, data management, and software/services for telecom industry. Dr. Chen earned his Ph.D. in computer science from Southeast University, Nanjing, China. Dr. Chen served as the member of program committee and was invited as external reviewer for several international conferences, workshops, and journals. He has published widely in international journals and conferences. Dr. Chen can be reached at yingch@cn.ibm.com.

Rada Chirkova is an assistant professor in the Computer Science Department of North Carolina State University in Raleigh. She got a B.Sc. and M.Sc. in applied mathematics from Moscow State University (Moscow, Russia), and a M.Sc. and Ph.D. in Computer Science from Stanford University. Her current research focus is on improving query-processing efficiency, by designing and materializing views, and on evaluating queries using derived data, such as materialized views and indexes.

Xuefei Cao is a Ph.D. candidate in the telecommunication engineering at Xidian University. She received his B.S. and M.S. degrees in telecommunication engineering from the Xidian University in 2003 and 2006, respectively. Her research interests are in e-commerce, security, and e-payment.

Lanjun Dang is a Ph.D. candidate in the telecommunication engineering at Xidian University. She received his B.S. and M.S. degrees in telecommunication engineering from the Xidian University in 2003 and 2006, respectively. Her research interests are in e-commerce, security, e-payment, and mobile communications.

Daniel Kou is a student of computer science at the University of Waterloo, Canada. He is interested in RFID and smart card technologies.

Francis C.M. Lau received his Ph.D. in computer science from the University of Waterloo in 1986. He is currently an associate professor and head of the Department of Computer Science at the University of Hong Kong. His main interests are in parallel and distributed computing, Internet and the WWW, mobile computing, operating systems, and computer music. Contact him at fcmlau@cs.hku.hk.

Wei-Bin Lee received his Ph.D. degree in 1997 from National Chung Cheng University. Since 1999, he has been with the Department of Information Engineering at Feng Chia University, where he is currently an associate professor. Presently, he is also the director of the Information and Communication Security Research Center at Feng Chia University. His research interests include cryptography, information security management, steganography, and network security. Dr. Lee can be reached at wblee@fcu.edu.tw.

Bing Li is a Ph.D. candidate at Arizona State University, and expected to graduate in December, 2004. His research focuses on the areas of distributed computing, ontology oriented programming, knowledge discovery, Internet software, mobile computing, e-commerce/e-business, and software engineering. In the summers of 2004 and 2002, Bing Li, worked with research staffs and senior engineers at the IBM T.J. Watson Research Center. In 1998 and 1999, he worked for Bell Labs and Motorola Research Center in China. He can be reached at lblabs@gmail.com.

Victor O.K. Li received SB, SM, EE, and ScD degrees in electrical engineering and computer science from the Massachusetts Institute of Technology in 1977, 1979, 1980, and 1981, respectively. He is the chair professor of Information Engineering at the University of Hong Kong, Hong Kong, and formerly the managing director of Versitech Ltd, the technology transfer and commercial arm of the University. Previously, he was the Professor of Electrical Engineering at the University of Southern California (USC), Los Angeles, California, USA, and director of the USC Communication Sciences Institute. His research interest is in information technologies, focusing on the Internet and wireless networks. He is a fellow of the IEEE, and a UK Royal Academy of Engineering Senior Visiting Fellow.

Dong Liu received his bachelor in radio electronics, master and Ph.D. in remote sensing from Peking University in 1990, 1993 and 1996. From 1996 to 2004, he was a research staff member, research manager, and senior research manager at IBM China Research Lab, where he led high performance web server, pervasive computing middleware, database and VoIP related research projects with important technical contributions to IBM DB2, WebSphere, and Lotus product lines. He joined Intel in 2004. His team is working on advanced system management capability across Intel platforms. He has published widely in peer reviewed journals and conferences. He has over 10 patents issued or being reviewed.

Jiming Liu is professor and head of computer science department at Hong Kong Baptist University (HKBU). He directs Centre for e-Transformation Research (CTR), a government-funded centre focusing on research in Web intelligence (WI) and autonomy oriented computing (AOC). Prof. Liu holds a B.Sc. from East China Normal University, an M.A. from Concordia University, and an M.Eng. and a Ph.D. both in electrical engineering from McGill University. Prof. Liu's present research interests include: web intelligence and the wisdom web, multi-agent systems and autonomy oriented computing paradigm, social networks computing, self-organization and complex systems modeling, and distributed data-mining, learning, and reasoning methodologies. Prof. Liu has published over 180 scientific articles in refereed international journals, books, and conferences. In addition, he has published 26 books and proceedings, among which 7 are research monographs. Prof. Liu is the editor-in-chief of Web intelligence and agent systems (IOS Press), annual review of intelligent informatics (World Scientific Publishing), and The IEEE intelligent informatics bulletin (IEEE Computer Society TCII). He is an associate editor of IEEE Transactions on Data and Knowledge Engineering (IEEE Computer Society), Knowledge and Information Systems (Springer), International Journal of Web Information Systems (Troubador Publishing), International Journal of Web Services Research (Idea Group), and Frontiers in Artificial Intelligence and Applications book series (IOS Press). Prof. Liu is the co-founder of Web Intelligence Consortium (WIC) and the IEEE/WIC/ACM International Conference on Web Intelligence (WI) and the IEEE/WIC/ACM International Conference on Intelligent Agent Technology (IAT) series.

Yi Liu is a Ph.D. candidate in the telecommunication engineering at Xidian University. He received his B.S. and M.S. degrees in telecommunication engineering from the Xidian University in 2003 and 2006, respectively. His research interests are in e-commerce, security, and e-payment.

Filip Perich is a Senior Software Engineer at Shared Spectrum Company and an Adjunct Assistant Professor at University of Maryland Baltimore County (UMBC). His primary research focus is in applications of Data Management and Artificial Intelligence to problems in distributed systems, particularly with an emphasis on wireless mobile / pervasive ad hoc networks. Currently, he is developing next generation (XG) technologies enabling tactical mobile users to use available communications radio frequency spectrum with minimal interference to existing legacy radios. He received Ph.D. and M.S. degrees in Computer Science from UMBC, and A.B. degree in Mathematics from Washington College in Maryland. Perich is an author of over 25 refereed publications. He is professionally active in advising graduate students, serving on Ph.D. committees, and in organizing conferences and workshops on Artificial Intelligence, Data Management, E-Commerce, Networks, and Semantic Web.

Thiruvengadam Radhakrishnan is a professor of computer science and software engineering at Concordia University in Montreal, Canada. He obtained his engineering degrees from Guindy Engineering College in Madras and from IIT Kanpur. For the past 30 years he has been at this University and served in many different capacities. His current research interests are in real-life applications of the agent technology, distributed information processing, and human–computer interfaces. He has published research papers, co-authored text books, and holds patents. His email address is krishnan@cse.concordia.ca.

Dongxu Shen received the B.S. from Harbin University of Engineering, Harbin, China, in 1995, M.S. and Ph.D. from Rensselear Polytechnic Institute, Troy, New York, USA, in 1999 and 2001, respectively, all in electrical engineering. From

2001 to 2004, he is a research associate at the Department of Electrical and Electronic Engineering of the University of Hong Kong, Hong Kong. His research interests include smart antenna, OFDM systems, media access, scheduling, and cross-layer optimization.

Pauline P.L. Siu received her Master of Philosophy in computer science from the University of Hong Kong in 2004. She developed the context-aware state management system (CASM) for the Sparkle project. Contact her at plpsiu@graduate.hku.hk

Song Song is a senior manager at IBM China Research Lab, where he led pervasive computing and wireless application research projects. Mr. Song received a master degree in biomedical engineering from Tsinghua University in 1988. Before he joined IBM in 1995, Mr. Song had been doing researches in medical informatics and imaging systems in Chinese Academy of Medical Sciences as a professor for many years. Mr. Song can be reached at soong@cn.ibm.com.

Yu Song is a software developer at MathWorks, developing software tools for analysis, design, and simulation of communication systems. He earned his Ph.D. in Signal Processing from Tsinghua University, Beijing, China, and conducted postdoctoral research at University of Texas, San Antonio, Texas. He can be reached at yu.song@acm.org.

Cho-Li Wang received his B.S. degree in computer science and information engineering from National Taiwan University in 1985. He obtained his M.S. and Ph.D. degrees in computer engineering from University of Southern California in 1990 and 1995, respectively. He is currently an associate professor of the Department of Computer Science at the University of Hong Kong. His areas of research include parallel architecture, cluster and grid computing, and mobile and ubiquitous systems. Contact him at clwang@cs.hku.hk.

Rong Yan is a staff research member of IBM China Research Laboratory. She earned her Ph.D. in electronic engineering from Beijing Institute of Technology, China, in 2002. Her research interests are in the areas of video coding, error resilience technology, and DRM. Dr. Yan can be reached at yanrong@cn.ibm.com.

Tao Yan is a Ph.D. candidate in the telecommunication engineering at Xidian University. He received his B.S. and M.S. degrees in telecommunication engineering from the Xidian University in 2003 and 2006, respectively. His research interests are in smart card, RFID, and e-commerce.

Bo Yang is an associate professor of computer science department at Jilin University. Now he is doing postdoctoral research at Computer Science Department of Hong Kong Baptist University. He received his B.Sc. degree (June 1997), M.S. degree (June 2000) and Ph.D. degree (June 2003) from Computer Science Department of Jilin University. His present research interests include: autonomy oriented computing, social networks computing, mobile agent systems and multi-agent systems.

Yudong Yang is an Advisory Research Member at IBM Research China. He got his Ph.D. in Computer Science from Tsinghua University, China, in 1997. He was with Microsoft Research China before join IBM. He began his academic career in areas including virtual reality and computer vision and later moved to Internet content analysis and delivery. His current focuses are embedded system and media accelerator architecture. Dr. Yang can be reached at yangyud@cn.ibm.com.

Chow Yuk received his Master of Philosophy in computer science from the University of Hong Kong in 2002. He developed the lightweight mobile code system (LMCS) for the Sparkle project. Contact him at ychow@cs.hku.hk.

Liang-Jie Zhang is a research staff member and the founding chair of the Services Computing Professional Interest Community (PIC) at IBM T.J. Watson Research Center. Dr. Zhang is a member of Business Informatics with a focus on service-oriented architecture and Web services for industry solutions and services. He has filed more than 30 patent applications in the areas of e-business, Web services, rich media, data management, and information appliances, and has published more than 80 technical papers in journals, book chapters, and conference proceedings. Dr. Zhang chairs IEEE Computer Society Technical Committee on Services Computing and serves as editor-in-chief of the International Journal of Web Services Research (JWSR). He was the general co-chair of the 2005 IEEE International Conference on Web Services (ICWS 2005) and the 2005 IEEE International Conference on Services Computing (SCC 2005). He can be reached at zhanglj@ieee.org.

Xiaolei Zhang is a Ph.D. candidate in the computer science at the University of Hong Kong. She received her B.S. and M.S. degrees in computer science from the Nanjing University in 1996 and 2000, respectively. Her research interests are in mobile and pervasive computing. Contact her at xlzhang@cs.hku.hk.

Kewen Zhao is a MS student in the telecommunication engineering at Xidian University. He received his B.S. degree in telecommunication engineering from the Xidian University in 2003. His research interests are in e-commerce, security, and e-payment.

Index